Unitarianism:
Its Origin and
History

Also from Westphalia Press
westphaliapress.org

The Idea of the Digital University

Dialogue in the Roman-Greco World

The History of Photography

International or Local Ownership?: Security Sector Development in Post-Independent Kosovo

Lankes, His Woodcut Bookplates

Opportunity and Horatio Alger

The Role of Theory in Policy Analysis

The Little Confectioner

Non Profit Organizations and Disaster

The Idea of Neoliberalism: The Emperor Has Threadbare Contemporary Clothes

Social Satire and the Modern Novel

Ukraine vs. Russia: Revolution, Democracy and War: Selected Articles and Blogs, 2010-2016

James Martineau and Rebuilding Theology

A Strategy for Implementing the Reconciliation Process

Issues in Maritime Cyber Security

Understanding Art

Homeopathy

Fishing the Florida Keys

Iran: Who Is Really In Charge?

Contracting, Logistics, Reverse Logistics: The Project, Program and Portfolio Approach

The Thomas Starr King Dispute

Springfield: The Novel

Lariats and Lassos

Mr. Garfield of Ohio

The French Foreign Legion

War in Syria

Ongoing Issues in Georgian Policy and Public Administration

Growing Inequality: Bridging Complex Systems, Population Health and Health Disparities

Designing, Adapting, Strategizing in Online Education

Gunboat and Gun-runner

Pacific Hurtgen: The American Army in Northern Luzon, 1945

Natural Gas as an Instrument of Russian State Power

New Frontiers in Criminology

Feeding the Global South

Unitarianism: Its Origin and History

A Course of Sixteen Lectures
Delivered in
Channing Hall, Boston
1888-9

by the
American Unitarian Association

WESTPHALIA PRESS
An Imprint of Policy Studies Organization

Unitarianism: Its Origin and History. A Course of Sixteen Lectures Delivered in Channing Hall, Boston, 1888-9
All Rights Reserved © 2018 by Policy Studies Organization

Westphalia Press
An imprint of Policy Studies Organization
1527 New Hampshire Ave., NW
Washington, D.C. 20036
info@ipsonet.org

ISBN-13: 978-1-63391-637-1
ISBN-10: 1-63391-637-5

Cover design by Jeffrey Barnes:
jbarnesbook.design

Daniel Gutierrez-Sandoval, Executive Director
PSO and Westphalia Press

Updated material and comments on this edition can be found at the Westphalia Press website:
www.westphaliapress.org

UNITARIANISM:

ITS ORIGIN AND HISTORY.

A Course of Sixteen Lectures

DELIVERED IN

CHANNING HALL, BOSTON,

1888-89.

BOSTON:
AMERICAN UNITARIAN ASSOCIATION.
1890.

Copyright, 1889,
BY AMERICAN UNITARIAN ASSOCIATION.

University Press:
JOHN WILSON AND SON, CAMBRIDGE.

PREFACE.

THE full and discriminating Introduction which Mr. Spaulding furnishes, renders anything more than a brief Preface superfluous. When these lectures were delivered in the winter of 1888–89 they were held by many to be of unique value, furnishing in a concise, popular, and yet trustworthy form information which could otherwise be gathered only by the comparison of many authors and the reading of many books. With this opinion the Directors of the Association agree. They put these papers in a book form, that they may interest and profit, not only the limited audience which heard them in Channing Hall, but a wide circle of readers, both within our borders and outside them, who may desire to know how Unitarianism came to be, and what has been the course of its history and influence in the Christian centuries.

G. R.

INTRODUCTION.

THE Channing Hall Lectures were established in 1886 in the new Unitarian building in Boston, by the Unitarian Sunday-School Society. They were designed to furnish instruction to Sunday-school teachers and others, not only in the methods of religious teaching, but also in the subject-matter of such instruction. In pursuance of this general plan, it was arranged in the fall of 1888 to have a course of sixteen lectures delivered upon the Origin and History of Unitarianism. Those lectures, substantially as they were then given, are published in the present volume. Two of the lecturers appear twice in the series. Rev. Joseph H. Allen, after delivering the opening lecture on Christian Doctrine in the First Five Centuries, kindly consented to take the place of Rev. Dr. F. H. Hedge, the state of whose health would not allow him to prepare the lecture which he had hoped to give upon the Contact of American Unitarianism and German Thought. The third lecture of the course was an extemporaneous talk by Rev. Edward H. Hall, the accomplished author of a volume upon "Orthodoxy and Heresy in the Christian Church." Mr. Hall being prevented from supplying a written paper for the present volume, Rev. Dr. Andrew P. Peabody furnished the valuable lecture upon Christianity from the Fifth to the Fifteenth Century.

The general purpose of these lectures may be briefly stated. They were intended to give to those who might attend the course a sense of the worth of Unitarianism as a faith which has deep historic roots, and from the beginning has had great allies.

The early lectures are devoted to the historic aspects of Unitarianism. Mr. Allen has shown conclusively, we think, that in the first Christian centuries the theology of the church was not Trinitarian. He dissipates, indeed, the fancy that modern liberal Christianity is in any doctrinal sense the revival of *primitive* Christianity; but he makes it equally clear that there are moral and spiritual affinities which are deeper and stronger than any doctrinal ties. No dogma of the church, however, as Dr. Peabody clearly shows, has any claim to be designated as *quod semper, quod ubique, quod ab omnibus*. In point of fact this very phrase was first used not by adherents, but by opponents, of what is usually spoken of as the Orthodox faith.[1] Dr. Peabody's lucid exposition of the history of ten centuries of Christian doctrine sets more than one favorite dogma of the so-called "defenders of the faith" in a light so repell-

---

[1] See pages 36 and 37.

ing that almost any heresy appears attractive by the side of the orthodoxy of such dark ages. The Catholic theology, of which the doctrines of Luther and his co-workers were supposed to be a reformation, Mr. Beach rightly declares to have been much nearer the Unitarian standard than was the Reformed doctrine itself. Yet in ways they knew not of the Reformers were fostering, in the very soil of Lutheranism and Calvinism, the growth of two of the leading ideas of Unitarianism, — the belief in reason as the highest tribunal of appeal, and the belief in the supreme worth of character. Mr. Beach's story of Unitarianism in Transylvania, and Mr. Herford's account of the same faith in England, show Channing to have had forerunners and co-laborers in other lands than our own. With Mr. Allen's second lecture begins the history of the last sixty years of American Unitarianism, admirably supplemented by Dr. Peabody's sketch of those New England Unitarians who lived too early to be affected by contact with German thought. The intervening paper, contributed by Rev. Dr. George E. Ellis, is an interesting account of those relations between the Church and Parish in Massachusetts Usage and Law out of which came, in so many instances, the schism whereby the Orthodox church-members were separated from the majority of the members of the parish, who in turn formed a new and "liberal" church fellowship. Dr. Briggs's sketch of Channing, and Mr. Stewart's lecture on Parker are admirably fitted to introduce the reader to the valuable memoirs that have been written of these two great leaders of liberal thought in the United States; while Mr. Tiffany's account of the New England Renaissance sets forth in lively colors that picturesquely noble movement known as Transcendentalism, — one of the strongest currents that reinforced the on-flowing faith of the soul in its own competency and in its nearness to the divine life. With the suggestive paper on Unitarianism and Modern Literature, a series of five lectures is entered upon in which not alone the best literature of our modern world, but its Biblical criticism, its scientific thought, its ethical ideals, and its deepest philosophy are shown by able thinkers and lucid writers to be *en rapport* with what is best and most enduring in the Unitarian faith of to-day. To mention the fact that the lectures just referred to were contributed by Rev. F. B. Hornbrooke, Rev. James De Normandie, Rev. T. R. Slicer, Rev. George Batchelor, and Prof. C. C. Everett is to assure the reader that a rare intellectual treat is therein offered him. In the closing lecture, Mr. Reynolds points out the new departures which Unitarianism is now making in strengthening the bonds of union among its adherents, in awakening a sense of denominational responsibility, and in entering upon a career of greater usefulness as a helper of the moral and religious life of the world.

The reader of this book, whether he be merely a student of Unitarianism or a member of its household of faith, will hardly lay the volume down without a profound feeling of gratitude to the Society that planned these Channing Hall Lectures, to the men who delivered them, and to the Association that has published them.

H. G. S.

BOSTON, December, 1889.

CONTENTS.

LECTURE I.

EARLY CHRISTIAN DOCTRINE.

BY REV. JOSEPH HENRY ALLEN.

	Page
Perspective of five centuries	1
Organic growth	1
Primitive Christianity misunderstood	2
Ancient thought and modern terms	2
Scientific and religious attitude of study	3
Composite historic photograph	4
Ancient inward and modern outward revolution	5
Central thought of Christianity from Paul to Leo	5
Discussions in third and fourth centuries	6
Trinitarian treatise by the schismatic Novatian	6
Level stretch of two centuries	7
Overthrow of the national Messianic idea	7
Crisis of a revolution in Christian doctrine	8
Justin's discussion of the subject	9
First statement of the Logos-doctrine	10
Germ of Trinitarian doctrine	10
Definition of the *Logos*, or *Word*	11
Three classes of thinkers, Gnostics, Confessors, Fathers	12
Belief essential to salvation	13
Cause of this error not merely speculative	14
Two streams of theology	15
The practical side developed in the Western Church	15
Crises of speculative interest in the Eastern Church	16
Germ of the Trinity in Athenagoras	16
Reason personified as the Word, or Son of God	17
Unintelligible controversies about persons and attributes	18
Variance caused by ambiguity	19
Steps of development	19

CONTENTS.

	Page
Pendulum swings toward Alexandrian mysticism	20
Sabellianism and its opponents	20
Hypostatical independence	20
Council at Nicæa	21
Homo-ousian and Homoi-ousian debate	21
Arian controversy in four councils	22
Heresy of Apollinaris	22
Nestorian opinions	22
Heresy of Eutyches	23
Pope Leo's formula of faith	23
Outward troubles lead to union in creed	23
A symbol of faith needed	24
Augustine's consoling work	24
Broad result of doctrinal evolution	25

LECTURE II.

CHRISTIANITY FROM THE FIFTH TO THE FIFTEENTH CENTURY.

By Rev. Andrew P. Peabody, D.D.

Two causes of the Dark Ages	26
Demoralization of Rome	26
Christianity made a State religion	26
Sins of the early Church Fathers	27
Asceticism exalted above truth	28
The new religion imperilled by its supporters	28
Two seed-plots for Christianity	28
Monasticism a necessity	28
Good influence of anchorites	29
Pure religion from the cloister, not the throne	30
Service to art, agriculture, and humanity	30
Conservatories and seminaries of literature	31
Scholasticism	32
Preservation of the Scriptures	32
Roman law the other cradle of Christianity	32
Influence of ecclesiastical symbolism	33
Power of the mustard-seed	34
Growth of liberty, philanthropy, chivalry, benevolence	34
Culmination of local dissensions in the Athanasian Creed	34
Homo-ousian debate	35

CONTENTS.

	Page
The *procession* of the Holy Ghost	35
Spanish revolt against the Creed	35
Metaphysical discussion of the Trinity	36
Predestination virtually set aside	36
A dogmatic test widely misunderstood	36
Double predestination preached by Gottschalk	37
John Scotus teaches that evil is a process of good	37
Doctrine of Original Sin embraced by the Latin Church	38
Abelard's opposition	38
Conditional Predestination taught by Duns Scotus	38
Vicarious Atonement established as a dogma	39
Anselm's theory in conflict with one more liberal	40
Arian heresy	40
Paulician, or Gnostic, belief in Dualism	40
The Cathari ascetics	41
Supremacy of the Bible maintained by Peter de Bruys	41
Pure morality preached by the Henricians	42
Rise of the Waldenses	42
Wiclif as a Reformer	43
Church and Scripture	44
Maintenance of the clergy	44
Opposition to mendicant fraternities	45
Posthumous martyrdom	45
Wesley as the founder of a sect	46
Wiclif's translation of the Bible	46

LECTURE III.

UNITARIANISM AND THE REFORMATION.

By Rev. Seth C. Beach.

Meaning of Unitarianism	48
Protest against Total Depravity and Predestination	48
A horrible decree	49
Belief in Human Nature and Free Will	49
Luther's rejection of these liberal ideas	50
His opponents nearer the Unitarian standard	51
Lutheranism a theological reaction from Augustinianism	51
Adherence to the Trinity as heavenly	52
Liberal debt to Luther	52
Theoretical and practical Salvation by Faith	53

	Page
Justification an inward process	53
Courage involved in belief in Character	54
Unwitting advocacy of the reliability of Reason	54
Luther's theology progressive and retrogressive	55
Human Will a factor in the Work of Grace	56
A cloud of Unitarian heresy noted by Melancthon	56
Liberalism of Zwingli	57
Description of childhood's purity	57
The Fall of Man	58
Zwingli's recognition of universal righteousness	58
Warrant of a larger hope in the divine mercy	59
Views of Calvin and other Swiss reformers	60
Differences as to Predestination	61
Rationalism in Zwingli and Socinus	61
Calvin's authority	62
Reactionary logic against the drift of the Reformation	62
His moral sternness a help to rational faith and character	62
Arbitrary predestination advocated	63
Martyrdom of Bolsec	63
Predestination rejected by a second martyr	65
Protest and career of Servetus	65
Modern progress in Geneva	67
Servetus second to Jesus in the army of martyrs	67
Blandrata, the Italian Liberal	68
The first Unitarian society	69
Socinian a term of contempt	69
The uncle, Lælius Socinus	69
The nephew, Faustus Socinus	70
Unitarian ascendency in Poland	72
Catholic persecution of the younger Socinus	72
Unitarianism nearly extinguished in Poland	72
Exiles in Holland, Germany, and Transylvania	73
Good work of Francis David	74
The government's liberal decree	75
Supremacy among the upper classes	75
David's doctrines, imprisonment, and death	75
Two centuries of trial followed by triumph	76
Churches of the Reformation	77

LECTURE IV.

UNITARIANISM IN ENGLAND.

BY REV. BROOKE HERFORD.

	Page
Early churches and earlier advocates	78
Continental and English pioneers	78
Primitive English Unitarianism difficult to trace	78
Unitarians confounded with Anabaptists	79
Suffering for Unitarian ideas	79
The death of Joan Boucher	79
Martyrs petty and great	80
Last burnings for heresy	81
Undercurrent of Puritan thought	81
John Biddle's service	81
Cromwell's belief in religious liberty	82
Three great minds	82
Broad Church view held in the closet	82
Spiritual lethargy and new life	83
Era of toleration, dissent, and chapel-building	83
English Presbyterians free from binding creeds	83
Natural and inevitable results	84
Joseph Priestley's startling position	85
Two kindred movements	86
Liberality of the General Baptists	86
Lindsey's emergence from the Established Church	87
The Feathers' Tavern Petition	88
Essex Street Chapel founded	88
Connection with Unitarian churches in America	89
King's Chapel	89
Priestley's sojourn in the United States	90
Early conquest anticipated	90
Obstacles and discouragements	90
Controversy and social prestige	91
Two causes of a new movement	91
Tuckerman's visit and missionary influence	91
Liberal movements in Lancashire	92
The Christian Brethren	92
Liverpool Controversy, "thirteen against three"	93
Pew-rents and free seats	94
Three theological schools	94
Helpfulness of lay-preachers	95
Home prosperity and foreign sympathy	96

LECTURE V.

THE CONTACT OF AMERICAN UNITARIANISM AND GERMAN THOUGHT.

By Rev. Joseph Henry Allen.

	Page
Distinctive Unitarianism not found in German theology	97
Reminiscences of personal interest	97
A special crisis	98
Norton's conservatism and Brownson's change	98
Controversy not over miracles but over the new order of thought	99
Vast and unmanageable topic	99
Three great departments	99
Speculative theology	99
Critical theology	100
Prominence of Schleiermacher	101
His first strong impression	102
Study of Deistical writers leads to Transcendentalism	103
Its ideas and terms distasteful to Norton	103
Effect on American ideas	105
Three leaders of thought influenced	105
Miracles widely discarded	106
Need of a philosophical method	107
Three methods of Biblical interpretation	107
Theological tone caught from Germany	108
Influence over four noted ministers	108
Theodore Parker's attitude	109
Furness's view of miracles	109
Sears as a reflection of Olshausen	110
Small influence of Strauss	110
The Tübingen School	111
The name German no longer a reproach	112
Alternative of dry-rot or a launch into wider waters	113
The more excellent way of Furness, Hedge, and Clarke	113
The pivotal appeal to the religious life	113
Scepticism caused by science, not theology	114
Debt to German thought for survival of religious life	115

CONTENTS. xvii

LECTURE VI.

THE CHURCH AND THE PARISH IN MASSACHUSETTS.
Usage and Law.

BY REV. GEORGE E. ELLIS, D.D.

	Page
Two grave questions	116
Why did not the Papal Church reform itself?	116
Its power and opportunity	117
Its past service and perfect system	117
Reformers before the Reformation	118
The question answered	118
Corporate sanctity vitiated by falsity and greed	118
Real cause of Protestantism	119
Vital corruption and lack of will	120
Worthy cause of sectarian discord	120
Varying influences unified in the ancient Church	120
Second serious consideration	121
Reforming party unmindful of inevitable consequences	121
The Bible conducive to piety, not to doctrinal unity	122
Purely historic interest in an old quarrel	122
Loss of supposed rights	124
Root of the difficulty in ancient Christian history	124
Two classes of Christians in the New Testament	125
Signification of the word *mass*	125
Pledged disciples essential to Christian continuity	126
Original distinction between Church and Congregation	126
Romanist extreme	127
Equality of clergy with laity in Congregational fold	127
Priestly dictation in the Roman Church	127
Sacraments and covenants indispensable to corporate life	128
Special prerogatives of communicants	129
Historic sympathy with defeated party	129
Primitive jurisdiction of the General Court	130
Ecclesiastical conditions in land-grants	130
Opportunities for petty parish feuds	131
Ministers and parishioners in first townships	131
Usages and statutes leading to complications	132
Independent rights of each company of believers	133
Congregationalism not identical with any creed	132
Colonial regulations	133
Different methods in different places	133

xviii   CONTENTS.

	Page
Franchise restricted to church-members	134
Four confusing enactments by the General Court	134
Maintenance of pastors involving right of choice	135
Harmony not at first disturbed	136
Restrictive laws of 1641	136
Choice of ministers regulated	136
Antagonistic provisions	137
Ecclesiastical councils mischievous	138
Actual connection of Church with Parish	138
Natural privileges of communicants	139
Church and Parish defined	139
Abundant occasions for friction	140
Doctrinal changes underlying legal decisions	141
Defection from Calvinism	142
Deepening causes of dissension	142
Sacramental rights of non-professors	143
Life-tenure of pastors a cause of trouble	143
Withdrawal of disaffected members	143
Two Dedham pastorates preceding the lawsuit	144
Dissension as to the settlement of a new minister	144
The wording of the Letters Missive	145
Parish property	145
Remonstrance by majority of church-members	146
Suit against the dissenting deacon	146
The one question recognized by the judges	146
No rights of churches separate from parishes	147
This decision a shock to multitudes	148
Natural indignation	148
Trespass upon vested rights	149
Parallel cases	149
Adjustment of old privileges to new times	150
Protestantism startled by the results of its own principles	150
Tendency of the law to subordinate the Church	150
Religion supported by non-communicants	151
Differing judgments	151
Growing disability of the Church	152
The Dedham seceders	152
Control of ecclesiastical property	152
How the Church lost its prestige	153
Character of covenant members	153

LECTURE VII.

EARLY NEW ENGLAND UNITARIANS.

BY REV. ANDREW P. PEABODY, D.D.

	Page
General silence in regard to the Trinity	155
Great change in the Eighteenth Century	155
Influence of thinkers not nominally Unitarian	156
Anti-Trinitarianism of two ancient creeds	156
Limitation of the subject to biographical sketches	157
I. Ebenezer Gay, of Hingham	158
Three clerical brethren	158
II. Charles Chauncy, of First Church	159
III. Jonathan Mayhew, of West Church	160
Professional culture	161
Independence and eloquence	162
Patriotism	163
Opposition to English missionary society	163
Steadfastness in death	165
Portrait	166
IV. Jeremy Belknap, of Federal Street Church	166
V. James Freeman, of King's Chapel	167
No open dissent in Connecticut	169
Three leaders	169
I. John Sherman, of Mansfield	169
Change of opinions	170
Unitarians in the Holland Land Company	171
Earliest printed defence of Unitarianism	172
II. Abiel Abbot, of Coventry	173
III. Luther Willson, of Brooklyn	174
Choice fruits of the vineyard	177

LECTURE VIII.

CHANNING.

BY REV. GEORGE W. BRIGGS, D.D.

Acknowledged leader and ideal theologian	178
Reminiscences of his pulpit eloquence	179
Preordained for his work	180
Love of freedom hereditary	180

xx CONTENTS.

	Page
Continuous religious experience	181
Early ministry	182
Inevitable protest for liberty	182
Congregational schism	183
Domination of certain great truths	184
Moral perfection of God	185
Mission of Jesus	186
One forever-burning light	186
Dignity of human nature	187
All minds in one family	188
Enrapturing faith	189
Naturalness of redemption	189
Truths and Bibles	190
Nourisher of noble souls	190
Anti-slavery sentiments	191
Higher expectations of truth	193
Other characteristics	194
Inspiring scenery of Narragansett Bay	194

LECTURE IX.

TRANSCENDENTALISM: THE NEW ENGLAND RENAISSANCE.

By Rev. Francis Tiffany.

Enlarged subject	196
Second birth of Europe	196
Double discovery of inner and outer world	197
Protest of conservatism and selfishness	198
Champions of the old and new	199
A word for the retrogressive party	199
Sublime sentiments and opaque understanding	200
The Puritan pioneers	200
Current and eddy	201
The questioning habit	202
Retarding effect of isolation	202
Attempt to found a theocracy	202
Giants of aspiring thought	203
Commonplace level	203
Liberalism creeping in	204
A quarry for Unitarian polemics	205

CONTENTS.

	Page
Noble charities and wide thoughts	206
Stagnation	206
Paralyzing influence of trade	207
Philistines	207
Children of Light	207
Confidence of spirit in itself	208
Characteristic features of the Transcendental movement	209
Reverence toward foreign thinkers	209
A Mont Blanc of thought	210
Scholars crossing the ocean	210
The movement not merely imitative	211
Spontaneity and freshness	212
Intellectual, æsthetic, and spiritual ferment	213
A stimulating address	213
Antagonistic effect	214
Relation to supernaturalism	215
External authority and inward recognition	215
Illustrations from art	215
No single theological issue	217
Far-reaching question	218
Priceless service	219

LECTURE X.

THEODORE PARKER.

By Rev. Samuel Barrett Stewart.

Early Unitarianism outgrown	220
The symbol remains a constant	220
Parker not included within a denominational cordon	221
Representative of an influx of new thought	221
Inheritance of life	222
Two great nurses	223
Habits of study	223
Boyhood and early manhood	224
Professional preparation	224
Analysis of the human spirit	225
Special characteristics	226
Not the originator of the new thought	226
His theology the outgrowth of himself	227
Four significant questions to be answered	228
Searching problems	228

CONTENTS.

	Page
An awakening sermon	228
Abstract of the five parts of his great book	230
I. Religious consciousness in varying forms	231
II. Inspiration not phenomenal but continual	231
III. Christianity not the Absolute Religion	231
Traditions and accretions	232
IV. Bible as literature	232
V. Church-history	232
Obvious heresy	232
Defects and prophetic grandeur	233
Public effect	234
Helpfulness of thought	234
Greatness of heart	235
New aspect of old ideas	235
A living deity in nature and man	236
Irrepressible satire	236
Onslaught upon impiety	237
Practical theism	237
Estimate of Jesus and his religion	238
Assurance of future life	238
Non-reliance upon external testimony	239
Belief in immanent providence	240
Pursuit of truth	240
Crusade for freedom	240
Inspiration to fresh study	241
Broader Unitarianism the result	242
Effect upon pulpit oratory	242
Parochial tranquillity disturbed	242
Martyrdom	243
Not a poet or philosopher	243
Death " without the sight "	243
Burial-place	244

LECTURE XI.

UNITARIANISM AND MODERN LITERATURE.

By Rev. Francis Hornbrooke.

Two methods of treatment	245
Serious difficulties	245
American literature and Unitarianism	246
One great name	246
Fiction in the early part of the Nineteenth Century	246

CONTENTS. xxiii
Page
Later works 247
Historians 247
Five great orators 248
Poets and essayists 249
Literary excellence 250
American poetry united with liberal theology 250
Remarkable hymns 251
Value of the inquiry 251
Changed literary conditions 252
Second part of the subject 253
Unitarianism in literature 253
Three difficulties 253
Individuality of utterance 254
What Unitarianism stands for 255
These ideas in literature 256
Emerson and Holmes 257
Liberal tenets in poetry 257
The Quaker Poet 258
Robert Browning 263
Lewis Morris 266
Underlying thoughts 269
Liberalism in fiction 269
Religious novels 270
The past a cause for rejoicing 271

LECTURE XII.

UNITARIANISM AND MODERN BIBLICAL CRITICISM.

By Rev. James De Normandie.

Parable of chaff and wheat 272
Value of detecting errors 272
Ungracious aspect of criticism 273
Nothing to fear for truth 273
All things subject to the laws of thought 274
How the Bible is to be understood 275
The Dutch School 275
Law of historic research 275
Use of reason in interpretation 275
Inspiration inferior to virtue 276
Important part of criticism 277
Controversial period 277
Something deeper than textual criticism 278

xxiv   CONTENTS.

	Page
Legendary element in the Scriptures	278
First results of German inquiry	278
Influence of natural science	279
Development Theory	280
Scientific separated from spiritual truth	281
Geology and Genesis	282
Comparative Theology	283
Sympathy of Religions	284
Oriental and Christian ritualism	285
Effect on missionary work	285
Another important question	285
Chronology of sacred books	285
Difficulties increasing with exact criticism	287
New hypotheses	288
Distinguishing privilege	288
Value of critical study	289

LECTURE XIII.

UNITARIANISM AND MODERN SCIENTIFIC THOUGHT.

By Rev. Thomas R. Slicer.

Limitation of the subject	290
Definitions of Theology and Science	290
Two questions	290
Three possible answers	290
The universe necessarily true	291
Answers of Unitarianism and Science	291
Changes in science	291
Honor among scientists	292
A noteworthy declaration	292
Devout confessions of scientists	293
One exception	293
Confidence in the world's orderliness	294
Claims, duties, and characteristics of Unitarianism	294
Thought and life more than opinions	295
First point of contact	296
Principles affirmed but beliefs not stereotyped	296
The universal spirit	296
Loyalty to divine will and moral character	296
Man's adjustment to the universe	297

CONTENTS. XXV

	Page
World not evolved from moral consciousness	298
Present attitude of science	298
Scientific methods not hampered by Unitarians	298
Mutual misapprehensions by religionists and scientists	299
True sphere of materialism and metaphysics	299
Religion confirmed by science	300
Fundamental hypothesis of religion	300
Devout belief not gainsaid by scientific facts	300
Agnostic theories unsupported	300
Analogy of God's will to man's	301
Human and divine thought	302
The Development Theory leading to the doctrine of Evolution	302
Will and thought coetaneous	302
Two great principles in modern science	302
Conservation of Energy	303
Correlation of Forces	303
Vital force no exception	303
Relation of these twin principles to supernaturalism	304
The soul dwelling in an enlarged universe	305
Working hypotheses in science and theology	305
Reasoning beyond facts	306
Tendency towards belief in Evolution	306
Not universally accepted	306
Relation to progress	307
Modest affirmations of science	307
Man not accounted for	308
The past of humanity a prophecy of its future	308
Perfect correspondence indicative of a perfect life	309
Moral and spiritual experiments	309
Discontent with secondary causes	309
Equipment of Unitarians for spiritual enterprise	309
Personal illustration of the harmony of devout science with broad religion	310

LECTURE XIV.

THE LAW OF RIGHTEOUSNESS.

By Rev. George Batchelor.

One way of treatment adopted	312
Motive-power in ethical life	312
Morals a better word than Ethics	312

xxvi   *CONTENTS.*

	Page
Righteousness better than either	313
Relation of right-wis-ness to expediency	313
Practical illustrations	314
Higher advances in the same direction	314
Exceptions to the law of trustiness	315
Manhood leading to gentlemanliness	316
Unitarian belief in the genuineness of human goodness	316
False conventional ideal	316
Incomparable examples of integrity and culture	317
Moral and educational soil of human nature	317
Patriotic devotion	317
Only a few models for imitation	320
Virtue enhanced by belief in immortality	320
The need, the deed, and the man	321
Two differing motives of action	321
Ethics and Religion equally honorable	321
Highest Utilitarianism shallow	322
Growth of virtue from within	323
Noblest conduct dependent upon religion	323
Seeming exceptions	324
Winning ideals heaven-born	324
Right feeling based upon right thinking	324
Deterioration of moral ideals when divorced from religious faith	325
Belief in immortality leading to humanity	325
Disproportionately generous fruits of our denominational faith	326
External inducements to virtue	326
Final sanctions of duty	327
Beneficent results of total culture	328

LECTURE XV.

THE RELATION OF UNITARIANISM TO PHILOSOPHY.

By Rev. Charles Carroll Everett, D.D.

This union of subjects not meaningless	329
Some philosophy belonging to every one	329
Unitarianism the simplest philosophy of religion	330
Two great antagonists	330
Different meanings of Agnosticism	331

CONTENTS. xxvii

	Page
Akin to Scepticism	332
Change of name but not of front	332
Spencer's Agnosticism	333
Varying use of the term Unknowable	333
Material illustrations	334
Significance of terms	334
Unknowability of the Absolute	335
Paradoxical position: the Agnostic is the Gnostic	335
Philosophical Agnosticism impossible	336
Disguised materialism	336
Commendable but doubtful simplicity	337
Materialistic questions hard to answer	337
Spiritualistic questions equally perplexing	337
Problem of Consciousness	338
Helplessness of the materialistic argument	338
Superior brightness of the Unitarian faith	339
Contrast with the elder Orthodoxy	340
Integrity and sanity of human nature	340
Reason a God-given instrument	341
The heart repressed by narrow systems	341
Intellectual and spiritual freedom	341
Wholeness of the world	341
Continuity of divine power	342
Spiritualistic philosophy represented by Unitarianism	342
Manifested in opposing systems	342
Background of the universe	343
Vast difference between matter and sentience	344
Development arising from self-assertion	344
Controlling power of love	344
This result the outcome of a spiritual source	345
Nature animated by controlling mind	345
Man bound to the universe by closer than intellectual ties	346
New aspect of inexorable law in human consciousness	347
Spiritual presence veiled in nature	347
Something above spirit and matter	348
Transcendent freedom of spirit	349
Loftiest moral force	350
Problem of Evil	350
Dualism sunk in profounder knowledge	350
Nature's tendency not capricious	351
Lower suffering exaggerated	351
Witness of personal judgment	352
Assumptions and conclusions	352
Ideal philosophy	352

LECTURE XVI.

ECCLESIASTICAL AND DENOMINATIONAL TENDENCIES.

By Rev. Grindall Reynolds.

	Page
Stint of our religious body	354
Co-existence of church activity with religious liberty	354
Individual and congregational freedom achieved	354
Impression made by early Unitarian leaders	355
Milder creeds	356
Fear of organization	356
Growth of Unitarianism in spite of itself	357
Definition of terms	357
No definite church polity	358
Absence of creed	358
What we are leaving behind	359
Former plainness of worship	359
Dogmatic training distrusted	360
One question which the fathers needed not to consider	360
Richer tendency	360
Ancient meeting-houses and modern chapels	361
Fine edifices demanded	361
Ecclesiastical festivals	362
Ritualism the inevitable reaction	363
Juvenile instruction formerly neglected	364
Change in this respect	365
Wider church hospitality	366
First efforts to reach outsiders	366
Three ecclesiastical tendencies summarized	367
Sectarianism not originally intended or favored	367
Tendency toward external coherence	368
Denominational gatherings	368
Past achievements and divided plans	369
Superficial differences and fundamental agreements	370
Spiritual union no excuse for inactivity	371
Duty to communicate truth	372
Truth, Freedom, and Usefulness	372
Chief problem of to-day	373

UNITARIANISM:

ITS ORIGIN AND HISTORY.

ORIGIN AND HISTORY OF UNITARIANISM.

EARLY CHRISTIAN DOCTRINE.

BY J. H. ALLEN.

THE process which proved such a thorny and tangled one, of casting the early Christian doctrine in shape to give the type of the world's best life for a thousand years, may be reckoned to have taken about five centuries before it was finished. A little more strictly, we may set the two boundaries of that process at the middle of the First Century, when Saint Paul set seriously about the task of interpreting the Messianic office of Jesus, and a little past the middle of the Fifth, when Leo the Great, of Rome, had laid strong and deep the foundations of the ecclesiastical structure that was to be. This large perspective ought to make our first step, in trying to understand as we may the nature of the slow growth of opinion that was meanwhile taking place.

This wide way of looking at it does not serve to the scholar quite the uses of the elaborate study which he has been used to spending upon that period, — or, more likely, upon some detached fragment of it. But it is well to look upon the growth of opinion as an *organic* growth; and that means, to see it first as a whole, before dissecting it to find the shape and uses of its several parts. That study is oftenest made too purely analytical and erudite. Think of the learning, for example, — literally microscopic, — that has been spent in interpreting a single group of texts, the New Testament Epistles or the Fathers of the Second Century, wholly detached from the soil they grew out of or the life they grew into! Think of that eager, anxious, controversial motive which made a great scholar like John Henry Newman stake his faith on the right reading of the documents of the Fourth Century, — doctrinally speaking, the stormiest and most passionate of all! Primitive Christianity has been identified not with the pulse of that strong, brave, spiritual life which went forth upon the world in those early centuries in a purifying and invigorating though turbulent stream, but with the opinions, necessarily transitory and crude, in which a credulous, ignorant, and excited time of revolution tried to express its sense of the one transcendent fact of its moral history, — to interpret to the understanding what its own eyes had seen and its own hands had handled of the Word of Life. Each later student of that astonishing phenomenon, launched as he probably was upon the swelling flood of modern controversy, was naturally anxious to claim those opinions as his own; and in this temper our Christian scholars of the Nineteenth Century have tried to identify themselves with the mind of the First, and to make good their claim of finding their own belief identical with "primitive Christianity."

If we would escape the fallacies and confusions that have grown out of the one phrase last quoted, we must first of all clear our mind completely of all such controversial motive. For example, it was a pardonable thing on the part of Unitarian critics half a century ago, but would be most unwise in us, to look for modern Unitarianism, or anything like it, in the early beliefs of Christendom. Negatively, indeed, we should be quite right; for, truly, we must look long and late into the history of doctrine, before finding anything like the Trinitarian creed of modern Orthodoxy. But our modern terms do not hit the ancient thought. Thus, to say (as in the title of an ingenious doctrinal tract) that "the Apostle Peter was a Unitarian" can only mean that the apostle was — as he certainly was — quite innocent of any such notion as that symbolized in the modern Trinity. But we should doubtless be very much astonished if we could see just what his thought really was about the kingdom of God that was immediately to appear, and compare it with our own way of thinking about the kingdom of God we are looking for. We may strip away the errors and accretions that came about in the course of centuries; and we may find, indeed, a human heart that beats very much like ours, but a line of thought almost as hard for us to follow as if it were written in Chinese.

In the task before us, then, we shall not once try to identify our own doctrine with that held by anybody at any point in that early age, — excepting only so far as the holders of it appear to us to read correctly their own experience, or to deal frankly and intelligently with the religious phenomena of the time they lived in. We may call this, if we will, a "scientific" attitude or temper in the study of opinion. But, in fact, that expresses it very imperfectly: the scientific temper is only one element in what we need; and, standing alone, is quite as misleading as a non-scientific or controversial temper, — perhaps more so. For, whatever else we do, we must deal with religious matters *religiously*, that is, sympathetically; and even the polemic temper is not half so far away from that as the non-religious or agnostic. We must be as frankly ready to accept a fact in the religious life, however strange and even repugnant it looks to us, as to discern an error or a truth in religious thought. We will see with the eyes of the early Christians if we can, and think with their minds as well as we can; but at least we ought to find in our own hearts something of the life they lived, and then put it to our thought in as much clearer language as we can.

And for this, instead of studying with the help of learned commentary that vast library of what we call by courtesy "the Christian Fathers," with a view to manipulate their scattered and floating hints into intelligible shape, it is quite possible that we may get a clearer notion of what we really want, if we follow somewhat *swiftly* that great current of religious life, and watch the bold navigators in that flood, or the trusting multitude that confided in their skill, with the motive not at all of taking sides with one as against another, but simply of seeing what is the point they all want to make, and how they are working towards it. In the period I have named, I roughly reckon (after the New Testament times) about fifty names of Christian writers,[1] some of them very voluminous, with whose lives, writings, and opinions the student of such things ought to be fairly well acquainted, in order to make that rapid review of any value. We must rely, in good part, on the broad impression taken from them all, — a sort of composite photograph I may call it; though it may be necessary to point out a few individual features, in order to make it clear that we are looking at the *human* likeness of a period at all.

Now I have noticed that when an artist sets about to draw a portrait, he wants first of all a clear thin outline that just hints the likeness, and guides himself by that while he works out the different features in due prominence and proportion.

---

[1] Migne's "Patrologia" contains the writings of something more than two hundred and sixty Christian authors of the period in question, from whose names a select list of fifty may easily be made out by the student. To this should be added a list of from twenty to thirty Pagan writers.

EARLY CHRISTIAN DOCTRINE.

Something like this is necessary, if we would take in at once so broad a view as that covered by four or five centuries. The general fact before us is a revolution of human opinion with which there is nothing whatever to compare, except that revolution of scientific opinion which has come about in the four or five centuries since the modern era of thought had fairly set in. But the radical difference of the two cases is here: that the modern revolution deals mainly with men's views of the universe and the laws of life seen *from the outside;* the revolution we are dealing with dealt mainly with men's view of their own relation to the Divine government and the law of the spiritual life as felt inwardly. Moreover, it went along with that most stupendous of all political and social revolutions, the complete dissolution of the fabric of ancient society, religion, morals, and empire, and the coming-on of the great wave of barbarian conquest, which changed the very raw material of the populations Christianity had to work on. We see the whole thing falsely, unless we see it in its bearings with that most memorable convulsion of all that have ever happened in human affairs.

I have mentioned the names of two men, Paul and Leo, — possibly the greatest, and certainly the most significant of the long series, — as standing at the beginning and the end of the four centuries' process of development. The process was one that, as we must remember, transformed the Christian doctrine from the prized possession of a little Palestinian sect to a great shaping spiritual force, of energy enough to dictate and control the lines on which a new civilization, of vastly greater might and splendor than the old, was slowly taking form and substance. What we wish to understand is, how the central thought — the "formative type," as a naturalist might perhaps call it — was growing and changing under such influences as I have hinted at. For that is really what we mean when we speak of the development of early Christian doctrine.

We have to do, as you will remember, with a period of some four hundred years, from the middle of the First Century to past the middle of the Fifth. Looking along that line, from our particular point of view, our eye is first caught by two groups, one about the middle of the Third Century, and one about the middle of the Fourth. Is first caught, I say; for the eager discussion going on in these two groups, respectively, represents to us the Sabellian and the Arian controversies, — the first, touching the nature and office of Christ, that are likely to have any definite meaning to modern ears. It will be convenient, therefore, in our wide perspective, if we let our eye rest a moment on these two cardinal points, and fix the date of them distinctly in our mind.

The earlier of these two dates, again, is interesting to us, from our point of view, in two ways: first, it is exactly at the middle of the line of development we are considering; and secondly, it is marked not only by that controversy, the earliest that has weight in the modern history of doctrine, but also by the earliest formal treatise on the Christian trinity. This is not, it is true, quite the trinity of the later creeds, though it speaks of Jesus — for the first time, I believe, distinctly — as "a god;" and it was not written by Sabellius, an Alexandrian Greek, but by Novatian, a Roman schismatic, a Puritan of ill health and (as he was charged) of "wolfish" temper, a man whose impracticable and eccentric opposition to the church authorities reminds us strongly of Roger Williams, and who, like that vexer of the Pilgrim church, entangled himself in an interminable snarl of controversy touching the right and wrong of baptism and the true conditions of church membership.

So we find that in the middle of the Third Century, more than half a century before Constantine, under the very stress of the martyr-age, or at least in a short breathing-space of rest from persecution, active and acrimonious controversy is going on, that touches both the central doctrine and the visible organization of the Church. We are already two centuries away from Paul; and in this long interval we have not, at first view, caught sight of anything that specially arrested us as a landmark of Christian doctrine. At least, the names scattered along that line are the names not of men who handled sharp weapons in the strife of opinion, but of Apostolical Fathers, — writers for edification merely; Apologists, — defenders of the faith against alien enemies; Fathers, — commentators, philosophical lecturers, and so on, who did a busy preparatory work, but who do not stand in especially sharp relief as the expounders of controverted doctrine. And so those two centuries are a comparatively level stretch, of little account to us until we look a little more sharply, and then we see that they are intersected by a line which, in truth, marks the most clearly defined and significant boundary in the whole development of Christian theology.

This cross-line cuts the course of our history at a point just a century after the beginnings of the Church of the Apostles at Jerusalem; and it marks, really, the starting-place of the rapid development of Christian doctrine, as such, contrasted with those first efforts, which we find in the Epistles of Paul, to draw the line between Judaism and Christianity. Clearly, throughout the New Testament, the leading idea is that Jesus was the Messiah of the Jews, in however spiritual fashion this office might be interpreted; and so long as the Jewish nation existed, however feeble a remnant it might appear, the deliverance and glory of the chosen people under its Divine Leader would remain the central point of faith, at any rate with a large proportion of the disciples. Indeed, in the time of the apostles, it is not quite clear that in the average Christian mind the Messianic hope was altered essentially from its early Jewish meaning, except that it was definitely fixed upon Jesus of Nazareth, and that its fulfilment was to be in a second coming, visibly, in the clouds of heaven, in the lifetime of the generation that had seen and heard the Master. It is common to say that that hope was extinguished in the tragical overthrow of Jerusalem under Titus. But it would be more correct to put the date sixty-five years later, — when a Messianic pretender or enthusiast, calling himself Son of the Star of Jacob (Bar-Cochab), having reigned three years as Messianic prince in Jerusalem, was suppressed, and the Jewish nation was bloodily extinguished under Hadrian, in 135. Up to that date, it seems quite certain that there was a sect of Palestinian Christians who looked distinctly to see a restoration of the "kingdom unto Israel" under the risen and triumphant Messiah. After that date, this hope was definitely blotted out, and the independent growth of Christian doctrine, as distinct from a more or less altered and spiritualized Judaism, may be said to have begun.

The year 135 is to be taken, then, as the crisis of the revolution which established Christian doctrine as an independent force in shaping the religious opinions of mankind. The moment is so well defined, and the narrative which relates it is so explicit and precise, that one might almost think it a myth, half-consciously created (as such things are) to tell the intellectual event in the terms of personal adventure. On the contrary, the story has every appearance of being plain matter of fact; and it is told by one of the most calm, plain, and thoughtful of all writers of that time, — I mean

Justin the Apologist, who died as a martyr somewhere about thirty years later. The dialogue is a long one, but I will just indicate here the cardinal point on which it turns.

Soon after that great catastrophe of the Jewish people, Justin — an educated Greek, now a zealous Christian of the philosophic type coming to be common — meets an elderly Jew, Trypho, a teacher and man of mark among his people, who (we may suppose) has been cast into a great despondency by that hopeless overthrow. Such, at least, we may imagine to be the motive of his patient listening; though, in truth, the part he holds in this dialogue is curt, captious, and dry. But to put it a little more dramatically: "Alas!" he says, or seems to say, "where can we now look for the fulfilment of that divine hope, that promise of God to his people?" The younger man takes up the topic, and enters with him at great length into the true interpretation of that prophecy: it is, he urges, a spiritual fulfilment of that hope, not a literal or carnal one, which has been meant from the first. And so, having prepared the way, he enters with frank enthusiasm upon that doctrine of the eternal Word of God — such as Philo had expounded it in Alexandria a hundred years before, and such as we find it in the Gospel of John — which, he insists, is the very Spirit that was in Christ. The language in which he states this is so important to my present purpose that I must give it, as nearly as I can, in Justin's own words: —

Before all created things God begat from himself a certain mighty Word ("might of the Word," δύναμις λογική), which is also called Holy Spirit, or Glory of the Lord, sometimes Son, sometimes Wisdom, sometimes Angel, sometimes God, and sometimes Lord, or Word. And [not][1] so it is with us: for

[1] The word "not" is found in the Greek, but is omitted in the versions as unintelligible.

when we utter any word, we *beget* that word — not by a cutting-off [or act of separation], such that the Reason in us is thereby diminished, but rather like one flame kindled from another, while the first remains no less [than it was before]. — Chap. 61.

This, with what follows, is probably *the first attempt* at a formal statement of the Logos-doctrine as a cardinal point in Christian theology; the Proem to the Fourth Gospel (whether written a little before or a little after) being an eloquent and noble *religious* expression of the same general thought. What is important for us to note is that, with this deep religious and philosophic idea, — suggested in this new application (apparently) by the final extinction of the Messianic hope, — the first stage of Christian doctrine passes away; the decisive second step is taken, that makes Christianity a new and independent force in the world of thought: the second step, as we may rightly say, since Justin's doctrine of the Word completes and follows out Paul's doctrine of the Spirit, which was the first.

We seem here to have found the germ, out of which came the rapid and astonishing growth of Christian doctrine in the three centuries succeeding. During all this formative period, we find that the chief task of interpretation, and the motive of every later Christological controversy, turned not at all upon the points familiar to us in the New Testament and in the so-called Apostolical Fathers: the simple acceptance of Jesus as a Saviour from sin; repentance, regeneration, and the rest; but upon the question, In what sense are we to understand the cardinal fact, the advent of the Divine Life among men in the person of Jesus? That the disciples were deeply persuaded of such an advent, as witnessed in their own experience and in what they knew of the world about them, we may accept without any cavil. The faith was real: the task of reason was to bring the theory of it within range and harmony of their general way of thinking, — which was far enough away from ours. The first attempts were, as we have seen already, a little vacillating and crude. We must try, however, to see how the doctrine looked *to them*, — not merely the shape it grew to afterwards. We find, for example, no hint of a formal Trinity; no distinction, even, of which they were conscious, between Son and Spirit. Thus the most definite statement we get from Justin's "Apology," written some fifteen years later, is this, — defending the Christians from the charge of impiety: "We worship and adore both Him [God], and the Son who came forth from him and taught us these things, and the host of other Angels who follow and are made like him, and the prophetic Spirit." A few years later we find these words of another Apologist (Athenagoras), who attempts to make the doctrine more explicit: "The Son [is] in the Father, and the Father in the Son, by oneness and power of the Spirit. Mind and Reason (*Logos*) of the Father [is] the Son of God" (chap. 10).

So far, the thought we have to deal with is simply religious; that is, it is an attempt to make plain to the understanding and put into intelligible speech a real experience, which the believer is first conscious of in his own religious life. For there are times when any of us who are capable of such emotions feel as if sharers of a Life higher than our own, and as if our thoughts were suggested to us by a Wisdom greater than our own. By the easiest turn of phrase, we call that prompting voice the Word of God. The Word so spoken in us is the voice of the Spirit; and the revelation of it through some nobler life we easily think of as the Word of the Most High "made flesh." With us, indeed, the terms are apt to be symbolic and vague, — if, indeed, we do not prefer other terms to express the same thing; but with those who received it then there were two things that made them take it in a much more literal way than we are apt to do. One was a habit of mind which made what we should call an abstract idea a real "objective" thing to them: thus Day or Night, Life or Death, by a sort of natural poetry, seem to such minds more an actual person or power than a mere impression on the senses or a mere fact of life. The other was a law of the language in which they thought, which carried the same thing farther out, and made the thing a person: the term "*Logos*" in Greek is masculine, not neuter, as Word or Reason would be in English; and it was clearly much harder for them than for us to think of it as a mere abstract quality. Thus, in the sentence I have just quoted, it was the most natural thing in the world for Athenagoras to say that the Mind (νοῦς) or Reason (λόγος) of God is his Son. I do not suppose that this way of looking at it can ever be made easy and natural to us as it was to them. But we constantly meet it in early Christian theology, — which we may, if we will, call vividly imaginative instead of coldly rational, — and we shall very soon see how important it is in the understanding of doctrinal controversy.

Meanwhile, as we have to remember, there are three classes of interpreters, all calling themselves Christian, each very different from both the others. Nay, in these early times of unchecked speculation about a very momentous fact in human history, we find a formal list of more than forty different "heresies," or fashions of free interpretation, before the creeds were fixed. Those who were intellectually fascinated by the theory, and attempted — often wildly and crudely enough — to work it out in systems of metaphysical philosophy, we call Gnostics. Those who simply laid it to heart as a gospel of life, and tried to live faithfully up to it, we call Confessors. Those who tried to interpret it into a coherent system of opinion, and to make it the basis of an organized and regulated religious life, were the Fathers, the teachers, the theologians of the Christian Church. The first of these classes ran fast into all manner of differences and extravagances, and in not much more than half a century had almost wholly disappeared. From the second class came the multitude of Martyrs, humble and unknown, most of them, who fill the record of three Christian centuries with glory and with pity. The third class have exhibited, too often, the passions of mere subtile and angry disputants that have grown out of their almost incredible notion of belief in doctrine as essential to salvation; but it is they who have also given the dignity, the intellectual strength, and the enduring vigor to the organic life of Christendom. The history of Christian doctrine is given in the lives of a few of these men.

But now that great and mischievous fallacy, — *belief in doctrine essential to salvation*, which has brought so much calamity, guilt, and shame upon the Christian ages, — how ever did it come about? It will not do to let it go with mere reprobation and abhorrence. We must see, if we can, how it was possible for some of the noblest and most enlightened of men to hold that opinion in good faith, and to open the way (as Saint Augustine did) to grievous crimes against humanity, even if they did not walk in that way themselves. And, in trying to answer this question, we shall hit upon the double current of motive, which it will be necessary to follow, to get any right understanding of what the history of Christian doctrine really is.

I do not think so shocking a belief as that, with all the horrible consequences it led to, would ever have come to pass, if the Christian doctrine had been held as a mere intellectual opinion. It was something very different from that. The Word was not made flesh, the Son of God did not dwell visibly among men, above all, a being higher than all the angels did not submit to the sorrows of humanity and the ignominy of a cruel death, merely to teach a theory of speculative knowledge, which we might compare to our modern science about the sun and stars! The whole thing meant deliverance from some impending calamity which was threatening all human society and the soul of every man. At the bottom of all religious feeling, nay, as a background to their joy of pardon and assurance of salvation, lay a deep sense of terror and gloom. Just what men feared we cannot always tell. Perhaps it was a great horror and dread of hell, which it certainly was in many: men's apprehension of a future life is always deeply colored by their experience of this. But it is not necessary to suppose it was so in all, or always. At any rate, we can look back and see what a doom — the destruction of a whole order of society, complicated with miseries and terrors like a French Revolution spread out over three whole centuries, with a mystery of iniquity before which the conscience stands aghast — was in fact slowly coming on, overwhelming and resistless; and it is impossible not to think that the *tone* of their feeling may have been a sort of foreboding of that almost infinite disaster. At the bottom of their religious conviction, at all events, and a motive of their deepest gratitude, was the sense that the Christian gospel was the way of rescue from some overwhelming doom. The Lord's people were safe, — how or why they knew not, — safe under a Divine Leader and Deliverer, while the world outside were cut off "in eternal ruin[1] from the presence of the Lord." It was not for them to dispute the terms of

[1] αἰώνιος ὄλεθρος.

safety; and these, they no doubt thought, implied at least as scrupulous homage, at least as accurate an observance of every form and title of reverence, as that demanded by the Roman emperor and his court. I do not go into their possible or probable theory about it, but only suggest this by way of illustrating what was evidently their state of mind.

With this motive, we need not be surprised that it became the keenest point of conscience with them, and the strictest condition they exacted of one another, to hold right doctrine concerning the true rank and majesty of their unseen Sovereign, and to vie with one another who should carry their homage to the most exalted pitch. I say that all these motives are to be found: I do not say what was always the theoretical ground of them. Their theology ran in two streams, not one, following this double line of religious motive: on their part, by what discipline or organization, by what rites and obligations, by what spiritual exercises of contrition, penitence, worship, or human duty, should they assure themselves of the Christian salvation; on the Lord's part, how should they rightly esteem and how most fitly honor the Author of the great deliverance?

In a broad way we may say that the former, the practical side, was taken up rather by the Western Church: the chief crisis it came to was in the work and life of Saint Augustine, about the year 400, which, beginning in a passion of remorse and a deep sense of native sin, went on to an absolute surrender of will and self to God, as its consummate work was that wonderful ecclesiastical structure, built up under Cyprian and Ambrose, confirmed by Leo the Great, and standing in vigor almost unimpaired down to our day. Of this, the more social, human, political task of the Christian Church of the first five centuries, with its more earnest and profound development of moral doctrine, I shall have little to say, though it is the historic fact best of all worth keeping clear in mind.

For my immediate purpose, I must keep to the line of speculative development, which is found chiefly in the Eastern Church, and which wrought out within these five centuries the great historic creeds of Christendom. The chief crises of interest are at or near the middle of the Third Century, the middle of the Fourth, and the middle of the Fifth. These are the dates of the Sabellian controversy, the Arian controversy (at its height), and the controversy respecting the Double Nature of Christ, which was brought to a term at the Council of Chalcedon, last of the Four Great Councils, in 451. From the point of view I have taken, a very brief review, I hope, will make these main points of the doctrinal development sufficiently clear and intelligible for the purpose we have just now in mind, and perhaps make the completer study of this period a little easier.

I must now go back to the point I had come to before, — the doctrine of the WORD, which came in early in the Second Century to fill the void left by the perishing of the Messianic hope. Let us here recall the words of Athenagoras, repeating with a little more precision those of Justin; namely, that "the Mind and Reason of the Father is the Son of God;" or, as we are free to read it, "The Son of God is the Mind and Reason of the Father." I have said something of the state of mind which made such a definition more natural and reasonable then than it would seem now. It has, in fact, to do with a system of philosophy (known as "Realism") held unconsciously, and prevailing from antiquity down to nearly six hundred years ago, but which has been blotted almost out of our memory and imagination by the analytic science of modern times. I wish to have as little to do as

I can with that line of pure speculation; but we cannot understand in the least what the creators of the Christian doctrine meant, or thought they meant, unless we make a little effort that way. The words just quoted — "the Son of God is the Mind and Reason of the Father " — are *the germ of the Christian Trinity*. If we were to use such words now, we should at once be understood to use them figuratively. Athenagoras uses them literally, — that is, as far as any symbolic language can be literal. And so we must understand them, too, in as literal a sense as they will bear.

Mind or Reason, we say, is an attribute of God. Now the Son of God, we also say, is certainly a person, not an attribute. But the early dogmatists did not see the difficulty as we do. To them, it is clear, it was perfectly easy to think of Mind or Reason as having an individual, almost we might say a personal, existence, — not of course independent of the Father, but "in the bosom of the Father." This fiction of speech, as we should call it, is what theologians call *to hypostatize the Logos*, — that is, to regard the Divine attribute as if it were a living person, a real thing. This is, in fact, what is meant by the true mystical doctrine of the pre-existence of Christ, — not that he existed (as the Arians say) as a conscious individual Person before the world was ; but that the Divine Word which "became flesh" in him was from eternity a quality of the Divine Nature, the same thing (so to speak) with the self-conscious intelligence of the Eternal. But this quality, or attribute, was so strongly individualized in the habit of mind I speak of, that there was not the least difficulty, or objection, in conceiving that it took in the most literal sense the place of a human soul in Jesus, and made him the Son of God exactly as Athenagoras declares that Mind or Reason is the Son of God. We, as I just said, have left wholly behind the habit of mind which makes such a conception possible to us; but to the early Christians it was evidently quite easy and natural, and we must see it so if we would understand anything of their doctrine.

I shall not take up here the story of those long, weary, unintelligible, and often scandalous disputes known as the Controversies of the period we are now looking forward to. I wish, just now, only to point out the difficulty or ambiguity of language which they turned on. For all the parties to these controversies contended, with equal zeal, that they were both orthodox in their belief, and the true interpreters of the Christian formula which all accepted alike. The difficulty lay in the nature of the thing to be expressed, and the language in which it was expressed. The hard, pious, and rather narrow Novatian, indeed, is content to say, bluntly, that " it would be an offence to deny that God the Father can beget a Son who is also a God," and lets it go at that. But those of a more metaphysical turn must needs look a little closer; and then they found there were two elements in the conception, instead of one; and whichever we give weight to, the other presently goes out of sight. We are agreed (we will suppose) to say that the Word of God — that is, the divine wisdom, reason, or thought — is the Son of God; and that the Son of God, in the flesh, was Jesus Christ. Now, when we say the Divine Reason, are we really speaking of an Attribute or quality of the Godhead, or are we speaking of a Person? If the first, then we are speaking of what is necessarily eternal, as God himself is eternal; for God cannot even be thought of without his Wisdom, his Reason, or his Word, which is strictly, therefore, co-eternal with him. But again, we are agreed in calling that Word his Son: his Eternal Son, therefore? This might be, and in our modern way of thinking would be, a pure figure of speech, as we have seen ; but it was far from being such with these ardent Realists, who saw in it, on the contrary, the most positive and objectively real of existences. And so at once the subtile question confronted them, in a sense that could not possibly occur to us : How can a son be co-eternal with his father? The very word "sonship" implies an act and a beginning : Christ, as Son, must then be, if ever so little, lower than the Father, and later in order of time, — that is, not literally eternal.

Such, as nearly as we can see it, was the equivocation, or ambiguity, which set the believing Christians at endless variance, — each (as I have said before) being convinced that his own belief was essential to salvation. Those more mystically inclined would dwell rather on the Eternal Word and its identity in essence with God himself; those more rationally inclined would draw the line where I have marked, and, in defending their position, would insist on a wider separation of Christ from God than the general conscience of Christians would bear. And so the story of the controversies of those three succeeding centuries is the story of the slow swing, as of a pendulum, first to one and then to the other of these two interpretations, till, as I said, its point of rest was determined, on authority then held good, at Chalcedon,[1] in the year 451.

With this hint for our guide, I will now go rapidly along the line of those obscure and acrimonious disputes, in such a way as to show, I hope, that they were not mere accidents of bigotry and passion, but were steps in a natural process of development, — stroke and counterstroke, thought balancing against thought, — such as all history shows must be, where

[1] Chalcedon is to us a mere geographical expression, of no particular account. It was, in fact, a small suburb of Constantinople.

any great revolution of opinion is going on. The passion and violence involved in it are neither more nor less disgraceful, neither more nor less surprising, — perhaps rather less, — than the passion and violence called out by the labor-battle of to-day; certainly, on a higher intellectual level.

Naturally enough, the first great swing of the pendulum was towards the more mystical and speculative view. What we call the School of Alexandria, with its two great teachers, Clement and Origen, spent its main strength (along with other and most important services of criticism, interpretation, and moral instruction) in developing, with all its bearings human and divine, the doctrine of the Divine Word, making it effectually the central doctrine of the Christian life. Even in the lifetime of that mighty teacher and commentator, Origen, the doctrine had been run out into a pious mysticism by Sabellius, who taught that the Christian Trinity — Father, Son, and Spirit — is purely a trinity of Attributes, just as light and heat are one with the splendor and power of the sun. This was to merge Christ in God, and either wholly lose sight of the historic Jesus, or else leave him a man like ourselves, only illuminated by the Light that shines upon all alike. This is the Sabellian heresy, condemned at Alexandria, and its author excommunicated, in 261.

"The chief adversary of Sabellius," we are told, "opposed him so earnestly as almost to fall into the opposite error of a hypostatical independence of the Father and the Son." Now, to explain the strange term "hypostatical independence," we most conveniently take the account given by a great and famous theologian, Gregory of Nyssa, a hundred years later, who tells us that *hypostasis* corresponds to the individual as *nature* to the race or species: thus we say the "nature" of a man, but the "hypostasis" of John or Paul.

EARLY CHRISTIAN DOCTRINE. 21

This error, then, of making Christ an individual wholly distinct from the Father, which was " almost " committed by the opponent of Sabellius, was quite fallen into, unawares, some sixty years afterwards, by Arius, a presbyter of Alexandria, who in like manner assailed his bishop, Alexander, as a Sabellian. The matter was more important now, as it was just when Constantine the Great had come to be sovereign of the Roman world; and the stress of debate grew so violent that, for reasons of State, Constantine — who had just (324) declared the empire Christian — resolved that it must be decided by a representative Council gathered from all Christendom. And so was summoned the first " Œcumenical " or World Council, which met at Nicæa, some forty miles from Constantinople, in 325.

Fortunately for Alexander, he had a keen and vigorous defender in a young deacon of his church, Athanasius, — who for nearly fifty years bore himself intrepidly and not unworthily as the champion of the contested faith. The story of his life is very dramatic, and wins genuine homage from us all, whatever we think of his temper or his opinions. But I can stop to tell only the point or two bearing directly on our subject. Arius was defeated in the Council, if not convinced; and, to guard against his error, the Nicene Creed (then adopted) carefully states that the Son is " of one substance " (*homo-ousian*, or *con-substantial*) with the Father. The Arians, or semi-Arians, — who were long in great favor at the Imperial court, — would compromise only so far as to say that the Son is of " like substance " (*homoi-ousian*) with the Father. And the degree of separateness, or independence, which they thus asserted, was held by the more orthodox to be a most dangerous concession to the decaying Paganism, — as if, in fact, it made Christ an inferior divinity, a Son of God in the same sense as the Roman pantheon made Hercules a son of Jove. Under that stigma — an illogical and monstrous compromise between a devout mysticism and a sober rationality — Arianism has labored to this day.

The Arian Controversy, which lasted for some forty years with great heat and violence, is not only the chief and most dramatic event of this Fourth Century, but is the only one of these great ecclesiastical campaigns which is well fastened upon modern memory. It was not, however, at all conclusive of the matter in debate, but only opened the way to further refinements and further quarrel, lasting till past the middle of the Fifth, and was then only settled by authority, not reason, — for in reason the battle goes on till now. Successive points of this debate came up to be determined by successive Councils, — the four (which it may be convenient to sum up here) held equally in authority in the Eastern and in the Western Church being those of Nicæa (325), Constantinople (381), Ephesus (431), and Chalcedon (451). I will recite, as briefly as possible, the doctrinal decisions made in the latter three.

The heresy of Apollinaris, condemned at Constantinople, was that Christ had, properly, *no human personality:* the Logos being his soul, and his body being specially created of celestial substance. The same Council condemned the heresy of Macedonius, which denied personality to the Holy Ghost: thus was made complete the formal doctrine of the Trinity, — the Nicene Creed being expanded accordingly.

The heresy of Nestorius (Patriarch of Constantinople), condemned at Ephesus, was that Jesus was not essentially Divine in his own person, but was made so by the "indwelling" Word of God. Hence Nestorius refused to the Virgin Mary the title (beginning to be ascribed to her) "Mother of God."

The heresy of Eutyches (a pious and mystical monk, a great fanatic), condemned at Chalcedon, was that the divine nature in Christ *wholly absorbs* the human, leaving it inoperative. The formula by which the faith was here defined was dictated by Leo the Great, bishop of Rome. Its essential declaration is as follows: —

We confess and with one accord teach one and the same Son, our Lord Jesus Christ, perfect in his divinity, perfect in his humanity, truly God and truly man, consisting of a reasonable soul and body; of one substance with the Father according to his godhead, and of one substance with us according to his manhood; in all things like to us, sin only excepted; . . . who is to be acknowledged one and the same Christ, the Son, the Lord, the only-begotten, in two natures, without mixture, change, division, or separation; the difference of natures not being cancelled by their union, but rather the property of each nature being preserved and running together into one person (πρόσωπον) and one substance (ὑπόστασιν), so that he is not divided or separated into two persons, but the only Son, God, the Word, our Lord Jesus Christ, one and the same Person.

Into this prodigious definition came to be evolved the simple proposition of Justin we started with, by a process that is seen to be strictly natural and inevitable, as soon as we take into view the ambiguity that lurked in the simple proposition itself, and the condition of mind to which it was addressed. Not that the controversy stopped here. Under the form of disputes concerning "a single nature" and "a single will," it continued still for a century or two to vex and divide the Eastern Church: in fact, the "one-will" heresy continued in the little sect of Maronites down to the time of the Crusades, possibly down to our day. But the decision of Chalcedon is the last that has any interest for us. It was, as I just said, dictated in almost its exact terms by Leo the Great, of Rome, called also "First of the Popes." It was the same year with the great invasion of the Huns in western Europe. Under the terrors of the barbarian flood that poured in successive waves, each bringing the final overthrow more certain and more near, it was fit that the moral strength of Christendom should not be wasted in that war of words; and so the voice of Rome, still strongest and most formidable of all, was heard, bidding the vain conflict to cease, and the Christian nations to unite in one formula of faith. And — whatever the abstract veracity of its terms — it is well that it was so; well for the world, and well for us.

What was wanted was a symbol, or type, under which the spiritual force educated and trained by four Christian centuries could rally, to organize and maintain an Authority that would serve as some sort of guide and defence in the awful three centuries' convulsion that was already seen to be impending. Thirty years before, Saint Augustine, looking out upon the storm-clouds that were gathering, — having already given the strength of his life to show that true liberty must be had not by the wayward will of man, but by absolute surrender to the awful sovereignty of God, — had proclaimed that the refuge of souls may be found not in any city of earthly foundation, but in the CITY OF GOD, eternal in the heavens. He meant it (writing as he did when the Gothic invasion was yet fresh and that of the Vandals was just about to burst) to show that men's strength is only in a Power that is spiritual and unseen. But his words were generous and brave, and they closed in a strain that is musical in its serenity and sweetness. And as the great conflict with barbarism went on, and as it was found that, after all, the race and states of men did not wholly perish, those words were taken more and more to heart, and had their weight in giving men good hope and courage for the future.

It is well then to see how this great moral force, that had been growing up side by side, though almost out of hearing of that passionate theological debate, at length accepted its result as the symbol of its own faith. GOD WITH MAN is the meaning which it conveyed to them; and so it made the long development of the early Christian doctrine no mere barren conflict in the dark (as an observer had once said of it at Nicæa), but the prelude to an organization that saved Christianity itself to the modern world,· and held in itself all the moral forces of civilization for the coming thousand years.

CHRISTIANITY FROM THE FIFTH TO THE FIFTEENTH CENTURY.

BY ANDREW P. PEABODY.

THE period covered by this Lecture comprehends what are commonly called the Dark Ages, — rightly so called, — shrouded in a darkness historically inevitable, yet immeasurably to be preferred to the light of the immediately preceding centuries, and fraught with light-producing agencies for the centuries to come.

For this darkness there were two concurrent causes. In the first place, Roman civilization was suicidal in its very nature. It culminated in a prodigality which exhausted the plunder of the vast empire, and in a moral degradation and depravity no less fatal to genius, art, intellect, and liberal culture than to individual and social well-being.

Christianity would have anticipated the gathering shadows by her purer light, had not that light been for the time wellnigh extinguished; but we must name for the second cause of the Dark Ages the adoption of Christianity as the State religion. There can be no better commentary on the words of Christ, " My kingdom is not of this world," than is furnished in the history of the Church whenever and wherever it has been organically incorporated with the State. I will not except even the English Church, which has owed to its political relations its periods of declension and of overshadowing worldliness, and to the nomination of bishops by the prime minister the appointment of sundry prelates who have shone, if at all, not in the beauty of holiness; while it was indebted to Methodism for its awakening from what seemed a death-slumber, and has at the present moment for its most efficient ministers men who would gladly draw a sharp dividing line between "the things which are Cæsar's" and "the things that are God's."

There is less a marked difference than a broad contrast between the sanctity of eminent Christians under the ban of the empire and the traditional sainthood of those under its patronage or protection. Of the former there is hardly one for whose name the term "saint" does not seem the appropriate prefix; of the latter, there are few for whom it would now be claimed, were it not already given. Jerome was mean, tricky, truculent, quarrelsome, and entirely oblivious of the axiom, as true in ethics as in geometry, that a straight line is the shortest distance between two points. Augustine, while profoundly and bitterly penitent for the sins of his youth, was by no means free from the then besetting sins of the episcopate. Basil and Gregory of Nyssa deemed it their duty to lie most atrociously in the interest of the Church, and in the case of Gregory, Archdeacon Farrar, who ascribes to him no less than three forged letters containing such deliberate falsehoods as in a Christian of earlier time or of our own would admit of no possible excuse, credits them to "the innocence of his heart, combined with imperfect moral views." Certainly he had "not so learned Christ." Most of the ordinations and episcopal consecrations that have left a record in history were effected or attended by force or fraud. Chrysostom, by far the best man of his time, was compelled to receive what was miscalled consecration at the hands of Theophilus of Alexandria, as vile a wretch as ever lived, who performed this office under threat, in case he declined it, of a criminal charge of which his life would have been the forfeit. Augustine was ordained by brute force against his will. Strange indeed it is, that the superstitious people of that day believed, and still more strangely is it maintained by credulous prelatists now, that spiritual grace was actually transmitted by violent hands laid on reluctant heads; and yet if the validity of such ordinations be not admitted, the entire fabric of unbroken apostolic succession, at best precarious and without adequate support, falls to the ground, stultified and annulled.

Meanwhile asceticism was held in higher esteem than truth, integrity, or mercy; men were taught to regard filth and squalidness as of supreme religious value; and there were among the foremost ministers at the chief altars of Christendom men whom what we now term common decency would not tolerate in the outermost courts of the sanctuary.

None of these things appear strange when we remember that the first imperial "nursing father" of the Church was a man who postponed baptism till he was close under the shadow of death, that he might, without peril to his soul, heap up the fuller measure of sin to be washed away. Under such baleful influences all that remained for Christianity was to "fall into the ground and die," in the only sense in which that which is God-born can die. But the seed of the Kingdom had life in death. It "took root downward," and deep root too, before it began to "bear fruit upward," or even to pierce the hardened soil under which it lay.

There were two seed-plots which proffered a specially congenial soil for the germination of Christianity. One of these was the monastic institution. Of this, as of any other institution, the worst that can now be said is that it is obsolete; for whatever survives its usefulness lives on as an obstruction and a nuisance. But monasticism, though even then not without gross excesses and abuses, was an early necessity of the Church. There were places and conditions in which it was impossible to be with the world without being wholly of the world, — to walk with man without ceasing to walk with God. All the ways of common life were so blocked up by compliances offensive to an enlightened conscience, that it was hard for a disciple of the new faith to buy or sell, to command or serve, to hold military or civil office, to sail or travel, to mingle in promiscuous society or to accept the hospitality of kindred or friends. For one determined to be consistently a Christian, the only alternative often was retreat or martyrdom.

Nor did one lose the opportunity of faithful Christian work by forsaking the haunts of men. There were many recluses whose eminent piety drew disciples into the deserts, caves, and mountain-clefts, to seek counsel and comfort; and not a few hermits and cenobites reappeared at intervals, as preachers of divine truth, always with a prestige of sanctity which made their word a power. Then, too, there is in sincere devotion a diffusive and penetrating efficacy, felt even when not recognized. It is as utterly impossible to suppress the radiance and to veil the outshining of a saintly spirit as it is to smother fire with linen garments. The pure light of the life eternal, once kindled in a recipient soul, may, like the stars of heaven, be a guiding light, though seen only from afar. To thousands whose outward vision never rested on one of these holy men, their multitude, their concurrent testimony, the report of their self-denial, vigils, and prayers, the mere existence of this cloud of witnesses in near and constant view of an open heaven, fixed an else wavering faith, confirmed an else flickering hope, and maintained in the arduous duties and frequent sacrifices of the Christian profession a strenuousness of purpose which might else have succumbed to incessant trial or temptation.

Nor was monasticism less a necessity after Christianity had mounted the throne of the Cæsars, and was thus rapidly lapsing into a baptized semi-paganism. It was even more difficult to lead a Christian life in the Church triumphant than it had been in the Church militant. Ritual conformity then became a substitute for duty, and penance was the sufficient remedy for sin. Some of the emperors, both of the culminating eastern and of the fast declining western empire, were just, honorable, God-fearing men, and now and then an empress left a record of purity, beneficence, and care for things sacred; but when the thrones were not filled, the courts were crowded, with brutality and profligacy; and example, which, while it tardily creeps up, runs rapidly down the social scale, paralleled and multiplied patrician vices among all sorts and conditions of men. There was very little that even Christian eloquence could accomplish. The great preachers were admired and applauded to-day, and imprisoned or banished to-morrow; and we cannot learn that they had any influence in stemming the swelling current of corruption and turpitude. Still less could a fervently devout man in private life make himself felt as a power for good, where there was hardly anything that he could do or enjoy without being or seeming in complicity with evil. The cloisters were, therefore, peopled by the most saintly men that bore the Christian name. Almost all the fathers and ecclesiastics of whom history gives a good report were monks or hermits at the outset, entered the active service of the Church with the utmost reluctance, and in nearly every instance lost in the outside world much of the simplicity and integrity of soul which they had brought from the cloister.

The monasteries retained whatever of generous culture in the useful arts and in letters had survived the subversion of the Roman Empire. To be sure, there sprang up about the

Byzantine court and in the provincial capitals a barbaric splendor, such as in the East has always surrounded royalty and official rank; but the frequency of wide-spread famine and pestilence indicates the decay among people at large of the practical knowledge and skill, which had in earlier time insured prosperous industry and had set limits to inevitable calamity. Nor yet was there any lack of such military science as related to the equipment and movement of forces, to siege and strategy. But agriculture and all its subsidiary arts found refuge in the purlieus of the monasteries. Their soil was well tilled, and their crops seldom failed. Their tenants, too, learned how to live and thrive, and every large monastery thus became a centre of civilization for a surrounding population in an ever increasing circle. In every work of propagandism, also, monks were the pioneers, and exercised on previously pagan soil a humanizing influence far beyond the capacity of conquerors, magistrates, or the secular clergy.

They also kept in existence such of the remains of ancient literature as have not perished beyond the hope of restoration, and — perhaps an equal service — they not improbably destroyed much of it which would have made the world no richer, had it been spared. The monasteries gradually became seminaries, and were long the only seminaries, of learning. The novitiates destined for the cloister received, of course, from their seniors such instruction as would fit them to replace their preceptors; and in the absence of all other means of education, boys in training for civil or military functions were placed under their tuition. But for them, writing would have been a lost art; for there were several centuries during which kings could not write their own names, and the (so-called) coats-of-arms in which some of us take pride, if indeed they are rightfully ours, indicate that we had ancestors who used these grotesque devices in lieu of the signatures of which they were incapable. Scholasticism had its birth in the monasteries, and all the older universities sprang from them. They were, at the same time, the almshouses and hospitals to whose shelter and ministries need was always a sufficient claim; and the great charities of these latter days are but the natural outgrowth of the humane and philanthropic spirit cherished in these homes of mercy.

Here too, and only here, were preserved the Scriptures, and here were transmitted, from century to century, the ability to read them, a not wholly inadequate, though imperfect comprehension of their contents, and no little of their redeeming and sanctifying efficiency.

The other "procreant cradle" of Christianity to which I referred is the Roman law as codified by Justinian, — the most truly Christian legislator that the world has yet seen. Without his code it is hard to say what Christendom might not have become. In the whole Roman world the tendency had been toward the unsettling of domestic life and the destruction of all that can make home sacred. In exclusively Christian circles there had grown up a better feeling and habit, and the earlier Christian emperors had somewhat limited the license of divorce, and taken some cognizance of the rights of wives and children as to their property and earnings. But Justinian nearly completed the work which they had begun. The marriage covenant received under his auspices the most stringent legal sanction, and could be dissolved by no means so easily as now in the greater part of Christendom. Little was wanting, and that little was soon supplied by the canon law, to make marriage absolutely indissoluble except by the one crime which in its very nature disowns and annuls it. Nor has there been in countries whose legislation has been founded on the Roman law any room for or need of the demands that under the English common law are perpetually made for the protection of the rights of women. It is impossible to overestimate the worth of these legal safeguards for domestic purity during ages of violence and misrule; and it reflects great honor on the hierarchies of both the Eastern and the Western Church that they employed in this behalf the enormous power of ecclesiastical inhibitions and penalties, that at no other point of discipline were they so nearly inflexible, and that the instances in which they were constrained by force or induced by bribery or intrigue to sanction with reference to marriage or divorce aught that was not in full accordance with the words and spirit of the Gospel were so few as to have been marked historical epochs.

During the Dark Ages the secular clergy were in part recruited from the monasteries; but, when not so, they were in general of a much lower order of intelligence and character than the monks. Few of them were capable of giving positive religious instruction, and such as was given related oftener to the mythology in which the saints were heroes, and virtually demigods, than to the contents of Christianity or its records. Still, reverence and worship, even when most ignorant, have a hallowing power; religious symbolism is of immense didactic value to minds of slender capacity or imperfect training; and the mere sense of things unseen, though it be utterly indefinite and vague, has a restraining and elevating influence. It was not, then, without substantial and cumulative moral benefit that the Church service retained and increased its outward splendor while there was but little sense of its meaning, and gave to Christianity a stronger hold on the imagination and the affections than it could gain on the rude and unnurtured intellect.

Then, too, there is an untold wealth of significance in the parable of the mustard-seed. In the minutest particle of Christian principle or sentiment there is a marvellous germinating power; the shoot that springs from it grows rapidly into an overshadowing tree, and not only so, but as with the banyan-tree, its branches drop into the loosened soil and take root, so that a forest may grow from a single seed. Thus during the period when art, literature, and intellectual life seemed paralyzed, and there were hardly as many illustrious men as there were centuries, domestic slavery ceased; kind feeling for suffering humanity, at first confined to the monasteries, was diffused through communities and nations; chivalry, with its keen sense of honor and its reverence for woman, came into being; large funds were contributed for the redemption of captives from Mahometan lands; the savageness of war was mitigated, its prisoners spared, and often generously treated; and the world that emerged from the darkened centuries was rich in elements of hope and promise which gave no visible tokens when the shadows fell.

As regards Christian doctrine there were, during the earlier part of the period under review, ecclesiastics who were interested in maintaining the controversies bequeathed to them from previous times, and there were councils, no longer œcumenical, generally local and embracing representatives of but a small portion of the Eastern or the Western Church, which issued dogmatic decisions no less than mandates as to discipline and church government. The Athanasian creed (so-called), which cannot be traced farther back than the Seventh Century, may be regarded as marking the close of the Arian controversy, and is, so far as I know, the earliest expression of an absolutely co-equal Trinity, though from the time of the Council of Nicæa the Western Church had been constantly gravitating in that direction. The Nicene creed had received the assent of many (so-called) semi-Arians, as it taught the derived and therefore subordinate nature of Christ. For a long time the chief point of controversy between orthodoxy and heresy had related to the single Greek letter ι (i) in the creed, the Homo-ousians, or orthodox Christians, maintaining that the Son is of the same substance with the Father; the Homoi-ousians, or semi-Arians, holding that he is of like substance, — a distinction in which it is hard to trace a difference.

There still remained the controversy concerning what is termed the procession, or the constant proceeding or flowing forth of the third person of the Trinity, — an idea which in any form it is difficult to reconcile with distinct personality; for though a person may proceed from another person, the continuous proceeding of one person from another is conceivable only to a mind that has been fed on theological subtilties. "Proceeding from the Father" was the phrase in the Nicene creed, though the words "and the Son" were added in a forged copy shortly after the adjournment of the Council. The original form is still in use in the Greek Church. In the Western Church usage varied; the Roman court gave ambiguous utterance so long as the Popes retained any hope of reuniting entire Christendom under their pastorate; and the words "and the Son" did not come into universal and unquestioned use before the Ninth or Tenth Century.

The principal revolt against the Athanasian creed when once established was in Spain, in the Eighth Century. The supreme deity of Christ, and such phrases as "the mother of God" and "the suffering God," were found to be insuperable obstacles in the attempt to convert Mahometans. This experience gave rise to a theory termed "adoptionism," according to which Christ, the Son of God in essence as to his divine nature, became so as to his human nature by adoption, so that his humanity and his human relations were genuine and real. This dogma had a brief currency in the West, and found some disciples in the East; but it was condemned by a council, and its principal champion, the Spanish bishop Felix, was imprisoned in Rome till he signed a recantation, which, on his return to Spain, he retracted, seeking refuge for his heresy in one of the provinces under Moslem sway.

With the revival of learning, which may be said to have begun in the Ninth Century, the scholastic philosophy and theology had birth and nourishment in many of the monasteries and in semi-monastic schools founded under the auspices of Charlemagne. The Trinity was thenceforward a favorite subject of metaphysical discussion and philosophical definition. There were scholastic divines who incurred, and not unjustly, the charge of tritheism; there were others, who, like Abelard, were virtually Unitarians, seeing in the three persons of the Trinity only three aspects of the one God,— in the Father omnipotence, in the Son omniscience, in the Holy Spirit perfect love.

As for predestination, during the early portion of the time covered by this lecture, while Augustine himself was lauded to the skies, his doctrine, without being formally disowned, was virtually set aside, and that, not so much in the interest of man's free agency and capacity of a right moral choice, as in the unwillingness to cast doubt on the universality of the redemptive power of the Church through its sacraments. It is worthy of notice that the test of strict orthodoxy propounded by Vincent of Lerins, and in our time often quoted in behalf of the severer types of dogmatic belief, *quod semper, quod ubique, quod ab omnibus,* " what has been believed always, everywhere, by all," was shaped in special antagonism to the Augustinian theology.

In the time of Charlemagne theologians recommenced the careful study of Augustine's writings, and one of the earliest results of this study was the discovery of a deficiency in his system. This was announced by the monk Gottschalk, who maintained, with a logic that cannot be disputed, that the predestination of a certain portion of the human race to salvation implies a'like eternal decree for the damnation of the residue of the race. He deemed the preaching of this double predestination so sacred a work, that he procured ordination in an uncanonical method, and began a course of missionary propagandism. He was in 849 condemned by a council, and compelled by a well-nigh fatal flagellation to throw his writings into the fire; but he refused to recant, and on his death-bed rejected the offer of restoration to the communion of the Church, considering all that had befallen him as foreordained for his salvation. He had some defenders and followers; and Hincmar, who had been the most active in procuring his condemnation, engaged John Scotus (surnamed Erigena, or Ireland-born) to write in refutation of his doctrine. This service John Scotus performed in a way very unsatisfactory to his employer, and with a philosophy which anticipated the positivism and pantheism of our own time. He wrote: " We cannot speak literally of prescience and predestination, inasmuch as with God there is no distinction of time; nor can we in any proper sense ascribe to him consciousness or knowledge. For him there is no evil. He is the cause only of good. Evil comes from one's isolating himself from God. It carries in itself its own punishment, if hidden in this life made manifest in the life to come. In the last analysis evil is a stage of development which leads to good, and the ultimate term of development is necessarily the return of all to God;" that is, reabsorption into the divine essence. In 859 a council condemned the heresy of John Scotus, and proclaimed Gottschalk's double predestination as eternal truth.

As regards original sin, while the Greek Church showed no tendency toward Augustinianism, the Latin Church from the Fifth to the Eleventh Century acquiesced in the transmission of sin, and of its penalty except as specially remitted, from Adam to his entire posterity. Among the earliest opponents of this dogma was Abelard, near the beginning of the Twelfth Century. He maintained that sin is in its very essence a voluntary act, and that children and persons incapable of free choice cannot in the sight of God be chargeable with sin or susceptible of punishment. Human nature he regarded as in no wise vitiated by Adam's sin. Like the early Alexandrian fathers, he expressed profound admiration for the virtue and piety of the Pagan sages, as contrasted with the vices of a portion of the monks and clergy of his own time. He evidently had no doubt that the characters of those non-Christian worthies placed them in a salvable condition; but if any maintained that faith in Christ is necessary to salvation, he challenges those who think so to prove that these men did not believe in Christ, as revealed in the Old Testament, or in the Sibylline oracles which he evidently supposed to be genuine and of great antiquity. His doctrine met with little acceptance, and was duly condemned by one of the frequent local councils that guarded the purity of church dogmas.

From his time for several generations the Augustinian doctrine maintained its hold. The next serious attack upon it was by Duns Scotus, in the Fourteenth Century. According to him, Adam's original righteousness was due, not to his nature, but to special gifts and graces with which he was supernaturally endowed. These he forfeited in his fall, and, of course, could not transmit them to his posterity, whose nature is what his was in its essence, inclined to evil, but not bad in itself, and capable of free choice, and thus of virtue and goodness. Man, according to him, cannot be regenerated without the grace of God; but he can by his own free choice put his moral nature into a condition in which he may be sure of God's regenerating grace, which is conferred only on those who of their own will seek it and in a certain sense deserve it. Predestination is thus conditional, — contingent on the divine foresight as to the use which man will make of his own free agency.

As to the doctrine of vicarious atonement or satisfaction, I find no proof of its having been established as an essential dogma till it was elaborated, in nearly its present form, by Anselm, the Archbishop of Canterbury, in the Eleventh Century. He first attempted to demonstrate, and did demonstrate to the satisfaction of his readers generally, that there was an intrinsic necessity for the payment of an infinite equivalent for the infinite punishment incurred by those predestined to redemption, — that it would be weakness in God and a sacrifice of his own glory to forgive man without the suffering in his stead of one whose co-equal divinity with the Father could alone make the price equal to the claim of justice. Augustine had taught the dogma of expiation by the death of Christ, but said that it was not intrinsically necessary, — that omnipotent wisdom might have provided other ways of redemption. It had been generally maintained that Christ paid a ransom for man; but the more common opinion was that he paid it to Satan, to whom men had virtually sold themselves. This was the opinion of men no less eminent than

Saint Bernard and Peter Lombard; though Peter Lombard and some other of the scholastic divines laid great stress on the sanctifying influence of the death of Christ on the soul of man.

Abelard openly impugned Anselm's theory of the atonement. He asked: If God was angry for the sin committed in the tasting of a single apple, must he not have been infinitely angry with the human race for the murder of Jesus Christ? He maintained that the justification of man by the death of Christ consists in Christ's kindling by this sublime act of love a kindred love in the human heart, — a love capable, not only of triumphing over the power of sin, but of investing the redeemed with the holy liberty of the children of God, and enabling them to fulfil the divine law under the impulse, no longer of fear, but of love.

As to (so-called) heretics in the period under our present consideration, the Arians, in the Sixth Century, were still in the ascendency among the Goths, Vandals, and Burgundians, and the kings of these nations were not slow in following the example set them by orthodox emperors and magistrates, in persecuting the adherents of the Nicene creed, demolishing their churches, sending their bishops into exile, and employing various modes of torture and mutilation on those who clung resolutely to their faith. In the Seventh Century Arianism prevailed extensively in Lombardy. In subsequent centuries, under its own name, it has left slight traces of itself in the history of the Church.

In the Eastern Church the most powerful heretical sect was that of the Paulicians,[1] whose creed was a revived and inten-

---

[1] This sect probably had its origin as early as the Fourth Century, and is said to have been founded by a widow in Samosata, named Calinica, from one of whose sons, Paul, the sect derived its name.

sified Gnosticism, of the Marcionite type. They carried the Persian dualism to the last extreme, regarding the external world and the human body as created, and the Old Testament as inspired, by the semi-omnipotent principle of evil, from whose dominion it was Christ's mission to rescue the souls of men. They were most numerous in Bulgaria, whence they spread all over the Eastern empire. They were suppressed, so far as vigorous measures of persecution could suppress them, by Alexis Comnenus, in the Eleventh Century; but it is said that there are still some remnants of the sect, its name unchanged, in the region of the Balkan Mountains. They were succeeded by the Bogomites,[1] whose dualism was less entire, but in its details somewhat more absurd, than that of the Paulicians.

In the Western Church the Cathari,[2] dualists like the Paulicians, rigidly ascetic, chargeable with no immorality of precept or practice, numbered many disciples in the Eleventh, Twelfth, and Thirteenth Centuries, and were severely persecuted by the Inquisition, which was established, in part, with a view to their extermination. Little is heard of them after the Fourteenth Century.

Early in the Twelfth Century, Peter de Bruys, in the South of France, was the founder of a sect called from him Petrobrussians. Their distinguishing feature was the rejection of the authority of the Church and the Fathers as to whatever cannot be proved from the Scriptures. Their founder was said to have been a disciple of Abelard, and, like him, to have

[1] A name said to have been derived from the Bulgarian words *Bog Milui*, "God, have mercy," — a favorite and wonted form of invocation among the members of the sect.

[2] Cathari, that is, *pure*, — a name assumed by the members of this sect to denote their ethical aim and profession, and at the same time to mark their separation from a church that had become *impure*.

disclaimed the dogma of vicarious atonement. He protested, not only against the details of the established ritual, but against all forms of public worship, and especially condemned prayers and offerings for the dead, maintaining that the conduct of a man in this world alone can determine his destiny in the world to come. About the same time, the Henricians, the disciples of a French monk named Henry, without the extreme notions of the Petrobrussians, were earnest propagandists of Christian morality, and of a simple faith in the sacred records independently of church tradition and patristical authority. Peter de Bruys was burned at the stake, and Henry was immured in a dungeon. They left few nominal disciples; but it cannot be supposed that their influence perished, though it may not be distinctly traced.

Later in the same century the Waldenses had their origin. Waldo, to whom they owe their name, desirous of knowing something of what he heard in an unknown tongue in the public service of the Church (for the Latin was no longer understood in France, even by the greater part of the clergy), employed two priests to translate for him into the then vernacular Gallic dialect several books of the Bible and sundry edifying passages from the Christian Fathers. Unwilling to hide what he found precious for his own soul, he devoted himself to reading and preaching the Gospel wherever he could obtain hearers, and succeeded in procuring at his own cost several willing and earnest coadjutors. He did not mean at first to create a rupture with the Church; but the Archbishop of Lyons took the alarm, and issued an imperative mandate, forbidding the laity to bear any part in the reading and interpretation of the Scriptures. Waldo and his associates appealed to the Pope, and were then formally excluded from the communion of the Church, and exposed to every form of unrelenting persecution. They grew under this harsh discipline, and were purged and refined by suffering. They have maintained through all these centuries a record of single-hearted piety, pre-eminent moral excellence, and immovable faith in Christ and his Gospel. No longer tolerated in the great religious centres, they gravitated toward the mountain-regions of Dauphigny and Piedmont, where they still have numerous churches, and hold in various small communities the controlling influence; while they now have also flourishing congregations in the larger Italian cities.

Of the principal precursors of the Protestant Reformation, Wiclif[1] alone wrought his life-work before the close of the Fourteenth Century. He deserved the name of a reformer even more than Luther. The disinterestedness of the motives with which Luther commenced his attack on the papal hierarchy is at least questionable; Wiclif undertook to expose the errors and follies of a church from which he was deriving great and increasing honor and emolument. Luther was as bigotedly attached to his own rashly formed and incoherent creed as ever was an honest Roman Catholic to that of Athanasius; Wiclif seems to have considered sanctity of life as the sole test of Christian character. Luther, though he verbally admitted, practically denied the sufficiency of the Scriptures, excluding from Christian fellowship those who, appealing to Scripture alone, dissented from him in matters of secondary importance; Wiclif professed distinctly and without limitation the fundamental principles of Protestantism, the sufficiency of the Scriptures, and the right of private judgment as to their interpretation.

[1] The following paragraphs relating to Wiclif are copied from an article on Wiclif which I wrote for the "American Monthly Review" of September, 1832. On making a fresh study of Wiclif's life, I have found no reason for changing what I then wrote.

Not only did Wiclif recommend and facilitate scriptural research; he took the lead in it, and in the midst of a dark and corrupt age he drew from the Bible a comparatively pure system of faith. He revived the almost forgotten doctrine of a righteous retribution, and maintained that "in the presence of his Judge each man must stand or fall by his own personal doings, not by those of his confessor, or of his mass-priest, or of any other spiritual agent." While he considered images as "the books of unlearned men," and admitted their lawfulness, he deemed the use of them unsafe and tending to idolatry. He censured it as folly to ask any intercession except that of Jesus Christ. Auricular confession and papal indulgences he utterly denounced. He scrupled not to pronounce the Pope Antichrist. The doctrine of transubstantiation he disclaimed, though he does not seem to have receded farther from it than Luther did.

With these enlightened views of Christian doctrine he united the utmost diligence and punctuality in the discharge of duty. He did not regard himself as absolved by the position which he assumed as a reformer from the proper work of a Christian minister. He thought that the clergy ought to be supported, not by ecclesiastical endowments, but by voluntary contributions, and was ready to apply to them Saint Paul's precept with reference to the laity, "that if any would not work, neither should he eat." In Lutterworth, of which he was rector, tradition represents him as having regularly devoted a portion of each morning to the relief of the necessitous, the consolation of the afflicted, and the discharge of every pious office by the bedside of sickness and death. More than three hundred of his parish sermons are preserved. They are plain, practical expositions of Scripture, and exhortations to the duties of common life. At the same time, while discharging thus indefatigably all the appropriate functions of a parish priest, he was issuing those attacks upon papal usurpation and corruption, which made the pontiff tremble on his throne, and stirred up the ire of his menial prelates throughout Christendom. He deemed himself an instrument in the hand of Providence, and that assurance made him strong. He was the inflexible enemy of the mendicant friars, and never failed to inveigh against their rapacity. He was at one time, when worn down by incessant labor and by the anxiety attendant on a recent prosecution before the ecclesiastical authorities, seized with a dangerous illness. While he was apparently on the verge of the grave, a deputation of the exulting mendicants was sent to urge him to confess his sins against them and to recant his denunciation of them. He listened in silence to a long exhortation addressed as to a dying man whose soul's salvation depended on his answer. When it was concluded, he ordered his servants to raise him on his pillows, and, fixing his eyes on his unwelcome visitors, he said calmly and firmly, "I shall not die, but live, to declare again the evil deeds of the friars."

It is matter of surprise that a man thus intrepid and so far in advance of his age should have died upon his bed. His escape from martyrdom can be accounted for only by the fact, that at different times he gained the confidence of the king, the respect of Parliament, and the protection of John of Gaunt, the most powerful man among the nobility, by his opposition to the temporal sovereignty and the pecuniary exactions of the Roman See. He, however, underwent a kind of posthumous martyrdom; for forty-eight years after his death something supposed to be his remains was disinterred, burned, and then cast into a neighboring brook. "The brook," says Fuller, " did convey his ashes into Avon; Avon into Severn;

Severn into the narrow seas; they into the main ocean; and thus the ashes of Wiclif are the emblem of his doctrine, which now is dispersed all the world over."

Wiclif's course, as virtually the founder of a sect, resembles that adopted in the last century by Wesley. They both were regularly ordained and fully qualified priests in the Established Church; they both authorized, employed, and superintended an unordained, unlicensed, imperfectly educated itinerant ministry. There can hardly be a doubt that Wesley took the idea of such a ministry from the "poor priests" through whom Wiclif organized an extensive, efficient, and enduring missionary enterprise in the interest of pure religion. Wiclif was the foe of ecclesiastical establishments, and denied the divine right of episcopacy. He would have favored the remodelling of the English Church on the basis of independent congregationalism. He therefore regarded his missionaries as virtually ordained of God, and as ministers of the true church of Christ, though not so recognized by the existing ecclesiastical organism.

Wiclif's most important work was his translation of the Bible, which he in dying left still incomplete, and which was finished four years after his death by Purvey, his successor at Lutterworth. The version was made directly from the Vulgate, and it does not appear that, though he had been Professor of Divinity at Oxford, he understood either Greek or Hebrew. His translation of the Beatitudes will serve as a specimen at once of his version and of the English of the Fourteenth Century: —

"Blessid be pore men in spirit: for the kyngdom of hevenes is herun. Blessid ben mylde men: for they schulen weelde the erthe. Blessid ben thei that mournen: for thei schal be coumfortid. Blessid be thei that hungren and thirsten rightwisnesse:

for thei schal be fulfilled. Blessid ben merciful men : for thei schal gete mercy. Blessid ben thei that ben of clene herte : for thei schulen se god. Blessid ben pesible men : for they schulen be clepid goddis children. Blessid ben thei that suffren persecucioun for rightwisnesse: for the kyngdom of hevenes is hern. Ye schul be blessid whanne men schul curse you, and schul pursue you, and schul seye al yvel agens you liynge for me."

UNITARIANISM AND THE REFORMATION.

BY SETH C. BEACH.

IN its restricted sense Unitarianism means belief in the personal unity of God instead of in a community of divine persons. Evidences of this belief more or less outspoken in the period of the Reformation are not wholly wanting; but considering that, in the second Protestant generation, the doctrine of one supreme divine person was burned at the stake in the body of Michael Servetus, it must be allowed that primarily the Reformation was not a Unitarian movement. In its larger meaning Unitarianism has been an advance along all the lines of religious thought. Among the articles of Unitarian faith so understood, besides the doctrine of one supreme divine person, may be enumerated belief in human nature, in moral freedom, in human reason, in character as of more worth than ritual or creed, in the equal justice not to say mercy of God, in the unreality of a devil, not to say of evil, and in the ultimate salvation, or evolution into something better, of all souls. Without being in any sense the first article of the faith, either in the historical order as having been the starting-point, or in the logical order as underlying the whole system, or in the order of importance as being with us the doctrine of doctrines, it has happened in spite of a thousand protests that belief in God's personal unity has given its name to the entire confession.

The movement first called Socinian, then Arminian, and finally Unitarian, began as a protest of the "natural man" against two particularly hateful doctrines of Calvinism, that of total depravity and that of predestination. The doctrine of total depravity is perhaps the most revolting article ever formulated in the name of faith. It confused the natural distinction between good and evil, right and wrong. It denied the name of goodness to the kindly instincts, generous impulses, and high-minded endeavors which even in the savage it could not wholly ignore. These things in the natural man, because in the natural man, were sin. They came from a corrupt heart. In the sight of God they had not the smallest moral worth.

Predestination was, as even Calvin declared, a "horrible decree." It was impious language, but Sir Walter Scott says "satire exquisitely severe," which Burns puts into the mouth of a Calvinistic saint who says in a supposed act of worship,

> "Wha as it pleases best thysel'
> Sends ane to heaven and ten to hell
> A' for thy glory;
> And not for onie guid or ill
> They 've done afore thee."

"Not for onie guid or ill they 've done afore thee" indicates the vice of the doctrine of predestination. It is the assumed arbitrariness of the divine decrees. Things follow one another in accordance with conditions, not in contravention of conditions. No one to whom a belief in a providential government of the world is a source of comfort, objects to the doctrine that God has foreordained whatsoever shall come to pass. What one asks is not to be wholly ignored in the process; that God shall not simply impose upon us a condition and destiny, but work through us to the given result; that the God who works in us shall not be a mere butt or toy of the God who rules over us. A predestination which sends "ane to heaven and ten to hell" regardless of any merits and conditions, simply effaces the individual.

The revolt against these two doctrines of Calvinistic theology was distinct and outspoken before any popular dissent from the Trinity had been formulated. In the order of their coming a belief in human nature, in its moral and spiritual possibilities, and a belief in what is not very happily named "free will," that is, in man's power in shaping his conditions and destiny, are the first articles of the Unitarian confession.

What quarters were given to these two articles in the characteristic theology of the Reformation every one knows. The denial of both in the squarest terms, and the assertion of the most unequivocal doctrine of total depravity and of predestination were the first fruits of Luther's theological activity. It is common to date the era of the Reformation from the posting of Luther's theses against indulgences, in 1517. His first thesis, his first challenge to the Catholic theologians, had appeared a year earlier. It is there we find the matter of theological difference which was at the bottom of his discontent. It is there he formulated the platform upon which he fought his great battle. He says, " A man who has no part in the grace of God cannot keep the commandments of God, or prepare himself either wholly or in part to receive grace; he rests of necessity under sin."[1] The answer to this is that such a man, a man that had no part in the grace of God, never existed; but that clearly was not the doctrine which Luther held. In a second series of theses, also before the battle over indulgences, the father of Reformation theology thus lays down the law: "It is true that man, who is a corrupt tree, can will or do nought but evil. . . . The excellent, infallible,

[1] D'Aubigné, i. 230.

and sole preparation for grace is the eternal election and predestination of God."¹

The theology of which this was supposed to be a reformation is much nearer the Unitarian standard. Doctor Eck, the Catholic champion, against whom at this stage Luther was pitted, justly replied, "Your doctrine converts a man into a stone or log incapable of any reaction. . . . By denying that man has any natural ability you contradict all experience."² The scholarly Erasmus, a Catholic champion against whom, ten years later in this controversy, Luther was arrayed, met the reformer of theology with an argument drawn from his favorite oracle. It is written, "Choose ye this day whom ye will serve." "It would be ridiculous," says Erasmus, "to say to any one, Choose, when it was not in his power."³ This is precisely what a Unitarian would say. That is, the Catholic position was much nearer the present Unitarian standpoint, in what we may call its native state, than it was after it had been "reformed."

Upon the doctrine of human nature and of man's moral agency the received Catholic theology had made great progress during the one thousand years that had elapsed since the days of Augustine. The doctrine which Luther was again launching upon the world was a reversion to the doctrine of Augustine. Neander says that Luther "set out from the Augustinian scheme,"⁴ and that "if the relation of God and man were such as it was represented by Luther and the other reformers, we must go beyond Augustine."⁵ Upon these doctrines then, whatever it may have been in other respects, the Reformation, instead of an advance, was a theological reaction, which carried back the fifteenth century to the fifth.

¹ D'Aubigné, i. 240.   ² Ib. ii. 49.   ³ Ib. iii. 323.
⁴ Neander: Dogmas, 666.   ⁵ Ib. 668.

With reference to the doctrine of the Trinity, Luther remained a Catholic. He accepted the received Athanasian definition exactly as it stood in the ancient creeds of the Church. If Unitarianism, in its more restricted sense as the doctrine of one only divine person, owes to Luther any direct furtherance, it is not in any qualification of the statement of the Trinity, but in a disposition to leave the definition of the doctrine in entire abeyance. "It is a heavenly thing," he says, "which the world cannot understand. Therefore have I taught that you ought to ground even doctrine not on reason or comparison, but on the words given in Scripture. The schools have devised many distinctions, dreams, and fancies, by which they have tried to set forth the Trinity, and have thus become fools."[1] There would never have been a "Unitarian Controversy" if all who have followed Luther in the Protestant dispensation had exercised this forbearance and discretion. How much of forbearance and discretion Luther himself would have exercised if in his day the Trinity had become a matter of controversy, our knowledge of what he usually was in controversy puts in doubt. It may be said of Luther that he accepted the Trinity in whole and in part, in substance and definition, but he accepted it by an effort of will, with that touch of misgiving out of which in the space of three centuries Unitarians were made.

Unitarianism owes to Luther a more considerable debt, an immeasurable debt, for his contribution toward what perhaps we would all agree is — faith in a good God possibly excepted — the most precious article of its confession, the supreme worth of character both as the way of salvation and as its substance. It may seem strange that a man who laid at the foundation of his theology the doctrine of salvation by faith, meaning

[1] Unitarianism in its Actual Condition, p. 228.

by faith, belief in the saving merits of Christ, should by that very doctrine have helped to the conviction that whatever the merits of Christ, one must save himself by his own life and deeds. What help to an enlightened faith is given by a man who, as Luther did, puts ecclesiastical ceremonies and the Ten Commandments on the same plane of religious significance or insignificance, and says that though " they may, it is true, produce a Fabricius, a Regulus, and other men perfectly upright in the eyes of the world," yet without faith in Christ " they deserve as little to be called righteousness as the fruit of the medlar to be called a fig"?[1] What better is it for me to look for salvation to the merits of somebody else, be it Christ, than to go into the market and buy it from the Pope? Theoretically the doctrine of salvation by faith in the merits of Christ, which is what to Luther the phrase meant, is not a whit more moral than the doctrine of salvation by buying papal indulgences.

Practically, however, the difference was very great. Though salvation was wholly by faith and not at all by works, yet works, it was held, were the sure fruit of faith. Keeping the Ten Commandments had nothing to do with your salvation, but your salvation would have and must have to do with keeping the Commandments. This laid, not a value but a stress upon morals which made such faithful stewards as the Puritans, and which after them has led Unitarians to feel that what the Psalmist calls " a clean heart and a right spirit" are the best possible preparations for either life or death.

The doctrine of justification by faith worked toward this result in another way. Faith is an experience, a part of the inner man. The purchase of an indulgence is wholly an outward transaction, except as it involves one's hopes or fears.

[1] D'Aubigné, i. 225.

When the business of salvation was shifted from a booth in the public street to the silences of one's own soul, and made to depend upon something in its inmost condition, an entirely new point of departure had been gained.[1] What it is in the inner condition in which salvation consists or on which it depends, may be open to debate, but the discussion is upon the right ground. Luther was very far from holding the doctrine that what one is, in spirit and purpose, is of more consequence to his soul than what he believes; the doctrine he held was directly and squarely opposite, but the two were in the same sphere, washed by the same sea, and if he had not made the right harbor, a better anchorage could be found by a longer voyage.

If belief in the supreme worth of character is with us — except that God is good — the most precious article of faith, another has perhaps done us the greater service. It has given us the courage to dare to believe in character. We owe the courage of this belief to the conviction that we can trust our intelligence, may and indeed must believe what is reasonable. Belief in the essential rectitude of human reason went with faith in human nature, was indeed a part of that faith. That reason could deal at first hand with matters of faith was not claimed by our Unitarian fathers. In theory they accepted the supremacy of a written text, but in practice they often went beyond and sometimes against their text. Indeed, the protest against the doctrines of total depravity and predestination was a revolt of the reason in the face of the text of Paul. Though not yet formulated as an article of faith, reason was even then accepted in practice as the highest tribunal of human appeal.

No article in the whole Unitarian confession would have been rejected by Luther with more contempt and scorn. His

---

[1] J. H. Allen: Christian History, Third Period, p. 131.

belief in the corruption of human nature was too complete to leave man any soundness or health in his understanding. He makes short work of confidence in what he would have called "the flesh." "In a word," says one of his theses, "nature possesses neither a pure reason nor a good will."[1] And yet no one since Paul had done so much as Luther was destined to do to quicken and confirm the faith in the purity of that reason which he despised. He made his contribution to the cause of a growing rationalism, not by his theory but by his example. He turned his reason to the poor business of putting reason down, but even that was a tremendous service. He had the intellectual courage to trust his reason to throw off entirely the authority of popes, councils, and church. Nothing that he could say in a thesis or a treatise of the insufficiency of the human reason could counteract the contagion of such grand self-sufficiency as this. That Luther would have claimed for his reason something more than he allowed to the natural human faculty, that for himself he assumed a reason enlightened by grace, made it possible for him to discredit the general understanding while exercising his own; but the distinction set up was invisible, and one which the world could not be expected to respect. Luther's splendid use of reason, sanctified or not, has been to the world as a city set on a hill.

Of Luther's relation to the beliefs which in distinction are called Unitarian, it may be said that he would have hated every article of the confession, which is not strange considering that he was cradled and nursed in the Fifteenth Century. It may further be said that with reference to the doctrines of predestination and total depravity he carried back the standard of enlightenment a thousand years, though happily it has not

[1] D'Aubigné, i. 242.

taken a thousand years to something more than recover the ground. Toward the conviction that character, the state of the inner man, is the supreme thing, his doctrine of justification by faith was a great step; and toward rationalism, the conviction that reason must at last decide, his example was an incalculable help. Add to this that he stirred the pool of thought, and you have most of what can be credited as Luther's contribution toward the working out of the Unitarian confession.

Melancthon, though a better scholar, a keener intellect, and a finer nature than Luther, was his confessed disciple. "Luther alone can decide," was his characteristic saying. Yet he neither repeated his master like a parrot nor followed him as a slave. His most important divergence from Luther was upon the doctrine of predestination. He returned very nearly to the then current Catholic position, and recognized the human will as a factor in the work of grace. He explained salvation as a result of the joint activity of God and man. This was a vast amelioration of the arbitrary over-riding of the creature, which made the doctrine of predestination so intolerable.

Like Luther, Melancthon accepted the doctrine of the Trinity, but apparently with a shade more of misgiving. A memorable sentence deserves to be quoted as indicating not only his own feeling but also the undercurrent of his age. "You know," he writes to a friend, " that in reference to the Trinity I have always feared that these things would again break out. Good God! what disturbances will be raised in the next age whether the Logos and the Holy Spirit are hypostases. I abide by those words of Holy Writ which direct to pray to Christ, and attribute to him divine honors; but I do not feel compelled to examine more accurately the assertions respecting hypostases."[1] A denunciation in the

[1] Neander: Dogmas, p. 651.

Augsburg Confession, drawn by Melancthon, shows that an outbreak against the Trinity was even then not wholly an imaginary peril. Among those whom the confession condemns are "the Samosatians old and new, who, when they earnestly contend that there is but one person, do craftily and wickedly trifle, after the manner of rhetoricians, about the Word and Holy Ghost that they be not distinct persons, but that the Word signifieth a vocal word, and the Spirit a motion created in things." It is evident that the Unitarian heresy was already a well-defined fact, a little cloud like a man's hand. It is further evident that though Melancthon had a philosopher's repugnance to use the term *hypostasis* (person) in speaking of the Word and Spirit, it was not a word over which he stumbled when there was a call to speak. When we add that in his mature age he applauded the burning of Servetus for denying the doctrine of the Trinity, Melancthon's relation to Unitarian heresies is perhaps sufficiently defined.

Among the three or four greatest names of the Reformation, the man with whom a Unitarian will find most points of contact and sympathy is Zwingli, the Zurich Reformer. It is however upon other articles of his confession, and not upon that which has given him his name, that a Unitarian will find in Zwingli a kindred intelligence. Zwingli accepted the Trinity, apparently without any of the misgivings which we have seen in Luther and Melancthon. Upon most if not all other articles of the Unitarian confession Zwingli made an advance which was remarkable for his age.

Upon the doctrine of human nature his view was entirely modern and rational. He seems to have known as little of the doctrine of total depravity as if Luther had not been his contemporary and Calvin his successor. How far away from Zwingli was such a conception of man, and especially of the child, let a few sentences show. "The human mind is like a garden, which if not cultivated is soon overgrown with weeds. From youth up, therefore, it must be trained and cultivated. . . . Many busy themselves in hanging their likeness everywhere, that their names may be made famous and their families illustrious, while they neglect and despise at once God's image and their own. . . . Satan desires to nestle in the hearts of the young, and to defile these as yet pure vessels."[1] One sees that this is not Calvinism. "Though often loud in praise of Luther, Calvin," says one of his biographers, "seldom speaks well of Zwingli." Calvin must have looked upon Zwingli as wanting the first element of theological capacity.

Zwingli accepted the tradition of a fall of man; but as he understood the atonement, that event had neutralized the fall. He says, "If the question be put, Did Christ restore the whole human family or only the church of believers? I answer, Christ brought by his salvation as much good into the world as Adam by his sinning brought evil; or Adam infected the whole mass with original sin, consequently Christ has restored the whole mass." It follows that the child starts to-day morally exactly where the first man started. An inheritance of evil had descended from the first man, but according to Zwingli it is not sin. Original Sin, so called, he says, is not in a proper, but only in a metaphorical sense, a crime; it is only a moral weakness. So Neander summarizes his doctrine.

Consistently with this view of human nature, Zwingli heartily recognized good wherever found, in Gentile or Jew, Pagan or Christian. "Religion," he said, "has not been confined within the boundaries of Palestine, since God did not alone

[1] Christoffel: Life of Zwingli.

create Palestine; he created the whole world. . . . I venture even to call that divine which is borrowed from the heathen, in so far as it is holy, tends to piety, and is undeniably true." He made bold to say that Plato had drunk from the "heavenly spring," that Seneca was a "holy man," that Pindar "throws light upon our Gospels," and that part of his heavenly hope was, along with Peter and Paul, to meet "Socrates, Aristides, Numa, Cato, and the Scipios."[1] A generation has not passed since he would have been counted an advanced Unitarian who had said as much. It is a narrow circle, a mere fringe of orthodox Christendom, in which to-day such opinions would be, not approved, but even tolerated. What a man then was Zwingli, who, more than three hundred and fifty years ago, without doubt, hesitation, or reserve, spoke of the heathen not as heathen, but as men, in the manner of the most enlightened of our time!

That the divine mercy will be equal to human need, and that the Father's welcome will yet be rewarded by the return of the last Prodigal, is a faith which has given name to another denomination, the Universalist; but to-day it is not less a part of the current Unitarian confession. It is curious to see how close Zwingli came to this large hope while respecting to the uttermost the text which says, "He that believeth not shall be damned." "Reference is only made," he said, "to those who have heard and yet have not believed. Of the others we cannot judge. . . . Whoever has heard the doctrines of faith proclaimed and yet continues and dies in unbelief, him we can *perhaps* count among the lost." There is meaning in that "perhaps." It indicates a degree of reluctance to damn an unbeliever which is incompatible with the full enjoyment of Christian orthodoxy. It indicates that while

[1] Christoffel.

Zwingli was not prepared to speak with the confidence of a modern Universalist, he was not without his hope that the door would be kept open till every sheep had returned to the fold. This is better than if he had made up in dogmatism for what at that time he lacked in light.

Upon the doctrine of predestination Zwingli held essentially the same view as Luther and Calvin. If we say that Luther's doctrine of predestination was a theological reaction, a return to Augustine, we must say the same of Zwingli's. Neander's remark is this: "Zwingli expressly declared that predestination extended even to Adam's sin. It is therefore erroneous that the harshest and most logical form of this doctrine was derived from Calvin."[1] It might have been supposed that Zwingli's unadulterated predestinarianism would have imparted to his memory, at least to Calvin, an acceptable fragrance. Strange to say, Calvin's keen sense detected, in Zwingli's doctrine, an unsavory element. And it may be added that Zwingli's disciples found Calvin's doctrine equally offensive. After Zwingli's death a warm controversy broke out between his colleagues, the pastors of Zurich, and the father of Calvinism then reigning at Geneva. It would seem that if Zwingli and Calvin stated their doctrine of predestination in the same words, it did not feel like the same doctrine. Every one knows that the practical effect of a doctrine depends even less upon its statement than upon the way it is held, the emphasis laid upon it, or the scheme of faith of which it makes a part. It is plain that the doctrine of predestination loses most of its horror when, as Zwingli was able to do, you eliminate total depravity, neutralize original sin, and reduce, "He that believeth not shall be damned," to a mere "perhaps," which does not exclude a hope. This was one of

[1] Dogmas, 668.

the points which Zwingli's disciples made in their controversy with Calvin. They said, "According to the sentiments of the apostles, God wills the happiness of all mankind."[1] That is predestination, but it is not an insufferable doctrine.

Of Zwingli's doctrine of predestination Neander remarks, "There is an approach in it to pantheism." Now, the nearer you come to pantheism, the more you free your doctrine of predestination, if you have one, of mere outward, arbitrary domination, which was so offensive to Burns, and others of his generation. Pantheism is the doctrine of an overruling, who is also an indwelling, God. Of this kind of predestinarianism there is a good deal to-day, both in Unitarian pulpits and pews.

Zwingli also differed much from Luther, more from Calvin, in the place which the doctrine of predestination held in his teaching. Calvin, it is truly said, "regarded it almost as the basis and foundation of religion;" Zwingli taught his full doctrine, yet with a certain reserve: "But let these things," he says, "be stated with moderation, and only seldom; for only a few can attain such heights of spiritual insight." Doubtless we shall do well to exercise that caution still.

How far Zwingli had gone in the admission of reason to the field of faith, we have seen. Lecky says there were "two theologians" in the period of the Reformation who "were accustomed to form their notions of truth and goodness by the decisions of their own reasoned conscience and, disregarding all the interpretations of tradition, to mould and adapt their creed to their ideal. These theologians were Socinus and Zuinglius, who may be regarded as the representatives of Rationalism in the first period of Protestantism."[2] Lecky says "Socinus and

[1] Dyer: Life of Calvin, New York, p. 233.
[2] Lecky: Rationalism, i. 369.

Zuinglius," an order which fails to suggest that Zwingli had finished his career when the elder Socinus was a child in the nursery, a boy of the age of six. Zwingli fell by the sword in a Catholic assault upon Zurich, in 1531; and with just appreciation it has been said, "the career of this most interesting of the Reformers was thus brought to an abrupt close."[1]

In 1541, ten years after the fall of Zwingli, and within five of the death of Luther, Calvin, after an exile of three years, was recalled to Geneva for a second term of power. During the next twenty-three years, until his death, if Calvin had worn a crown his authority could hardly have been more absolute. With this ascendency of Calvin began a new chapter in the history of the Reformation; Geneva became its centre, and Calvin its head.

In Melancthon, in his later years, it is possible to discover very distinct marks of a weakening of the stern and rigid dogmatism in which the Reformation began. The pupil of Luther was perceptibly loosening the yoke of his master and giving the theological current of the Reformation movement in the direction of a milder and more rational faith. In Zwingli this tendency had gone so far that he seems almost to belong to another age. Calvin set himself to stem this rising tide. He flung himself against the stream, and, so far as concerns the main current, reversed the flow. In other words, the great intellectual achievement of Calvin was to lead a theological reaction. He returned to the standpoint of Luther, which was also the standpoint of Augustine. Calvinism in its doctrinal purity is, with the difference perhaps of a more rigid logic, the master-stroke of the Fifth Century.

Not much in the way of direct contribution toward anything that has ever gone by the name Unitarian can be expected

[1] Hall: Orthodoxy and Heresy, p. 170.

from Calvin. As in the case of Luther, his use of reason even in the cause of unreason tended to Rationalism; and his strenuous insistence upon righteousness not as the substance, it is true, nor as the means, but as the fruit and sign, of salvation, did more than the fifteen centuries since Christ — Luther included — to lift the moral element to that transcendent place in religion which is its due. It would be ungrateful to a great benefactor not to recognize Calvin's contribution toward the most important and precious conviction in any religious confession. Spite of the formal logic of his creed, even to Calvin himself character was more than doctrine. Vigilant as was his inquisition into matters of faith, his inquisition into matters of conduct was more searching and relentless still. Stern as was his rule against heresy, his methods with the loose and immoral were more summary. He could be indulgent, even paternal, toward a quiet, circumspect misbeliever like Socinus; but no sinner, however quiet and circumspect, was safe in the indulgence of his little private vice. There can be no doubt that Calvin's stern discipline had the effect, and that he intended it to have the effect, to put questions of character above questions of creed in the conception of religion.

The development of other elements of the Unitarian Confession during Calvin's ascendency came not so much through him as in spite of him. The revolt of human nature against mere arbitrary predestination, against a God who, to take Calvin's words, "in saving some and condemning others has no regard to their merits," found champions in Bolsec and Castellio both able and respectable.

Bolsec was a physician by profession, and, until he meddled with theology, a man of standing and reputation. If he had confined his activities to the practice of medicine, we have reason to believe that he would have been permitted to enjoy his religious opinions undisturbed. On the contrary, he ventured to dissent from the doctrine of predestination, — at first, it would appear, with great moderation and in the privacy of friends. He was summoned before Calvin and privately admonished. For a repetition of the offence he was called before the consistory and publicly rebuked. The indiscreet layman ventured upon a more open transgression. At a week-day service for which a large congregation had assembled, one of Calvin's colleagues and disciples had stated the doctrine of predestination in what seemed to Bolsec extremely offensive terms. The fiery layman made bold to controvert the preacher both with invective and argument. At that inopportune moment Calvin entered the church, and quietly seating himself listened to the rebellious heretic. Bolsec done, Calvin took the floor. Bolsec was finally taken from the church in the custody of an officer, and after a protracted imprisonment, in which for some time it was a question of life or death, was expelled from the city.[1]

Castellio, a man of rare accomplishments, had been placed by Calvin at the head of the schools of Geneva. On account of too much freedom in the criticism of the Scriptures he incurred the displeasure of Calvin, and on account of an equal freedom in the criticism of the clergy he was condemned and sent into banishment. He obtained a professorship at Basel. At this apparently safe distance he opened a controversy with Calvin upon the doctrine of predestination. Not only the churches of Basel and Geneva, but also of Bern and Zurich, were distracted by the hot dispute. The scale turned in favor of Calvin. Castellio wrote a book against predestination, the publication of which Calvin had enough influence at Basel to have forbidden under penalty of death. The victory of Calvin

[1] Dyer: Life of Calvin.

was fatal to Castellio, who died in disgrace and poverty. "I learn, to the great shame of our age," said Montaigne, "that under our view two persons distinguished for learning have died of starvation."[1] As one of these he mentions Castellio. The doctrine of predestination had triumphed, but the triumph had in it the seeds of coming defeat.

Unitarianism proper, belief in the personal unity of God, found confessors in Servetus,[2] and in Lælius and Faustus Socinus.[3] Servetus was a Spaniard by birth, of the same age as Calvin, born indeed the same year, 1509. He studied at the university of Saragossa, accompanied the confessor of Charles V. to Germany, and, deserting both the confessor and his creed, appeared at the age of twenty-one in Basel as a disciple of the Reformers, — a disciple considerably more advanced than his masters. "You obtrude yourself upon me," Œcolampadius wrote him, "as if I had nothing else to do than to answer your questions. . . . You do not admit that it was the *Son* of God who was to come as man, but that it was the *man* who came that was the Son of God." A year later, at the age of twenty-two, Servetus printed a book entitled "Errors of the Trinity," which was sufficiently creditable to draw from Melancthon the statement, "I read Servetus much, though I am well aware of the fanatical nature of the man."[4]

The sale of the book was summarily forbidden by the Basel magistrates. A year later the youthful theologian attempted a restatement of his views in a series of "Dialogues concerning the Trinity." The result of this second venture was the sudden disappearance of Servetus not only from Basel but also for

[1] Audin: Life of Calvin, p. 420.
[2] Early Sources of English Unitarianism, Bonet to Maury, p. 81.
[3] Ibid., p. 178.
[4] Willis: Servetus and Calvin, p. 45.

the space of twenty years from the knowledge of mankind. Two years later a brilliant young Spaniard by the name of Villeneuve, no longer known as Servetus, presented himself at the university of Paris as a student of mathematics and physics. He subsequently entered the college of physicians at the same university for the study of medicine. In due time he became assistant to the professor of anatomy, who makes mention of him as "a man distinguished in every species of learning, and scarcely second to any in the doctrine of Galen."[1]

A species of learning in which unhappily Servetus was too proficient, upon which he gave lectures at the university with too much success, for which he fell under the censure of the faculty and the parliament, was astrology. Active, learned, and original, let it be confessed that Servetus had not exactly a sober intellect.

Invited to Vienne, near Lyons, as physician to the archbishop of that see, "M. Villeneuve" spent twelve years of honorable life in the quiet and successful practice of his profession. Meanwhile he opened a theological correspondence with Calvin, then at the head of Protestantism. Thirty letters of Servetus are extant, not always written in the manner in which Calvin was accustomed to be addressed. The manuscript of a book entitled "The Restoration of Christianity" was also forwarded to Calvin for examination. With this material in hand Calvin was able to discover the identity of his correspondent with the famous or infamous author of "Errors of the Trinity." Calvin communicated his discovery to the Catholic authorities at Lyons, and set the detectives of the Inquisition on the hunt. Servetus, no longer "M. Villeneuve," was arrested and thrown into prison, from which,

[1] Willis.

however, by the indulgence of his jailer, he was permitted to escape. Attempting to reach Italy, the fugitive entered Geneva, stayed a day too long, was recognized and thrown into prison, from which no friendly jailer permitted his escape. After a trial of thrilling interest, lasting more than seven weeks, for an offence committed in another territory, — for an offence for which at Geneva banishment was the highest penalty known to the law, — Servetus was condemned to be burned at the stake, and the sentence was executed. Strange to say, a Unitarian was safer from that day. "It may be said," says Hallam, "that the tolerant spirit rose out of the ashes of Servetus."

The reign of Calvin may be said to have continued at Geneva a century and a half. In 1706 the clergy were excused from their old engagement to teach and preach the creed. In 1817, the era of our own Unitarian controversy, it was forbidden at Geneva to preach "in a disputative style, on the doctrines of the Trinity, the imputation of Adam's sin, and predestination."[1] In 1847 "the old Protestant Church of Geneva was abolished, and an almost creedless church established."[2] Castellio and Servetus were avenged.

By common consent, Jesus holds the first place among the martyrs of history. Judged by the test of fruitfulness, it can hardly be doubted that the second place belongs to Servetus. The seed which Jesus watered with his blood dropped upon inhospitable soil at Jerusalem; in the hot-bed of Jewish tradition it met the fate of seed scattered among thorns; transplanted to Asia Minor, Macedonia, and Rome, it took root and ripened to a harvest. Something very similar happened in the case of Servetus. The seed fertilized by the ashes of the

[1] Christian Examiner, xv. 151; xxvi. 320.
[2] Encyclopædia Britannica, Art. "Geneva."

great martyr came to a late harvest, it is true, even at Geneva; but under the heel of Calvin for more than a century, like a trampled vine, its promise was slow in coming. It found its good ground in two countries where the heel of Calvin, if it touched, rested with less weight. What Asia Minor, Macedonia, and Rome had been to the gospel of Christ, that in kind, if not in degree, Poland and Transylvania were to the doctrine of Servetus.

In 1556, three years after the martyrdom of Servetus, Giorgio Blandrata, an Italian physician, — the third physician we have met in this history, — driven out of Italy for his opinions, settled at Geneva and entered into relations with the church of Italian Protestants there established.[1] At the time of his arrival he claimed to be and probably was in substantial agreement with Calvin. It is one of the signs we have of continued vitality in the ashes of Servetus, that at the end of two years Blandrata found Geneva an uncomfortable residence, and went forth to win for himself the distinction of "founder of Unitarianism in Poland and Transylvania." In both countries, but especially in Poland, the doctrine of the Trinity had already been openly challenged; but with the arrival of Blandrata in 1558, the spirit of Unitarian dissent entered upon a career of marked activity and success. Discussions were held, nobles and scholars espoused the cause, synods were assembled to settle the controversy with such success as synods are wont to have, and in 1565, after seven years of active fermentation, a division of Polish Protestants took place by that process with which the world is familiar, — Protestants who chose to consider themselves orthodox excluding Protestants whom it suited the majority to consider heretics.

[1] Chambers's Encyclopædia, Art. "Blandrata." Encyclopædia Britannica, Art. "Socinus."

This date, 1565, ought to be memorable in our annals, as it marks the establishment of the first Unitarian Church since the disappearance of Apostolic and the breaking up of Arian Christendom. Ten years later Faustus Socinus took up his residence in Poland, and under his leadership Polish Unitarianism achieved what it is not too much to call a brilliant history. Poland, at that date, was not the prostrate province which it is to-day; in the age when Germany was giving us Luther, Poland was the country that gave the world Copernicus.

The name of Socinus is of great importance in the history of Unitarianism. For three hundred years the word "Socinian" has been a term of contempt in Christendom. The word has perhaps ceased to be a symbol of hate, but not of contempt, when Carlyle speaks of Harriet Martineau as writing him "saw-dustish, Socinian, didactic little notes," of " her brother James, a Socinian preacher of due quality,"[1] and of "Socinian Preachers" who "proclaim Benevolence to all the four winds, and have Truth engraved on their watch-seals."[2] As this is perhaps the most respectful reference to Socinus in literature for three centuries, it becomes interesting to know what the man, or men, did to make the name so infamous.

There were two Italians of the name, uncle and nephew, both illustrious in the annals of heresy.[3] Lælius, the elder, was a man of independent fortune, — apparently of attractive person, amiable spirit, and gentle manners, too much of a free-thinker to live in Italy, — who travelled through nearly every country in Europe, lived on terms of affectionate intercourse

---

[1] Reminiscences of Jane Welch Carlyle.
[2] Essays, " Characteristics."
[3] Early Sources of English Unitarianism: Bonet-Maury, pp. 179-198.

with Melancthon, was "my dear Lælius" to Calvin, even while raising questions concerning the resurrection of the body, salvation, and, to Calvin perhaps his most tender point, predestination. There is a tradition that in his youth Socinus had belonged to a club of free-thinkers in Italy, who, among their other heresies, rejected the Trinity; but no misgivings concerning this cardinal doctrine have been discovered in the writings of Socinus earlier than 1554, — that is, the year following the martyrdom of Servetus, at which time he is known to have uttered what are called "incautious remarks" upon the Trinity, and to have given more decided expression to his doubts in his correspondence. This is another evidence that Servetus did not suffer in vain. The heresy of Socinus was of that mild kind which enabled him a year later at Zurich to subscribe to an orthodox confession, not, however, without the right reserved of further investigation. He died at Zurich, in 1562, at the age of thirty-seven, respected and beloved. His significance in the history of thought comes from the happy circumstance that he bequeathed his manuscripts to his more aggressive and more distinguished nephew.[1]

Like his uncle, Faustus Socinus was a native of Siena, in Italy. At the age of seventeen he fell heir to a fortune which placed him in independent circumstances. At the age of twenty he was suspected of Lutheranism. In 1562, at the death of his uncle, he was residing at Geneva, and was enrolled as a member of the Italian Church. He was then a young man of twenty-three, and so little the man he afterward became, that, inheriting the ample fortunes of his uncle, he conformed to the Catholic Church, and returned to Italy to enjoy his possessions. After a residence of twelve years as

[1] Encyclopædia Britannica, Art. "Socinus."

man of the world at the court of Florence, he retired to Basel, turned theologian, systematized the heresies of his predecessors, — especially the fruitful suggestions of his uncle, whom he ever gratefully acknowledged as master, — and worked out a scheme of rationalized, if from the modern standpoint not always reasonable, faith which for more than two hundred years was familiarly known by his name. He denied the Trinity, the deity of Christ, the personality of the Devil, the native and total depravity of man, the vicarious atonement, and the eternity of punishment. His theory was that Christ was a man divinely commissioned, who had no existence before he was conceived by the virgin Mary; that human sin was the imitation of Adam's sin, and that human salvation was the imitation and adoption of Christ's virtue; that the Bible was to be interpreted by human reason, and that its metaphors were not to be taken literally.[1] "He anticipated modern philanthropists by insisting upon" the unlawfulness, not only of war, but of the taking of human life under any circumstances; and "the candid spirit and the freedom from passion with which he writes in an intemperate age" is acknowledged to his praise.

In 1579, being then at the age of forty, and having a name known throughout Europe, Socinus took up his residence in Poland, and from that date until his death in 1604, a period of twenty-five years, was the able and recognized head of Polish Unitarianism.

He left a vigorous and flourishing church. "The noble and the opulent, the learned and the eloquent, crowded to his standard." A Unitarian college was established at Racow, the headquarters of the church, in 1600. A printing-press was also set up, and kept busy in publishing books and tracts for the propagation of Unitarian or Socinian principles. Every

[1] Chambers's Encyclopædia, Art. "Socinus."

member of the church contributed to a fund from which were paid the salaries of ministers, the expenses of "colleges," the support of widows, orphans, and aged ministers, the printing of books, and the maintaining of missionaries. During the century of its existence the Polish Unitarian Church, popularly known as the "leper church,"[1] was a church perhaps the most efficiently organized that Unitarianism has ever had. Under the Sigismunds I. and II., the most enlightened princes then upon any European throne, Poland enjoyed complete religious toleration, — the first to attain that distinction in Christendom. As has happened elsewhere when Unitarians have stood upon an equality, the Unitarians of Poland by their energy and intelligence attained an ascendency out of all proportion to their numbers. They succeeded, we are told, " in obtaining possession of all those honors in the State which were the reward of eloquence, art, or learning."

But Poland was a Catholic country, and the Unitarian Church experienced the vicissitudes which were to have been anticipated. In 1598, at the instigation of the Jesuits, a mob attacked the house of Socinus, dragged him from a sick-bed through the streets, and threatened him with death. He was rescued; but his papers had been destroyed, and among them the manuscript of a book which he regarded as his most important work. He lived in retirement at the house of a friend for six years, and died by disease and not by violence, one is glad to know, in 1604.

For another generation the Unitarian Church maintained itself under increasing difficulties. In 1638 two reckless students of the college at Racow demolished a crucifix at the entrance of the city. The authorities of the college disavowed the offence, but the populace demanded vengeance; and the

[1] The Unitarian, November, 1887. Art. " Unitarianism in Poland."

Diet of Warsaw decreed the banishment of the professors, the destruction of the college and printing-press, and the closing of the Socinian churches. Twenty years later, under complete Catholic ascendency, a decree passed the Diet of Warsaw expelling all Socinians from the country. Strange to say, the date of this barbarous edict, 1658, happens to have fallen upon the centennial year of the arrival of Blandrata, the apostle of Polish Unitarianism. In 1661 the decree was executed with a rigor which has been compared to that which attended the expulsion of the Jews from Spain. The profession of Socinian opinions, or the harboring of a Socinian, was made an offence punishable with death. In spite of this penalty, and the rigor with which it was executed, confessors of the faith still lingered in the country, maintaining a regular ministry, educating their pastors at Leyden in Holland, and holding their services in private houses, in fields, and in forests. At the partition of Poland they were included by Russia and Austria among other Dissidents, since which time, I find it said, "they have been permitted to enjoy their religious opinions;"[1] but I do not find it said whether at this date any remnants of the once vigorous Polish Unitarian Church survive.

The exiled Unitarians found refuge in England, Holland, Germany, and especially among their co-religionists of Transylvania. The planting of Unitarianism in Transylvania followed its planting in Poland by only a half-dozen years, and was the work of the same apostle. John Sigismund, heir to the throne of Transylvania, passed his youth in exile at the Polish court. In 1556 he returned to his kingdom, and enjoyed a brief but enlightened reign of fourteen years. It

[1] Dictionary of Christian Churches and Sects. Marsden. Art. "Unitarianism."

was during this period that Unitarianism took root in Hungary.[1] In 1563, Blandrata, the founder of Polish Unitarianism, not less eager in the propagation of his faith than in the practice of his profession, was invited to Transylvania as court physician.

The most fruitful achievement of this eccentric apostle was the conversion of Francis David, one of the most able, most noble, and most eloquent of Transylvanian Protestants, who in his intellectual progress passed from Lutheranism through Calvinism to Unitarianism, and to whom the Unitarians of Hungary point with just pride as the real founder of their church. Francis David, a native Transylvanian of Saxon ancestry, was born in 1510, seven years before the outbreak of the Reformation, and educated at Wittenberg under Luther and Melancthon at the high tide of their career. Returning to Transylvania, he threw himself zealously and effectively into the cause of the Lutheran Reformation in that country, with such distinction that he was made bishop of the Lutheran church. In the controversy between Lutherans and Calvinists concerning the Lord's Supper, David took the more rational view of the Calvinists, that no outward miracle takes place in the bread and wine. In 1564 he was made bishop of the Calvinistic church, as he had been of the Lutheran. At the synod which chose David to the Calvinistic bishopric, the king was represented by his favorite, Blandrata, and the two religious innovators were drawn to each other. Two years later, by the influence of Blandrata, David was appointed chaplain to the king, and was preaching to the court that "he who divides Christ into two, man and not man but

[1] Unitarianism in Hungary (in the Unitarian for November and December, 1886; February, March, May, October, and November, 1887). George Boros.

God, he is a deceiver;" commonly self-deceived, it ought also to have been said.

Unitarian opinions were in the ascendant at the court, and spread rapidly among the nobility and gentry of the kingdom. A decree passed the diet and was approved by the king, granting toleration in the broadest terms : " The preachers shall be allowed to preach the gospel each according to his understanding ; " the people " shall be allowed to keep the preachers who please them. On account of religion shall no man be misused." This decree is memorable. Its date is 1568. It made Transylvania the second country in which religious freedom was established by law, and it made the Unitarian Church of Transylvania possible. Its anniversary was celebrated in 1868 with great enthusiasm by the Unitarians of Hungary, as marking the completion of three hundred years of their history.

Excluded from the Calvinistic synod and having organized a synod of their own, Francis David was made the first bishop of the Unitarian Church. The two years that followed were a kind of golden age for Unitarianism in Transylvania. Twelve great schools, or gymnasia, and in nearly every congregation an elementary school, were founded, and it is broadly stated by an Hungarian writer that " there remained scarcely a trace of Catholicism, and Calvinism had withered before having taken root." There seems abundant evidence that for a few years Unitarianism was among the aristocratic and educated classes the prevailing confession. Three years after the edict of religious equality the enlightened prince of Transylvania died suddenly at the age of thirty-one. His Catholic successor confirmed the Unitarians in the exercise of their religion, but forbade the propagation of their opinions. The Unitarianism of this period, while rejecting the deity of Christ, had continued reverently to pay him adoration not unlike the adoration of Mary among Catholics. In this practice, Servetus, Socinus, Blandrata, and at first Francis David, were at one. But the rationalistic temper of David soon threw off this Catholic tradition. A fatal breach occurred between the two great champions of Transylvanian Unitarianism over this issue, and at the instigation of Blandrata, David was thrown into prison, where, already broken in health, after a few months of languishing he died in 1579.

The two centuries that followed, though always succeeding in maintaining their right to a legal existence, was a period of great trial to the Unitarians of Transylvania. Blandrata, to whom after Francis David more than to any one else they owed their existence, deserted them in his old age and conformed to the Catholic Church. Their darkest hour was in 1716, when, under Austrian rule, their printing-press was suppressed, their publications forbidden, their cathedral taken from them by force, and their churches and schools throughout the country turned to Catholic uses. Under the heel of this rigorous despotism the devoted church lay for three quarters of a century, until the accession of the liberal Emperor Joseph II. in 1780. This enlightened monarch forbade the seizure of their churches, indemnified them for the loss of their cathedral, placed them in offices of trust and power, and authorized the printing of their confession and the publication of their books. The same liberal policy was continued by his successors. Under Francis I. the four established religions, Catholic, Lutheran, Calvinist, and Unitarian, were again placed upon an equality; in 1792 a wealthy Transylvanian nobleman, dying childless, left his entire property, a large fortune, to the Unitarian Church; in 1837 another Hungarian magnate did the same. Under these changed conditions the Unitarian Church began to rehabilitate itself. In 1845 its membership was reckoned at 45,000; in 1887 the number of registered Unitarians in Transylvania and Hungary was 57,516, with a gain from the preceding year of 918. The number of congregations was 108.[1]

Of the organized movements dating from the time of the Reformation, the Unitarian church of Poland, after a century of struggle, was completely wrecked; the church of Geneva, founded by Calvin, having first become essentially creedless, as has also the church of Zwingli at Zurich, has, as happens with all creedless churches, been for more than half a century prevailingly Unitarian; and the brave church of Francis David in Transylvania, planted originally upon a Unitarian confession, after the fiery ordeals of three centuries still maintains a vigorous existence.

[1] Unitarianism in its Actual Condition, Transylvania, pp. 296–315. Unitarian Review, August, 1885. Bixby. Unitarian Year-Book, 1888.

UNITARIANISM IN ENGLAND.

BY BROOKE HERFORD.

THE establishment of distinct Unitarian churches in England dates back to 1774, when Theophilus Lindsey left the Church of England and went up to London to start the first avowedly Unitarian place of worship in the country. But that was not the beginning of Unitarianism. Centuries before this, Unitarianism began in England as an individual opinion, had first its martyr-age, then a period when it was a great ferment of controversy, and finally the distinct development of it which stands to-day in our English Unitarian body.

The names of some of the Unitarian martyrs on the continent of Europe are comparatively well known, — Servetus, burned by Calvin; Valentine Gentilis the Italian; and other isolated students here and there, who had been stirred up by the Reformation spirit to read the Bible for themselves, and who could not stop where Luther and Calvin stopped. But even before these men's names were known in England, there were English men and women who were reading the New Testament in the same plain, straightforward way, and who could only find there the old simple teaching, of One Almighty God, and Jesus Christ as a great holy teacher, but not God.

It is not easy to trace this earlier Unitarianism. The name "Unitarian" was not then known. On the Continent we recognize them by the popular charge that they were turning Jews, — modern Jews in disguise, — that being the idea created by their opposition to the doctrine of the Trinity. In England all sorts of heretics were put in the one great category of "Anabaptists." That was the great hateful name which was the watchword of contempt and persecution; and it not only included those who were for adult baptism, or re-baptism, but any who were unsound about the Mass, or who rejected those ideas of Christ's deity on which the Mass was founded. The old historian, Stowe (1525–1605), tells us how a number of these Anabaptists came over to England from Holland about 1535 to escape from persecution; but the persecuting laws had just been revived in England, and they were soon taken off to prison and then — sometimes three or four at once — they "bore their fagots," as the phrase was, and were "brent" at St. Paul's Cross. We have a glimpse of their opinions in the enumeration of heresies for which such things were done, among which the following are named: (1) The denial of the Trinity; (2) That Jesus Christ was only a man, but not the true God; (3) That the only benefit men receive from Christ consists in their being brought to the true fellowship of God, — just an anticipation of the "moral influence" theory which was held by Unitarians long before it became one of the doctrines of the New Orthodoxy. These were poor unknown foreigners, however, and little notice was taken of them or of their sufferings; but it made more noise when, in 1550, Joan Boucher, a lady of Kent, and one of the ladies of the Court, was charged with heresy, — some opinion contrary to the Incarnation it seems to have been. She had been an earnest student of the Bible, and was one of those who had welcomed Tyndale's forbidden translation of the New Testament into English, doing all she could to spread it, and even taking copies to Court, tied, like smuggled goods, under the voluminous skirts of the period. So well known was she at Court, that the young king, Edward VI., refused at first to sign the warrant for her execution, and only did it at last on Archbishop Cranmer's urging. A brave, fearless woman she was, speaking right up in court, reminding her judges that they had already had to change from Catholics to Protestants, and that in the end they would have to come to this for which they were condemning her when they should have read the Scriptures and come to understand them. And in Smithfield, when the priest standing by the pile of fagots tried to convert her, she told him to let her alone and go home and read his Bible. And so she died the death.

But flames could not extinguish the truth, or put into the New Testament anything but the old simple truth, — Christ a great holy teacher, but not God! The story of all that struggling time — through the Catholic reaction under Queen Mary, and on into the Protestant revival under Elizabeth — is dotted with the names of Unitarian martyrs. "Arians" they now began to be called, reviving the well-known name of the Fourth Century. Even when the other Protestants were themselves being persecuted by Mary, they still had no mercy for these heretics who went a little further in their Protestantism; and when Philpot, Archdeacon of Winchester, was in prison for Protestantism, he became so angry with one of his fellow-prisoners on this account, that he spat upon him! The man's offence was that he had argued that God was no otherwise in Christ than in other men; and the story comes to us in a quaint old pamphlet which is extant, called "An Apology of Jhon Philpot: written for spittynge on an Arian; with an invective against the Arians, the veri naturall children of Antichrist."

So, even under Protestant Elizabeth this was the one

heresy that could not be tolerated. In 1579 W. Hamont, a plough-wright, and in 1583 John Lewis went the same fiery road for the same heresy; but the public feeling was beginning to be sick of this kind of thing, and in a few years it ceased; but be it remembered that the last two burnings for heresy in England — Bartholomew Leggatt and Edward Wightman, burned in 1611, only nine years before the sailing of the "Mayflower" — were for Unitarianism.

Now came a new period in the development of liberal thought. Unitarianism, which had hitherto, in England, been the heresy of a few isolated and daring thinkers, became a strong undercurrent of thought, running through the whole of the Seventeenth Century. It was a century of great individuality in religion. Puritanism was working in the nation, setting men looking earnestly into religious questions. Into this ferment of thought came the Latin treatises and catechisms of the Socinians, the Unitarians of Poland. Poland was still in its glory, and the centre of Polish Unitarianism at Racow was the centre of a widespread propagandism. These Polish Unitarian books came to England, found their way among scholars, were read at the universities, and began to influence great numbers of thinkers. The church synods of London and York forbade the importation and sale of such books. But they still came in. One man, especially, is associated with this Unitarian controversy of the Commonwealth time, John Biddle. He was a reputable clergyman educated at Oxford, and with him Unitarianism was not an undercurrent. He openly espoused it, wrote tracts in favor of it, even organized a little church in London, really on the basis of the simple worship of one God. A pertinacious controversialist, too, he was. He was prosecuted, he was imprisoned. His books were ordered to be burned by the common hangman, — nay, so bitter was the feeling aroused by him, that his opponents procured from Parliament a new law against heresy and blasphemy which would have put Biddle himself, as well as his books, into the hands of the hangman. But then Cromwell stepped in. Cromwell was not a Unitarian, but he was almost the only leader of the time who thoroughly understood and prized religious liberty; and with his strong hand he kept the persecuting Act from being put in force. He let Biddle live quietly in the country, and when the feeling against him was too strong, sent him away into a sort of friendly exile in the Scilly Isles. Eventually, on Cromwell's death, he was again thrown into a prison — a prison so loathsome that disease soon carried him off; but the work that he had done, and the books he had introduced, did not die. In the time of the Long Parliament it was being openly preached here and there that "Christ was a prophet and did miracles, but not God." And Dr. Owen, the great champion of Congregational orthodoxy, complained in 1655 that "there is not a city, a town, scarce a village in England, where some of this poison is not poured forth." It is curious, indeed, to recall some of the names of those who came to hold Unitarian opinions, though there was no Unitarian "body." John Milton, John Locke, and Sir Isaac Newton, three of the greatest minds of the century, were all really Unitarians, so far as rejecting the doctrine of the Trinity went. More curious still is it to remember that William Penn, the Quaker, had come to the same conclusion, and his tract "The Sandy Foundation Shaken" is simply an able argument against the Trinity. It all led to nothing, however. It was a sort of Broad-Church view, held in the study and the closet. No church was founded on it. All the churches continued bound to the old creeds and articles. Still the old services went on, and the broad stream of the old Calvinism swept forward. And when at last the era of toleration came, with the final overthrow of the Stuarts in 1688, a sort of religious lassitude succeeded to the feverish strain of conflict and persecution of the Seventeenth Century; so that, with the beginning of the Eighteenth Century, there came about the deadest time that the English churches have ever known.

It was in the still water of this dead time of the Eighteenth Century that we find the beginning of the organic movement out of which grew the present Unitarian churches of England.

Figure to yourselves the state of things. What is called the " era of toleration " began immediately after the overthrow of the Stuarts in 1688. The sects were now at liberty to go quietly on in their own way. On the one hand there was the great established Episcopal Church, — at a pretty low ebb in religious life, for its most earnest life had gone out of it on that " black Bartholomew's Day, 1662," when the two thousand Puritan clergy were ejected. On the other hand were these Puritans, — " Dissenters " they began now to be called, — divided into three great sects, Baptists, Independents, and English Presbyterians. Now, these were all free. They could build churches, and they did. From 1693 to 1720 was the great " chapel "-building time. " Chapels " was all they ventured to call their meeting-houses, for fear of rousing up the old persecuting passion of the established and dominant Episcopacy; and the name clings to them to this day, so that the Dissenting bodies commonly talk of " going to chapel," while " going to church" means attending the Church of England.

But now, in this great development of chapel-building by these three denominations, a curious thing took place, which unexpectedly affected their after history. That curious thing was, that while the Baptists and Independents (or Congregationalists) tied down all these new chapels to perpetual orthodox uses by rigid doctrinal trust-deeds, — like that at Andover, for instance, — the English Presbyterians left theirs free. It seems strange that they should do so; for the Presbyterians had begun by being the narrowest sect of the Puritans, and the Scotch Presbyterians always remained so. But the English Presbyterians had very little to do with the Scotch ones, and through all the changes and sufferings they had had to go through they had become broadened; and so it came to pass that now, when they were building their churches or chapels up and down the country, they left them free. Let it be clearly understood that they were not Unitarians. They were steady-going orthodox folk, — Calvinists, even, most of them. They had not even any idea that their descendants would ever become Unitarians; but they did not want to tie them. They had themselves felt the evil of creeds, and they would have none of them, and so they left their churches free.

Mark what followed. The English Presbyterians, thus left free, began to grow more liberal. It was natural they should; for they had no exact lines to keep, no creeds or articles to be periodically brought out and compared with what they might be preaching. So their minds, free, began gradually to work in a more liberal direction. From the first, the old rigid Calvinism began to melt away. Then they went on to thoughts of God which led to their saying very little about the Trinity. A general reverence for Christ took the place of the old distinct belief in his deity. First, they gave up preaching the orthodox doctrines, and then they gave up believing them. They opened the communion to all; they no longer insisted on the old professions of "church-membership," but counted all who worshipped with them "the church." Thus things were going on all through the middle of the last century. Of course it was not the same everywhere; some still held the old views, while many began to be spoken of in the ministers' meetings as Arians, and a few — regarded as far-going radicals — talked flat Socinianism. There were differences, too, among the people. Some saw the liberal drift with dismay. "Sir," said Mr. Crook, one of the old conservative hearers, to Rev. Mr. Haynes, minister of the Presbyterian chapel in Sheffield, — " Sir, I like the old doctrines." "So do I, Mr. Crook," replied the minister; "the older, the better, sir. Mine is as old as the Apostles." In truth, these English Presbyterians, having no creeds to take their bearings by, but only the Bible, were almost unconsciously feeling their way back toward the simple Christianity of the New Testament.

There was one man among them, however, who could not feel his way unconsciously. Dr. Joseph Priestley was too open-eyed to go in any direction without knowing it. He was one of the leading scientists of his time, — a restless investigator, and at the same time an earnest religious thinker and student, just as eager to make out the truth about religion as to investigate the properties of oxygen or electricity. So he investigated Christianity, studied the creeds of the churches, came to the conclusion that they were a long way from the Christianity of Christ, and gradually came to be a thoroughgoing Unitarian. When he came to this conclusion he did not hide it; he proclaimed it and preached it. It startled the old steady-going Presbyterian churches; they were hardly ready for it. The older men held up their hands in horror; the timid advised caution. But Priestley went right on; proclaimed that the Trinity, the deity of Christ, and the substitutionary sacrifice of Christ were corruptions, and declared Unitarianism the original doctrine of Christianity. Gradually he forced our old Presbyterian churches to hear and to think; and the upshot of it was, that at length he aroused a large part of the body to the consciousness that they were really Unitarians. They still did not take the name; they disliked sect-names altogether. It had always been their pride that Presbyterians did not condition their fellowship by any creed, and they did not like being identified specially with this new Unitarian doctrine any more than they had liked being tied fast to Calvinism; but the logic of facts was too strong for them. The fact was, that these new thoughts of God's simple unity, and of Christ's inspired humanity, and their altogether more reasonable way of looking at religion, — these thoughts were of more importance to the world just then than the mere process of liberty by which they had come to them. And so, though they mostly continued to call themselves English Presbyterians, or simply Presbyterians, all the world began to call them Unitarians; and more and more the Baptists and Independents, or Congregationalists, who had formerly fellowshipped and worked with them, drew apart, and left them, as they are to-day, in the reluctant isolation of a separate Unitarian body.

Two other movements of thought of a somewhat similar kind increased and strengthened this development of a separate Unitarian body, — one among the General Baptists, the other in the great Episcopal Church itself.

The Baptists in England had always been divided into the "Particular" Baptists, holding the old Calvinistic doctrine of particular salvation, or the election of particular individuals, and the "General" Baptists, that is, those who believed that salvation was a general thing, open to all who would repent. The Particular Baptists have always been tolerably rigid Calvinists, — though of late they have not been rigid enough for their great leader, Mr. Spurgeon, who bewails certain growing tendencies to liberalism. But the General Baptists had that one germ of liberalism in them from the beginning, — hope for *all*, not merely for the elect, — and that germ grew, until, about the time when the Presbyterians found that they had practically drifted into Unitarianism a large part of the old General Baptist body found out the same thing. So there came a split in the old General Baptist Assembly; the main body standing for Liberalism, the orthodox minority seceding (about the year 1770) and forming the New Connection of General Baptists. The Unitarian General Baptists have continued their separate organization, and their churches hold to their old distinctive rite of adult baptism by immersion; but in other respects they are part of the Unitarian connection, being included in the English Unitarian "Year-Book," and generally acting with us in conferences and associations.

A still more interesting movement, however, was that in the Established Church. It brought us only one man, but that man did a great deal to reconcile our churches to the Unitarian name, and make them appreciate the value of that which it stood for. Indeed, the name of Theophilus Lindsey must always stand with that of Dr. Joseph Priestley as practically the co-founders of our liberal church. Lindsey was an Episcopal clergyman, a modest, quiet country parson in a little Yorkshire vicarage, — a gentle, refined man, but with a mind and a conscience. He was one of those who were helping a great Broad-Church movement in the Church of England in the last century. "Latitudinarians" they were called in those days; but they went every bit as far as Dean Stanley and the Broad Churchmen of our time; there were numbers of things in the Prayer-book and Creeds and Articles which they could not believe, in any plain natural meaning; and so strongly did they feel this, that a movement sprang up for getting Parliament to relax the terms of subscription to the Church Articles. Lindsey was one of the movers in this, and they held a meeting in London at the Feathers' Tavern, and drew up a petition to Parliament. That Feathers' Tavern Petition was a famous matter a century ago. But the result was that Parliament not only would not do anything, but refused by three to one even to let the petition be presented! People said, "What will the petitioners do now?" They did nothing; simply stopped in the Church; said they must go on trying to widen the Church,— but stayed in. All but one man. Alone of them all, Theophilus Lindsey saw his duty and did it; he saw that there was no real chance of any widening, and that it would not do for him to go on repeating prayers and creeds about the Trinity which he no more really believed than his friend Dr. Priestley did; so he sent in his resignation to the bishop. It was dreadfully hard. Everything was against him. The bishop wrote him a long, kind letter, urging him to stay in the Church. His brother liberals protested against his deserting them. His wife's rich Episcopalian friends stormed, his poor parishioners pleaded and wept, but all in vain. In December, 1773, he gave up his vicarage and went up to London with just twenty pounds in his pocket (and that got only by selling his furniture and books) to start a Unitarian church. It is not easy to realize in these days what that meant. There was not an avowed Unitarian church in all England, though there were many that were generally known in their neighborhoods as holding that position. The thing was illegal. To deny the Trinity was still a crime punishable by law, though the law had for a long time not been enforced. Still, Theophilus Lindsey went right on. He hired an old auction-room in a little street off the Strand (Essex Street), and the room was fitted up for worship; but he had hard work to get it licensed for preaching, and for months an emissary of the government attended to report what was said and done.

This was the first avowed Unitarian church in England, and this was its founder. It is an instructive history. For see: Lindsey's Broad-Church friends had prophesied that if he left the Church, his usefulness would be gone, and that he would do more to advance the truth by remaining in, like the rest of them. Time showed which was right. Of all those Broad Churchmen who petitioned for the Church to be widened, the only one who made any mark on the religious thought of the time was Theophilus Lindsey, who went out. The rest are forgotten. Their whole movement died away. On the other hand, Lindsey in that little auction-room succeeded beyond any one's expectation. Essex-Street Chapel became a notable place; to it gathered numbers of the leading liberals of the time, barristers, scientists, members of Parliament; and for nearly a century it remained the leading Unitarian church of London.

That was in 1774. I think it was from 1785 to 1800 that some of the American Congregational churches began to occupy a distinctly Unitarian position, about a quarter of a century later than the movement among the Presbyterians in England. The real connection between the two is this: not that the English Unitarianism was in any sense the cause of American Unitarianism, but that the open movement in England helped the open development of the movement in America. In the preface to the King's-Chapel Prayer-book (1785) we find that Dr. Freeman in making that revision of the "Book of Common Prayer" acknowledges the assistance he had obtained from the similar revision just eleven years before by Theophilus Lindsey. The fact is, however, that among thoughtful men in America a similar process of liberalizing to that in England had also been for a long time going on. This process was helped by Dr. Priestley's coming to America. It was in 1794 that, virtually driven out of England by the intolerance which had burned his home in Birmingham and which dogged his steps in London, he came to New York on his way to settle in Pennsylvania. He was received with the greatest honor. A company of New York citizens wanted to keep him there, promising to form a church for him if he would remain; and again in Philadelphia friends procured a wide hearing for his lectures on religion; and these things must have helped to bring out "into the open" the growing Liberalism which was already seething in Boston and the New England Congregational churches. So that, though it was in 1785 that Dr. Freeman, in Boston, altered the old Prayer Book so as to leave out everything Trinitarian, and so planted the first clear landmark of Unitarianism in America, it was not till 1800, and after, that the new departure became a marked and definite thing. In fact, it may be said that Unitarianism in England was about a quarter of a century before Unitarianism in America. Since that time, however, its development has been very much the same in each country. There, as here, the earlier Unitarians felt it was so clear that Unitarianism is the Christianity of Christ, that they thought a few generations would convert the country. There, as here, the actual path has been full of difficulties and discouragements, and the actual number of our churches is about the same in each country, — some three hundred and sixty-five or three hundred and seventy, large and small, all told. There, as here, any direct work and church building has been crippled by a morbid dread of sectarianism; we have been afraid of working alone for religion, even when that has been the only way for us to work at all: and men who would only give fifty dollars for their own church have often given five hundred dollars to Methodists or Episcopalians to show that they are not illiberal. Abroad too, as in America, we have been cramped in our own life by the attitude of controversy, which for long was a necessity forced upon us. So our work has been halting and clumsy, and hardly ever have we yet brought our full power to work upon the religious life of our time. In England, too, Unitarians have labored under difficulties, unknown here, from the tremendous social prestige and attraction of the great "established" Episcopal Church. As the last half-century has also seen a great revival of religious earnestness in the Episcopal body, it gradually drew away from us many of the great county families which had held by the "Old Dissent" as a sort of tradition, and who would never leave it as long as it was under any of the old persecuting disabilities. Still, the Unitarian churches have gone forward, to some extent in numbers, to a still more striking extent in spirit and active religious life. If they have lost somewhat among the wealthy and cultivated classes, they have gained far more among the people; and now, almost everywhere in England one of their strongest elements is the thoughtful, intelligent artisan-life which has gathered to them during the past forty years.

Two influences combined, half a century ago, to set the life of our churches in this new direction. One was the visit of Dr. Tuckerman to England in 1835. His preaching, and the story of his own ministry-at-large in Boston, interested our English churches very deeply. He awoke our people in the large city churches to a new concern for the sad, ignorant, perishing masses around them. Within two or three years of his visit similar ministries-at-large — "Domestic Missions" they are called in England — were started in London, Manchester,

Liverpool, Birmingham, Leeds, Bristol, and several other places. This was done not as a sectarian movement, nor with any idea of increasing our churches or their attendance. Indeed, the Unitarian name was put almost absolutely in the background. They were to be pure agencies for helping and doing good, without a thought of any sectarian gain. It was about as noble a kind of sectarian self-abnegation as has ever been seen. But perhaps on that very account its benefit reacted all the more upon the doers. It put into our strongest city churches a new interest in doing good, and with that came new life, more interest in religion every way. Then, about the same time, other influences were at work. Richard Wright and several others of an earnest missionary spirit had been going up and down the country preaching Unitarianism to the common people with an eagerness which some of the old Presbyterian families regarded as fanatical and vulgar, but which roused up a great deal of wholesome controversy, and started a few new churches of quite different calibre among our artisan populations; not mission congregations, but regular churches of plain, homespun people, often holding together and keeping up a Sunday-school without any minister. All this brought home to our churches a new sense of there being whole classes, especially in the manufacturing districts, whom Orthodoxy was failing to hold, who were the strength of secularistic and anti-religious movements, and who might be won to Unitarianism; but for whom Unitarianism had hitherto done almost nothing.

Concurrently with this awakening of an interest in the religious needs of the people, our churches were brought into contact with several very interesting religious movements right among the people themselves. Right in the heart of the woollen manufacturing villages of Lancashire it was found that there was a group of half a dozen little churches, — come-outers from one of the Methodist bodies, — who, entirely by their own reading of the Bible, had found their way to Unitarianism without knowing that there were any Unitarians, and who, moreover, still retained their old fervent Methodist ways. Great was their delight at finding out at last that there had been for generations a strong body of churches, standing for the same views, and heartily disposed to fellowship with them. And so these congregations, calling themselves "Unitarian Methodists," came right in with us. Then a little later (about 1844) came another of these popular movements — another secession from Methodism — under the lead of the once well-known Joseph Barker. A number of the groups of his sympathizers, almost all plain laboring men, formed themselves into little churches under the name of "Christian Brethren." At first they would not identify themselves with Unitarians, declining any sect-name, and many of them being strongly set against any professional ministry. But they gradually found themselves more and more in sympathy with us, and at last, when their leader Joseph Barker swung clear away from religion, they mostly, instead of following him, drew more closely to their Unitarian neighbors, and within a few years were heartily united with us as part of the general denomination.

Another event which drew attention to Unitarianism among a different class was what was called the "Liverpool Controversy." In 1839, thirteen of the Episcopal clergy of Liverpool announced a course of public lectures against Unitarianism. The Unitarian ministers of Liverpool had been, for some few years past, James Martineau, John Hamilton Thom, and Henry Giles, afterwards well known as a public lecturer in America. Their ministry had been entirely the opposite of controversial, and indeed they none of them liked the name "Unitarian."

But such a public attack could not be left unnoticed, and they accordingly invited the public to hear the other side, and gave a corresponding series of lectures in Paradise-Street Chapel, the precursor of the later Hope-Street Church. This discussion — "the thirteen against three," as it was called — excited very wide attention among thoughtful people, and led many to embrace Unitarianism; while the collected volume, "Unitarianism Defended," has been ever since one of the standard works on the Unitarian side, and derives special and permanent interest from its containing some of the earliest published writings of Dr. Martineau, so long the leading mind of our church in England.

The usual method of support in the English Unitarian Church is by pew-rents. The American plan of *owning* pews is practically unknown in England. In some of our churches the pew-rent is put at a very small sum (perhaps from half a dollar to two dollars a sitting), so as not to prevent any one however poor, from belonging to the congregation on terms of equal membership; and then those members able to afford more assess themselves for yearly subscriptions in addition. Of late years a good many of our congregations, nearly one tenth of the total number, have adopted the "open church system,"[1] leaving the seats entirely free and unappropriated, and asking for no fixed or pledged subscriptions, but simply having an offertory at each service, — in some cases in closed bags, so that no one knows what any one else gives, in other cases in envelopes.

The ministry of all these churches, apart from those who come over from other denominations, is drawn from three sources, — three Theological Schools.

[1] First introduced among our churches in 1864, in the Strangeways Unitarian Free Church, Manchester.

First, and chief, for a century past, has been "Manchester New College," just removed[1] from its quarters in London to Oxford; at its head Dr. Martineau, with a group of noble scholars around him, — Dr. James Drummond, Prof. J. Estlin Carpenter, and others. It is a school of free, untrammelled theological study, often impugned by some of the more zealous Unitarians as not sufficiently concentrating its force on providing ministers for the Unitarian churches, but still really giving us our strongest and most scholarly ministers.

Secondly, is the "Unitarian Home Missionary Board" (about analogous to the "Meadville Theological School"), designed to afford a ministerial and theological training to men who have not been able to take a college course.

There is, besides, an old Theological College at Carmarthen, in Wales, a relic of the old Presbyterian days, before the development of Unitarianism. It is mainly in the hands of Unitarian trustees, but is managed on a broad catholic plan, so as to include both Orthodox and Unitarian professors and students, both of whom teach and study side by side in entire friendship.

One point in relation to the ministry that may be of interest, is that the missionary work of the regular ministry is supplemented in England, to an extent quite unknown among our American churches, by the help of lay-preachers. At quite a number of our new and mission churches the services are conducted usually by laymen, one or other of the neighboring ministers giving perhaps some occasional services. In that way most of our District Missionary Associations (or "Conferences") cover a great deal more ground, and keep up the services with much greater regularity than would be possible with churches entirely dependent upon ministers.

[1] October, 1889, — henceforth named "Manchester College, Oxford."

Such is the history, and such are some of the most interesting features, in the growth of Unitarianism in England. Its progress is slow, but steady. Its thought is leavening other churches more and more, and meanwhile its own churches are gradually increasing in numbers, and are generally better supported and better attended than they were fifty years ago. Nearly half of them have been rebuilt within that period, and all are brighter, more beautiful homes of worship than they used to be. And, alike in their closer association with the old Unitarian churches of Transylvania and with the newer churches of America, and in strengthening union and extending activities among themselves, they are more living than ever before, and find around them an ever widening opportunity.

THE CONTACT OF AMERICAN UNITARIANISM AND GERMAN THOUGHT.

BY J. H. ALLEN.

IN order to bring the vast topic of German Theology in any intelligible way within the limits of my hour, I must confine myself to the very narrowest interpretation of the words in which my subject is announced. And these must be understood to mean, not how Unitarianism is to be found in German theology "from the time of Schleiermacher;" for it is not there at all — at least in name. The German theologians, for reasons which I need not explain, are generally bound by Lutheran or other State traditions and conditions; and, while it may often be said of the best of them that their way of thinking is quite in harmony with ours, their form of doctrine is wholly different. I shall not, therefore, trouble myself or you about that; but take what is the only serviceable rendering of the words of my title, namely: How, when, and where has the course of Unitarianism in America been affected by contact with German theology from the time of Schleiermacher?

This brings me, again, to a very precise date, which I must take for my starting-point. That date I shall take, for reasons of convenience, at just fifty years ago. And, as there is a personal equation in all these things, which more or less warps our judgment of them, perhaps you will pardon me the impropriety of a word to explain what those reasons of convenience are. I was at that time a student in college, among circumstances that led me to take an eager interest in the discussions then going on, and to look forward with eager hope to the part I might possibly be afterwards called to take in them. I was in the dear and serious household of my mother's brother, Henry Ware, Jr., who affectionately encouraged such early hopes in his kindly but taciturn way. I had listened with a vague but exhilarating delight to Mr. Emerson's Divinity School Address, given that summer, — which had, as you know, shocked some, while it had charmed others, as the first clear word of " another gospel, which yet was not another." So that I was already prepared, when a year later the battle of the books began, to follow its changing fortunes with a degree of personal feeling as to the issues involved which has not been in the least diminished to this day. In short, to speak with still greater precision, the exact crisis that brought to the front the bearing of German theology upon American Unitarianism was the publication, in 1839, of Professor Andrews Norton's Divinity School Address on " The Latest Form of Infidelity."

Here, perhaps, I ought to add a further word of explanation. First as to myself; for by nurture and habit I clung strongly to the more conservative side in the debate that followed. I have always considered that Professor Norton had the better of his opponents in scholarship and logic; till the age of twenty-five I intended, or expected, that my place would be on that side; and if I have altered from this position since, it has been not so much due (as I think) to the course of that discussion as to a passage of argument with that rude logician, Orestes A. Brownson, during the crisis of the notable change by which he became a Catholic. Next as to others; for the real point at issue in that debate has been often misunderstood, as if it had been the question of admitting the supernatural or miraculous in Christianity.

On the contrary, in one of his letters addressed to Professor Norton, Mr. George Ripley says: " For my own part, I cannot avoid the conclusion that the miracles related in the Gospels were actually wrought by Jesus;" and in a pamphlet of the same date, understood to have been written by Theodore Parker, he says, " I believe that Jesus, like other religious teachers, wrought miracles." And, as neither of these men has been accused of Jesuistry or moral cowardice, it appears that the question at issue was not as to their opinions, which at that time were in the main conventional and customary, but as to a new and unfamiliar order of thought, which was seen to be powerfully affecting the principles and foundations of men's religious belief. What this new order of thought was, and what has been its effect among us during this past half-century, it will be my duty to make as clear as I can within the limits allowed me.

That influence, whatever it was, we ascribe in a vague and general way to German theology, especially " from the time of Schleiermacher." But German theology of that period — that is, of the last ninety years — is (as I said) a very vast and unmanageable topic; and I must therefore narrow my field still further, by pointing out three great departments into which it may be roughly divided.

First is that which especially dates from Schleiermacher himself, though it also has to do with those famous philosophical schools which appear to have had absolute control in the higher thought of Germany down to about forty years ago, — chiefly the school of Hegel. It was these that gave the great intellectual impulse, and that appeared to open up an entirely new interpretation of religious thought and the religious life, and hence created that fresh enthusiasm among some of our younger men half a century or more ago, which we call Transcendentalism, and Professor Norton called "the latest form of Infidelity." This (as I just said) did not so much affect men's particular opinions as their whole way of looking at the subject of Religion. We may call it, if you please, the German *Speculative Theology*.

Second, and producing its effect more gradually, is a movement which started still farther back, largely from the impulse given by the German poet and critic Lessing. I may describe it in a general way by saying that its effect has been to take the Bible out of that sanctuary where it was regarded as a holy thing by itself, never to be judged, but only to be explained and then accepted reveringly by the human mind, — to take it, I say, from that sanctuary, to class it among our other literary treasures, and to interpret it just as we do other books of history, of legend or tradition, of moral exhortation, or of religious poetry. I say nothing for or against this result, which I suppose that we are all at this day fully agreed to accept. I only say that to bring it about took something like a century of controversy, often very angry and bitter; and that during this time there was evolved a mass of erudition, argument, exposition, speculation, literally unspeakable in its dimensions, which makes the field of German *Critical Theology*. And it is the diligent cultivation of this field among our own best scholars — including Professor Noyes, Dr. Hedge, Theodore Parker, and James Freeman Clarke, against the strong protest of the elder school represented by Professor Norton — that has brought about the most marked changes in the body of opinion known as American Unitarianism.

Third, we must reckon a field with which I have nothing whatever to do here, although in some ways it is perhaps the most important of all. For German theology, in its large sense, has been one of the greatest and most remarkable educating influences of the last half-century to a very large class of minds. Every topic suggested in both the lines of discussion I have described has been taken up, and with infinite painstaking, erudition, and patience followed out to the last slender filament of inference or investigation on which it was possible to string an opinion or a guess. It would be mere pedantry to cite the names of the innumerable laborers in that wide field;[1] and any attempt to explore it would only lead us away from the strict and narrow line we have to follow. That portion of the field we may call the German *Theology of Erudition.* With it, as I have said, I have for the present nothing to do.

I must now go back, and explain the prominence which has been given in my topic to the name of Schleiermacher.

Frederick Daniel Ernst Schleiermacher was born in 1768, and died in 1834, at the age of sixty-six. He was a man of the very finest religious genius, a preacher of extraordinary fervor and wealth of thought, of a moral nature singularly clinging, sympathetic, and emotional, a scholar of vast erudition even for a German, a student of great and indefatigable industry, and a teacher, or intimate adviser, of personal weight and influence almost unparalleled. Professor Philip Schaff calls him, without qualification, "the greatest divine of the Nineteenth Century." To understand the ground of his unexampled and unique influence upon the religious thought of his day, we should take into account that very early in life he saw clearly these two things: first, that the doctrinal system built up during the Reformation had completely gone to seed, and existed only as a lifeless and sterile form, — at least in

---

[1] Tholuck and Neander are perhaps the names which will be most widely and gratefully recognized.

Germany and among the educated classes, where his work was, as we see in the life of Lessing, — and must perish unless a new soul could be breathed into it; and second, that the idea, the method, the discipline, embodied in the Christian Church and known to the Christian conscience, must form the type, the model, the condition, under which such new religious life could be had, — and this, if it must be, independent of all doctrinal forms whatever. To show the intensity of his conviction on this point, I copy here his own words: "Religion was the mother's bosom,[1] in whose sacred warmth and darkness my young life was nourished and prepared for the world which lay before me all unknown; and she still remained with me, when God and immortality vanished before my doubting eyes." This, I say, is his characteristic testimony to the reality of the religious life, wholly independent of all doctrinal forms whatever. And we must take it as our starting-point, in estimating both the peculiar nature of his influence upon the mind of his time, and the peculiar dread of that influence which we find among those who, like Professor Norton, honestly held that very clearly defined opinions were essential to any hold at all upon the Christian faith. To such minds that language sounded merely vague, delusive, and sophistical.

The date of the first strong impression made by Schleiermacher upon the mind of his time was the year 1799, when he published a series of eloquent pamphlet "Discourses" on Religion, addressed to "the cultivated among its despisers." As to this date we have to bear in mind that it was just at the coming in of the tide of reaction that followed the extravagant anti-religious fury of the French Revolution, and set so strong towards conservatism in politics and religion: so that he was

[1] Germ. *Schoos,* "womb."

doing in Germany a like task to that attempted just then by Chateaubriand in France. But we must look back of that date, to see how this religious reaction took just the shape it did in his mind. The father of Schleiermacher was a good old-fashioned Calvinistic preacher, chaplain to a regiment; and for convenience in some of his wanderings, he put the boy at school among the Moravian Brethren. These made the most pious of religious communities. In spiritual descent their tradition came down from Bohemian exiles, who carried into their retreat the same religious ardor that had flamed with such obstinate fury in the Hussite wars; but in them, or in their followers, it was tempered to a sweet, somewhat austere, and most nobly self-sacrificing piety. It was the placid faith of a company of Moravian missionaries in a storm at sea that had touched John Wesley more profoundly than ever before with the reality and power of a religious life. And this obscure community was "the mother's bosom, warm and dark," which nourished the germs of that young life given to its charge.

The later experience of university life, and the deliberate study of the Deistical writers (then making a good deal of noise), which he undertook against his father's earnest protest, did not, as we have seen, extinguish the deep sense that religion in the soul was the most profound and blessed of realities; while they did convince him that it must be interpreted to the educated mind in a way very different from the old doctrinal scheme, — a way in which the form of expression should be, avowedly, not the adequate statement of a fact of human knowledge, but the symbol, or image (*Vorstellung*), of that which far transcends all human knowledge. Hence he chose such phrases as seemed to minds like Professor Norton's a mere playing fast and loose with sacred things, sophistry or conscious self-deception, "veil-weaving"[1] about one's real opinions, so as to hide their true meaning from others' eyes. Thus, departing from the common language of theology, Schleiermacher speaks not of "God the Creator and Moral Governor" (which are the terms insisted on by Martineau and English thinkers generally), but rather of "the Divine Life" and our "communion with the Living God, — a sharp distinction," he says, "is to be drawn between the Living God and a personal God," — not of "a Future Life of Judgment," in the terms familiar to most Christians, but rather of the "Eternal Life," or deathlessness of the spiritual principle in man, and of its blending in the Hereafter with the Universal Life, in language that implied, or seemed to imply, that its conscious identity would be lost.[2] In short, his whole system of doctrine (*Glaubenslehre*) — which is developed at great length and very elaborately — appears to be built on the interpreting not of any written word, but of the actual experience of the religious life. Its data are purely the facts of Christian consciousness; and, as a countryman of his has said of him, it was "quite uncertain whether Schleiermacher believed or not in revelation, miracle, the divinity of Christ, the Trinity, the personality of God, or the immortality of the soul. In his theological phrases he would avoid all that could distinctly mean this or that." In his exposition of faith he starts with this one point of fact: I am a Christian; this I am by nature and inheritance. By introspection and analysis, not by study of the letter of the gospel, he will then determine what that fact implies; what is the meaning of incarnation, atonement, resurrection, in the terms of religious experience; and this

---

[1] *Schleiermacher* (as Professor Norton reminds us) is a German word signifying "veil-maker."

[2] Compare Martineau's Study of Religion, ii. 355-360.

shall be his Christian creed. Of course, all sharp bounds of doctrine disappear; and this simplicity of method, carried out with the wonderful wealth and fervor of his exposition, makes him the great master of liberal theology, by whatever name his disciples may be called.

But it is not my business here to expound Schleiermacher's method or doctrinal system, however briefly; only to show how the order of thought I have been trying to describe came into effect on New England Unitarianism at that particular time, why it fascinated some while it alarmed or offended others, and in what ways it has modified the character of it ever since.

This order of thought was (as I have already hinted) further strengthened by those schools of German philosophy so powerful in the first half of this century, which came to be eagerly studied among us about fifty years ago. I have nothing whatever to do with them here as systems of opinion. I only speak of them because they shared the same obloquy with the new theology from those who imperfectly understood them; and because they have strongly affected the current of opinion since, — more strongly than most of us are apt to think. Not directly; for few cared to study them, or could possibly understand them if they did. But those few have in a very special sense been the teachers of our generation, and have influenced even the popular way of thinking among us more than we are often aware. James Freeman Clarke, for example, was strongly attracted by these philosophies and by the theology founded upon them. Then there are two well-known works of two very accomplished students in this direction: "Reason in Religion" by Dr. Hedge, to whom German came to be almost a second mother-tongue during his school-days passed in Germany, and who had as much to do as anybody in naturalizing the new order of thought among us; and "The Science of Thought," by Professor Everett, which is understood to be a product of the philosophy of Hegel, — that philosophy held in especial dread and abhorrence by sober thinkers among us half a century ago. Just in proportion to the seriousness and the religiousness of their way of thinking have the men of a younger generation been influenced by such books as these.

But the philosophy I speak of has had another effect among us, more direct and more intelligible. Fifty years ago, as I have shown, Unitarians were substantially all agreed in accepting Christianity as a special and supernatural revelation, in the common sense of those terms. I have quoted both George Ripley and Theodore Parker, in their controversy with Professor Norton, as professing, with the utmost apparent simplicity, their own belief in the Christian miracles. At this day, on the contrary, not only (with very rare exceptions) those who are regarded as leaders of thought among us — such as Martineau in England and Hedge in America — have quietly dropped or openly discarded the argument from miracles; but Broad Churchmen in England, like Bishop Colenso, who never forfeited his bishopric, like Charles Voysey and Stopford Brooke (before the secession of these latter), have done the same; Matthew Arnold, openly a member of the Church of England, says without rebuke that "miracles do not happen." The way for this remarkable change of opinion among men in general has no doubt been opened by scientific habits of thinking; but as a change in religious opinion, the way for it had to be prepared by philosophy. Schleiermacher, as usual, speaks both ways: "Insulate any natural fact," he says, "and it becomes a miracle; repeat any miracle, and it becomes a natural fact."

And, for a time, the religious scruple is pacified by such a compromise.

Clear and honest thinking, however, demands something more than this tampering with words. It demands, first, a fixed habit of mind in harmony with the best opinion or knowledge of the day : this we call " a philosophical method " in our thought; and second, a careful study, with the best helps of modern learning, of the documents and evidences of our faith : this we call "a scientific criticism" in our theology. I have just spoken of the great change that has come to pass in the opinions of the thinking world, in the common understanding of the Bible history. I have now a few words to say of the way in which this change has been helped among ourselves by the study of German critical theology.

To go into the subject properly, I ought to show how there have grown up in Germany, more or less directly as the fruit of different philosophical schools, a great variety of interpretations, or ways of interpreting the Bible records, most of them more or less rationalistic; and how these may be divided into three main groups : the non-miraculous, pure and simple, represented by the name of Paulus; the mythical or poetic, represented by Strauss; and the historical or scientific, of which the best exponent is the school of Baur. Now the story of these groups is extremely interesting and instructive, but I have not time to give it here;[1] and besides, my subject seems to make it more proper for me to illustrate it by examples taken among our own students and theologians, instead of those that come to us across the water in a foreign tongue.

Strictly speaking, there has been no scholarly investigation of this field among ourselves. The best that any of our stu-

[1] It is given in "Christian History in its Three Great Periods." iii. 227-238.

dents have done has been to study according to their ability, and appropriate as far as they thought good, the learning which has been poured forth in unstinted measure from the German press. German has for this half-century been the favorite, I may say the indispensable, language in which to follow up any of these lines of investigation. And whether our own writers have borrowed their opinions out and out, or whether they have thought them out for themselves under the atmospheric pressure of that great world of learning and speculation, the result is one : the general, even the popular, way of looking at the subject, with or without knowing it, has taken its tone from Germany.

The earliest signs of this influence among us were an essay on "The Messianic Prophecies," by Mr. (afterward Professor) George R. Noyes, in 1834; critical "Lectures on the Old Testament," by Professor Palfrey, published in 1840; and a "Note on the Old Testament," by Professor Norton, in 1844. These, however, though expressing the extreme of radical opinion in their day, were addressed only to scholars, and hardly reached the general mind; then, too, they did not directly touch the Christian records, and so excited little or no particular alarm. The first book I remember, showing clear traces of German influence upon critical opinion, — less by its argument than by the fact of its publication, — was a tale called "Theodore, or the Skeptic's Conversion," translated by James Freeman Clarke from the learned and famous theologian, De Wette. Theodore is an ingenuous young theologian, beginning to be troubled with doubts of the supernatural, — a sort of Robert Elsmere of that period, whose spiritual struggles are mild, indeed, compared with those of a later day, and who easily finds comfort in such pious compromises as those we have seen in Schleiermacher. There could not have been a gentler or kindlier introduction among us of the line of thought which controversy was to make so familiar afterwards. De Wette was one of the earliest, one of the most devout and pure-minded, as well as most copious and learned, of the new school of commentators; and his writings, though long left behind by the rushing current of speculative exegesis, did perhaps more than any others to instruct the students of that generation.

It is natural to speak next of the work of Theodore Parker, whose chief task of erudition was to translate and expound, from his immense range of reading, De Wette's commentary on the Old Testament. He had already, in his South Boston sermon on "The Transient and Permanent in Christianity" (1841), cast these topics of learned discussion into the waters of popular controversy; and his name, more than any other, came to be the watchword of the change of opinion that was slowly coming to pass upon the popular mind: a change which was strikingly shown three years ago this month, when the American Unitarian Association published a large volume of Theodore Parker's writings, including that very discourse, under the editorship of James Freeman Clarke.

Two other Unitarian scholars, especially revered and beloved among us, have shown in different ways and more obscurely something of the German influence in their commentaries upon the Gospel, — Dr. William Henry Furness and Mr. Edmund Hamilton Sears. "Jesus and his Biographers," which is the completest and best statement of Dr. Furness's exposition, recognizes with extreme gratitude and respect his obligation to his instructor, Professor Norton; but its characteristic view — that the miracles, taken in their most literal sense, were *the natural acts* of such a soul as Jesus — not only was a great shock to the received opinion, but no one can read the rationalistic commentary of Paulus without seeing how the two differ in their method only by a hair's-breadth, and how (consciously or not) the one has caught the manner and spirit of the other whom apparently he means to contradict. They have the same matter-of-fact way of taking the detail of narrative and of giving it a "natural" explanation, each in his own fashion. Allow for the thick, clumsy, dingy, ill-printed German volumes, and set beside them the fair, clean, trim, compact pages of the American press, — compare the scholastic method of the German erudite, who chiefly rejoices and expands in the dry light of criticism, with the religious beauty and tenderness that mark the later exposition, — and you have in the one, in many a familiar passage, only a transfigured likeness of the other. Mr. Sears's "Heart of Christ," I should say on the other hand, with perhaps a little less confidence, reflects, in the great sweetness and spiritual beauty of its exposition, the tone of Olshausen, that most devout and mystical of learned commentators, whose orthodoxy of belief seems purely a phase of his sentimental piety, and whose spirit is wonderfully winning as you begin to read him, whether or not you are long content with his intellectual view. Mr. Sears's refined and beautiful intelligence was the gracious channel through which that vein of influence flowed in, to the delight and comfort of many a kindred mind.

I do not know of any theologian among us who has accepted seriously Strauss's mythical theory of interpreting the gospel narrative. It was taken up by Theodore Parker, while it was yet new, in the "Christian Examiner," in an admirable exposition and confutation; and I do not remember any discussion of it as a living issue among us since. In brief, it would make the supernatural parts of the Gospels a sort of allegory or philosophical poem, founded on ideas current in Jewish tradition, and embodying in symbols certain facts and phases of the higher life of man. Especially such transcendental facts of the Gospel narrative as the Incarnation, the Temptation, the Transfiguration, the Resurrection and Ascension, are expounded frankly as "myths," — that is, philosophical ideas, or facts of the religious life, put in the form of narrative of real events, which are regarded as purely symbolic or allegorical. It is understood to be the product of what is called the school of Hegel "of the Left" in philosophy; and, if one wishes to see how that general line of symbolic interpretation is carried out through the field of fact and dogma, he might be advised, instead of studying the words of Strauss himself (which are foreign in tone, and more or less repellent to us), to find it in the writings of Drs. Hedge and Everett before cited, especially the former.

Of far greater importance at this day than the schools of criticism yet spoken of is what is known as the "Tübingen School," established and still largely controlled by the massive learning and masterly mind of Ferdinand Christian Baur. I have myself several times given public exposition of the method of this school and the results it seems to lead to, and shall say nothing of it now, except that it has been most fully, most intelligently, and best set forth before our public by that graceful scholar, that widely read theologian, that accomplished man of letters, Octavius Brooks Frothingham, — a man who inherits the elegant and fastidious refinement of our elder New England scholarship, and has added to it an intellectual breadth, a moral courage, and a mental vigor, which put him conspicuously in the front rank of a younger school of theologians.

I have now, as time allowed me, passed in review the influences, both religious and dogmatic, or intellectual, which have come upon American Unitarianism during the last fifty years, while I have been a close and interested spectator in the field. There is one other thing which seems to me necessary, in order to make this survey complete. I have said already what were the dismay and repugnance with which that influence was first seen to be coming on. To quote from Professor Norton's address on the Latest Form of Infidelity: "In Germany the theology of which I speak has allied itself with atheism, with pantheism, and with other irreligious speculations, that have appeared in those metaphysical systems from which the God of Christianity is excluded." Some of you may no doubt remember when the very name German was a sort of reproach, and any suspicion of that line of speculation was a stigma from which it was not easy for the young theologian to get absolved. Yet you have also lived to see one who as a young theologian most eagerly and with warmest sympathy followed that line of speculation, come nearer perhaps than any other man of education among us to the common thought and heart; for, when I recall those early influences, I seem to find the popular embodiment of them all in James Freeman Clarke.

Again, it seems to me clear that the life of religious thought which has come down to us survives not in spite of, but in virtue of, those influences I have attempted to describe. I do not mean that the opinions of the present day are in better harmony with the true religious life than those which prevailed fifty years ago. I do not think they are. At any rate, it is not for us to disparage that body of opinion which stayed the religious life of Channing, Tuckerman, and Henry Ware. What I do mean ‘is, that to have shut down the gates against an intellectual tide so genuine and strong as was then setting in, would have been to turn what till then had been an open channel into a little land-locked creek, and to shut us out effectually from the large intellectual currents of our age. The alternative in that case would have been to strand in dry-rot, or to effect a breach by violence into the wider waters. There were those then who were willing to do either, — Norton the one thing, Parker the other thing. But all of us, I think, are now agreed that the more excellent way was that taken by the younger scholars of that day, — Furness, Hedge, and Clarke being conspicuous in the group, — who set themselves to deepen the channel and keep it open, and won for us who follow them the free navigation of the sea.

And this service of theirs turned, as you will have seen, upon the same point which Schleiermacher made the pivot of his first appeal to the German people : I mean his assertion that the religious life — with all there is in it of beauty and joy, of comfort, aspiration, strength, and hope — is its own evidence and its own exceeding great reward ; and that, while it is not without intellectual foundation of its own, it is yet independent of all form of speculative opinion. It was (humanly speaking) of infinite importance for us at that time that this conviction should be well established. Doubtless it has had the ill effect of making some men loose, reckless perhaps, about holding firmly any clear conviction at all about anything. But it has had the good effect, with very many more in whom opinion was wavering, to hold them still within the blessed circle of Christian fellowship, till character should be ripened, principle braced, and the mental tone invigorated. Thus it has quickened and refreshed the springs of spiritual life in the veins of our religious organization itself.

Besides, as we must remember, the opinions then most

dreaded — opinions touching the supernatural and miraculous in the ministry of Jesus — were not opinions invented by theologians, however radical. On the contrary, the most radical of theologians used every art of forced interpretation, of evasion, and of intellectual compromise, to escape the pressure of those opinions. If the old doctrinal view of the Incarnation, the Atonement, the Resurrection, and the miraculous works of Jesus has in any mind been weakened, dissolved, or washed away, it has been not by the theology which first exhausted every shift to save it, but by the science which in a pitiless flood beat and encroached upon it, in spite of those poor makeshifts. Within these fifty years many of us have had thrust upon us, again and again, firsthand testimony from believers of facts as distinctly miraculous as anything in the New Testament, — facts which one or two hundred years ago would just as distinctly have received that interpretation; yet we know perfectly well that such testimony, however vouched, would not stand an hour in any civilized court of justice, and so we quietly lay it by, whatever be our private opinion of its validity. It is just so with our treatment of the miracles of the New Testament. Thousands among us receive them with the same faith, comfort, and reverence as of old. But not one of us thinks of defining the line of Christian fellowship by the acceptance of them; not one of us would stake a single point of his own religious faith upon them; not one of us appeals to them as argument for the spiritual truth, but at most as what that " truth as it is in Jesus " may help us to accept.

This change in the general intelligence has come about, reluctantly and with infinite protest, during the entire scientific revolution of the last two centuries. It has not been frankly accepted, among those calling themselves Christians, till comparatively late in the fifty years' period we have been looking back upon. But it had to reach not our scientific opinions merely, but our religious opinions. If the religious life survives among us in spite of it, this result is due, in no small part, to the influence upon our elder Unitarianism of German theology from the time of Schleiermacher.

THE CHURCH

AND

THE PARISH IN MASSACHUSETTS.

USAGE AND LAW.[1]

BY GEORGE E. ELLIS.

AMONG the suggestions and reflections which oppressively crowd the thoughts of a diligent and well-furnished student of Christian history, especially that of the last four centuries, there are two of the gravest import. The first comes in the form of this question: Why was it that at the period of that distracting convulsion in the political and religious affairs of Europe called the Reformation, — why was it that the Roman Catholic Church did not in itself, by itself, and for itself, institute a thorough and searching process of purification, renovation, and even of reconstruction? It seems as if, within the limits of practical possibilities, it might have done so. In so doing it might have won reverence, glory, and gratitude from its noblest members, and have silenced and discomfited its enemies. What deplorable strifes, woes, and tragedies might then have been averted from our common humanity!

That church stood for and claimed to be representative on the earth of the kingdom of God, — a divinely constituted

[1] This Address was delivered at the Commemoration of the 250th Anniversary of the Gathering of the First Church in Dedham, Massachusetts, on Nov. 19, 1888, and repeated in the present Course during the season of 1888–89.

society, with truth, virtue, and piety for its foundation pillars, with justice and righteousness for the methods and the ends of its rule. That church, as yet unshattered in its august fabric, seemed to present the only opportunity and agency there had as yet been in history — must we say, also, the only one there ever will be? — for uniting a family of Christian nations, the most advanced and steadily progressive states and kingdoms of the civilized world, into one Christian commonwealth, ruled in all their highest concerns by an inspired superearthly authority.

That church then, always, and now, had and has some of the noblest and most awing elements and principles for holding the love, reverence, and obedience of all classes of men and women. Its claim and purpose of unity and universality gave it grandeur and dignity. Its marvellous organization rivals in earthly gradation and order the rankings of a solar or planetary system. It improved with aptitude and skill its grand opportunity to substitute a unifying spiritual sway over the fragments of a wrecked political empire. By conciliation and thraldom, by temporizing arts and mediating interventions, it established a more than feudal rule over royal vassals. It made itself needful and powerful in the balancings of political strategies. It had ingenuity in intrigue, and for provoking wars, campaigns, and insurrections, from which it gathered in the spoils. It was for centuries the only mediator and arbiter in all diplomatic intricacies. Its intervention, invited or obtruded, decided the smallest and the largest issues. What splendid service that church had wrought in rekindling civilization in Europe; in restoring, preserving, and extending all learning; in turning quarries of stone into cathedrals of majestic sublimity and beauty; in spreading upon the radiant canvas the whole Bible and all sacred history, with saints and heroes, men and women, in truth and in fond legends, in richest tints and pigments. What a galaxy of starry witnesses, servants, and disciples makes up the church calendar of sainthood, of orders, fraternities, and sisterhoods, of scholars, of statesmen, of the wise and valiant, of lonely missionaries in all their heroisms! These were the mighty and splendid possessions and achievements of that church, fitting it to guide and consecrate the civilization of the world.

Why, then, did not that august and potent hierarchy, in the crisis of peril to its sway and unity, assume the faithful work of its own purification and renovation, repudiating and casting out of it all that made it hateful and false and insufferable among men? It had had solemn remonstrances and warnings from wise, sagacious, and holy men within its as yet unbroken fold. "Reformers before the Reformation" is the familiar and honorable designation of a role of faithful disciples, but stern censors, within its yet unsundered fellowship, — men, some of whom the church has since beatified, — who pleaded in vain for self-renewal and purification from its enormities and scandals.

The answer to our question, which includes the most of the grounds and reasons why the church could not avert the assault and rupture and humiliation of the Reformation, is expressed in the sentence that it had become entangled, diseased, and corrupted by the things of this world. It was vitiated through and through by an element of falsity. There was not left in it the soundness and energy of wholesome, recuperative life. It had lost its corporate sanctity. It had entered into leagues, and bargains, and plottings, and rivalries with states and princes, espousing their strifes, introducing astute churchmen into their cabinet councils, and guiding their military campaigns. It put to service, for ends of worldly ambition, all the trickeries of artifice, policy, intrigue, and double-dealing with an ingenuity which perplexed and baffled the most cunning diplomacy. Its greed and grasping for land had made it the largest territorial proprietor and temporal potentate in all Europe. Internally it was riven with dissensions, with popes and antipopes contesting for the sovereignty. Simony, nepotism, sensual vices, and every form of unrighteousness and crime made popes, cardinals, and ecclesiastics of every grade the subjects of scandal and reprobation. Marriage being forbidden to the clergy, free concubinage was the consequence. Fraudulent and fabulous pretensions underlay the very foundations of the papacy, and grovelling and childish superstitions were the most potent elements of its sway over its docile and credulous disciples.

All these fatal and condemnatory verdicts against the church came from accusers and revelations within its own fold, from the "Reformers before the Reformation," before a single word had been uttered or a single line had been written by an avowed Protestant. It suits the modern champions of the Roman Church to ascribe the convulsion of the Reformation in our mother England to the resentment of Henry VIII. of the refusal of successive popes to sanction his divorce from his lawful wife. As if the lustful passion of one man, monarch though he was, could have kindled Europe into revolt from the papacy. But moral and religious scruples against a sanction of divorce were the least of the motives which wrought with the pontiffs. Their entanglements with imperial and royal policies and rivalries were the obstructions. We can hardly assign moral scruples to the pontiffs of that era, when we have seen their successor, this very year, granting to a ducal applicant permission to commit the sin of incest, for a money consideration.

The alternative is open for those who choose to decide, either that the church lacked the will and the resolution for its own purification, or that corruption in its very organism and vitals would have made the process fatal to its life. But this internal reform failing, the consequences were division within, assault and protest from without, and an irreconcilable rupture.

The able and eminent French bishop, Bossuet, thought he had exposed a fatal and irremediable error in Protestantism, more than a century after it had been showing its fruits, by setting forth with vigorous raillery its "variations." Protestantism was the parent of Discord. Its divisions and subdivisions into fragmentary sects, with their contentions, were a scandal upon religion, bringing it into contempt. By some Protestants these variations have been lamented and condemned as just occasions of reproach. Others, wise and serious observers, even in view of all the discord and contentions of sects, have been reconciled to them as the results of sincere and earnest apprehensions of the manifold elements of truth.

At first view it might seem remarkable that the old church should have apparently been so wholly free of sectarian divisions; but on a keener study of the matter we are brought to recognize the sagacious policy of that church in contrast with the scattering tendency of Protestantism. However rigid may be the rule of doctrine and discipline in a church maintaining strict unity, there will always appear from time to time, in its fold, men and women of strong individuality of opinion, temperament, impulse, or zeal, emphasizing some single virtue, habit of life, rule of observance, method of devotion, or type of piety. These would break off into sects under Protestantism. But the Roman Church, with an adroit and wise balancing of indulgence and restraint of freedom and authority, allowed all these threatening individualisms to spend their energy and zeal in organizing orders, fraternities, sisterhoods, with their rules, statutes, occupations, preferred devotions, and special garb, — all held, however, to the root of unity. They were like little rills, rising and swelling from distant and independent springs and hidden fountains, but quietly led on in their channels to the one full stream. But in Protestantism every eccentricity and individuality in active and restless minds has produced a fissure and a fracture, splitting off into a sect.

This leads us to recognize the second of those gravest reflections derived from the study of our Christian history of the last four centuries, and which will bring us nearer to our special theme. It is a profound impression of the entire lack of apprehension and consciousness in the whole reforming party, of the consequences to themselves and to all who should follow them, of their repudiation of a long vested authority in religion, and of their utter lack of any adequate substitute for it. It was as when part of the company on a well-furnished but imperilled ship desert it for the open sea, leaving behind them compass and charts, pilot and commander. Little did those Reformers realize the infinite distractions which were to follow, to vex them with discord and strife, with endless alienations and divisions, and the bitterness and iniquity of mutual persecutions. Long wonted to the restraints and guidance and forced adhesions of authority, they knew not how to use freedom for common ends of harmony. Every single step in the inevitable series of progressive stages of development, expansion, enlargement, and liberalization under Protestantism, which ought to have been looked for as the most natural and reasonable consequences of parting from authority, has come even upon the most intelligent and rightly intentioned men as a shock or surprise, exciting amazement and horror, and prompting them, when it was possible and feasible, to call in force, penalties, punishments, and the terrors of the law for suppression or vengeance. The series of controversies, variances, and quarrels, with or without the interference of legal processes through which the history of Protestantism leads us, alike in the councils of nations and in the feuds of little villages, far exceeds in length and in sadness of retrospect the revolutions, convulsions, and catastrophes which make up civil and political history. Protestantism has no finality.

In leaving the ship of the church for the open sea, the Reformers took with them the Bible. Precious, beyond all expression or estimate is that sacred volume. Above the church on earth, with its hierarchy, better than the tubes and lenses of the astronomer with which he pierces to the secrets of the upper world, is that revealer and witness of things divine. That volume serves with inexhaustible and ever-opening wealth the uses of piety and edification for men. But it is of no more use for preventing or reconciling the doctrinal diversities or contentions of its devoutest readers within the field of opinion and discipline than would be an unabridged dictionary. It furnishes indeed the material and provocation, the catchwords and symbols of all the sectarian divisions, the controversies and contentions of centuries in the history of religion.

It is with one of these, a trivial or a serious one, as you may regard it, in the infinitely varied series of such successive developments, that I am now to deal. This then fair village was the scene and the occasion in which a legal tribunal was called upon for judgment concerning one of these (shall I call them?) developments and results of Protestantism. Many years ago I had come to the resolve — after much thought, time, and labor, privately and through the press, given to such subjects — that I would never again concern myself with, or speak, write, or publish anything connected with our old religious controversies. It is difficult to reach the hard-pan through those bogs and underlying quicksands. It is doubtful if there is any bottom to those soundings. So, when I was invited to the slight service which I am now to undertake, my first prompting was gently to release myself. But on reflection, the quality, the kindness, and the courtesy of the invitation, coming from two representative parties, gave to it an urgency for me. Nor was I long in reminding myself — indeed, the thought was spontaneous — that time and change and charity had so calmed and chastened the once embittered feelings of a sharp conflict, that its ashes might be analyzed without rekindling the fire. Not a word nor a moment would I give to the rehearsal of the alienation between townsmen, families, neighbors, and life-long friends attendant and consequent upon the variance. I have read the documents about it, but they have an ill flavor and odor in them which I will not cast upon this pleasant autumn air. All those once inflamed grievances are now as absent from the living in these scenes as they are stilled in the passionless dust of those sleeping in the village burial-ground.

Our subject has interest for us simply as putting before us a chapter or incident in the history and religious usages and legislation of Massachusetts. A judicial decision reached here established a legal precedent for all like cases that did or might arise in a period of strong excitement among the old Congregational societies of the State. The question which was opened was: What were the respective rights and privileges, as derived alike from history and traditional usage, and from constitutional and statute provisions, of two associated bodies in one of our old religious societies : the one, the members and the proprietors in a corporate parish, compelled by legal enactments to support a public teacher of religion and morality; the other, an unincorporated, voluntary, and self-constituted fellowship within the parish, of men and women united by a covenant of their own appproval, as a church for maintaining and enjoying Christian ordinances? The two parties here could not dispose their difference by concession or compromise, and as questions of property were concerned the interposition of the judiciary was inevitable. The decision was a shock and a surprise to the discomfited party. It was received as depriving the members of a church in covenant of a supposed inherited and established right. That is the point of view from which I approach my subject.

Let me ask you to withdraw your thoughts for a few moments from the local bearings of this subject, to which we will return with its special interests, and to engage them on its far wider, comprehensive relations. It was not at all strange that a church here in the wilderness, in the Seventeenth Century, in the line of the generations of Christian discipleship, should regard itself in its relations to a local parish as a privileged body, with distinct and important rights. We shall have to look far back into Christian antiquity, even to the first promulgation of the religion, to find a full explanation and reasons for a special church prerogative. This is most vitally concerned with the continuity and the transmission of the religion of Jesus Christ. All through the centuries of its course we may trace the existence, the presence, and the relations to each other of two distinct classes of persons, who gave it degrees of their attention and interest, and put themselves into quite different attitudes of discipleship and duty towards it.

We should have to begin with the Gospel narratives. We there read of selected, attached, and avowed followers and intimate attendants on Jesus, who shared his privacy and were favored by his confidence; and we read also of another class, chance and irregular listeners to his teaching, called "the multitude," or "the people," pausing near him from curiosity or momentary prompting. We trace the presence of the same two parties with the same relations to each other in the subsequent ministry of the Apostles. In synagogues and market-places were ready and curious listeners to preaching and exhortation; and in private houses, apartments, and upper chambers were groups of avowed and earnest adherents, with Christian convictions, faith, and mutual discipline. The distinction was soon drawn, or rather, drew itself, between covenanted and uncovenanted disciples, between those who "gladly heard the word" and nothing further, and those who were known to each other as pledged, committed to constancy in intercourse and observance. Then came in what we know as covenants, ordinances, sacraments, recognized by these pledged disciples as methods for their mutual recognition, and the basis of their fellowship, their reliance on each other for sympathy, steadfastness, and support. For this inner fellowship were reserved confidences and privileges.

The term "mass," as attached to the most august and solemn of the rites of the Church of Rome, carries in its definition the whole breadth and depth of the distinction drawn between companies and attendants on Christian teaching and exhortation, and the covenanted fellowship of disciples. The word "mass" is from *missa* or *dimissa;* pronounced by the officiating minister it was a signal for the uninitiated to depart, that the inner fellowship might engage in a privileged and reserved service.

Among the mountain heaps of Christian literature there may be — though I do not recall any such — a strong argumentative essay which might deal very ably with this theme; namely, that the survival and continuity in living presence of the Christian religion were vitally dependent from the very earliest age upon a pledged and covenanted body of avowed and constant disciples. Would anything be known or extant beyond a mere historical tradition of an instituted Christian religion had it not been for this original and perpetuated covenant body of pledged disciples, as distinct from a random series of assemblies, congregations, listeners to preaching and exhortation?

If we were to follow up this subject it would lead to a clear, emphatic statement of the immeasurable influence which covenants, observances, communion rites, and sacraments have had in perpetuating Christianity. The old peripatetic philosophers were well named, — travelling, wandering teachers. They had hearers, after a sort disciples. But they had no covenants, no sacraments. They founded schools, but not churches. Some of the old pagan religions had their "mysteries," but the only quality in them was mystery. The distinction between Christian churches and congregations was no after device. It was original from the first, drawn between listeners to, hearers of preaching, and those who charged themselves with assumed and avowed obligations by covenant. This distinction has reached its extremest — it may be its unnatural and objectionable — division in the Church of Rome. In view of what we shall, by and by, have to recognize as the limited and subordinate relation into which the legal decision put our Congregational churches in their connection with parishes, we may well take note of the complete inversion of the relation of the two parties among the members of the Roman Church, with which the laws of our State do not interfere. In that church, now so strongly established by Irish immigration into this old Puritan heritage, the existence of two parties, representing the church and the congregation, presents itself substantially as the distinction between the priesthood and the laity. In this respect the Roman discipline is in complete antagonism with the rule established by the decision of our Supreme Court.

In the Congregational fold the ministers were the servants, at best the equals, of the members of their flock; not their masters, or in anything their superiors. In all that concerned instituted religion, providing edifices and appliances for public worship, the collection and use of money, the choice and ordination of religious teachers, the establishment of a platform of faith and discipline, and the recognition of sister churches, the laity, the brethren, either took the initiative or had a joint participation in all affairs. Titles to land and edifices were vested in lay trustees.

Observe how all this is wholly reversed in the usages of the Roman Church here. The priests constitute a fellowship as close and reticent, and as free from legal visitation and oversight, as are our secret fraternities, — to which in all other respects but its own the church is so inimical. The laity know of their conferences, methods, and purposes only so far as the priests choose to disclose them. The creed, the things to be believed in summary and detail, is imposed authoritatively. The construction and application of it are made by the priesthood. Docile obedience to discipline is the prime condition of discipleship. All ceremonies, rites, and observances are of exaction. The laity have no choice in the selection or institution of their pastors or teachers. The parish is made up and bounded for them. The laity contribute all the funds and resources, but have no voice in the allotment or disposal of them, and no treasury report of amount or use is ever returned to them.

You pay your money, but you do *not* take your choice. Churches, colleges, schools, parsonages, seminaries, hospitals, and cemeteries spring forth like magic all around us, revealing to us only the energetic activity of the priesthood and their marvellous success in gathering money. All this property of every kind is vested in the bishop of a diocese, and passes by an open will to his successor. The church may become the largest landholder in our country. Here, in the priesthood, then, we have the church, infinitely transcending in functions and authority the covenanted fellowship among the Puritans. And where, meanwhile, is what answers to the congregation among them? It is composed of a consenting and docile flock, responsive to priestly counsels and requisitions, reverently kneeling before the altar, receiving the fragment of the holy wafer, and passing the ordeal of the confessional as the condition of a saving shrift in the solemn parting hour of life.

Certainly, in the old, once dominant, but now shattered church, the distinction which I have historically traced between church and congregation has reached a most radical and dividing result. Going back to our own original Puritan usage seems like a return to primal simplicity. I have had in view merely to indicate that in some way, or by some method, through the succession of Christian generations, there has prevailed something answering to a distinction between church and congregation, marked by covenants and sacramental symbols, for those who, so to speak, avowed discipleship and made themselves responsible for maintaining Christian observances, while they were associated more or less intimately or dependently with chance assemblies of so-called "hearers of the Word." The inference has been intimated that the living perpetuity and discipleship of the Christian religion has been secured, as otherwise it would not have been, by the continuity of this pledged and covenanted body with sacramental symbols. There have been, as there are to-day, associations and assemblies on Sundays and other days for instruction, worship, sympathetic and ethical culture, and benevolent activity, which do not call themselves churches, but which are more or less under Christian baptism. They dispense with pledges and sacramental observances. Some of these have ceased after trial. It remains to be proved whether any such experiment can attain to Christian continuity.

My aim has been so far to lead on to the question which our Puritan ancestry asked, and in their way answered, — whether the church which had done such service was not entitled to some privilege and prerogative? That was the real issue involved in the controversy with which we have to deal.

Before I proceed further, and in view of what is to follow, I must here frankly avow that I feel a measure of sympathy on the side of those who were deeply aggrieved, as under a sense of wrong, by the practical workings and effects of the decision of the Supreme Court in the case that is to come before us. After considerable study and reading of subjects of intensified strife and contention, making up so largely what is called Christian history, I have learned the value of candor, of constraint upon the indulgence of preferences and prejudices on my own side, and of large allowances for the lights and shades of all party conflicts. The decision of the court bore heavily and grievously upon religious relations and beliefs, associations and fellowships, which had become most dear and sacred to many devout hearts.

But let me explain that the personal sympathy to which I refer is not from preference or approval of the doctrinal tenets of either party, nor from any better temper or conduct of either party in the strife which followed. I would define it rather as an historic sympathy arising from a full view of facts, usages, traditions, and recognized methods with which the legal decision seemed to deal roughly.

Let me repeat, the matter for adjudication concerned the respective prerogatives, privileges, and legal rights of parishes and of churches composed of some of their members gathered in the old Congregational societies in this State. The original General Court of the colony claimed the right of jurisdiction over the whole territory and the inhabitants within the bounds of the charter. It soon began to grant parcels of land within the wilderness, with valleys and meadows, to companies of petitioners for settlement.

With a healthful dread of allowing bodies and groups of strolling, straggling adventurers — such as within our own century penetrated our western frontiers — to plant in lawlessness and disorder, the court in all cases made it a primary and requisite condition of its grants, that each company should have with them, and should maintain, a competent minister of the gospel. This and other municipal provisions constituted our old towns parishes. The internal history of these early parishes offers matter of interest, including two very different classes of occasions and subjects, — the one of gracious and edifying tenor, the other of variances, feuds, and quarrels. The one class presents us with noble and elevating themes, showing the origin and transmitted influence of principles and habits in religion, morality, and education, in the training of men and women and households in domestic fidelity and purity, in neighborly virtues, and in all that secures prosperity and good government, — which has made Massachusetts the most privileged heritage on the earth. The ministers and the ministers' wives were the guardian angels of these wilderness settlements.

But while all this excellent work of training and influence went on, one who is curious in such things may trace through parish and church records a series of petty strifes and vexations, sometimes sharp alienations, even on matters which look to us as of very trivial interest. In isolated, torpid, and humdrum scenes of laborious life, little things loom largely. Each parish had one or several of the following excitements to stir it: The choice for life-long settlement of a new minister, and the apportionment of his salary in beef, pork, corn, wood, and silver; the site for the rebuilding of the meeting-house; the seating of the people in it according to social rank; changes in the mode of conducting public service; whether the Scriptures should be read with comments or without them; the deaconing of a psalm or hymn, line by line, when the people could not afford psalm-books; the exchange of one psalm-book for another; the use of a pitch-pipe in starting a tune; the introduction of instruments, viol or organ; the placing of singers, male and female, together; the piques and discords of choirs, and the innovations in warming the house. These and how many more occasions were there for parish feuds, before there were yet separation and division by sects.

We must now take another step in dealing with our subject. I have spoken of each of our early townships as being a parish for the compulsory support of public worship and instruction, and of an internal body or fellowship of men and women covenanted together and constituting a church in each parish for the observance of ordinances. What were the relations between these bodies, on which in 1818 a judicial decision was found necessary?

It was in preparation for meeting this question that I began with a brief historical reference to a distinction drawn, from the first preaching of the gospel, between those who listened to it and those who were covenanted in discipleship to it. It was in full recognition of that distinction that congregations and church fellowships were from the first gathered in Massachusetts. The matter, simple at first, became complicated. Usages, allowed or tolerated, methods, asserted claims and rights well-nigh having the force of common law, and then a succession of legal statutes, frequently changed and coming into direct conflict with each other, had brought in the elements of confusion.

The theory and practice of Congregationalism, by which the churches of Massachusetts were planted, as distinguished from Episcopacy or Presbyterianism, was the full and perfect right, under the New Testament pattern, for each company — of convenient size — covenanted together to choose, institute, and ordain all officers, pastors, teachers, ruling elders, and deacons needed by them in a congregation or church for teaching and ordinances.

It has been often claimed that Congregationalism was organically and vitally identified with a certain system of doctrines in a formulated creed. The only ground for that claim is that, in the revival and restoration of the New Testament Congregationalism by the Puritans, a certain formulated creed and system of doctrines were then prevailingly accepted. But that was no organic element of Congregationalism, which may consist with different doctrinal beliefs and usages. Democracy is distinguished from monarchy and aristocracy in government. But democracy is not identified with one special platform of principles or with a set of political usages and opinions. We shall have to refer farther on to the elements which came in to complicate the main issue in the contest, from the changes of doctrinal opinions and beliefs where there had once been substantial agreement.

We must briefly review the methods, usages, and legal enactments which, from the first settlement of this colony, disposed of the relations between the two parts of a parish, — the congregation and the covenanted inner fellowship, the church.

We are at once reminded of the lack of uniformity, the variety of method adopted in this matter at different times and in different places. Sometimes a covenanted body, the church, was the original nucleus around which gathered a congregation, and the proportion of numbers in the membership of each was constantly changing. Sometimes a church was formed within a previously assembled congregation that had maintained worship. Governor Winthrop, the Deputy Governor, " and many others, men and women," formed at Charlestown, July 30, 1630, the First Church of Boston. They had then no minister or other officers, which they elected and instituted a month afterwards. They called the body which they thus formed "a Congregation or Church." They signed a very simple and tender covenant without any doctrinal articles, which continues in use unchanged to-day. In other cases, as for example in this First Parish of Dedham, there had been worship under a tree and in a rude meetinghouse by a congregation, within which was afterwards gathered a church.

When the famous order of the court was passed, May 18, 1631, restricting the civil franchise to church members, the whole matter seemed to be decisively disposed of. For if church members were to have exclusive authority in all civil affairs, they might well exercise their prerogative over congregations in parishes. It seems to me that the tenacity with which church bodies afterwards asserted their rights in the initiative choice and institution of ministers is to be referred to this original exclusive enjoyment of the franchise. This restriction upon citizenship was stoutly clung to till the royal order of Charles II., in 1665, positively insisted upon the enlargement of civil rights. Even then the sturdy court rather circumvented than complied with the order, by requiring that any man seeking a citizen's rights and not a church member should present such a certificate of character and orthodoxy, as well as property, as might have secured his admission to a church, if he had chosen to seek it. It was not strange, therefore, that when church members were deprived of their exclusive civil rights they should infer that, as the king had not interfered with their church affairs, they could retain in entail their own precedency in the choice of their ministers.

There were, however, four orders passed by the General Court within a space of ten years (1636–1646), by which confusion was introduced in the relations between inhabitants of a town and the churches in them. In the exercise of its authority by the court, first came in a provision that proved fatal to harmony and an element of injustice. This furnished a rightful and effective plea by which parishioners, not church members, could claim to have a voice in the choice of their ministers. The first of these orders was a requisition, in 1636, applying to a single town (Newbury), that as the church members in it could not bear all the expenses they had incurred in building a meeting-house and for their minister, the cost should be assessed, *pro rata*, upon all the inhabitants of the town. The second court order, 1638, made that same exaction for the support of churches and ministers applicable to all the towns; the hint being dropped to reluctant persons that they might avail themselves of religious ministrations if they chose to do so.

The third of those orders (1643) provided that the churches should be written to, to enforce upon their members their duty of voting in civil affairs, when for any reason they failed to exercise it. The fourth order (1646) imposed upon every inhabitant of a town the obligation to attend on public worship under a penalty of five shillings fine for each occasion of absence. The penalty in England for the offence at that time was only sixpence.

Obvious enough it is, and reasonable enough it appears to us, that the court in these exactions — unwittingly, it doubtless was — provided the grounds and the materials for the strife which subsequently arose between parishes and churches as to the management of their joint affairs. The time was to come when churches would protest: "We will not have a pastor set over us whom we have not ourselves chosen and put in office;" and when members of the parish would plead: "If you compel us, it may be against our will, to maintain and listen to a minister, we ought to have the privilege of selecting him."

We can understand how, under the circumstances of changing times and opinions, harmony might first exist in the relations between parishes and churches, and then how that harmony would be disturbed. A continuance of a general accord in doctrinal belief would be one condition; another would be the preponderance in a parish of the number of those who were under the church covenant. Where the church embraced nearly the whole or a large majority of the male members of a parish, any variance between the two bodies in the selection of a minister would be ineffective if it showed itself. We must remember that the range of choice of ministers in our early years was limited.

The following enactments are found under the head of Ecclesiastical Laws, in 1641 : The *inhabitants* of any town, "who are orthodox in judgement and not scandalous in life," not as yet "in a church way," receive full liberty to enter into such in an orderly and Christian way, after having notified neighboring magistrates and churches of their intention, and receiving approbation. Each church so formed was free to exercise all Christian ordinances, to elect and ordain all officers, — "able, pious, and orthodox, " — and to admit, discipline, and expel members on due cause, "according to the Word ;" support of and attendance on all occasions of public worship are required under a penalty, and habitations for and maintenance of ministers are to be provided for by a town tax. To make sure of its intent in this matter, the court in 1668 declared that the *church* to which it had assigned such powers was to be understood as meaning only members in full communion, and the minister chosen by them should be such to the whole town. Any one not a church member, who presumed either to take part in or to dispute the choice, should be proceeded against under civil process. This law, it will be observed for further reference, made the minister thus chosen both the religious teacher of the whole town and the pastor of the church.

Restiveness and dissatisfaction soon prevailed under this legal disposal of some delicate matters. So we find a Province law, thirty years later, vested the choice of a minister in the inhabitants of the town at large, with the singular proviso that if a town neglected for six months to choose a minister, then the court should provide and settle one. Thus the church was cut off with a *salvo* securing to it "all its privileges and freedom in worship, church order, and discipline." The next change in the law made a concurrent choice of parish and church requisite. Finally, another law enjoined that the church should initiate the choice, and if the town did not concur, then the church should call a council of three or five neighbor churches, whose decision should dispose of the variance for either party. I know of no case in which this reference to a council was used. The Legislature next gave the right of choice to the parish, independently of the church. This not working well, the church was allowed a concurrent vote, and the next year was reinstated in its exclusive privilege of electing the minister. A statute of 1754, proceeding on the fact that churches, as not being corporate bodies politic, could not hold property in succession, constituted deacons trustees of all church and parish property. Our State constitution and statutes gave the right of electing a minister to the parish from which he derived his support.

There certainly was occasion enough in these frequent and radical changes in the legal interference with the relations of parishes and churches for provoking variance and strife. But there came in another complication in the case. The law rested in the provision that each town should have and maintain "a public teacher of morality and religion." But it was contended that while such a minister might serve the use of a parish at large, he could not, as a matter of course, be constituted by the parish the pastor of the church to officiate in ordinances. This sacred official character could not be given to him by vote of the town, for the earliest law had made covenanted members in communion the electors and ordainers of their pastors. So prescription and usage had come to require that ordination to a pastorate should be the solemn act of the church as such, calling in the presence and approbation of a council of sister churches.

The court was responsible also for all trouble from this source. In its natural desire to secure harmonious, sisterly, and even unity of methods and discipline among the churches, to prevent their becoming eccentric and antagonistic individualities, the court had prompted and approved the making of a platform of constitution and discipline with rules for neighboring churches, represented by pastors and delegates, to gather in councils to recognize the initiation of a new church body, the institution of a new pastorate, and to mediate and give advice where there was variance. So far as these councils confined themselves to friendly, advisory, and unassuming offices they might serve excellent uses. But the moment they assumed authority they struck at the very foundation of Congregationalism, the full, complete independency of each Christian fellowship. Even laymen in the congregation might, and often did, ordain their ministers and other officers. True, these laymen represented a covenanted body, not the mere parish. But the parish had no need of a council except as matter of courtesy. Still, this call and intervention of a council came by usage to be regarded as an ecclesiastical ratification and solemnity, which added to the teaching of morality and religion the quality of an ordained pastor of a church.

We have now to inform ourselves, as fully as the materials in our hands will admit, as to the actual connection and relations between a parish and a church formed or existing within it, when the matter came up for judicial decision. We have seen that these relations had been regulated and disposed both by legal orders and by usages. The law had been frequently changed. The usages were traditional, embracing alike claims of right, reason, and courtesy.

I am prompted by historic candor, as I have said, to admit a strong basis for the claims of prerogative and privilege set up by the church in the choice of a pastor. The claims were by inheritance. We have traced the origin of them in the first Christian age. There had been no break in the succession, in the assertion, or the allowance of them down to the date with which we are concerned. A fellowship of covenanted disciples, when brought into connection with those not pledged as they were, assumed special responsibilities. A church was the voluntary, spontaneous, earnest agency for upholding pious and sacred usages in a community. It charged itself with solemn and momentous obligations. By many offices and observances, by occasions of fasting, renewals of its covenant, mutual reawakenings of its membership, and the quickening of zeal and labors, it constantly sought to reanimate and edify itself, and to be the medium of many benefits to a community. Well, therefore, might a church hold itself distinguished in privilege as to Christian institutions above the wholly unpledged members of a congregation or town parish, a proportion of whom might be indifferent, chance attendants on preaching when they liked it, and often grudging their compulsory support of it. Thus stood the case at the crisis which we are reaching.

In the parishes and churches to which the legal decision, as a precedent, was applicable, the relations stood as follows: The church had become an *imperium in imperio*, and the issue came to be raised whether it was supreme or subordinate. The parish was a body politic, with consequent rights and obligations. It was compelled by a public proprietary tax to support a minister of religion for the inhabitants. The church was a self-constituted, self-perpetuating body, of both sexes, of minors and adults. It might have members who were not proprietors, not taxable in the parish. It might include servants transiently in the families. New-comers moving in from other towns, who were church members there, might commune by sufferance, though by usage expected to present a letter transferring relations. The church, not being incorporate, as was the parish, could not hold or transmit property in perpetuity. Its individual members had no transfer rights as pew-holders or sharers in a fund. The church used the parish or the congregation as, so to speak, a feeder from which to add to its own membership. It was wholly for the members of the church, for the time being, to decide on the terms and conditions for the admission of new members. These were an assent to a covenant, a confession of faith, and a profession of religious experience. These terms as concerning doctrinal beliefs might be free or rigid; they might from time to time be changed, reduced, relaxed. There might be devout and earnest men and women in a parish who were ready and even desirous to partake of church ordinances. If their consciences or convictions withheld them from assenting to certain doctrines or terms of the covenant, they could not become church members. If the number and weight of character of such persons induced the pastor and covenanted members to make the formulas of admission unobjectionable to them, they gladly availed of the privilege.

We come now to the most delicate matter of our subject.

From our historical review, thus far, we have seen how abundant were the occasions and materials for friction, for variance and contention in the relations between parishes and churches as regulated by law and usage. The choice and institution of a new minister might draw heavily upon them when there were preferences and partialities between different candidates. It was at the discretion of a candidate to keep aloof if he could see that there was to be contention about him. All that we have been concerned with thus far has related to a period in our church history when the congregational body had all been in substantial accord with the Puritan, Calvinistic, orthodox system of doctrinal faith under which all our early churches were gathered and covenanted.

But radical and very serious changes, modifications, and softenings of doctrinal belief had now come into the churches and furnished the occasion of division, acrimony, and strife. And here it is to be distinctly and emphatically noted that, though underlying and prompting the litigation to be referred to were doctrinal differences between the parties to it, the court did not and could not deal with the case with the slightest reference to or recognition of them. They were wholly waived and unnoticed. Not a plea nor an argument upon the right or the wrong, the truth or the error, the legality or the illegality of religious opinions or beliefs came into the case.

I repeat, the issue turned upon the legal rights — whatever might have been the developments of historic-traditional usage and prescription — which a body of covenanted church members, connected with a parish, had in the call and institution of a minister, and in the control and disposal of parish and church property, such as the parsonage, ministerial lands, funds, plate, etc.

No reference whatever was made to the mode in which this church was constituted, the terms of its covenant, the method of admission to it of new members from the congregation, or matters of creed or doctrine. It was even admitted in the issue opened between parish and church, in the case before us, that it was not raised with any reference to matters of doctrinal belief. Yet none the less the prime occasion of the discord and dissension which then prevailed in the old Congregational churches of the State, and which made litigation and a judicial decision seemingly inevitable, was furnished in the changes and variances of doctrinal belief which had come to announce themselves and to find recognition alike among ministers, church members, and parishioners.

These changes had come in gradually, quietly, and for a time unchallenged. They were at first undefined and not sharply asserted. But they proved, as they advanced, to be radical, threatening, and burdened with matter of discord and strife. We define the issue sharply enough by saying, in the phrases of the time, that it was an alarming "defection" in the churches from their original basis of Calvinism or orthodoxy, and a "decline" into a relaxed and vague form of so-called Liberalism. It is true such a process had been long advancing, and that the full recognition of its results could not but be attended with amazement, grief, alienation, and contention.

We have seen what materials and occasions for variance there were between congregations and churches, as their relations were disposed by laws and usages, while as yet there were no questions opened in the communities which they represented in matters of doctrine. But when most serious and radical changes in doctrinal belief presented themselves for assertion and recognition, a wholly new element of strife came in, with interminglings of passion and bitterness.

As I have intimated, ministers, church members, and parishioners were found to be divided and classified under the two parties, the old and the new, the orthodox and the liberal. By friendliness, neighborly regards, and tolerance, peace was for a while continued in many parishes. As there were known to be, in the congregations, men and women who were ready and desirous to share in church ordinances, but who shrank from the public relation of their religious experience or from the acceptance of the rigid doctrinal confession, if the minister and the church consented these terms might be relaxed by changing the matter of the covenant. If such change were resisted by the minister and a majority of the church, those of the congregation thus excluded from the ordinances would have their grievance. To this cause we must attribute jealousies and unfriendly relations between members of the congregation and the church in some parishes at that time.

As ministers then had a life tenure of office, the election of a new minister was the occasion of calling out and intensifying differences which had been repressed. In cases, of which there were many, including the strongest old parishes in the State, in which minister, congregation, and church had shared in the relaxing of the original orthodox standard, the transition of the pastorate was peaceful. Such was the case in the First Church of Boston in its passage from Calvinism to Liberalism. There is not a word or a trace on its records of any shock or variance in the choice of its successive ministers in accordance with the views of those whom they were to serve. In the contemporary church and congregation of Charlestown, in the ferment of the controversy, the majority of the legal proprietors preferred the old standards. So the minority withdrew and instituted a new church and society. In Cambridge the majority of the parish took the liberal side in the choice of the minister, while the majority of the church dissented and set up another organization.

The pastor of the First Church in Dedham had resigned to assume the presidency of a college, and in 1818 a successor was to be chosen. It appears that the changes in doctrinal opinion and belief, which had been working for many years in the Congregational societies of the State, had manifested themselves here. Under the pastorate of the minister preceding him who had now retired, and who, in the phrase of the time, was classed among the so-called "moderate," there had been modifications in the covenant and terms of admission to the church, under which many persons who had shrunk from accepting the previous terms had come into communion. Among these was that honored patriot statesman, Senator Fisher Ames. The succeeding pastor, now retiring, had been regarded, by some at least of the parish, as of the same "moderate" views and temper on points then so sharply contested. But it proved as time went on that his convictions and preferences and sympathies were with the old beliefs. There was likely then to be a variance in preference in the choice of a new pastor. Cambridge and Andover were the sources for the supply of candidates.

The parish here voting as legal proprietors, including of course both those who were and those who were not members of the church, by a majority of two thirds — representing four fifths of the taxable property of the town held by law to the support of the ministry — made choice of a Cambridge candidate. The communicants meeting separately, after the parishioners, dissented from the choice. It was doubted and disputed at the time whether the dissentients were a majority or a minority of the actual membership of the church. The numbers on either side — subject afterwards to readjustment — seemed to stand, of male members, fourteen in favor of the candidate and eighteen in opposition.

After the intensity of the variance was passed, a majority of the church members appear to have retained their connection with the parish and the new minister. But as the dissentients in the church claimed to be a majority, the letter-missive, summoning neighbor or sister churches, by pastors and delegates, to gather in a council — after the prevailing usage of Congregationalism — for the ordination of the pastor-elect, could not go forth in the name of the " First *Church* of Dedham."

So the invitation went forth from the " First *Parish* of Dedham." Of course the dissentients urged that a minister thus instituted to office filled merely the legal requisition of "a preacher of morality and religion," and was not thereby ordained as pastor of the church. The church, therefore, a month afterwards called a council of its own, which did little more than pronounce the proceedings of the parish council irregular, express sympathy with the aggrieved, and advise moderation.

In the litigation which followed between the parties, for the sake of defining the legal question, the point was yielded that the dissent of the church was the expression of the majority of its members. There were at the time three deacons in office. One of these soon died; of the others, the junior remained with the parish; the senior one, who by law was the trustee of the parish and church property, of considerable value, withdrew, carrying his vouchers with him. Of this property it is to be said, as of similar funds in other towns, that it had long been gathering from various sources and donors, gifts from the town and individuals, — parsonage, lands, wood-lots, money, and church vessels. This deacon with the disaffected portion of the church claiming, as before said, to be a majority, and therefore entitled to hold the property, instituted a new fellowship and society and settled over them a pastor. This new pastor gives on his records, as "remonstrating" against the recent ordination of the minister of the First Parish, the names of ninety-five persons, constituting, as he says, a majority of the church. Of these names twenty-four are of men and seventy-one are of women. The first name is that of the pastor, whose resignation of the First Church and removal to another State, preceding the division, might seem to have released him from further responsibility in the case. How many of these names, men and women, were legal members of the parish it might be difficult to decide. Still, the allowance before the court was that they constituted the majority of the church.

The portion of the church remaining with the parish removed the deacon who had withdrawn from it, and chose two new deacons, in whose name a suit was instituted against the retiring deacon for the recovery of the parish and church property from his trusteeship.

It is interesting to note with what strict precision of rule and method the court, amid the intense excitement of the time — a more than local one — rigidly confined itself to the single point for adjudication. Not only, as has been said, were the underlying elements of contention wholly out of view, but there was reserve on other matters. The question was not adverted to of the doubtful elements of majority or minority between the parties, nor were the sources of the property in contest, as derived from persons in or out of the church, referred to. The question recognized by the court was simply this: whether the claimants had been lawfully appointed deacons of the First Church; that is, whether the body which had appointed them was by law the First Church.

The decision of the court was as follows : —

"When the majority of the members of a Congregational church separate from the majority of the parish, the members who remain, although a minority, constitute the church in such parish, and retain the rights and property belonging thereto."

This legal decision would have been regarded as a momentous one had it applied only to the single case then in hearing. But it was the establishment of a precedent which would dispose of all like cases then to be expected to present themselves in the troubles of the time between parishes and the churches gathered within them. So far as it averted further litigation and induced a recourse to other methods of disposing of those like cases, it might be welcomed. The full purport of the decision was that the law did not recognize a church independently of its connection with the parish in which it was gathered, from which it might sever itself and carry property with it. Even the withdrawal of all the members of the church from the parish would leave free opportunity for a new church fellowship to be formed within the parish, which would accede to all the rights and property of the body that had retired.

Such was the disposal of a contested issue which was made by the supreme legal tribunal of the State. Doubtless, as to lawyers all things are possible, there were lawyers then, and there may be lawyers now, who would dispute the decision. Those of us who are not lawyers would at least, as I myself certainly should, be diffident about any questioning or discussing of it. But none the less the decision caused a shock to the feelings and convictions of thousands in this community, of the most painful and exasperating character. Even were I to offer to you — as I shall not — extended relations and quotations from the documents of the time, I should fail to reproduce in you the sentiments and passions, the dismay and the indignation roused in multitudes then living.[1]

After the brief historic reference which I have made to the traditions, usages, and statutes concerning the privileges and prerogatives of covenanted church bodies as connected with miscellaneous congregations, I need not attempt to account for the indignation and the deep sense of grievance and wrong excited among those who fondly clung to the old ways of piety here. I understand it, I appreciate it. Historically, as I have said, I sympathize with it. The sting of that legal decision was sharp and deep. Had it then come to this, — that the old churches of the fathers of the Puritan colony, the covenanted bodies, the elect religious fellowship, the pledged disciples of faith and piety, were the mere tenants on sufferance of the meeting-houses, the appanages of parishes, dependent upon them for roof and shelter, and upon the ministrations of teachers that might be set over them as pastors perhaps by unconverted tax-payers in the towns? There was no disguising the fact that the decision availed

---

[1] I quote but a single one from the many impassioned outbursts from those who felt outraged by the decision of the court. It was made by Rev. Dr. Enoch Pond, afterwards of the Theological Seminary of Bangor: "We call the proceeding by the hard name of *plunder*. And we call upon the courts of Massachusetts to revoke these unrighteous decisions, and put the Congregational churches of the State upon their original and proper basis" (Half Century of the Unitarian Controversy, p. 415).

to the countenance of the liberal or innovating party in the churches.

But more than this, the decision, rightfully or not, was believed by very many sincere and earnest persons to be a grievous trespass upon vested rights sanctioned by usage, allowance, and law in the churches. It may be that we may find help towards an appreciation of the sense of wrong felt in this matter of religious interest by the aggrieved party by illustrating it, not from parallel, but from similar cases by the decision of the law in secular affairs.

Soon after the recuperation following the Revolutionary War the Legislature of this State gave an exclusive, favorable, and perpetual charter to an incorporated company for what was then regarded as a stupendous enterprise. It was the building of the first bridge over the Charles, between Boston and Charlestown. It proved a safe and vastly profitable investment. Faithful trustees and guardians of the property of others, the sacred securities of widows and children, committed to it their funds, purchasing the stock at a high premium, relying upon a pledged legal covenant. Some years afterwards, constraining reasons of business and convenience induced the Legislature to violate its own covenant and to charter a rival parallel bridge. Dismay and indignation for the old proprietors naturally followed. The case ran through all our courts, and the Supreme Court of the nation gave validity to the trespass.

A similar case presented itself of complaints of outrage of vested rights when the Legislature, by its charter of the Eastern Railroad, struck at the value of the property invested by a previous charter in the Salem Turnpike. These are secular affairs. But we know well what intenser wraths may stir in heavenly spirits about sacred things. *Tantæ ne iræ?*

The difficulty of adjusting vested rights and institutions to changes of opinion in religion has been met in every age of developing civilization and knowledge. It is the province of a special department of civil law. Antiquated designations of trust funds have to be readjusted. The old Jewish synagogues and the Roman basilicas, with or without law, became Christian churches. At the Reformation, millions of acres of land, cathedrals, churches, universities, schools, and uncounted sums of endowed benevolences, the monuments of Roman Catholic piety, were made over by Parliament to Protestantism. Hoards of wealth, yielding its proceeds to the English Church, were originally consecrated for the saying of masses for the repose of departed souls. What a disquieted and restless place that purgatory must have been conceived to be, when such wealth and intercession were needed to bring peace to its inmates!

Calvin found no qualms of conscience in preaching in the old Roman Cathedral at Geneva, and I have myself attended upon Unitarian ministrations there. But Protestantism, as I said at the start, has always been amazed and shocked by developments natural and inevitable from its own first principles. And so the law took away from our old churches the privileges which it had once granted to them.

We need pursue our subject no further than to take note of the fact that the law, as law, may have led the way to what has become the most marked characteristic of our time in the order and conduct of our religious institutions. The legal decision, without any such intent, but none the less effectively, did tend to discredit the old historic relation between a covenanted sacramental body and the congregation within which it was gathered. The law seemed to intimate this: You must keep the teaching of religion and morality in a parish distinct, as the prior and paramount object, from the concerns of an inner fellowship for some special observances of its own.

Has not this had the effect of throwing into the shadow the church bodies in our old congregations? Certain it is that in no one of those congregations, however closely it might abide by the old standards of faith, would the church for one moment think of inducting a minister without having made sure first of the approval of the society. Nor is this all. We have in these days of ours, here and around us, become wonted to a state of things which may be regarded, from one point of view, as a recognition of the noblest religious liberalism, independently of all bonds of creed and covenant.

Among us especially, here and now, and largely elsewhere, religious institutions, methods, and benevolences are sustained — yes, I will say it — most generously and heartily sustained by those who are not committed by any personal pledge, creed, or covenant; even by many whose modesty or conscience would lead them to shrink from assuming the Christian name. Still they may have read or heard the words, "Ye are my disciples, if ye do the things which I have commanded you."

Political, military, and religious conflicts constitute in history the larger and the most exciting portion of its records. While they are passing they engage one class of feelings and passions. The review of them by wise and calm reflection is more favorable to sober judgment. Our minds are capable, if we will so train them, of a degree of impartiality. In reviewing the local though intense dissension which we have sought calmly to apprehend, of course we cannot look for harmony and accord of opinion.

Yet a reasonable candor may prompt the friends and sympathizers with the party aggrieved by the legal decision to allow for the practical embarrassments with which it had to deal. The real root of the difficulty was this: the church had failed to draw in or to retain, as it once did, the majority of the legal members of a parish. Indeed, in many cases the membership of the church was but a small minority of the parish. Certain feelings, prepossessions, prejudices, unsympathetic and even repelling, had made a connection with it unattractive to considerable numbers of persons. The communicants too were disproportionately women, who were not voters in business affairs.

As we have seen, the seceders from this parish were seventy-one women and twenty-four men. Had women voted, there might have been direct antagonism with their husbands. Under the circumstances, constituted as a church was, it could hardly have been expected that even if all its members were of one mind the parish would yield to them the choice of a minister. If in this or in any other society the church had embraced a majority of the legal members of the parish, there would have been no occasion for an appeal to the law; it would then have been for dissatisfied communicant and non-communicant members to withdraw, as in some cases they did.

But why could not a church seceding by a positive majority of its members carry with it church property? The reason for denying that, as of right, seems to have been that that property was of a very miscellaneous character, not admitting of discrimination in its parts. It might have been long accumulating from the town treasury, from individuals, and joint contributors. It had always been identified with and used in common by the local central place of worship for the parish.

The funeral bier and pall, the meeting-house, the parsonage, the ministerial lands, charity funds, the baptismal font and other sacred vessels, had been held and transmitted through that parish, and must through it go down to the succession. The church members might have the benefit of it, but could not transfer it.

I have sought with candor and impartially to do justice to that feeling of amazement and protest which followed the adjudication subordinating an old Congregational church to a parish. The same spirit of candor requires that a word be said on the side of those who approved the decision as under the circumstances of the time right and reasonable. It was judged by them as not just that the affairs and the funds of a parish should be controlled by a self-constituted body of church members, few or many, formed within it. There are many evidences in our records that in several old parishes a grudge or jealousy was long perpetuated from the restriction of the civil franchise to church members. The relative numbers of the communicants had been steadily decreasing in many parishes. To have retained its power the church should have retained its weight of influence. In some cases it did not. Had there been in a church a steady, strengthening growth in numbers and in the character of its members to secure the respect and confidence of a community, there would have been no lack of deference to it.

It would be safe to say, historically, that the church members in a town were generally the more exemplary and estimable of its people. But all were not such; and the free, inquisitorial spirit of our community was critical in such matters. Meanwhile it was undeniable that equally estimable and exemplary persons in a parish could not or would not pass the ordeal of admission to a church. The issue, in the view of such persons, then became a plain one; it was whether the owning of a covenant and the partaking of an ordinance should secure in a parish the same exclusive right which it once had in citizenship. Subsequent legislation has put it fully within the power of corporate covenanted religious bodies to hold their funds securely.

EARLY NEW ENGLAND UNITARIANS.

BY ANDREW P. PEABODY.

IT is hard to trace the early history of Unitarianism in New England. The name was seldom used, yet not omitted with any view to concealment; for we have abundant proof that the ministers to whom it belonged preached what they believed clearly and fully, and it is in great part to still extant passages from and accounts of their sermons that we are indebted for our knowledge of their opinions. But a marvellous change had taken place in the last century, at the beginning of which the denial of the Trinity would have seemed no better than blasphemy; while at its close nearly all the clergy of Boston and its vicinity and many others in Massachusetts were known to dissent from the ancestral creed, to have ceased to use Trinitarian doxologies, and to preach what was then known as Arianism, regarding Jesus Christ as the greatest and oldest of created beings, but in no proper sense as God. At the same time, so little stress was laid on the Trinity by its professed believers that, with two or three exceptions, these Arians remained in full church fellowship with those of the orthodox faith. In the territory now within the limits of Boston there were, a century ago, but two professedly Trinitarian ministers, one of them being Dr. Thacher, of the liberal Brattle Square Church, while Dr. Eckley, of the Old South Church, was known to entertain doubts as to the deity of Christ.

This state of things is to be accounted for in large part by the intimacy with England, English scholarship, and English thought, which was closer in Boston than anywhere else in America. I doubt whether the professed English Unitarians had much influence here; for, though men of eminent piety, ability, and learning, and politically on the side of the colonies in their conflict with the crown, they were, with the exception of Dr. Price, of a type of theological belief which has found little favor here, and has long been obsolete on its native soil. They were materialists, and regarded the literal resurrection of the body as a condition antecedent to the renewed and eternal life of the soul. But a tidal wave of liberal thought had swept over the English Church and overflowed into the quarters of the orthodox dissenters. Samuel Clarke, the greatest divine of his age, had given publication to opinions adverse to the deity of Christ, and had even drafted such amendments of the Prayer Book as might be consistent with his non-Trinitarian belief, and he had many sympathizers among the higher ranks and the more learned members of the clerical body in his own church; while Doddridge and Watts, without disclaiming the term "Trinity," professed opinions under that head which are not in accordance with its ordinary meaning.

This tendency in the English Church was cherished by two of its creeds, — the Apostles' Creed being simply Unitarian, while the Nicene Creed is expressly anti-Trinitarian, making Christ a derived and thus, of necessity, a subordinate being, — God of God, or (more literally translated) from (that is, derived from) God: the only distinction between the Nicene fathers and the Arians having been that the latter believed Christ to have been created by God, while the former maintained that he was derived from God, — a distinction manifestly without a difference, though in the early time rivers of polemic ink and of martyr-blood were shed on account of it. The English Church prescribes, indeed, the use, thirteen times in the year, of the Athanasian Creed, which is Trinitarian, which was designed to correct the errors of the Nicene Creed, and in which, with a logical consistency worthy of all admiration, the English churchman calls down upon himself eternal perdition for belief in the Nicene Creed, which he has just repeated in the same act of worship.

It is little that a single lecture can do towards covering the field assigned to me; and while I should be glad, had I time, to speak of the growing definiteness of opinion and utterance, of the condition of the churches and the community under the more liberal dispensation of the Gospel, and of the quality of the preaching in liberal pulpits, I shall confine myself chiefly to biographical sketches of the principal Unitarian ministers who flourished before the marked historical epoch of Channing's Baltimore sermon.

The earliest place in the record belongs to Ebenezer Gay, minister of the First Church in Hingham, who died in 1787, in the ninety-second year of his age, and in the sixty-ninth year of his sole pastorate, on a Sunday morning, arrested by a sudden death-stroke while preparing for the usual pulpit-service, — the longest sole pastorate of which we have any knowledge. His mind retained unimpaired vigor to the last; and on his eighty-fifth birthday he preached a sermon, entitled "The Old Man's Calendar," which passed through several editions, was reprinted in England, was also translated into Dutch, and published in Holland. An edition of it must have been printed as late as my boyhood; for I well remember a fresh-looking copy which I read to my mother, as among the then new acquisitions of our church library. I doubt whether the century produced a better sermon, and it was but one of his very many printed sermons; for he was called upon on all the various public occasions on which superior ability is wont to be sought. He had a gift more prized in his time than now, — that of a punster in the choice and treatment of his texts. Thus, in a sermon at the ordination of a Mr. Carpenter, he took for his text Zechariah's "man with a measuring line in his hand." Again, in preaching at the ordination of Joseph Green, he said: "We trust that he will be a *Joseph* unto his brethren whom he is to feed with the bread of life;" and then, referring to Jacob's benediction on Joseph, he added, "The Lord make him a fruitful bough, even a fruitful bough by a well, and always *green* and flourishing in the courts of our God." At the time of the Revolution, suspected of lukewarmness to the popular cause, and called upon by a committee appointed to disarm the Tories, who asked what arms he had in his house, he took them into his study and showed them a large Bible, saying, "There, my friends, are my arms, and I trust they will always suffice for me." He outlived any temporary disaffection, if there was any, on political grounds, and left a precious memory as a man of rare gifts and graces, sanctity of life and power of usefulness. The elder President Adams enumerated him with several other ministers in that neighborhood as having been well known as Unitarians in the middle of the last century. But that there was no ban upon him on that account would appear from his life-long intimacy with Dr. Appleton of Cambridge, well known as a moderate Calvinist. Indeed, Drs. Gay, Chauncy, and Appleton, nearly coevals, were virtually as brothers, and the three performed the principal parts in the ordination of Dr. Howard, of the West Church in Boston, who was settled as a Unitarian.

In his own profession, as a writer, as a man of profound and varied learning, and as mighty in the Scriptures, Charles Chauncy, minister of the First Church in Boston, had in his time no equal. Though in the pulpit he was handicapped by a puny frame and a feeble voice, his services were claimed on all occasions of importance, and his printed sermons are reckoned by the score. It is related of him that in his youth, disgusted by noisy fanatics, he besought God never to make him an orator. His prayer was granted; yet with the weight of his words there was a discriminating emphasis which satisfied the understanding, together with a not infrequent intensity of earnestness which powerfully moved the sensibility of his hearers. He was a man of quick temper and strong impulses, yet of such perfect self-control that in a life of seldom intermitted controversy he was remarkable for uniform candor, meekness, forbearance, and courtesy in the treatment of his antagonists. He was an ardent patriot. In the Revolution he had so firm confidence in the justice of his country's cause that he was wont to say that, if the people of the land did not win the day by human might, a host of angels would be sent from heaven to fight for them. But he denounced in unsparing terms, and from an early period in his ministry, those fraudulent devices of baseless paper currency, enforced legal tender, and the like, which have disgraced civilization from the declining days of the Roman Commonwealth down to our own Civil War. As early as 1747 he preached an election sermon, which on this very ground gave such offence to the General Court that the question whether it should be printed by legislative resolve was earnestly debated. His reply, when he was informed of this discussion, was characteristic: "It shall be printed, whether the General Court print it or not; and do you say from me that, if I wanted to initiate and instruct a person into all kinds of iniquity and double-dealing, I would send him to our General Court."

Dr. Chauncy was not only of the most liberal school of theology as to the Divine nature, — he published several works in which he maintained the ultimate salvation of all men; and though in this he stood alone, so far as we know, among the New England clergy, he was so admired for his commanding ability, and so venerated for the beauty of holiness in his life, that he seems never to have been alienated from the cordial friendship and fellowship of those from whom he differed most widely. He died in 1787, after a ministry of sixty years, for the first twenty-two of which he was the colleague of Rev. Thomas Foxcroft, and for the last nine years was aided by Rev. Dr. John Clarke as junior pastor.

Jonathan Mayhew, of the West Church in Boston, was fifteen years younger than Dr. Chauncy, but died twenty-one years before him. He was the only one among the liberal clergy of his time who was not, outwardly at least, in full fellowship with his brethren, and in all probability it was due to his personal peculiarities rather than to his belief that he was an exception. I cannot find that in his opinions he was more latitudinarian than Dr. Gay, and he was less so than Dr. Chauncy. But, while singularly amiable, sweet, and lovely in character and in private intercourse, he seemed a born belligerent. Whatever he believed he presented in its antagonistic aspects. He had no tolerance even for honest error, still less for shams; and while, as I think, he had truth always on his side, his exposition of it was often better adapted to exasperate and imbitter than to persuade or convince. This tendency, so widely at variance with his genuine kindliness of heart, was due, no doubt, in great part, to his ancestry and training. He belonged to a kingly race, — to a family pre-eminently masterful, accustomed to rule, and unaccustomed to contradiction and antagonism. His great-great-grandfather was proprietor and governor of Martha's Vineyard and the adjacent islands, and, while exercising a benignantly absolute sway in temporal matters, because after the death of his son, who was a minister and missionary, he could obtain no successor in his place, commenced preaching himself, at seventy years of age, and often made a journey of twenty miles on foot to officiate at some remote Indian settlement. His son, grandson, and great-grandson, all ministers by education and profession, were missionaries to the Indians of Martha's Vineyard and pastors of such few white families as were on the island; and, though with no other authority than that of the greatest of servants, they were, of necessity, virtually autocrats, and held a royal priesthood, in which they were foremost in toil and self-sacrifice, and supreme in the allegiance and devotion of those whose souls they held in charge. Jonathan Mayhew's father was the most gifted of the series of missionaries, and, in the opinion of such men as Drs. Gay and Chauncy, would, if in as conspicuous a sphere, have won a reputation in no wise inferior to that of his son. He is said to have fitted his son for college, so that the son had had none of that contact and conflict with the outside world which might have tempered his ardor, quelled his self-assertion, and smoothed and rounded his statements of unacceptable beliefs and opinions. He must have exhibited something of this uncompromising plainness of utterance in his novitiate; for on the day appointed for his ordination only two of the invited council made their appearance, and they declined to perform the service, advising the summoning of another council. This was done; and of fifteen ministers invited, not one of them from Boston, eleven were present, and among them was Dr. Appleton of Cambridge, who undoubtedly had become acquainted with young Mayhew while he was in college, and prized him, in spite of his heterodoxy, for his sterling worth. Many of those who kept aloof from Mayhew at the outset subsequently became his warm friends, and were in professional, no less than personal, fellowship with him. But he never joined the Boston Association. It was, and, I believe, still is the custom for newly settled ministers to ask for admission to membership, and as there is no record of his application having been made and refused, the probability is that he omitted asking rather than incur the risk of a refusal. He, therefore, took no part in the Thursday lectures, but established a Wednesday lecture of his own, which drew large audiences from other churches. There probably lingered in his church some feeling adverse to the Boston Association, as Mayhew's successor, Dr. Howard, postponed application for membership for twenty-two years, and until the Association took the unprecedented step of appointing a committee to inquire of him whether he was willing to join them.

When the frieze of Sanders Theatre, at Cambridge, was to be graced with busts of distinguished orators, Dr. Palfrey, than whom no man was better fitted to be an impartial judge in such matters, urged very strongly the claim of Mayhew to the place assigned to Daniel Webster. I believe that he was in the right. I have no doubt that Mayhew was the most eloquent man of his time, and more efficient as an orator than Webster ever had the opportunity of being. During the nineteen years of his ministry he was by far the most conspicuous pulpit orator in Boston. Hearing him was deemed not a mere Sunday duty, but a privilege of the highest order, awakening, inspiring, uplifting, edifying. His printed sermons have nothing of the stilted formalism not uncommon in the last century. They are still live sermons, with nothing obsolete except what ought to be obsolete in sermons a century old, namely, that which makes every really good sermon fit for its own place and time; for the sermons which retain, after a century, all the life that they ever had are such as, whatever their other merits, lacked life at the outset.

But Mayhew's claim to enduring remembrance as an orator rests not solely on theological, though I will not say, not on religious, grounds. Patriotism was with him, as with the Hebrew prophets, an altar-fire, and its cause a sanctuary service. No one of his coevals had so deep an insight, so keen a foresight as he, as to the wrongs and needs, the rights and destiny, of these then British provinces. He voiced the earliest outcry of an oppressed people, and hailed the first faint dawn of freedom. He was in constant intercourse and correspondence with Otis, Bowdoin, the Adamses, and their coadjutors. His profession, so far from being a hindrance to him in the public service, only multiplied his opportunities and enhanced his influence as a leader and a guide in resistance to the usurpations of the home-government, and in the initial measures towards emancipation from it; and we have ample evidence that his counsel in public affairs was most prized by the wisest and best men.

The same vivid sense of right and justice which determined his political action led him into a controversy, which might have passed into oblivion were it not for a memorial of it of which I shall presently speak. The English Society for Propagating the Gospel in Foreign Parts, chartered by William III. in 1701, manifestly designed and endowed for missionary purposes, both for subsidizing the ministry in English settlements destitute of gospel privileges and for evangelizing the Indians, and recognized as so intended in sermons in its behalf by such men as Bishops Butler and Beveridge, had spent its annual income chiefly in establishing and maintaining Episcopal churches in places by no means destitute of the means of grace, such as Boston, Cambridge, Salem, Newbury, Portsmouth, Bristol, New London, and had repeatedly taken advantage of the disaffection of two or three members of a congregation to plant such churches where they were neither needed nor wanted. Indeed, there are still existing considerable church-funds derived from property of this society that remained in the country after the Revolution. So much had been incidentally said and written as to this mode of proceeding as to call forth a plausible pamphlet in defence of the society from one of its missionaries, Rev. East Apthorp, who had at Cambridge a congregation of ten or twelve families close under the shadow of the college and the parish church, and who was said to be bishop expectant, if not designated, of all North America. Mayhew replied to this paper in a pamphlet of nearly two hundred pages, intensely strong, wise, but without the meekness of wisdom, trenchant, sarcastic, stinging, speaking the truth, but certainly not in love, not with grace seasoned with salt, but all salt and no grace. He was answered by Dr. Caner of King's Chapel and Dr. Johnson of Connecticut, and also in some scurrilous doggerel, with a copious prose commentary, by a person who misnames himself "a gentleman of Rhode Island Colony." Mayhew rebutted the assault by the Episcopal divines in a reply of marvellous keenness and not unrighteous severity. Meanwhile, on the other side of the Atlantic the quarrel had been taken up by Archbishop Secker, who writes with no little power of sophistical argument, and at the same time very superciliously. In his lordly way he calls Mayhew "the poor man." To this pamphlet Mayhew's reply is scathing and withering. In the course of it he says: "I am indeed, even literally, 'a poor man,' as this gentleman calls me, I suppose, in another sense, and in that respect I have been publicly upbraided by some of the very decent writers against the 'Observations;' nor has even the honest, irreproachable memory of my father wholly escaped their insults." And then, alluding to the mole-paths by which Secker's enemies reproached him with having wriggled into place and grovelled into lordly rank, he adds: "I had much rather be the poor son of a good man who spent a long life in the humble and laborious, though apostolical, employment of preaching the unsearchable riches of Christ to poor Indians, and one, as I suppose, now at rest from his labors with the spirits of just men made perfect, than even the rich son and heir of one who had, by temporizing in religion and tampering with politics, by flattering the great and prostituting his conscience, made his way to a bishopric,— how large a bag soever he had carried with him through a life of idleness and pride, of intrigue and luxury, or left behind him at death, the black period of all his greatness and glory." This answer, unanswered and unanswerable, was printed in 1764.

Dr. Mayhew died in 1766. When he was at the point of death, Dr. Cooper, himself a Calvinist, asked him if he retained the opinions that he had taught. He replied firmly and earnestly, though with difficulty of utterance, "I hold fast my integrity, and it shall not depart from me." It is worthy of note that the first prayer ever offered at a funeral in Boston, except by Episcopal ministers, was offered by Dr. Chauncy at Dr. Mayhew's funeral, our fathers having dreaded even the appearance of praying for the dead.

On receiving the news of Mayhew's death, Thomas Hollis, the third of the name among the benefactors of Harvard College, who already possessed a likeness of Mayhew, procured an engraving of him, in the best style of the time, with Mayhew's two pens crossed over the Archbishop's mitre, the pens expanding at the feather end into ripened wheat-stalks, and girt with a laurel wreath enclosing the legend, " I am indeed a poor man," with the inscription beneath the whole : " Jonathan Mayhew, D.D., pastor of the West Church in Boston, — an asserter of the civil and religious liberties of his country and mankind, who, overplied by public energies, died of a nervous fever, July vii., MDCCLXVI., aged XXXXV." Of this engraving I have a copy that was the property of Edward Wigglesworth, the second of the name, and the second Hollis Professor of Divinity in Harvard College, which I suppose to have been a gift-copy from Hollis to the incumbent of the professorship bearing the family name, and founded by his great-uncle.

Passing over several honored names which I have not time to mention, I come to Jeremy Belknap, the first Congregational minister of the Federal, now Arlington Street Church, which till 1787 had been a Presbyterian church. He was settled for nearly twenty years in Dover, New Hampshire, and while there published the first of his three volumes of the " History of New Hampshire," which, in point of comprehensiveness, thoroughness, and accuracy, left nothing to be desired, and half a century ago still retained its place as second to no historical work that had appeared on this side of the Atlantic. He left Dover on account of the utter inadequacy of his salary. In Boston he had the reputation of a sound preacher, a scholar of large and varied attainments, and a model man as to all the graces of the Christian character. He was a pioneer in the anti-slavery cause, in 1788 drew up a successful petition to the Massachusetts legislature for the abolition of the slave-trade, which in this State had survived the existence of domestic slavery, labored for the same cause in Providence in connection with Moses Brown of happy memory, and was elected an honorary member of the Society for Abolishing the Slave-trade in Rhode Island. His sense of the Divine goodness recoiled from the dogma of eternal punishment, and he inclined to the belief that the resurrection of those unfit for heaven would be to what he called "a mortal life," to be terminated by "a second death." His memory has the double association, on the one hand, of his warm and eloquent defence of the congregation of King's Chapel in ordaining James Freeman, and, on the other hand, of his friendly agency in procuring for the Charlestown church the services of Dr. Morse, for many years the chief leader of all assaults on liberal theology. Dr. Belknap performed a signal service in the compilation of a book of Psalms and Hymns for public worship, free from any recognition of the Trinity or of the supreme deity of Christ, — a book which remained in use in his own and in many other churches till it was superseded by Greenwood's collection. It was used in my church at Portsmouth when I was first settled, and contained not a few sacred lyrics which I have been sorry to miss in later hymnals. Dr. Belknap died in 1798, at the age of fifty-four.

The only remaining Massachusetts minister whom my limits will permit me to commemorate is James Freeman, whose name lingers in so recent, loving, and reverend remembrance that, were it not for the unique position which he held, it might seem superfluous to dwell upon his history. But while he was surrounded by Unitarian ministers, they were pastors of churches that had not so far committed themselves that they might not have settled pastors of a different type, while he was the first man who, as a publicly avowed Unitarian, was pastor of a church declared by its own corporate action to be a Unitarian church. For several years the people of the Old South Church, while their house of worship was occupied by the British troops, and afterward while it remained unrepaired, worshipped in King's Chapel alternately with the chapel congregation, the service of the Prayer Book being read once every Sunday. Mr. Freeman commenced his services as reader, and when in 1782 the Old South congregation returned to their own church, he was invited to become minister of the Chapel. He was permitted at the outset to make some changes in the English liturgy, and the more readily because there were portions of it which, as no longer British subjects, the American ministers of the English Church were compelled to omit or modify. He became convinced that the Trinity was not a Christian or a Scriptural truth; and after hearing a series of discourses from him on Christian doctrine, a majority embracing three-fourths of his congregation voted to adopt a modified liturgy conformed to their altered belief and that of their minister-elect. He, in vain of course, sought episcopal ordination; and at length, in 1787, the congregation took the ground sanctioned by the Cambridge Platform, that the greater right of election includes the lesser right of ordination, and the wardens were accordingly authorized to induct Mr. Freeman into the ministerial office, which he filled as sole pastor for twenty-two years, remaining senior pastor till his death, in 1835. He and his classmate, Bentley of Salem, though not materialists, were probably in closer sympathy with the English Unitarians than the men of whom I have already given sketches. They were not Arians. Dr. Freeman would probably have been in accordance with the more recent Unitarians who see in Christ all of the Divine that can be made human. As a preacher and a pastor he held as high and as dear a place as a Christian minister ever held; and while in his infirm old age his voice was no longer heard in public, his home at Newton was a Mecca for saintly pilgrimage. Of those who knew him, no one lives who does not deem having known him a subject for fervent gratitude; for with all the cardinal virtues of a mature Christian character he united those tender, delicate hues and tints of spiritual beauty which make goodness supremely lovely and shed on lengthened years the dawning light of heaven.

In Connecticut there was, during the last century, in the Congregational churches no open dissent from the established standard of orthodoxy, though there may have been in the very numerous Episcopal churches a wider latitude of opinion. In the early part of the present century there were three cases of trial for heresy, which may properly be regarded as historical, both on account of the extensive publicity given to them and on account of the signal merit of the persons accused.

The earliest of these cases was that of John Sherman, a grandson of the eminent patriot and statesman, Roger Sherman, — it may be, inheriting from him the spirit of protest; for there has recently come to light and will soon be issued from the press a correspondence between Roger Sherman, then a deacon of the New Haven church, and Dr. Hopkins of Newport, in which Sherman impugns the stern, repulsive, and now obsolete type of Calvinism which, under the name of Hopkinsianism, was rife in the New England churches. John Sherman, a graduate of Yale College, was settled in the First Church of Mansfield, Connnecticut, in 1797. Before his ordination he drew up a rigidly Calvinistic confession of faith, and insisted on its being signed by all the members of the church. At any early period of his ministry, however, before he began to doubt the truth of that confession, he recommended and obtained from his church a vote, "That our creed is only a manifestation of the general sentiment of the church, and not a test of communion in church privileges; but that we will hold Christian fellowship with all, whatever may be their particular theological opinions, who afford, by a life and conversation according to the gospel, a comfortable evidence that they are the friends of Christ." It may seem strange, but it is by no means a solitary case, that Mr. Sherman's first doubts as to the Trinity were awakened by Dr. Watts's treatise on the "Glory of Christ," in which he develops what used to be called "the indwelling scheme," and which, if published now, would be regarded as a Unitarian work, maintaining, as it does, that the divinity of Christ consists in the full indwelling of God in what else were Christ's pure humanity. Mr. Sherman subsequently became acquainted with professedly Unitarian English writers, was led by them to make a thorough and careful examination of the Scriptures, and came to the conclusion that they teach the unity of God and do not teach the Trinity. His ministry had up to that time been in the highest degree successful, and he was greatly beloved by his people. When they were informed of his change of opinions, a single deacon was the only man who was disposed to make complaint of him. In all probability his hearers recognized in his statement of belief the very impressions which, ignorant of controversy, they had derived from their own reading of the Bible; for where these questions have not been raised, it is only a very simple theology and Christology that the devout mind of average intelligence finds in the Gospels. But the clerical

Association to which Mr. Sherman belonged took the alarm. They proposed to convene the clergy and laity of the churches in the county, in Consociation, as a court for the trial of Mr. Sherman, a court of that kind having been authorized by the Saybrook platform, yet having never been regularly organized, nor even recognized as existing in any previous instance. The Association, finding that the Mansfield church as a body would take no action towards the trial of their minister, voted as a clerical body to suspend their ministerial connection with him. He then asked for a dismission; and a mutual council, friendly to him, advised the dissolution of his pastorate, with the expression of strong esteem and confidence, and a cordial recommendation to such churches as should see fit to receive him, at the same time declining to pass judgment on his opinions. The action of the Association had meanwhile increased the number of disaffected church members to ten; but the society as a body and a majority of the church adhered to him, expressed their undiminished regard for him, and manifested their attachment to him by a handsome pecuniary donation, and by other presents to him and his family. Not only so, but in less than two months after the meeting of the council, the society and the church passed votes inviting him to return and settle again as their minister.

He, meanwhile, was forming new relations. He went to Oldenbarneveldt, or what is more commonly called Trenton Village, in New York, and there became the first minister of the oldest Unitarian society in that State. The village was founded and named by Colonel Mappa, who came to this country as agent of the Holland Land Company, and Adrian Van der Kemp, a Dutch clergyman and refugee, who was said to have been one of the most learned men living, and as such was made Doctor of Laws by Harvard College, though I doubt whether he ever set foot in New England. The elder Mr. Huidekoper must have been there at that time. He came to America as Colonel Mappa's clerk, and was an inmate in his family till he went to Philadelphia, whence he removed to Meadville, still in the service of that same Holland Land Company. These men were earnest and devout Unitarians, and they gathered about them a congregation of superior intelligence and worth, and attracted to the village many visitors of eminence, and not a few permanent residents of like spirit with themselves. There remain on the spot no members of either family; but the Van der Kemp house is now the parsonage. Mr. Sherman was installed there in 1806; but his ministry was not of long duration. He removed to Trenton Falls, established an academy there, and enjoyed great popularity as a teacher. He built the oldest part of the hotel at the Falls, where he died in 1828. The house passed into the hands of his son-in-law, Mr. Moore, whose fine taste, large culture, musical genius, and gentlemanly manners merged the quality of an innkeeper in that of a courteous and generous host, and whose recent death must have saddened very many who have enjoyed his hospitable attention and kindness.

Mr. Sherman, about the time of his leaving Mansfield, published a volume the first few words of whose long title are "One God in One Person only," — the earliest formal defence of Unitarianism that was ever issued from the New England press. I have examined it with care, and find it indicative of profound thought, of a depth and accuracy of critical scholarship level with the best scholarship of its time, and of the directness and boldness of expression befitting one who feels the obligation of explicitness and honesty in dealing with sacred themes.

Abiel Abbot, a native of Wilton, New Hampshire, a graduate of Harvard College, and at one time a tutor, was ordained pastor of the church in Coventry, Connecticut, in 1795. He was a member of the council that dismissed and recommended Mr. Sherman, and was led to review his theological opinions by his interest in Mr. Sherman's case. In 1809 his preaching in accordance with his altered views on controverted subjects began to occasion uneasiness in his church, which, in 1811, by vote of a majority, applied to the Association of ministers in Tolland County to organize the Consociation of the county, for which authority was claimed as a tribunal of last resort. Mr. Abbot and the society denied the jurisdiction of this body, which by vote declared the ministerial relation of Mr. Abbot dissolved, and revoked the commission — which they certainly had not given him and therefore could not recall — by which he was authorized to preach the Gospel and administer its ordinances. Rev. Dr. Osgood, of Medford, strongly orthodox, yet as strongly liberal, advised Mr. Abbot to continue his ministration as if there had been no adverse movement, telling him that he had no more reason to tremble at the anathema of the Consociation of Tolland County than at a bull of the Roman pontiff. The majority of his society were of the same mind. But at his request, and on his part for the sake of peace, they joined with him in summoning a mutual council, which in accordance with his own judgment advised the dissolution of his pastorate, at the same time cordially recommending him to the churches.

Dr. Abbot, on removing from Connecticut, became principal of Dummer Academy, and subsequently returned to his native place. In 1827 he was installed as pastor of the First Church in Peterborough, New Hampshire, where he remained in active duty for twelve years, and as senior pastor for nine years longer. A few years after his resignation he took up his residence with his grandson, Rev. Samuel Abbot Smith of Arlington, and retained his full powers of mind till his death in 1859, at the age of ninety-four. In his pastorate at Peterborough he did more than all other men had done before him in the cause of education, in the improvement of the schools, in the establishment of school, church, and ministerial libraries, and in the diffusion of intelligence, not only in his own town, but in that whole district of New Hampshire. In these labors Rev. Dr. Leonard, the Unitarian minister of Dublin, was his efficient coadjutor. Dr. Abbot was a man of scholarly tastes and habits, enjoyed the reading of the classics till the last week of his life, and hardly ever passed a day without reading a portion of the New Testament in Greek, or without discovering some new shade of meaning here and there that had escaped his previous notice. He was a man of the Beatitudes, so pure, so gentle, so full of love to God and man, that there seemed nothing of him but the earthly tabernacle that was not ready for heaven years and years before he went to heaven. Rev. Dr. Sprague, the historian of the American pulpit, was the first child that he baptized, was afterward his pupil, and held him in such affectionate regard that for many years, and until the autumn before his death, he never let a year pass without visiting him. Though Dr. Sprague was a Calvinist of the old school, I am sure that, if he had made a catalogue of modern saints, Dr. Abbot would have headed the list.

The third case to which I referred is that of Rev. Luther Willson, father of Rev. Mr. Willson of Salem. He was settled in Brooklyn, Connecticut, in 1813, as colleague pastor with Rev.

Dr. Josiah Whitney, a moderate Calvinist. In 1816, Mr. Willson having formed and uttered from the pulpit theological opinions other than those of his senior, Dr. Whitney called a church-meeting for conference on the subject, which was discussed anew at an adjourned meeting at which a majority of the church, thirteen out of the twenty-three present, voted that "the Trinity is an essential or fundamental doctrine." At a subsequent meeting Mr. Willson agreed with his church to call a mutual council, to give fit advice under their peculiar circumstances. The council, all men of approved orthodoxy, say in their result that neither the church nor the society considers Mr. Willson as having forfeited his ministerial character by his change of opinions, nor does the church or the society desire his removal from office. They therefore recommend mutual charity, and the concession to one another of the liberty which each claims for himself. The church immediately declared by vote of the majority their approbation of this result. But outside influences were continually at work. Five brethren of the church were induced to apply, not to the Association to which Mr. Willson and his senior belonged, which had been formed by secession from the rigidly Hopkinsian members who were the major part of the clergy of the county, but to the original Association, who were asked, with delegates from their several churches, to sit in Consociation, or as a court of judicature. Mr. Willson denied the jurisdiction of this body, which, however, declared his pastoral office in the churches in its connection and fellowship to be ended. The society refused to regard the action of the Consociation as valid, and were ready to sustain Mr. Willson; but he, with a view to pacification, proposed the calling of a mutual council, with the understanding that his dismission should be recommended. The council sanctioned his dismission, with expressions of sympathy, approval, and confidence. The church subsequently excommunicated Mr. Willson and several of the members who had been his supporters. A minority of the society, with a majority of the church, seceded with the senior pastor, leaving the old church edifice and organization, with all legal rights thereto appertaining, to the First Church in Brooklyn, which, long the only Unitarian church in Connecticut, enjoyed for many years the ministry of Rev. Samuel J. May, and which, after a season of depression, yet never of discouragement, now gives promise of renewed and vigorous life.

Mr. Willson, on leaving Brooklyn, thought of abandoning his profession; but after spending some time in Boston, as Dr. Channing's guest for a week, and in intimate intercourse with other ministers of like faith with himself, he was induced to remain in the ministry, and in 1819 he accepted an invitation to the pastorate of the church in Petersham, which after fifteen years he resigned on account of impaired health. Having had in early life much and successful experience as a teacher, he took the schools of Petersham under his special charge, and is still lovingly remembered there by all who knew him, and by none more lovingly than by those who, as pupils in the public schools, had in their childhood the benefit of his double pastorate. Of what manner of spirit he was, may be known from the fact that at one time Dr. Tuckerman corresponded with him with a view to his becoming associated with himself in the Ministry-at-Large. He died in 1864, leaving the spotless record of a life passed in simplicity and godly sincerity, and in the close and constant following of his Saviour.

Of the men whom I have commemorated, the first four died before I was born. The last two are the only ones whom I knew, and them not intimately. I wish that I had time to speak of the ministers with whom I had a nearer acquaintance, who were advanced in years when I was young. But I have far exceeded the normal lecture-hour.

Permit me to say in closing : — Circumstances have placed me in intimate relations with many ministers and Christian men and women of all our leading denominations, and I am fully convinced that there is among the various portions of the Church a much more nearly equable distribution of God's choicest gifts and of the richest fruits of the Spirit than bigoted sectarians are willing to admit. I have in no quarter of the Church failed to find many whom I could both admire and love. Yet, were I to select special models as Christians and ministers, I should not need to look beyond the pale of those ministers of our faith whom I learned to love and honor in my youth, and whose memory is among the blessed and priceless privileges of my old age.

CHANNING.

BY GEORGE W. BRIGGS.

DR. Channing was the acknowledged leader of the Unitarian communion when it became a separate Christian body, and his name is still the foremost in the American liberal church. He died more than forty-six years ago; but though dead he is speaking still through the myriad copies of his works so widely circulated both here and abroad, often finding their way into other communions than his own, and carrying forward the work to which he gave his life. Indeed, the loving portraitures of his character, and the splendid tributes to his influence in elaborate discourses and glowing eulogies, both in England and America, on the hundredth anniversary of his birth, almost seemed actually to make him live again, — once more to speak with his former persuasiveness and power. I have been accustomed to think of him as in many respects an ideal man. An ideal theologian he certainly was, — neither the maker nor the servant of any system of opinions, ignoring all fetters for himself, imposing none upon others, — entirely consecrating himself to a constant search after higher truth. One closely allied to him in blood termed him an ideal American. And truly among the statesmen and patriots who laid the foundations of the Republic, or have nobly served it, I think of no one who was more inspired by that great hope for humanity, and that reverence for its sacred rights which are the basis of the nation, or more fully possessed by the spirit of liberty which is the breath of its life.

I must be pardoned for a personal reference. It would be absolute ingratitude if I did not speak of Dr. Channing with loving reverence. In my youth he was at the summit of his fame, and I owed to him the priceless benefit of new views of truth, — new thoughts that came as Heaven-sent helpers amid perplexity and doubt. When another's word has helped and saved us, we understand why the woman poured the costly ointment upon the Master's feet. At one period two preachers were of more help to me than any, or all, beside. One was Dr. Dewey, who made the pulpit truly a throne. The other was Dr. Channing. It was the writings of Dr. Channing that helped me, rather than his pulpit services. I saw him only three times in the pulpit, — once when he preached at the dedication of the church in Newport, Rhode Island, once when he gave the charge at an ordination in Northampton, and once when he simply read a hymn. The charm of his voice, the sweetness and fervor of his manner, the simplicity and grandeur of his thought, made both the sermon and the charge inspirations. And in this line of the hymn, —

"Blessings abound where'er he reigns,"

the way in which he uttered the word "abound" seemed to open to thought all the blessed results of the reign of Christ in all the Christian centuries. Perplexed, driven to the verge of unbelief by the only creed known to me in childhood, the words of Dr. Channing came like sunshine after tempests, flooding all things with light and beauty, revealing a new heaven and a new earth. It is hard for men to-day to realize the fascination of his earlier publications to those who were then groping their way out of the old New England creed, hungering and thirsting after a rational faith. No tale of fiction was more absorbing. How well I remember one early friend who pored over their pages far into the night, as well as in his days of leisure, with continual joy. He was the type of many beside. How little a truly inspired speaker may know of the minds he wakens, the hearts he subdues or calms, the souls he saves! Will not those to whom he has opened the book of life at some time come to him with blessing and praise, as the spirits in heaven are pictured coming to him who opened the book with the seven seals?

Dr. Channing was preordained by his parentage, by his early training, by all the circumstances of his life, for the work he was called to do. The man was fitted for the hour. All hereditary influences were auspicious. His father was a successful lawyer. Though he died in middle life, he had already attained distinction in his profession, and was at the time of his death not only the Attorney-General for the State, but also the United States District Attorney for Rhode Island. He had graces of character as well as high mental gifts, and although firmly attached to the Congregational Church was liberal in thought. The mother of Dr. Channing was the daughter of William Ellery, one of the signers of the Declaration of Independence from Rhode Island. She is described as a woman of rare excellence, inheriting her father's energy, — an embodiment of devoted generosity and strict conscientiousness, ot determined straightforwardness and cordial love, making her by the divine right of character an inspirer and guide.

The circumstances attending Dr. Channing's early days were auspicious also. Born in the midst of the Revolution, he grew up in the atmosphere of freedom, and heard in his boyhood the earnest discussions of the noble patriots of that time, and of the many eminent men who came to his father's house. The spirit of Roger Williams, the founder of Rhode

Island, demanding "soul-liberty," ruled the State; so that the love of freedom was infused into his blood.

Then, too, his whole experience was a religious experience. Even in childhood he was called "the little minister," and in college he made his decisive choice of the ministry as his profession. After he left college he went to Richmond, Virginia, for a year and a half as a tutor. Living there among men who had very different tendencies of opinion, he was impelled to a thorough study of Christian evidences and Christian truths, which confirmed his faith, and led him to consecrate himself in the most solemn way to the service of God. That solemn act of self-consecration was but the unfolding and flowering of the seed planted in his heart in his earliest life. While at Richmond, by his intense devotion to study — remaining at his desk far into the night — he laid the foundation of the ill health of his whole after life; so that thereafter, to borrow Dr. Bellows's felicitous expression, he had only enough of physical frame "to anchor his body to the earth." At first, his religious experience did not seem to bring religious joy. He had some ascetic ideas respecting physical culture, and tried to harden himself for difficult duties in the future. No saint in the calendar ever questioned himself more rigidly, or imposed upon himself stricter rules of self-discipline. But the religious joy soon came, and he lived in that sunshine of the spirit until the end. When asked in his latest days what is the pleasantest period of life, he answered, "About sixty-two." Truly his path was like the "shining light, that shineth more and more unto the perfect day."

When he came back from the South, he devoted himself anew to theological studies, reading much, but as the records of his life imply, giving himself more to writing and to thought in his desire to concentrate his mind upon the great spiritual truths, and to make them realities to his soul. In his twenty-third year he began to preach, at once attracting attention by the earnestness and fervor of his discourse and the purity of his thought. Almost at once he had the opportunity to become the minister either of the Brattle Square Society or of the Federal Street Parish, since removed to Arlington Street. Not deeming his health sufficient for the duties of the larger society, he chose the Federal Street Parish, then the smaller. But it could not remain small when he became its minister, and six years after his settlement his church was taken down and a larger building erected in its place in order to make room for the many who came to hear him. He constantly gained a widening influence through all the earlier years of his ministry, attracting the most intellectual by the grandeur of his thought and the charm of his speech, winning the most religiously disposed by his religious fervor. And therefore both his position and his course were predetermined when the changes in thought, which had been silently going forward for a long period in the Congregational churches in the eastern part of Massachusetts, became more pronounced, and the adherents of the older theology withdrew from ministerial intercourse with their more liberal brethren.

Trained in the air of liberty, he could not fail to protest with the utmost vigor against the system of exclusion then adopted, as he did in the paper entitled "The System of Exclusion and Denunciation in Religion Considered," published in 1815. So, too, it was natural that at the ordination of Mr. Sparks in Baltimore, in 1819, he should avail himself of such a conspicuous opportunity to give a distinct statement of the opinions generally held by his liberal brethren, — their mode of interpreting the Scriptures, their views concerning God and Christ, their idea of the nature of his mission and mediation. More than any one thing else, perhaps, that discourse brought matters to a crisis. Instantly the fires of controversy began to blaze. But controversy was entirely alien to Dr. Channing's nature, and he had comparatively little to do himself with that warfare. It was Andover on the one side — guilty herself of broaching one little heresy of hope to-day — and the elder Dr. Ware, as the principal disputant, on the other. One article was prepared by Dr. Channing for the "Christian Disciple," a magazine established two years before, in which he combated the objections to Unitarian Christianity; but then, and in all later years, he principally devoted himself to unfolding its positive excellences. Nevertheless, though so seldom a combatant in their behalf, his character and his distinction as a preacher gave him the leadership among his brethren. Indeed, he thus became a leader, as by a divine election, before there was any recognized company of men to follow him. For the way in which the liberal ministers of that time became in any sense a separate Christian body was unique in religious annals. They did not withdraw from their former religious fellowship. Their old associates withdrew from them, refusing all professional intercourse, thus turning them out of doors, and compelling them to form a separate organization, or else to have no religious brotherhood. It has been said that when all the rest of the State of Massachusetts had been made into separate townships, there was one small portion of its territory that had been left out, not organized into a distinct community. So the liberal churches and ministers were left out some seventy years ago; and they were very slow in uniting themselves together. It was not until 1820 that the ministers formed the Berry Street Conference for discussion among themselves alone, — the association now called the Ministerial Conference, meeting on the last Wednesday in May in Channing Hall. The Unitarian Association, embracing laymen as well as clergymen, was not formed until 1825. The liberal churches had had a bitter experience of exclusion and denunciation for opinion's sake. They were alive to the perils that might attend associations, so forcibly presented in an article by Dr. Channing, published in 1829, and it required years to convince them that they could really form themselves into a denomination without some danger to their individual liberty. Perhaps the fear of that peril is not absolutely banished even now.

Perhaps I have lingered too long among these introductory thoughts. The truer design of this paper is to present some statement of the opinions held by the liberal parishes when they were cut off from their old religious fellowship, — and Dr. Channing may be taken as their exponent. We have often heard in later years of Channing Unitarianism. What was that? Channing formulated no theological system, presented no creed. He would have been false to himself if he had attempted it. But there were certain great truths that dominated, and always inspired him, glowing before his mind in hours of thought, recognized more or less directly whenever he wrote or spoke. If we give to them the name of Channing Unitarianism, — Channing Unitarianism was a beautiful faith, nourishing many whom we remember as noble, saintly souls, bringing forth abundant fruits of righteousness. Glance at these inspiring truths. One central faith with Channing was the faith in the moral perfection of God. I am not sure that we might not call it his commanding thought, though it is not the one which is most frequently connected with his name. In his Baltimore sermon, and in the paper entitled "The Moral Argument against Calvinism," he vindicates the right of man to judge concerning the Creator, contending that God himself has made it a duty by giving us a moral faculty, and that if we decline to do it we violate a primary law of our nature. "If God is incomprehensible," he says, "he is not therefore unintelligible, and we may form distinct ideas concerning him, and can reason from those ideas as justly as from any others." And so it was that he took this idea of the moral perfection of God, and brought the old New England faith before it for judgment. Tried by that standard, the doctrine of depravity, either in its older form, asserting that man has an utterly corrupt nature at birth, or as modified, affirming that he comes into life under such circumstances as make it certain that he will become altogether sinful, was an impeachment of the divine character. So too was the terrible dogma that God of his sovereign will elected a certain portion of the race to be saved from the else universal doom, leaving the rest in a guilt that he himself had made inevitable. Such dogmas made God infinitely unjust, a being to whom man could owe no allegiance. The moral perfection of God, the idea of the divine fatherhood, were vital truths, before whose brightness the dogmas of the old theology fled away, as the earth and heavens were pictured as fleeing from the face of him that sat upon the great white throne, till there was found no place for them. In Channing's view unjust and unworthy ideas of God were the great spring of corruption in religion. In one place he says, "The great controversies in the Church may be resolved into one question: Is God perfectly good?" In his view the justice of God was the exact adaptation of spiritual discipline to the moral condition of every soul, and was thus only one phase of his mercy seeking to work out the highest good for his every child. How earnestly he pleaded against all dishonorable ideas of God! He cries, "We cling to the divine perfections. Leave us a God worthy of our love and trust, in whom our moral sentiments may find delight, in whom our weaknesses and sorrows may find a refuge." It was such a God that he learned to worship when he roamed along the beach of his native island in his youth, and whom he adored with ever deepening love to his latest day.

Another commanding idea with Dr. Channing was his conception of the great purpose of Christianity. In respect to the nature of Jesus, and the effect of his mission in procuring the remission of human sin, his views were never clearly defined to others, or as I think to himself. Writing concerning the ideas of Unitarians in a letter to a friend in 1815, he said that a majority believed that Jesus was more than man, and that he literally came from heaven on his mission to the world. In the Baltimore sermon in 1819, speaking of Jesus, and the influences of his death in procuring forgiveness, he said that many Unitarians, evidently including himself, " think that the Scriptures ascribe the remission of sins to Christ's death with an emphasis so peculiar, that we ought to consider this event as having a special influence in removing punishment, though the Scriptures may not reveal the way in which it contributes to that end." I do not know that he ever modified his views upon these points, or made any statement that was more distinct.

But one thought respecting Jesus was like a forever burning light, — the idea that he came to free men from sin, and to lift humanity to its divinest possibilities of life. He delighted to present Christianity in that aspect, as the ministry to raise men in the scale of spiritual being. No man had a profounder reverence, or a tenderer love for Jesus. Still to preach Christ, in his view, was not continually to dwell upon his person, but to unfold his religion, to diffuse his spirit, and thus to promote the great aim of Jesus himself, — the perfection of human character. The sermon at the ordination of Rev. Mr. Motte, in 1830, was entirely devoted to this theme. In the sermon at the ordination of Dr. Farley in Providence, in 1828, unfolding the sublime idea of likeness to God as the aim and end of religion, the purpose of life, the same truth was presented in a bolder form. He regarded Jesus as the great emancipator, who came to set free all our affections, faculties, and energies, to give perfect liberty, perfect development, to human nature. If we may borrow the illustration of a brilliant living preacher, as the sun pours its light upon the earth to call forth myriad forms of life into all their possibilities of beauty, so he thought Jesus, the light of the world, shines upon the soul to inspire and perfect its every germ of spiritual greatness, its every God-given power.

But there was yet another idea which is more frequently associated with the name of Dr. Channing, — the doctrine of the dignity of human nature. That thought indeed seemed to come to him as by a revelation in his early youth. One day when he was in college, while he was reading passages in a book that asserted man's capacity for a disinterested affection, for perfect self-devotion, the truth of the greatness of the human soul suddenly burst upon his mind, to be thenceforth, in the words adopted by his biographer, "the fountain light of all his day, the master light of all his seeing." The place and the hour of that revelation seemed to him forever sacred. He found confirmations of this doctrine of disinterestedness in the teachings of Dr. Hopkins, that theological champion, so stern in his theology, but so benignant at heart. For what was the startling declaration linked with his name, that the proof of fitness to be saved is to be willing to be damned for the glory of God, but a repulsive expression of the sublime idea of absolute self-devotion? When the prodigal came back renouncing every right and privilege of a son, condemning himself to a servant's place, he proved his fitness to receive the forgiving kiss.

It was a moment of inspiration when Dr. Channing made that splendid assertion of his conception of the dignity of human nature in the words, "I regard all minds as of one family." The words were simplicity itself, but the thought was sublime. If all minds are of one family, or, as he elsewhere says, "essentially of one origin, one nature, kindled from one divine flame, tending to one centre, to one happiness," then the old word that God made man in his own image asserts at once the simplest and the greatest truth, and the relation between God and man is truly that of father and child. Then the family in heaven and earth is one. Dr. Channing termed this the greatest of truths. It was a root idea with him, which budded and blossomed into the beautiful theological conceptions, the fair and sweet philanthropies, the splendid hopes for humanity on earth, and for souls hereafter, which found in him an expression and an advocate. It is interesting to see how modern researches are bringing indirect yet real confirmations of this inspiring thought. Channing proved it to himself by the thought that truth, which is the food and inspiration of the mind, is the same everywhere; a truth of mathematics, for example, being the same in all worlds, to man and God. Science is proving that the same substances exist in the sun and stars as in the earth. The same elements exist, one law reigns, in the boundless realms of matter. Is not the inference legitimate that one law also reigns in the infinite realm of spirit? Science, which sometimes seems to unsettle faith, is indirectly supporting its most ravishing conception, that the same truths exist in all spiritual spheres, to be the law and the life of all souls, to unite them into one family and brotherhood.

It is hard to tear one's self away from the consideration of such an enrapturing faith, and the inspiring thoughts which it suggests. If all minds are of one family, kindled by one flame, then there are no impassable gulfs to separate me from the grandest souls. Then there is nothing in Jesus himself of which we have not the possibility and the germ. Then if we should ascribe to Jesus only a human nature, we should not derogate from his spiritual greatness, or deny his divinity. Only a human nature? A true son of man is a son of God; and the true son of God must be the son of man. It is not strange that men were so impressed by the way in which Dr. Channing uttered the words, "The human soul." For that phrase, often so thoughtlessly spoken, always brought to him a vision of the infinite possibility of a diviner life, and all his faith, and aspiration, and hope, and joy, were in the tones of his voice when the words fell from his lips.

Another favorite idea with Dr. Channing must be distinctly named, although it has already been implied in what I have said. He regarded religion as natural to man. In his view all the great principles of human nature were its germs, and the great expressions of religious truths were the developments of the ideas that were wrought into the very structure of our being, if we may speak so, written upon the soul itself by the finger of God. In his Newport sermon he combated the assertion that religion was a human contrivance, and worship an unnatural service. And how well I remember the tone in which he said, "You tell me, my sceptical friend, that religion is the contrivance of the priest. How came the priest into being?" How many thoughts are suggested by this conception of religion as natural to man, and of its truths as the clear unfolding of ideas originally stamped upon his nature. Therefore how natural it is that we should find so many of the same truths in widely different faiths, sublime moral precepts outside of Christendom, in the words of philosophers and sages. Nobler, purer souls will discern the same truths, as those who climb the mountain heights will have the same prospects opening upon their sight. Therefore also the declarations of revealed religion, as we term it, the higher religious teachings coming from the lips of the inspired souls, prophets, apostles, Jesus himself, — all this is the natural religion in the divinest sense of the words. For what did Jesus do but tell the truths that came to the sight of a true son of man as he looked into the divinest things? There never were truer words than these of Emerson: —

> "Out of the heart of nature rolled
> The burdens of the Bible old."

These great declarations of truth are not made sacred because they are recorded in Bibles. They make Bibles sacred. They are not true because Jesus uttered them. Jesus uttered them because they are eternally true, their own witness and proof to the living, inmost heart of man. The burdens of the Bible are the record of the visions of the soul as it soars, inspirations that give it wings for a loftier flight.

I must leave this line of thought. Let no one confound my inferences from some of his favorite ideas with the views of Channing himself. But did I not rightly say that the central thoughts in all his teachings — the idea of the moral perfection of God, of the great purpose of Christianity as the uplifting of the human soul, of the dignity of human nature, of religion as natural to man — made Channing Unitarianism a beautiful faith? What noble souls it nourished. I recall them, commanding preachers, differing from each other as one star differeth from another star in glory, yet each one a light in his own time and place; distinguished laymen, leaders in life, often the rulers, always the safeguard of the State. Time would fail me to name them, as time failed the writer to the Hebrews to name the heroes of faith. And what fruits of righteousness that form of Unitarianism produced! What noble philanthropies it inspired! I turn to Channing himself as its illustration. During all the later years of his life he was not so much a preacher as a philanthropist. Possessed by the thought of the greatness of the human soul as literally the child of God, he longed to free men from every hindrance to their noblest life. When no longer able often to speak in the pulpit, he pleaded for the poor, for the elevation of the laboring classes, for education, for temperance, and repeated with deeper fervor his early denunciations of war.

Dr. Channing could not forget the slave. The wrongs of the bondman were burned into his heart, when he actually looked upon slavery for a short period in his youth. Earnest abolitionists at first denounced him because he seemed so slow to identify himself with their work. The harshness and severity of the antislavery leaders jarred upon his gentle nature. But one incident of that period gives a striking illustration of his magnanimity and greatness. Samuel J. May, that incarnation of love, went to him in 1834 to plead for the cause of the slave. Forgetting everything but his cause, he cried, "Is it becoming in you to complain because we speak in such an inferior way against what you acknowledge to be an awful injustice, when you, perhaps more than any other man, might have raised a voice of remonstrance that would have been heard through the length and breadth of the land? Why, sir, have you not spoken before?" Suddenly it then occurred to him to whom he was giving this rebuke, the man whom he revered more than any beside, and in trembling expectation he waited for his reply. At length the painful silence was broken by the meek answer, "Brother May, I acknowledge the justice of your reproof: I have been silent too long." I know not which of these men seems nobler as I read the story of that interview.

From the hour of that conversation Dr. Channing never was silent concerning the antislavery cause until his tongue was silent forever. He could not speak after the manner of Garrison. I detract nothing from Garrison's fame. This generation has honored itself in honoring him. Fifty years after a rope was put upon his neck in Boston, and men were almost ready to murder him in their madness, his statue was erected to give true dignity to one of the city's princeliest streets. Garrison spoke like him who came crying in the wilderness. Channing seemed to me to speak in the tone of the Christ. But the Christ was as fearless as John. Channing was as heroic as he was benignant and gentle. His fearlessness was proved at the memorable meeting in Faneuil Hall in 1837, which was called at his suggestion to condemn the murder of Lovejoy, the antislavery editor in Alton, Illinois, who was shot while defending his office against a mob. It was the meeting in which Attorney-General Austin expressed the feeling of many by asking, "Did not Lovejoy die as the fool dieth?" and Wendell Phillips, then comparatively unknown, but never forgotten afterwards, leaped upon the platform to denounce that recreant question with the burning eloquence enkindled by his righteous wrath. Dr. Channing's last public word was an address on the anniversary of West India Emancipation, given at Lenox, Massachusetts, on the 1st of August,

1842. Only two months later he died. Did he not go up into heaven with a true preparation to hear the welcome, "As you have done it to the least of these my brethren, you have done it unto me"?

I have omitted until now to name one thing that was as truly characteristic of Dr. Channing as anything in his life. He clung to his distinctive views of truth with steadfast, most loving faith. But still more earnestly, if that was possible, he clung to the hope, the faith, that there were still higher views, for which every free mind should be always striving. His spirit was pictured in the words of Paul, "This one thing I do; forgetting the things that are behind, and reaching forth to those that are before, I press toward the goal." Channing Unitarianism could never degenerate into "Unitarian Orthodoxy" in his hands. He protested against that in a letter to Martineau in 1841, writing that he had felt for years that old Unitarianism must undergo important modifications, or developments. John Robinson in Leyden could not have given the charge to the Pilgrim company with deeper earnestness, never to forget that there was more light yet to break from God's Word, than Channing would have given it to any who were ready to follow him. In his charge to Mr. Dwight, at Northampton, he said: "Do not feel as if Christianity had spoken its last word. It is the characteristic of divine truth that it is infinitely fruitful." One noble sentence in the preface to the volume of his "Miscellanies," published in 1830, must never be forgotten. Referring to the attacks made upon his works, he wrote that he had declined to answer them, not from contempt of his opponents, but because he believed that he should do himself and others more good by seeking higher and wider views, than by defending what he had already offered. "I feared," he said, "that my mind might become stationary by lingering around my own writings." That one sentence, written when bitter and biting censures were heaped upon himself, and the truths held dearer than himself, made him immortal. What higher truths must be revealed to a soul like his in the eternal heavens!

Of course there are many things that should be said of Dr. Channing which have not been alluded to thus far. No man was more possessed by the true spirit of patriotism. His name has a place in literature. His style was unlabored, for he only aimed to utter himself plainly, and to be true. His sermons had great literary merit. His few papers of a more strictly literary character attracted wide attention. In the article upon Napoleon, while doing justice to military genius, he discrowned that daring usurper, tearing away the veil that concealed his moral deformities. For what was that freebooter upon the land but the real brother of the freebooter upon the sea? The other principal literary papers contributed to the "Christian Examiner" were the articles upon Milton and Fenélon. But the purpose of the present paper was to speak of him as an exponent of Unitarianism, and therefore other aspects of his life have been put aside. How earnestly I hope that even this incomplete representation of him may bring some features of his character as distinctly before the mind as his portraits picture the features of his face.

I add one word more. Dr. Channing was a child of my own native State. I delight to think of him as one of her children, because her scenery and her history helped to make him what he became. He loved his native island, that gem upon the bosom of the Narragansett Bay. In the sermon that I heard at Newport he referred to the beautiful scenery around his birthplace, and spoke of the beach, so "dear to him in the sunshine, still more attractive in the storm." "No spot on earth," he said, "has helped to form me so much as that beach." The world of fashion visits it in summer days, hearing nothing, it may be, save the thunder of the waves. As Channing walked over it angels spoke to him. And then the spirit of Roger Williams, the apostle of soul liberty, rested upon this equally heroic soul, making him always devoted to, and in his own words, "always young for liberty." Rhode Island? Her territory is but a dot on the map of our mighty empire, but if her scenery and history could inspire such a noble soul, her name will always be dear to the lovers of truth, of humanity, and of liberty.

TRANSCENDENTALISM:

THE NEW ENGLAND RENAISSANCE.

BY FRANCIS TIFFANY.

THE subject given me for my brief hour in this course of lectures reads simply "Transcendentalism." I propose to enlarge the title into "Transcendentalism; or, The New England Renaissance." The especial designation, Renaissance, or Re-birth, I would emphasize from the outset, as starting in the mind a distinct class of conceptions, without the aid of which the New England movement cannot be treated with due sense of historical continuity.

This term, "The Renaissance," — the New or the Second Birth of the world, — is one we are all familiar with nowadays. In its broadest, its only scientifically historical sense, it denotes what Symonds, who has written the history of the movement in Italy, summarizes as "the whole transition from the conceptions of the Middle Ages to the conceptions of the Modern World." Its two grand achievements were, as Michelet puts it, "the discovery of the world and the discovery of man." High-sounding terms these, — "the discovery of the world and the discovery of man;" but in how vast a sense are they literally true! Go back in imagination to the Middle Ages, and ask yourselves, Did man then know, did he so much as dream of, this majestic universe which has finally become revealed to the modern mind? Question, again, man's actual knowledge in those days of the character and scope of his own indwelling powers. Did he so much as dream of the triumphs reason was to achieve, of the intellectual systems thought was to build, of the world of beauty art and literature were to create, of the order and stability law was to inaugurate, of the conquests of disease and misery medicine was to usher in, of the richness, variety, and charm all these were to impart to human life? No: as such potential miracle-worker he never suspected himself. He would have thought you were talking of wizards or demons, and have shrunk back in horror. Thus, in a thousand higher aspects of his being, man had not yet been discovered by himself.

And how was brought to pass this double discovery of the inner and the outer world? In the one only possible way, — of the foremost intellects and characters of Europe beginning to trust in and use their natural powers, thus finding out experimentally alike what these powers were made for, what they could hope to achieve, and to what marvels of marvels they were externally related. The compass, first heard of in 1302, gave the world later on the discovery of America, the rounding of the Cape of Good Hope, the circumnavigation of the globe. The telescope enabled Copernicus and Galileo to prove the revolution of the earth and the true theory of the planetary system. Printing began its marvellous career, and made accessible to thousands the works of the mighty spirits of Greece and Rome. Gunpowder revolutionized the art of war. Men of genius in sculpture and painting revealed the grace and glory of the human form. To France, to Germany, to Holland, to England, the movement spread, to break out in original shapes in Shakespeares and Bacons, in Erasmuses, in Luthers, in Descartes, in Spinozas. Was not all this in truth, then, what Michelet so accurately calls it, " the discovery of man and the discovery of the world"? Did it not inaugurate a new human consciousness, and bring to the lips the ecstatic cry: "What a piece of work is a man! How noble in reason! how infinite in faculties! in form and moving, how express and admirable! in action, how like an angel! in apprehension, how like a god!" How Transcendental, by the way, this last quotation sounds!

Meantime, however, while all this was going forward, there was another and a vastly larger class of people, who looked on with anything but eyes of favor. Nor is it to be wondered at. The smug citizen, who has been accustomed all his days to walk on level ground and with his head up in the air, — no wonder he has a vindictive word to say of the impious physicist, who makes his brain spin by telling him that, in the course of the next twelve hours, he will be where he will have to stand with his feet turned up to the bottom of a globe and his head hanging down into a frightful abyss. The Mediterranean sailor, with a love in every port, whom Columbus drags off to cross the boundless ocean; the routine student, who is contemptuously told to learn to think for himself, when he naturally supposed that others had done all that for him; the comfortable priest, whose whole needful stock in trade had been a string of beads and the mumbling of a few unintelligible Latin prayers; the splendid prelate, with stipends and dignities entirely dependent on the continued ignorance and superstition of the masses; nay, too, the earnest, self-consecrated, saintly man, — the Saint Bernard perhaps, — who does not care an iota whether the world is round or square, beautiful or ugly, learned or ignorant, so that it can only be saved from the leprosy of sin, and who feels that all possible hope of salvation is supernaturally bound up in the dogmas of the Church, — why should not from all of these break forth a fierce and infuriated protest against the advancing movement? "This blasphemous prying into what God meant to keep secret must be put down." So the infuriated Franciscans cried to Roger Bacon. Mobs, papal anathemas, inquisitions, were in the very air.

We are now getting on to ground upon which it behooves us to tread very carefnlly, in order to be at once appreciative and just. These two great classes of the human race, which we now see confronted face to face, and glaring at one another with angry eyes, persist in every age, — the champions of the new, the champions of the old; the believers in the future and the believers in the past; the men who trust in reason and think all things possible to it, and the men who distrust it, dread it, in certain fields abhor it. Each party has something to say for itself which it is well to heed. And so, first, a word for this latter party.

Not unlikely, quite a number of persons here present, addicted to pedestrianism, and yet short of stature, may — in the White Mountains, say — have noticed a certain tendency on the part of men six feet in their stockings to exaggerate the statement of the number of miles that may be reeled off per hour with positive comfort and without calling a halt. Laboriously accompanying one of these nine-league booters through a long day's march, does not the man of shorter stride and scantier breath feel, toward the contemplative hour of nightfall, irresistibly impelled to raise the question, "Is not my six-foot friend somewhat exposed to the danger of becoming the victim of what philosophers call 'his own subjectivity'? Does he not, in fine, take a somewhat too transcendental view of average legs, — a view too much lifted into the realm of the absolute and unconditioned, and freed from all impertinences of time and space?" Now here is a simple reactionary feeling, which, duly extended from mere pedicular to intellectual and moral considerations, will serve to interpret vast conservative and even retrograde movements in human history.

We can easily see, then, why a whole range of such sublime sentiments as that " Truth is its own evidence," " Beauty its own witness," " Virtue its own reward," should commend themselves very rapturously to a class of highly spiritual minds, and seem very perplexing and irritating to a denser and opaquer. "Oh, yes; only give us a picture," these last poor fellows pathetically cry, " in which, as in the earliest human efforts at art, it was plainly written over every animal in the landscape, 'This is a cow,' or ' This is a horse,' and then we will freely admit that a cow or a horse is its own intrinsic evidence." Now, for one, I cannot but feel a certain tender and loving sympathy with this particular mental condition. The first awkward, fumbling attempts of the human reason, like the first awkward and fumbling attempts at art, produce rather indiscriminate results. We all perfectly recall the bygone school-days, in which, after four times adding up a column of figures, and getting four entirely distinct answers, we felt a not unnatural uncertainty as to which one of the four might be in strictest accordance with immutable truth. But there was one infallible authority we regarded with as awful reverence as do devout Catholics the symbol of Saint Peter, — the Key to the arithmetic. One glance at this, and we could proudly say of the correct answer, " This is the cow," " This is the horse," and rejoice that truth now shone in its own light and had become its own intrinsic evidence.

But we are seemingly keeping too long away from New England, unless possibly it be on the principle that "the longest way round is often the shortest way home."

The New England colonies were settled by a class of men and women who were a salient illustration of one aspect of the grand uprising of the Renaissance, considered from the point of view of the "whole transition from the conceptions of the Middle Ages to the conceptions of the modern world." In flagrant defiance of the doctrine of the long-assumed divine rights of kings, here was a class of men on the high road to the discovery that kings had a "lith" in their necks. In many directions, their faith in the powers of human reason was emphatically pronounced. That men had abundant capacity for founding States, and that a town-meeting of ministers, lawyers, traders, and farmers was as august a body as a House of Parliament, — of this they rapidly became entirely convinced. In other directions, however, these self-same men were an equally salient instance of a distinct retrogression from the on-setting tide of the Renaissance, — a band of reactionary protesters against what they regarded as its inherent vice.

Every river has its current and its eddy, and so flows two ways at once. Look at its current, and you say it flows north. Look at its eddy, and you say, "No: south." Like flint had the Puritans of England — spite of a few exceptions — set their faces against the joyous, the poetical, the beautiful, the scientific, the speculative and critical aspects of the Renaissance. They would have put a very different estimate on Shakespeare and "all his works" than do you and I, and would have thought his chances in the world to come far more promising if Mr. Ignatius Donelly should only succeed in proving himself to be in the right.

Settled down on the hard soil of New England, with Indians to fight, forests to fell, communities to found, churches to build, forced more or less to become jack-at-all trades, — in farming, trading, legislation, law, medicine, and, erelong, even divinity, — a literally unexampled growth took place in practical confidence in the power of reason to deal with all kinds of emergencies. The Yankee habit of asking questions, and of always replying by asking another question, now made rapid headway. But at one point all this inquisitiveness, all this desire of learning something new, stopped short. The same man who would question with the most radical audacity the whole political tradition of past history would recoil in horror at the idea of questioning either the physical ability or the devout willingness of a foreordained whale to swallow Jonah. Here the mental arrest was absolute, here the paralysis of human reason entire.

Time will not serve me to enlarge on the logical consequences of a mental attitude like this, so radical and defiant in one direction, so conservative and submissive in another. You can readily see that it meant two distinct tribunals of judgment, — the tribunal of free reason, the tribunal of the written Scripture. Neither, further, will time serve me to dwell — as I would much like to — on the retarding effect exercised on the development of many sides of the New England mind by the almost utter isolation in which it so long found itself, cut off, as it was, from the great circulating currents of European life, — from its refinements, its science, its art, its philosophy, its literature, — and shut up to a monotonous diet of politics and technical theology. Enough that all this necessitated a very narrow and starved mental condition, and left whole sides of human nature unsolaced and uninspired by any stimulating environment.

Now, unfortunately for any long-continued success in the establishment of a rigid and inflexible theocracy in New England, the very worst book in the world had been chosen to found it on, — the Bible. Strive as you may to overlay it and load it down with a whole Ætna of burnt-out dogmatic slag, scoriæ, and ashes, the Titans within are ever rending the mountain flanks and pouring out their indomitable insurgent hearts in fresh streams of fiery lava. And so New England had its perpetual, even though sporadic, witnesses to the inextinguishable hunger and thirst of the spirit after a fresh, spontaneous, originally creative, eye-to-eye, soul to-soul, religious life of its own. The first Transcendentalist in New England, Emerson was always fond of saying, was Jonathan Edwards. "A grim, cast-iron specimen of the breed!" you will be tempted to say. Not at all. There are beautiful passages in his so generally lurid and terrific sermons, which I would agree — could I only make a private arrangement with Emerson's publishers — to insert in his Essays, and which would be read by his most ardent devotees without a suspicion that they had not flowed straight out of the mind and heart of the Concord seer. Of course Jonathan Edwards would have put in his proviso. "Yes, this glorious power to see God eye to eye, 'to glorify him and enjoy him forever,' is all true. God is his own divine witness, his own clear interpreter, — but to *the elect alone.*" Of the Quakers, too, the same might have been said, and in an even broader sense. Their doctrine of the Inner Light, of the Spirit that judges all things, even the deep things of God, — what was this but a still bolder assertion of the indwelling power of the soul to rise above book, priest, formulated creed, and cry to the Eternal, " In thy Light I see light!"

Spite, however, of these not infrequent incursions of a freer and more subjective spirit, — among which I would certainly rank certain aspects of the personal-experience doctrine of Methodism, under the lead of its fiery apostle, Whitefield, —

it will have to be confessed, I feel sure, that the tendency alike of thought and emotion in New England set steadily on towards a lower, a more literal, a more prosaic and commonplace level. For Calvinism in full eruption we must all feel, I think, the same half-sublime, half-terrific sense of glory and dread with which we look on Vesuvius or Ætna in fiery outbreak. For Calvinism, its craters dead, and its flanks one desert of monstrously contorted rocks and dreary, barren ashes, we must equally feel as we do when toiling up the sun-scorched heights of an extinct volcano of to-day. Such Calvinism in due time became, — a literal burnt-out volcano. Indeed, it would historically look as though the very capacity for deep and strong emotion had been annihilated in the New England heart, so long, so monotonously, and so remorselessly had the soil been religiously overcropped, so frightfully had it been seared and baked by revival fires. It must be suffered to lie fallow a generation or two, to recover heart.

Man shall not live by volcanoes alone. This, thousands on thousands were now beginning to feel. Parishes began negatively to express their sense of fatigue by seeking relief in *not* settling " men of strong doctrine." Life had grown to be far more comfortable. Material wealth had witnessed a great increase. A smug, unheroic, average-citizen temperament had been generated. The sensation philosophy of John Locke had won a numerous following. Reason — that is to say, reason within reasonable limits — had gained increased respect. Arminianism began to creep in, and gradually to work on towards Unitarianism. And never, perhaps, — as Rev. O. B. Frothingham so clearly points out in his invaluable " History of Transcendentalism," a book I would earnestly commend to your reading as the only full and adequate account of this important movement, — never, perhaps, had what I have ventured to call "reason within reasonable limits" so admirable a quarry to disport itself with as was now furnished to Unitarian polemics in the dried and desiccated mummy of Calvinism.

For a time "reason within reasonable limits" held high carnival. Now came the days of its young espousals. So delightful was the sense of the privilege of exercising reason on what had hitherto been forbidden fruit, such a fresh and unwonted sensation did it communicate, that no wonder it drew so many able men to embrace the profession of the ministry. The moral argument against Calvinism, — what a glory in heroically calling (and it was heroism then) right, right, and cruelty, cruelty, and tyranny, tyranny, in their own intrinsic nature! The contradictions and absurdities of the received doctrine of the Trinity, — what a fine intellectual invigoration in subjecting these to the canons of a rational logic! Then, too, the rehabilitation of a pure and good life, the loyal championship of it as above all creeds and professions, the stripping off from the dethroned and beggared heir of God the "rags of filthy righteousness," and throwing over his shoulders the royal purple, — who shall tell what a discovery of a new world, of a new man, this was to thousands! Perpetual honor to the early leaders of this movement, — the Worcesters, Channings, Nortons, Noyeses, Deweys, Greenwoods, Ephraim Peabodys, and a host of others. Without the solid foundations of sanity, character, and piety they laid, the more ebullient movement that was to succeed would have run great dangers of eventuating in license and excess.

As time went by, however, the original impulse of Unitarianism began to lose its first vitality. You cannot call a new thing new forever. There is a first cry of "Land! land!"

which not even a Columbus can raise a second time. People became accustomed to the exercise of "reason within reasonable limits," and to feel the stirrings of a call to "fresh hills and pastures new," — that is, a limited number did. As for the bulk of the body, it began to manifest a strong disposition to settle down in a traditional way. Channing, with his high-wrought prophetic sense of the new glory that was to break forth, expressed the keenest disappointment over this state of arrested development, and declared he felt less and less interest in Unitarianism. "Reason within reasonable limits" had grown highly respectable; its adherents were the prosperous and honored; it had its scholars, whose conclusions were to be insisted on as impregnable and final; it had established noble charities and entered energetically on the work of a more rational education and of wiser and better institutions for the pauper, the felon, the insane,— what more could reasonably be asked of it? Why could it not be suffered to enjoy its laurels?

Ah, friends, laurels wither, when long since plucked from the living tree. As a momentary symbol, and while green and glistening, how beautiful! when dry, sere, and rattling, what a mockery! Unitarianism had always carried with it one serious limitation and drawback. It had the note of provincialism; it was cut off from the grand circulating currents of the world's larger life; it lacked alike the prophetic sense of its own fuller mission and the spiritual imagination to build its inspiring ideal. It was abandoned to no infinite principle. It was to be the leaven of Orthodoxy, its work accomplished when it had taught Orthodoxy to make the same kind of bread with itself. This bread had come to be a certain regulation loaf, with whose size, weight, and easy digestibility the majority were entirely satisfied. Its Channing, whom it never half comprehended, and in many ways hampered and distressed, was to it the utmost limit of the horizon, if not a suspicious degree beyond. Its look was turned backwards. And so it began to ossify. Angry recriminations were now to be heard against any proposal of innovation; and while no hands were more munificent in subscriptions for building the tombs of its past prophets, none were handier with a brick or an egg for the reception of new prophets. The mercantile influence, the mercantile standard of spiritual values, was paralyzing it. I beg everybody's pardon, but one more generation of the like, and Unitarianism would have degenerated into a simple gospel for the Philistines. Transcendentalism, we now see clearly enough, saved it, by breathing into it the spirit of a newer and larger life.

Who are the Philistines?— peace to the shade of Matthew Arnold after all his effort to define them! They are an eminently respectable body of half-vitalized men and women, good fathers, good mothers, good citizens, exposed to the perpetual danger of perishing of dry rot through the prosaic, commonplace, and utterly unimaginative character of their constitutional temperament and actual environment. Woe to the world that does not possess solid masses of them; and woe equally to themselves, if, for their own best good, their Canaan is not every now and then invaded, conquered, and reconstructed by the children of light!

Who, again, are the children of light? They are the mobile, impressionable, and impassioned temperaments of every age; the diviners of the signs of the oncoming future; the cordial welcomers of every promise of a fuller, richer, more spiritually imaginative life; the believers in the things eye hath not yet seen nor ear heard. And such were the early leaders of Transcendentalism in New England. I need but to enumerate such names as those of Emerson, Alcott, Margaret Fuller, Elizabeth Peabody, Mrs. Ripley, Dr. Hedge, Dr. Furness, George Ripley, Dwight, Cranch, Caleb Stetson, Clarke, Bartol, — almost all Unitarians by nurture. Faithful to the best that had come down to them from their inheritance in the past, they yet turned eager, anticipating eyes towards a diviner future, and from their heart of hearts prayed the prayer, —

> "Let knowledge grow from more to more,
> But more of reverence in us dwell;
> That mind and soul, according well,
> May make one music as before,
> But *vaster*."

Now we have already taken notice of certain signs in the past of what Emerson recognized as having the note of genuine Transcendentalism, — the confidence, namely, of the spirit in itself. But it was only in a very restricted way that this confidence of the spirit in itself held true. The Quakers, with their emphasized doctrine of the function of the Inner Light, made the nearest approach to it. These Quakers as a body were, however, spite of a few very beautiful exceptions, a narrow, ignorant, and fanatical class of men and women, who most unhappily thought that the more completely they cut themselves off from nature, literature, beauty, art, science, and philosophy, the brighter would be the shining of the Inner Light. Indeed, in the Quaker horror of such profanities as music and dancing there could hardly have sprung up among them, and been told of one of their prophets and one of their prophetesses, such a myth as that which records the story of how, on witnessing together the exquisite aerial evolutions of the Viennese *danseuse*, Ellsler, as she came down tiptoe, with "a station like the herald

Mercury, new lighted on a heaven-kissing hill," Mr. Emerson bent over with effusion to Miss Fuller, and exclaimed, " Margaret, this is poetry!" while she, in turn, breathlessly ejaculated, " Ralph, it is religion!"

This, of course, is simple travesty. And yet what an ill historical student would he be, who did not reckon alike with the travesties and with the broadest comic caricatures of any period he studies, seeing how, under exaggerated and laughable aspects, these are so many illustrations of the popular feeling of the day! What is really hit at, in this especial one I have cited, is the entirely novel and unrestricted ranges of experience on which, in contrast with the sober earlier New England habit of mind, the Transcendentalists began to insist as sources of light and inspiration. In point of fact, we are here directly led to what must be emphasized as the *most characteristic feature* of the Transcendental Movement in New England; namely, that it took its rise among a class of men and women at once *highly impressionable* and *broadly cultivated*. Their Bible had to be a very large one, and with very little line of distinction between its canonical and apocryphal books.

Now, for all the clearly enunciated belief of the votaries of the new movement in their own eyes and ears, just as significant a fact was it that they believed equally in the eyes and ears of a vast range of other authoritative teachers. Their attitude was quite as much docile and reverential as it was self-assertive. Communications were beginning to be reestablished between isolated, provincial New England and the grand circulating currents of European literature, art, philosophy, and science. Through the writings of Coleridge — especially that epoch-making book of his, the " Biographia Literaria " — aspiring young minds in New England were beginning to get hints, and more or less satisfying outlines, of a grand order of thinking, inaugurated in Germany by men of the stamp of Kant, Fichte, and Schelling. Such shorter pamphlets of Fichte as "The Vocation of the Scholar" and "The Destination of Man" rang like the battle-call of the bugle in their ears. The volcanic mind of Carlyle had, moreover, broken out in full eruption; and in the lurid clouds of fuliginous smoke with which he seemed to fill the whole canopy, — clouds lighted up with the fiery glare of the crater burning in his own breast, — sensitive spirits seemed to read once more the revelation of a world sublime and awful as that of Calvinism, but with its symbols plucked out of the fiery heart of the Nineteenth Century instead of out of the heart of the Middle Ages.

Carlyle professed to have made an Alpine, a Himalayan discovery. A new mind had come into the world, an original creation fresh from the hand of God, — a mind towering to the zenith, continental in the base of its foundations, its flanks all glorious with forests and gorges and fertile valleys, teeming with corn and wine. This Mont Blanc, this Mount Everest, he named by the name of Goethe, and cried to the world, "Lo! the man who has experienced everything, suffered everything, closed in Jacob wrestle with everything, only to triumph at last in clear, loving, utterly reconciled Olympian serenity over them all!" There was in those days a note in the voice of Carlyle as of some Titanic Promethean sufferer, long riveted to the bleak rocks of Caucasus, to whom has at last come the glorious prophecy of deliverance; and mightily it stirred the hearts of others.

Still not alone in the way of indirect importation through the medium of the English intellect were the influences coming in that were to throw the more susceptible minds of New

England into ferment. Aspiring young scholars, like George Bancroft, were beginning to cross the ocean to learn the tongue of Germany, and to come into direct contact with its masters in theology, philosophy, and historical criticism. It may seem out of place to name Mr. Bancroft as a force in the development of the Transcendental movement; but such a force he indirectly was through the broader style of thinking, the more ideal philosophy, and the fresher and more vital views of the right interpretation of history he brought back with him from Germany. But along with him went, in a boy of thirteen, to be placed at school there, a boy who had got ready for college at so irrationally early an age that his father was at his wits' ends to know what to do with him till he should be old enough to enter, — one who was destined to exert a still more direct and profound influence on the New England movement. I speak, of course, of Dr. Frederic H. Hedge. There, on its native soil, he laid the foundations of that thorough and idiomatic acquaintance with the German language which, later in life, when he came to be settled as a minister in what is now Arlington, Massachusetts, enabled him to deal at first hand, and as one "to the manner born," with the treasures of German criticism, philosophy, and literature. Still another example in the same way I might instance in Mr. John S. Dwight, who, crossing the ocean and coming under the spell of Bach, Mozart, and Beethoven, did such invaluable work through a long lifetime in helping on the grand march of the Musical Renaissance, from the day of "Old Hundred" and "Coronation" to the day of the Saint Matthew Passion Music and of the Fifth and Seventh Symphonies.

A most serious mistake, however, would it be to regard the Transcendental movement as a simple importation from abroad, a servile imitation of English, French, or German ideas. It was at the last remove from this, and was full of the sap of a spontaneity and freshness all its own. Vasari's old story, of how one sight of a gloriously sculptured Greek sarcophagus in the Campo Santo of Pisa so wrought on the susceptible soul of Niccolà Pisano that, from the hour, all Italian sculpture was revolutionized, was simply repeated on New England soil. Nine tenths of the early Transcendentalists rubbed but lightly against Plato, Plotinus, Saadi, Firdusi, Kant, Fichte, Goethe, Schleiermacher, Schelling; but it was fructifying pollen they bore away from the contact, and by it their own minds were vitally impregnated. And so it was a genuine Columbus cry of, "The New World! the New World!" even though later voyagers were to discover that it was raised only over San Salvador, and not over the whole new continent. For better or worse, then, I repeat it, Mr. Alcott had got hold of Plotinus, Margaret Fuller of Plato and the Greek legends, Dr. Hedge of Kant and Fichte, Emerson of the Hindu and Persian mystics, Mr. Dwight of Goethe and Beethoven, Mr. Ripley of Schleiermacher and later on, of the works of great French socialistic leaders, Theodore Parker of De Wette, James Freeman Clarke and others of the ethics of Jouffroy and the writings of Cousin. From all alike came the cry, "O brave new world that hath such spirits in it!" Simply impossible was it that such men should not begin to see visions and dream dreams of a new and better order of things,— some of them confining themselves to trying to knead the new leaven into the old lump; others demanding, as in the Brook Farm experiment, the outright inauguration of a new social era.

It will be the pleasant task of other lecturers to speak to you in detail of the bearing on Unitarianism of the various special directions into which the new movement soon branched, and on their domain I must not trespass. Enough for me, if I can make vivid to you the essential spirit and inevitable trend of New England Transcendentalism. First and foremost, it can only be rightly conceived as an intellectual, æsthetic, and spiritual *ferment*, not a *strictly reasoned doctrine*. It was a Renaissance of conscious, living faith in the power of reason, in the reality of spiritual insight, in the privilege, beauty, and glory of life. Perhaps, when Emerson described it as the "very Saturnalia of faith," he touched the centre alike in the characteristics of its ecstasy and of its excesses. To understand its full significance, therefore, it is absolutely necessary that we summon clearly before the imagination alike what it reacted against in the past and what it sprang eagerly forward to greet in the future. And the readiest and most picturesque way to do this is to call to our aid the presence of two powerful personalities, — the Achilles and the Hector of the war of two distinct intellectual civilizations that had now joined in the issue of battle. They must unhesitatingly be Ralph Waldo Emerson and Prof. Andrews Norton.

When, in the summer of 1838, Mr. Emerson gave before the Cambridge Divinity School that marvellous address whose perennial beauty and perfume are as entrancing to-day as though exhaled from a fresh-plucked rose or lily, it wrought on a limited class of highly susceptible minds with a sensation only to be paralleled with that of an escape from the crowds, heat, and dust of the stifling city to the scent of the pines and balsams of the forest, or to the stimulating iodine and boundless horizon of the sea-shore. "Behold, new heavens and a new earth!" was their literally ecstatic cry. It had given them back, they said, nature, life, Jesus, God. Here was one, they declared, who saw these ineffable presences and shining ones with his own eyes, interpreted them from his own heart, and adored them in the sanctity of his own conscience.

Far differently, however, did this address act on the minds of others, notably on that of their most stalwart champion, Prof. Andrews Norton. To him Emerson's utterance stood for a wild, visionary, and utterly reckless assault on the very foundations of religious faith. Peremptorily did he challenge and deny its every premise. "Nothing is left," he declared, "that can be called Christianity, if its miraculous character be denied. Its essence is gone: its evidence is annihilated. . . . There can be no intuition, no direct perception of the truth of Christianity, no metaphysical certainty. . . . No proof of his [Christ's] divine commission could be afforded but through miraculous displays of God's power."

Now, of Prof. Andrews Norton no competent man will ever speak but in terms of the highest intellectual and moral respect. His piety, moreover, was of a deep, tender, and inward stamp, as is witnessed by some of his hymns, so uplifting to the devout heart. But here, nevertheless, he stood; and this was his philosophy, or reasoned account of his ground of faith. It was the old Lockian doctrine. Man gets all his ideas through the medium of the senses. These bear witness to the reality of the Now and Here. There must, then, be a direct outward sensation from another realm to introduce into the world trustworthy confidence in a commissioned revealer of the Elsewhere. A miracle is such outward sensation. The suspension or outright infraction of the order of nature is a sense-impression introduced from another realm. The teacher who can do what no other man can,— turn water into wine, rebuke the tempest, raise the dead,— has hereby produced his credentials from on high, and to him must all hearken.

I do not raise this issue here as a preliminary towards a discussion of the question of miracles, but simply in the way of the elucidation of my own subject, — that of Transcendentalism, — whose essential root-principle is here involved. A conversion by miracle ? Why, it is a profanation of the soul ! It is outright denial of the whole foundation of religion in the reason, heart, conscience, spiritual yearning of men. Such was Emerson's high-wrought and passionate feeling on the subject, and it was, I think, — in its broad implications, — the fundamental issue of Transcendentalism.

Ah ! this whole question of external authority and inward recognition, how infinitely wider a one is it than men suspect ! What endless practical issues does it raise in life ! How often I used to meditate its full import in the picture-galleries of Europe, where, in a fresh shape, it was forced on my attention ! There hanging on the walls are the masterpieces of Raphael, Titian, Correggio, Rembrandt, Rubens, along with no end of inferior works. What shall the poor, unaided mind do, turned loose in such a labyrinth ? What assurance that the soul shall not "dilate with the wrong emotion" before an inferior work mistaken for a superior, before a Palma Giovane mistaken for a Titian ? Ah ! is there not a commissioned and duly authenticated Baedeker, guide-book, philosopher, and friend ? Open his pages, and lo ! before every picture marked with *one star* you can feel peacefully assured that you are in the presence of something great, and before every one marked with *two stars* of something superlative. No fear then of abandoning yourself to an unjustifiable emotion. Yes ; and duly subordinated to the spirit, it is an admirable contrivance for saving time and for reserving one's vitality for what is presumably excellent. And yet — and yet — it must never be forgotten what inherent evils there are in having one's work thus done beforehand for him. The pictures one finds out for himself through vital elective-affinity, — those are the ones that make the fructifying impression. Only look at those poor mortals in the gallery who have yielded themselves unconditionally to the courses of the stars. What a lack-lustre in their eyes! What a barren conventionality in their tones!

Sometimes, indeed, this absolute subjection to accredited authority works utterly paralyzing results. There is, for example, in the Accademia of Venice, a picture by Carpaccio, about which Ruskin fulminates in his Mount Sinai way, — fulminates in substance, for I quote him from memory, and confess to far less proficiency in the use of thunder and lightning than he: "Whoever places himself before this picture will be judged by it forever. If he does not see at a glance that here painting reaches its highest culminating apex, let him lay it down as adamantine truth that he is by nature totally destitute of any and every capacity for ever hoping to cherish one true feeling for art." I have given only feebly what is expressed by Ruskin himself with all the vigor of the damnatory clauses of the Athanasian Creed. Well, we know how the Athanasian Creed has always worked on the free development of private sentiment in the Church. Now for the way in which its imitation works on the free development of genuine feeling for beauty. Here come along the gallery, for example, four or five sweet, peach-bloom, demure-looking English girls, each with her Ruskin devoutly in her hands. They have manifestly read their Athanasius; for *Dies iræ, dies illa,*—

"The Day of Wrath, that Dreadful Day,"

is visibly written on every face. And no wonder! "To be or not to be" in the glorious kingdom of beauty is now the question; and there hangs the painting, and over it the flaming sentence of the infallible Judge. They take their seats in awful silence, and hardly dare to lift their eyes. Do they really like the picture? It is hard to tell; for under such stupendous conditions the fledgling maiden mind does not work spontaneously. Anyhow, like it they must, or else, "without doubt, perish everlastingly." And so they think they do, and go away so relieved.

"Oh, you dear, sweet, silly girls!" I was often impelled to cry over such a group, "it is all right that you should be under authority, but why not under the authority of some one who has an inkling at least of the law of the natural development of the human mind? Why, instead of this annihilating Ruskin, should you not have some sensible father, uncle, or elder brother, who would merely turn you loose here, and say: 'Now girls, fearlessly and honestly, try for yourselves what you really enjoy and what you do not enjoy; no matter whether it be only the simplest face or the simplest figure, so long as it is your own genuine impression. From one genuine impression you may go on to another, and another, and still another; and who knows at what height you may arrive at last in your enjoyment of the beauty, pathos, and sublimity of these masterpieces? But this simple travesty of education, why, it is falsifying, it is paralyzing your natural capacities from the very start.'"

And now, in conclusion, let me say that I do not know of any better way of illustrating what seems to me the root-idea of New England Transcendentalism than through just this picture-gallery experience of my own in Europe. It is an illustration which gives to the discussion the real breadth I would like to impart to it. In truth, it was no simple theological issue these eager men and women were debating in the question of miracles or in the question of any external authority like that insisted on for the Bible. Many of them had no objection to the admission of miracles, so long as they were not made tests of truth. It was a far wider reaching question, and one that affects our attitude to all that is beautiful, noble, and divine in life,—namely, that of the competency of mind to spontaneously recognize it. At this point Transcendentalism took resolute and final stand. With your own eyes must you see. If color-blind, then in vain for you arches the prismatic glory of the rainbow, even though Iris herself should glide down to assure you it is beautiful. Now, in what way this differs from the absolute imperative of the Beatitudes of the Sermon on the Mount I confess myself constitutionally incapable of perceiving. But it was the crowning glory of the Transcendentalists that they made this principle co-terminous with the universe, prophetically anticipating in the spirit those later material revelations of the spectroscope, which proclaim how precisely the same elements that are burning and shining in our own little planet are burning and shining in Sirius and the Sun. What! shall we ban and bar a rose because it originated in Persia, or a lotus because it first floated on the bosom of the Nile? was their instinctive thought. Why, then, ban and bar any beautiful flower of the spirit, because first unfolding its petals and breathing forth its perfume in a Hindu, Parsee, or Sufi garden of the Soul? Theirs as Transcendentalists to justify their name by simply transcending all those arbitrary boundaries of creed, race, nationality, local self-conceit, which narrow, harden, and poison the human mind, till it becomes constitutionally incapable of truly knowing and loving Him of whom, through whom, and to whom are all things, to whom be glory forever. And so, in this direction, the service of Transcendentalism to the future development of Unitarianism was priceless; and for one, I most heartily concur in the words with which Rev. Joseph Henry Allen sums up his own conviction on the subject. "Transcendentalism," he says, "melted quite thoroughly the crust that was beginning to form on the somewhat chilly current of liberal theology. . . . Indeed, it is the great felicity of free religious thought in this country, in its later unfolding, that it had its birth in a sentiment so poetic, so generous, so devout, so open to all the humanities as well as to the widest sympathies of philosophy and the higher literature."

Am I not right, then, in characterizing Transcendentalism as the New England Renaissance?

THEODORE PARKER.

BY SAMUEL BARRETT STEWART.

IT is allowable to felicitate ourselves, I think, upon the fact that Unitarianism is now a symbol for many convictions of religion of whose virtue and sanity its earlier exponents were profoundly ignorant, or if not ignorant, sceptical; that it has at length agreed to many things that in years past it fiercely combated. How the family has multiplied, by birth, by adoption, by incorporation! The hardy pioneering little anti-Trinitarian colony of old is to-day like a republic, comprising as it were a multitude of separate States, as to its manifold speculative and theological discriminations, but held closely, fraternally together by a governing unit of tendency and purpose.

Best of all, the symbol remains a constant. Like the greater name Christian, that at first stood for a single fact, the name Unitarian now stands for an order of religious thought that unfolds and unfolds, a movement of thought that grows more critical and philosophic, at the same time it becomes more sympathetic, more inclusive, and more constructive. Narrow and constrained were the lines of thought as our Unitarian fathers projected them. How broad, free, and sweeping they are beginning to look! What variety of philosophy and criticism they now include! What range of scholarship, what reformers, what defenders, what idealists, what builders and organizers, what saints we have, and what martyrs!

It would be an indelicate presumption on our part to draw a denominational cordon around the free and lofty soul of Emerson. It would be equally so to draw it around the names of Parker and many of his dear friends and followers in liberty, did we restrict Unitarianism rigidly to its past or even its present definitions, to many of which they objected, and in consequence of which they either withdrew from or were left out of its household economies. Happily, however, "that great new star, a beauty and a mystery, that once rose in the winter nights and hung over Boston," has been a "perennial inspiration" not only to those who looked up then, but to those who now follow its luminous track. Happily, also, the daring and prophetic voice of Parker, to which men once listened breathlessly, and yet almost shrank from, echoing down the decades, has lost its harsher accents. Happily, also, the power of thought and the subtler power of the Time-Spirit have been so influential with us all that to-day we find ourselves sitting easily and sympathetically in the companionship of the great and noble dead. It is as if nothing had happened. In the essentials, in the profounder things, we have come to close understanding.

Theodore Parker is the popular representative of an influx of new thought into Unitarianism, and of a new impulse and energy imparted to its ethical gospel. The first large period of Unitarianism closed with Channing, and up to Parker's time its business was mainly to affirm anti-Orthodox or anti-Calvinistic teachings. These were found in new readings of the Testament, and especially in a nobler and truer conception of human nature and of the relations of man to God. All the earlier efforts to show the errors and cruelties of Orthodoxy, and to set forth the promises of the better faith, had been magnificently summarized by Channing, the moral grandeur of whose affirmations had advanced Unitarianism, intellectually at least, to a bold and commanding position. Nor was Unitarianism all the while strictly polemical; it was philanthropic also; and in nothing was Channing more sublime in expression, and a more permanent authority, than in his great discourses upon social morals, upon labor, culture, education, and, in general, upon intellectual and political freedom. What indebtedness Parker felt to this great man he has repeatedly expressed in his journals and correspondence, and especially in his sermon upon Channing's life and services.[1]

It was during these times, when Transcendentalism was leavening the New England mind, when the German philosophies and the varieties of Biblical criticism were getting in vogue, and in our Liberal schools men were at work upon the task of elucidating the history and traditions of Christianity, that there appeared among us a prodigy of learning, a rugged, warm-souled, eloquent preacher of piety and righteousness, ruthless of popular Christian traditions, a terror to the church and clergy alike, — Theodore Parker. He had sprung up in a little village rich in traditions of virtue and patriotism, himself full of the natural juices of the soil, outwardly shaped by physical toils, and in intellectual and moral fibre a firm, unbending, luxuriant, and (to use his own favorite adjective) "handsome" oak. A voracious, unsated plant, he had absorbed not only the wealth of his own surroundings, the knowledge of men and Nature and books, but the intellectual wealth of the living world and of ages past. It is almost impossible to dissociate him from the earth he loved and in which he everywhere felt the presence of law and

---

[1] Found in Dr. Clarke's Selections from his Writings, published by the American Unitarian Association.

love and beauty. More than most great men he seems of original derivation, a first-born son of the soil, like one of Deucalion's ready-made men out of the rocks, full-breasted, full-fed throughout with such noble instincts and passions as befit a lusty warrior to carry him through the battles of the world. If ever in any man's clay divine fire raged, it raged in his. And yet the smell of the earth was upon his garments; he was intensely human.

Parker was nourished equally at the breasts of Puritanism and of Patriotism; but whatever patriotic loves, whatever conscience may have reposed in his ancestry, whatever intellect or religious affection, they but feebly explain his tremendous mental energy, the moral tenacity and firmness of his lifepurpose, his great humanity, and the tenderness of religious sentiment generated in his strong manly nature by a spiritual chemistry that is the despair of knowledge. A man of inspirations, mental and moral, he indeed was, so little was there in his constitution of the traditional, so little of the conventional, so much, on the contrary, of the extraordinary. From very youth he was spurred and driven by an insatiate passion for knowledge. No plodding farm-life should bemire his quick, aspiring intellect! Long before the famous advice, he had "hitched his wagon to a star," and was driving on a celestial highway at white heat.

But if a man of inspirations, where one with such capacity for work, with such burdening sense of the necessity of it and such passion for it? Such work as Harvard College required of a man in those days he could despatch in a single year. Three hundred and twenty solid books were an easy year's work for his country-trained vigor. His resolutions were to respect six hours sleep, seven if possible, eight better still; but at no time was he capable of checking at the safe and appointed moment the momentum of a fearfully speeding brain. Nothing short of compassing the very globe, of comprehending the whole organic and historic development of mankind, would satisfy his inordinate ambition. His mother-tongue was not enough; he must know all languages, spoken, unspoken, accessible, inaccessible, the better to accomplish his purpose; the wonderfullest thing of all being the proficiency which he attained as a linguist, despite the isolation of New England and the scarcity of facilities.

Let us keep a few dates in mind. Parker was born in Lexington in 1810; was a farmer's boy at farmer's work until his twentieth birthday, when he entered Harvard College. Meantime he had taught a few winter schools and had read immensely. What was required of college work was easily done in a year; he left without a diploma: the degree of A.M. was conferred upon him some years later. The year following (1831) he instructed in a private school in Boston, the next two taught a school of his own in Watertown. Before he was twenty-four he entered the Divinity School nearly a year in advance. After graduation he "candidated" all the way from Cape Cod to the Connecticut River; projected an endless amount of work; followed up his reading and study with unintermitted zeal; and very naturally defeated the intention to restore his impaired health. In June, 1837, he was ordained at West Roxbury, when he was not quite twenty-seven years old.

The ten years of preparation for professional life, which was naturally determined upon in his own mind as the ministry, differ in no respect from later years in two things at least; namely, an unappeased ambition for the service of God and humanity, and an almost superhuman degree of toil in that service. And if in his early life he had poverty of means to contend with, the greater poverty under which it would seem that he chafed was the poverty of the days and the hours and the very moments.

Many things explain how it was that his thoughts and convictions grew into an armed host that was soon to spread anxiety and alarm in the quiet places of the churches of America and through the strongholds of human slavery. Parker's favorite analysis of the human spirit — he made it the framework of all his preaching — was into four primary faculties, the intellectual, the moral, the affectional, and the religious. " Love of truth is the piety of the intellect. Love of justice is the moral part of piety. Love is the piety of the affections. The soul has its own functions ; God is the object of it." I speak of this here, however, only to remark upon the large quantity of each and all these faculties that this man contained in himself. I have already intimated what was his intellectual piety, — his love of truth and hot pursuit of it, — and what huge masses of knowledge he had heaped up and now held in reserve to feed and sustain him in the effort to arouse the ethical and spiritual life of his countrymen. Of his moral passion and his strong piety toward God and toward man I can only say that to know it one must read the almost tragic story of his swiftly moving life, the confessions of his correspondence and the truer confessions of his solitude, go through the history of his heroic leadership in the great conflict for human rights, feel the fervor and the motive of his daily sermons ; one must linger over the little volume of " Prayers," the meditations of a tender soul breathing the Infinite Father's love and compassion, revealing the deeps of human love and pain, all the sources of gratitude, all the objects of duty ; one must learn how firmly held were his moral standards, and how loyally too, through strife and scorn and hatred ; must learn the tenderness and fidelity of his friendships, and the buoyancy of his courageous heart, — to know how completely what he called the primary functions of the soul had possession of his capacious bosom.

Many special characteristics served him. Whatever he felt to be truth and duty he held to with an iron grip. Fear was something of which there was no trace in his blood. To retreat would have been as impossible for him as for Mars to turn back in his orbit. Then he had spontaneous command of all his resources; knowledge more than he needed; method, — a natural, easy, telling method for work and for discourse; a prodigious memory, — a memory that could hold five hundred lines after a single reading; tact of living, native quality; sentiment, all kinds and degrees of it; logic and skill in argument; invective, wit, satire, humor, persuasion, — all these were at his instant beck and call. Beyond most men God had endowed him with language, and his natural expression he had cultivated after the best models of popular address; so that though lacking the graces of oratory, plain people and cultivated alike were enchanted by his speech. Few men have ever spoken to the masses with so much erudition and refinement of expression, so great copiousness of thought and illustration, at the same time so unaffectedly, so directly, so tersely, with so much simplicity, warmth, and affection.

It seems necessary to say these things in order that we may appreciate the sweeping force and contagion of interest with which the new notions of religion and of Christianity which he promulgated invaded New England and, indeed, America. It must not be supposed, however, that Parker was the originator of the new thought, or that he was the only worker in the field. A greater voice than his, a still, magnetic voice of Nature and of Life, the voice of Emerson, was already prophesying the same things in laconic and original phrase. What message Parker had to deliver was but the freight of Transcendentalism which had for a long time been afloat as a kind of phantom-ship to the eyes of New England church-going people. There were, moreover, inquiring Unitarians who had taken the risk to "reason beyond the limits of reason," whom Parker would seize by the hand and give courage for the leap. Contemporary with him were many brilliant and devoted men who in their own more reserved ways were at work on the same problems into which Parker had thrust the plough, and was furrowing with less sympathetic, less tentative, but more positive and, as it seemed to most persons, most audacious methods, — men, some of whom we now call venerable, and who receive our love and homage for scholarship and eloquence and for their heroism in moral causes, and for their contributions to the permanent literature of Liberal Christianity. And the fact that there were some persons determined that "Theodore Parker should have a chance to be heard," shows that there were elements of thought already in the popular mind that needed only an organizing and a crystallizing touch to become vital.

Parker wrote, "As for my theology, it has grown out of me as naturally as my arm has grown out of my body." A natural growth it was, no doubt; but it was a growth cultivated by a self-informing and originally working mind bent upon practical ends and applications. For little as we find to distinguish his earlier theological sense from that of the current Unitarianism in which he was reared and under whose tuition he received his first lessons, his mind was too receptive, too daring and inquisitive, to abide long the partial conquests that Unitarianism had made. His Divinity School studies, his early contributions to the "Christian Examiner" and the "Dial," and his studies of Biblical criticism at West Roxbury, show whither the tide was setting. Even before his settlement he had proposed to answer some significant questions; for example: What is the extent of known supernatural revelation made to man? What is the foundation of the authority of Jesus Christ? Is Christianity to be a universal religion? What is the foundation of religion in man, the design of miracles, and so forth?

These were very different questions from those which Unitarians had been usually asking. They concerned much more searching problems, not the accidental characteristics of Christian doctrine, but the traditional conceptions of Christianity; they concerned Christianity as a form of the Absolute Religion; in fact, the sources and practical meanings of Religion itself. In part they were philosophical, in part historical, in part critical; in the end they were to be made intensely practical, and, as a whole, to produce widespread and heated discussion.

The first expression that gave him great publicity, and brought on the unhappy controversy with his Unitarian brethren, was the South Boston Sermon on "the Transient and the Permanent in Christianity" (May 19, 1841). No better subject could have been chosen, no better title, to express what was to be the trend of his whole ministry of religious reconstruction; for his essential motive, as he subsequently stated it, was "to recall men from the transient form to the eternal substance, from outward and false belief to real inward life; from partial theology and its idols of human device to universal religion and its living, Infinite God; from the temples of human folly and sin which every day crumble and fall, to the inner sanctuary of the heart, where the still small voice will never cease to speak." "Looking at the word of Jesus, at real Christianity," he says, "at the pure religion he taught, nothing appears more fixed and certain; but looking at the history of what men call Christianity, nothing seems more uncertain and perishable." And this is what he unfolds, showing how form and dogma are but the accident and not the substance of Christianity, with what false idolatry the Bible is contemplated, how shifting men's notions have been of the origin and nature of it and of the nature and authority of Christ, and how Christianity is made to rest on the personal authority of the teachings of Jesus, and not on their immutable truth. Turning the picture, he shows the original word of Jesus, divested of historical accretions, "as a very simple thing, very simple; as absolute pure morality, absolute pure religion, the love of man and the love of God." Only could men and society be once rooted and grounded in these axiomatic, these intuitive, these universal truths, oh, how soon (was the purport of his faith) might we hope for their emancipation from the slaveries of vice and superstition!

At that time we should have listened, as we should to-day, spellbound, the utterance was so fluent and exhilarating, with such promise of new piety and new ethics. The sermon had its peccadilloes of expression; Parker was always apt to tease the sense of propriety in those against whom he was contending, by putting in incongruous juxtaposition things which they were wont to separate as sacred and profane. But all his irreverences, as people thought them, were but the spontaneities of a man who spoke his mind in homely and familiar terms, untempered by fine-spun, apologetic, or carefully considered phrase. The sentiment of the sermon was refreshing as a morning shower. But Orthodoxy raised the cry, "Infidel! Atheist!" and even Unitarians were disturbed lest the young enthusiast, for whose learning and eloquence and earnestness they had such admiration, and in whose career they were reposing the largest hopes, was tumbling the truths of Christianity, along with its errors, all together into a general wreck.

This sermon will always be marked as perhaps an unconscious introduction to a great life-work. It had its effect. And yet he had only "thrown out" a few things. It remained to expand and to fortify himself. The opportunity was afforded by a course of lectures which were almost immediately asked for by his Boston friends. These lectures were given in the winter of 1841-42, and were published the following spring as the "Discourse of Religion." Into them he threw his best thought and scholarship, and all the fervor of his soul. He had not taken his stand carelessly; he had had four years experience as a minister, and in study was sure of his ground. Moreover, the discussion of the *sermon* had stirred him, and he was tremendously in earnest. A few months before he had written in his journal, "I intend in the coming year to let out all the force of Transcendentalism that is in me. Come what may come, I will let off the truth as fast as it comes." And in the same vein, we may say, "let it off" he did, "just level to the people's ear."

I think I shall not mistake the purpose of this lecture in giving the briefest possible abstract of this celebrated discourse. It has five parts, and considers the "religious element and its manifestations," "inspiration," "Christianity," "the Bible," and "the Church." His starting-point is the spontaneously active religious consciousness as a primary element of man's constitution. This implies the existence of God, or an idea of God, on which we depend, as certainly as the senses imply the existence of a physical world; the universality of worship, experience, and the analysis of man's nature all pointing to it. The sentiment is universal; it transcends will and understanding; it is an intuition.

But the conception of God (the distinction between the idea of God and the conception of God is not made very plain) varies with the developing reason of mankind, so that we have fetichism, polytheism, pantheism, dualism, monotheism as historical phenomena of religion, and expressing it more or less completely. In other words, the consciousness of religion has taken a great variety of intellectual forms, wearing them as garments, casting off the old and putting on new, manifold errors, superstitions, and fanaticisms included in them; itself, however, the germ, absolutely good and pure, quick and vital, having been the secret of these unfoldings. This germ is the absolute religion; and it has often expressed itself most beautifully, in all historical religions, in the noblest and divinest individual characters.

As for the personality of God, our conception must necessarily be that of finite personality, personality limited by human imperfections; and we must separate the substantial from the phenomenal; then we shall contemplate God as Spirit, Being, Cause, Knowledge, Love. As such, God dwells in Nature and in man; law and beauty in the outward world, truth and love in the mind of man, being his perpetual manifestations. Nor is he transiently active, as in alleged miracles, but immanent and constant. Inspiration, therefore, is not phenomenal and special, but natural and universal, and depends upon the " quantity of our being and the quality of our obedience."

Thus he approaches Christianity. The main question is, Is Christianity the Absolute Religion? By eliminating transient dogmas from historical Christianity, he finds the permanent truth, that is, pure Christianity, or the Absolute Religion. If we take the current historical conceptions of the words of Jesus for Christianity, it is very far from being Absolute Religion; these conceptions are merely forms of it. But if we mean by Christianity the simple truth as Jesus taught and lived it, it is absolute morality, absolute piety.

It remains to inquire into the historical forms of religion, especially the Christianity of tradition and accretion. This is a matter of testimony. An examination of the Gospels yields imperfect and conflicting representations of Jesus; and testimony to the miracles upon which the authority of his message has been supposed to rest is defective. Still, it is easy to find the essential word of Jesus, — a word that responds to the universal consciousness of religion, and is inherent in all historical religions. It is plain, also, that Jesus is the purest manifestation of divine thought and of religious life in man, and as such the Gospels, in the light of reason and human sympathy, unmistakably represent him.

The concluding chapters have to do with the natural development of the Bible as a literature, disarming Orthodoxy of its infallible letter and text; also, with the speculative errors of Catholicism and Protestantism, closing with admonitions, to Unitarians especially, to advance a step farther and plant themselves on more stable ground.

Little as we should be disturbed now by the doctrine in the main, it did mean a complete overthrow of the traditional beliefs of the popular church. It was the signal for a revolution, and was too much even for Unitarians of that day; and it is not strange that matters turned as they did, and that Parker was left to fight out his battle comparatively alone. The heresy was obvious. He had denied the conventional belief in a supernatural revelation, in a mediatorial Christ, and in a miraculous attestation of Christianity. He had brought discredit upon the literal truth of the Gospel record. "If this teaching is to prevail," men said, "it is all over with traditional Christianity."

Undoubtedly it was a defect of the "Discourse" that it did some injustice to the values of many historical doctrines and institutions of Christianity that had been worked out of the profoundest religious experience and the highest sense of utility, — thoughts, sentiments, and ceremonials that had been wings and feet to the original gospel. Sublime and tender, also, as were its delineations of the character and spirit of Jesus, and of the ineffable beauty and the permanence of his teachings, almost no one was prepared to see swept away the old and trusted vehicles that had transported him, so faithfully and so punctually, from station to station of the developing life of Christendom. From this point of view the "Discourse" was desolating. But, on the other hand, it was a prophetic anticipation and announcement of a greater, a calmer, a juster thought that was soon to come and take possession of us, and which, happily, we see has been rapidly coming. Henceforth there were new thoughts of religion abroad. Parker had furnished New England with material for years and years of every-day discussion, — with Theism and the Absolute Religion, with universal inspiration, the human origin and transmission of the Bible, the natural and human Jesus, immortality its own witness, and with piety without sacraments. Here were great facts for examination; great truths to which men were to find their way with much difficulty and pain; great truths to be absorbed. Few were prepared to listen to them, much less to receive them; few had courage to utter them. Only the young Parker, with Luther-like independence, frankness, fulness of knowledge, positiveness of conviction, and power and grace of speech, could do it; only the young Parker, whose blood was aroused by a moral passion for the revival of that sincerity and nobility of religious life in the people — in the nation, let us say — which he believed that the excesses of ecclesiasticism, the painful theologies of the day, the blindness of the world to the imperishable truths of the original Christianity, and the timidity of the clergy were making impossible.

The "Discourse of Religion" is the only formal exposition of his theology. It was made when he was little more than thirty years old, and remained the unmodified, dogmatic groundwork of his whole ministry.

The enthusiasm with which this revolutionary and stimulating version of the real gospel of Christianity was received on the one hand, and the bitter denunciations of it on the other, together with his own desire to give it the widest possible publicity, soon brought him out of his secluded little country parish into this great centre of thought and life. Parker was made, as has been repeatedly said, for great "uses;" his large intellect was stanchly built to carry on commerce with great principles, with great duties, and with great men, — to deal with moral and social reformation in its largest aspects. The little West Roxbury meeting-house furnished but a toy pulpit for a giant preacher. The only pulpit commensurate with his magnitude was the platform of the Melodeon and the greater platform of Music Hall. No church could contain him; already he was outside the church; already his message seemed to be less a message to be given through the church than to the church itself, — a greater message also of righteousness to the nation which the church was refusing to deliver.

Indeed, from the study of the "Discourse of Religion" and, in fact, of all the sermons of Parker, one cannot help feeling how he was proceeding to help men to see the needed and always overlooked complement to traditional religion. The habit of mankind is to refer the revealing consciousness of God to the past; to look upon the creation as a thing of yesterday and not of the eternal to-day; and to feel that the only authoritative manifestations of truth and piety are those with which its traditions have familiarized it. To him the Christian world seemed to be everywhere and always looking backward, absorbed in the preservation of its creeds born of a less enlightened reason, and in the perpetuation of symbols once poetic but now prosaic, and devoid of beauty and utility; to him the church seemed to be a close, airless, tomblike sanctuary of memories, instead of a living organism throbbing with the heart-beats of a quick and healthy conscience, and directed in its activities by the cry of human despair and need. With his great warm heart intent upon the highest service, he was impatient with what he saw of the tithing of mint, anise, and cumin, and the forgetting of the weightier matters of love and righteousness. It was this habit he set himself to combat. His desire was to gain a recognition of the fact that the essential condition of the vitality of religion and of its usefulness is in the immediateness and the constancy of the manifestations of the Indwelling Spirit. Indeed, so powerfully was he exercised by the feeling that if men would but obey the voice of the living God in the conscience and in the affections, the end of religion would be answered, that, if he was sometimes driven to the extreme of scarcely crediting traditional and institutional religion with its real values, it was because the denial of it was made a condition of the popular theology. This faith was with him not only a fundamental conviction, but a moving force with which his whole being was agitated. Through this great and energizing conviction alone had he any hope for a living piety among men.

The doctrine was not new, but somehow it had never made that kindling impression which he felt that it ought to make, and which he happily caused it to make. For there was something in his elucidation of it and in the emphasis that he laid upon it, in his perpetual reiteration of it, in the dogmatic, positive, easily understood terms in which he put it, that gave an entirely new aspect to the old ideas of revelation and of inspiration with which people were laboring on in such ignorance, and with such pitifully anxious and timid minds.

Parker's God was a living God in Nature and in man. So real, so poetic was his sense of God in Nature that it was almost as if he were pantheistic. And yet everything that might imply this was but the extravagance of his worshipful sense of the Law, the Beauty, the Economies, and Providences of the natural world. His love of Nature was intense. So infinite was Nature, so sublime, so creative, so good, that he surrendered himself to it in the ecstasy of adoration. Greater yet was his adoration of the conscience. Conscience was a word constantly upon his lips, perhaps the oftenest repeated of his potent words. It was with sternest command that he bade men bow down before the absolute moral law of their being. Conscience was very God.

Now, to such a man it is no wonder that the inanities of speculative Christianity, the thoughtless reverence of ancient form and phrase, and the indirectness or the silence of the church as to the consuming sins of society, were an unpardonable offence. Scarcely could he restrain the withering satire that involuntarily sprang to his lips.

Moreover, it was in these things that he discovered the sources of a widespread impiety, both intellectual and practical. The denial of God, in a speculative sense, was as common then as it is now, as it is always, howsoever we may phrase it. And it was not very long before he found the occasion for a course of sermons on "Atheism as Theory and

Atheism as Ethics," and on "Theism as Theory and Theism as Ethics." As was his wont, he treats the subjects somewhat diffusely and spontaneously; they were levelled, as were all his addresses and writings of whatsoever sort, to the comprehension of the masses. The reader must not look for the acumen that he finds in modern discussions of the speculative part of these questions; but in practical meanings they have tremendous force and strength.

The scheme of God as perfect cause, as perfect providence working in the world of matter, in the world of life and being, in the world of humanity in its vast historical developments, in the experience of the individual, — this is the scheme of speculative theism. Then the scheme of practical theism is that the idea of God leads to the absolute love of him, to trust in him, to real joy and tranquillity and rest in him, these expanding the soul in well-proportioned parts for perfect beauty and piety. The sacrament of piety supplements the sanctions of the conscience. These together constitute the Absolute Religion which issues in obedience to physical, domestic, and social law whereby man has a perfect body, home becomes pure and woman elevated; whereby temperance and chastity prevail, and men deal justly one with another, and poverty and slavery and vice cease, and man grows truly worshipful.

This, I repeat, was a scheme of theoretical and practical theism which, filled out and clothed upon with his wealth of the knowledge of Nature and of man, vitalized with his moral vigor and made eloquent with his warm human feeling, constitutes one of the most powerful appeals to the popular heart for pure worship and pure conduct, to be found in the annals of the American pulpit.

But after all has been said, so far as Christianity is concerned, as the analysis of the "Discourse" plainly showed us, Parker did not expound the Absolute Religion at the expense of anything vital and essential in the ministry of the Founder of Christianity. Precious, indeed, did he hold the one sacred and idolized name of the Christian world. Only for the confused and confusing conception of Jesus that has been transmitted by speculative Christianity, he substituted the plain, honest, natural, tangible notion of his humanity. Unitarianism had not then escaped the dust of the speculative workshop, and the mediatorial office of Jesus was still felt to be in some sense necessary to the perfect adjustment of man's spiritual relations to his Maker. To abolish the office altogether required that the real nature and service of Jesus should be set forth in distinct and unmistakable terms. Who has ever done it more tenderly, more impressively? Who has ever drawn the portrait of the great Friend of Mankind in truer lines and in purer color? Who, rather, has called us away, as he has done, from the false and exaggerated drawings of speculative Christianity, to know and enjoy the original, so fathomless in its practical and spiritual meanings? Indeed, the service which he rendered in making the humanity of Jesus distinguished cannot be overestimated, inasmuch as his was one of the first reverent and effective efforts to rescue the ethical and spiritual utilities of his mission from the obscurity into which they were thrown by the mediatorial and sacrificial scheme of popular Christianity.

But time warns us to hasten on to another topic. There is a sense in which Parker contributed immensely to the vitality of the doctrine of immortality. There was no belief in which he was more impregnable than in his belief in the immortal life. He held the future life within the compass, as it were, of mathematical certainties. With him it was something that admitted of no doubt or question. "Let me be sure of two things," he said, "first, of thine Infinite Perfection, O Father in Heaven, then of my own immortality, and I am safe. I fear nothing. I am not a transient bubble on the sea of time; I shall outlast the Everlasting Hills." The very certainty, the very absoluteness of his faith in the immortal life is almost startling. For it is not merely a hope; it is not a yearning; it is knowledge itself. As Mr. J. H. Allen has finely said, — "With most men the best part of their religion is far from being that which lies in the clear, glaring light of consciousness, or what they could give the best account of to themselves. The twilight atmosphere of mystery in which our lives are wrapped — from clear light shading off imperceptibly to obscurity and gloom — is the sphere where most of our pious thoughts and emotions lie. In Theodore Parker it was almost as if this shadowy sphere did not exist. . . . He *knew* he was immortal. Any demand of proof was an impertinence. Any offer of historical evidence was an affront to his living faith."

And now it must be added how great a gain it was to the faith and piety of many that he did thus point out, absolutely and dogmatically it may be, a more unfailing source of assurance than the authority of historical revelation; namely, the universal consciousness of spiritual and immortal relations. To the unspiritual it might seem a less certain assurance than some historical and miraculous testimony; nevertheless, it must eventually have been a revelation to them of the unfathomable deeps and mysteries of their own being. And it was in this sense that to those who were sceptical of the supernatural evidences of the doctrine, the assurances of the Absolute Religion were of untold strength and comfort.

And it was not only of immortality that there was in his mind a practical certainty. There was the same practical certainty of the personal and immediate providence of God. Speculation never disturbed his practical sense of things. So human, so affectionate was his sense of God, that he must cry out "O Thou who art our Father and our Mother!"

Parker loved books, loved philosophy, theology, all sciences, indeed; loved the pursuit of truth for its own sake. But a mightier love swayed him, — the love of piety and righteousness in mankind; and ere his feet were planted upon the platform which afterward became the tribunal where the morals and motives of people and statesmen alike were brought to solemn judgment, his whole soul became absorbed in the eradication of the one great iniquity that from the beginning had been preying upon the vitals of the nation. In that holy crusade to break the chains of the slave his was a tireless voice to lead the brave, to shame the cowardly, and to outwit the politic. And it was by virtue of his power as a bold and uncompromising social reformer, that he gave new ethical impulse not only to the dull conscience of the people as a political body, but also to its ecclesiastical conscience. For somehow men began to see that there was a higher law than the traditional Christianity that had so long permitted or found excuse for a great crime against humanity. And thus the emancipation of the slave began to mean with us something more than emancipation from a form of human and political injustice; it began to mean an emancipation of the living conscience from the bondage of the ethics of a supposed supernatural revelation; the emancipation, also, of the saving, living Jesus of humanity from the vague inoperative notion of the mystical Christ.

There is no time, were it my purpose, to linger over the

sublime service of Parker to the cause of humanity and justice. His large sympathies soon exhausted his strength. All men were to him brothers, — the poor, the ignorant, the suffering; they came close to his heart. He remembered their cause in all his daily prayer and discourse. The service of the great and good and gifted, — that also he remembered. No opportune moment did he miss to declare to his fellow-citizens the service of their country's historic leaders, Franklin, Washington, Jefferson, Adams, Webster, Quincy; to instruct them in their virtues and to warn them of their follies. And if in his delineations of character and in his estimate of men's service, while he was tenderly eulogistic, he was stern and implacable, his motive was one of patriotism, and of fidelity to honor and sincerity. God had not made him to prophesy smooth things; he had made him to prophesy righteousness and truth.

In passing, we must also remember that Parker rendered no inconsiderable service in stimulating, to say the least, the desire among scholars to engage in the study of the common origins and characteristics of the historical religions in which many of our own clergymen have distinguished themselves. Though he did little of this kind of work in any formal way, it was one of his cherished but forbidden ambitions to do so; the whole range of it came under his belief in the common ethical and religious consciousness of mankind. There is no doubt, I imagine, that he was a great support and inspiration to his dear and life-long friend and defender, James Freeman Clarke, in his noble contribution to literature on the "Comparative Study of Religions." I suspect, also, that Samuel Johnson's "Oriental Religions" had some of the rootlets of its inspiration in this great preacher's exposition of the Absolute Religion. Then it must be added that he was one of the powerful, though distant, contributing causes of the Free Religious movement, whose ground is the Absolute Religion.

And through all these sources we see how our New England Unitarianism has been stimulated to larger and healthier life. Whatever may have been the heart-breakings over the conflicts between Theism and Christianity, or the Absolute Religion and Christianity, or Free Religion and Christianity, concerning the meanings of Christianity, and all the minor themes of miracle and historical testimony, over this and that method of criticism, unagreed as we still are, and shall always be, and ought always to be, if we have any desire of life and growth, there has been a manifest greatening of thought and broadening of fellowship.

Nor must we omit to mention the infusion of tonic into our pulpit expression, for which Parker must be in a measure credited. Most is due to Emerson, without doubt; but much is certainly due to Parker. The "Ten Sermons" are fresh as a handful of flowers gathered from meadows and hillsides; the west wind blows through them; the song of the birds lingers in them. There is nothing in his sermons scholastic, bookish, dry-as-dust. There could be no sleep where Parker was. Every sentence is succulent. There is vivacity, health, and an optimistic glow in every paragraph. Nor is there any shrinking from plain truth plainly spoken. If the truth offend, there is hope. Such plainness often cuts to the quick; and only those, I think, who drew near to the heart of this noble and heroic man knew that there was no malice in him.

Parker's influence among the Liberal churches around him was, in many instances, temporarily disastrous to their tranquillity. His fearlessness and sincerity were contagious. Young ministers caught new life; people in the pews caught it; and there were many breaches, personal and social, long in healing. These, however, were but unavoidable incidents attending the breaking up of the hard crust of traditionalism for the entrance of air and light, and for the germination of healthier fruit.

Parker was in some sense a martyr; and his martyrdom was followed by many lesser, and yet not less painful, martyrdoms. Through the influence of that sincere, outspoken, uncompromising, but scattered company of independent men, whose hearts and souls beat responsive to the moral enthusiasm of his voice, who refused to be tied to any creed or form, or to bow to any idols of wealth or society, there has come at last a kindlier tolerance, a warmer fellowship, and a more energetic effort to reach the world with a rational and comforting faith.

Parker was neither a poet nor a philosopher in the strictest sense. Deep answereth not unto deep as in his great contemporary, Emerson. He was a worker in the solid things of practical duty. He was, moreover, infinitely less a destroyer than a builder. If he drove the plough deep in, he turned up the soil in richer condition for the sower.

Parker was spared the awful spectacle of the long physical struggle which he foresaw, and into which his burning sense of justice helped to plunge the nation. Nor did he witness the morning sun-burst of freedom over all the land, and the quick awakening of the greater and healthier energies of the American people. Neither was he permitted to enjoy the broader theological sense, the higher criticism, the growing sympathy of religions, and the larger recognition of the validity of the eternal truths underlying all forms of faith for human salvation, which prevail more and more with the growth of knowledge and the closer intercourse of the peoples of the earth.

At the meridian of his manly powers he sank down in a foreign land, overworked and exhausted, but still clinging to the life he loved for the sake of its divine tasks, and rests surrounded by the tombs of many illustrious souls of the Reformation, to whom he was kindred in spirit and in work.

UNITARIANISM AND MODERN LITERATURE.

BY FRANCIS B. HORNBROOKE.

UNITARIANISM and Literature may be regarded in two ways. We may either review the names of those connected with the Unitarian movement who have won an honorable place in literature, or we may consider how much of the religious thought and feeling, which finds glad welcome in our Unitarian churches, also finds expression in modern literature. By taking the first course, and by trying to designate those Unitarians who deserve recognition in modern literature, one soon finds that he has chosen a pleasant but at the same time a most difficult task, — pleasant because so many praiseworthy names crowd upon the memory; and difficult, because in spite of the utmost care it is almost impossible not to omit names which may seem to others as worthy of remembrance as many who have been mentioned. There is another and more serious difficulty. Writers who deserve ample recognition for the work they have done in theology, or in science, or in historical research, often cannot be counted among those who have added to the wealth of our literature. The line which separates useful contribution from literary achievement is a shadowy one; and to make a definition which will justify the inclusion of one name and the exclusion of another is practically impossible. In matters of this kind much must be allowed to the undefinable tastes of individual minds. Names will be passed over by one which will seem to another to deserve notice. If, therefore, in the roll of names which I propose to call, some are not found, I trust the omission will not be regarded as implying any judgment with regard to the value of their work, but as my individual judgment that their work is not literature; and I must leave it with the reader to determine how far that judgment is correct. All that I can claim is that I am not conscious of being guided by any personal or theological considerations.

American literature and American Unitarianism began together. I doubt whether any religious movement was ever richer in the adherence of men and women eminent in literature than American Unitarianism during the greater part of the present century. Any account of American literature which failed to notice those who were in implicit or avowed sympathy with Unitarianism would not be worth the writing. This is evident the moment we begin to recall their names and achievements. At once there leaps to our lips the name of Dr. Channing, before whose day no sermon written in New England had any literary value, and owing to whose influence the modern sermon has been endowed with a grace corresponding to the preciousness of the truth it contains; then Emerson, for fifty years "the friend of all who would live in the spirit," whose quickening thought, conveyed in telling form, has made him the teacher of those who teach, and to whom hardly a man or woman who has tried to utter his or her thought is not more or less indebted.

The early part of our century was not rich in works of fiction. But such as they are there is nothing worthy of mention among them, with the exception of Cooper's novels, and later of those of Mrs. Stowe, outside the works of Lydia Maria Child and William Ware. For more than twenty years Mrs. Child was the representative woman in our literature. It may be that the attraction of her work has ceased, yet none the less the fact remains that she did work which satisfied the mind and heart of a generation of our people; and in our quickly moving century to do that is to do a great deal. The works of William Ware ("Zenobia" and "Aurelian") bear the impress of a master-hand, which will aid them in the struggle for a permanent place in literary history. The mention of Ware recalls another Unitarian clergyman, Sylvester Judd, whose novel "Margaret" takes a high place, and of which James Russell Lowell says, in his "Fable for Critics": —

> "'T is enough that I look
> On the author of 'Margaret,' the first Yankee book
> With the *soul* of Down East in 't, and things farther East,
> As far as the threshold of morning, at least,
> Where awaits the fair dawn of the simple and true
> Of the day that comes slowly to make all things new."

Later than these come the novels of Dr. Holmes, with their suggestive studies of those phases of human experience best known to the physician. Hawthorne had too little of the social element in him to deeply interest him in public religious movements; but his sympathies were all in accord with the Unitarian purpose. No one who has read "Marble Faun" and "The Scarlet Letter" needs to be reminded of the marvellous contributions he has made. Of living writers of fiction no one has surpassed Edward Everett Hale in the difficult task of making good short stories; while through such novels as "In His Name," "Ten Times One is Ten," and "Our New Crusade," Dr. Hale has done so much to promote general benevolence and to apply the ethical principles of the New Testament to modern life, that his name has become a household word throughout our land.

Among those who have aided in making history what it has

become in our time, a means of literary delight as well as an instrument of instruction, have been not a few who own the Unitarian influence and name. Parkman has thrown a flood of light upon the dark pages of Canadian annals, and by his spirit of loyalty to truth has done ample justice to the heroic labors of the Jesuit missionary. Prescott has unfolded with all the charm of romance the story of the conquest of Mexico and Peru, and the golden time of Spanish history under Ferdinand and Isabella and Philip II. Motley has portrayed with a vigor that stirs the blood of the reader the long resistance of the Dutch Republic to Spanish tyranny, and the early days of the Netherlands after they had emerged with success from the struggle for independence. Ticknor has told the history of Spanish literature with such clearness and beauty that the reader becomes as much interested in Lope de Vega and Calderon as in the great ones of English literature. Bancroft has endowed the history of his country with all the dignity of an epic poem, and has recited the great events of our national history with an eloquence seldom equalled and never surpassed. Dr. John G. Palfrey has written the history of New England so well that it will not need to be done again.

The five great orators of New England are Winthrop, Phillips, Webster, Everett, Sumner. Of these, Winthrop has always been a faithful adherent of the church which made his ancestors illustrious by driving them out of *Old* into *New* England. Phillips was, during his lifetime, although connected with Parker in the work of social reform and opposition to slavery, in sympathy with orthodox Congregationalism; but Webster, Everett, and Sumner were in accord with Unitarianism. For years Mr. Webster was a faithful attendant upon the services at Brattle Street Church, and in the last record of his religious faith there is no evidence that he had modified his religious opinions. Edward Everett, who more than any other New England orator, deserves a place in literature, and whose orations will always be read and enjoyed by the lover of what is best in rhetorical art, was through his whole life identified with the Unitarian body. So likewise was Charles Sumner, whose speeches will always have the interest which attaches to marvellous learning when it is inspired by undying devotion to a noble cause.[1]

Passing from orators, historians, novelists, let us now notice some adherents of Unitarianism who have added in other ways to our literary inheritance. In criticism we have Henry Giles, whose treatment of Shakespeare's characters is of the highest order, and whose works deserve, even if they do not obtain, a repeated reading. Here too we have Whipple, for so long a time the most potent factor in the formation of literary opinion. No finer specimens can be found in literary criticism than in the prose volumes of James Russell Lowell; and no more genial reports on the events and conditions of the times than in the writings of George William Curtis. Dr. Holmes has imparted to our literature a wit all his own in the Autocrat, the Professor, and the Poet of the Breakfast Table. There are also those who have imbued what they have done with a literary character who might have won a high place in pure literature. Among these is Dr. Furness, who has given so

[1] Other noted men among the orators of our country might be named as adherents of Unitarianism, — men like John Q. Adams and John C. Calhoun; but perhaps we would better pass them by, since we are dealing with literature; and the speeches of those whom we have named, however valuable in other respects they may be, are not literature. There are also those still living in full sympathy with Unitarian aims and ideas who occupy an honorable place among the orators of the country; but perhaps it is too soon to decide whether their speeches will find a place in literature.

much of his life to the sweet task of aiding those who "would see Jesus;" James Freeman Clarke, who sacrificed a career in literature to the work of establishing Unitarian ideas and principles; and Dr. Andrew P. Peabody.

It is the distinction of Dr. Hedge — " clarum et venerabile nomen " — that in his youth he brought from Germany the materials which have made our thought more profound; while in later years he has clearly shown in his own person how depth of thought may be wedded to masterly effectiveness of style. In the case of all these, theology and literature have become one. A religious body which on two continents can give to the world such specimens of literary excellence, united with the highest thought of the time, as are found in our day in Hedge, Furness, Clarke, Peabody, and Martineau, has reason for being somewhat proud of its place in literature.[1]

In poetry it may be said in one word, that with the exception of Whittier and Poe, every poet in this country in the highest rank is in accord with Unitarian ideas, a member of the Unitarian body. Longfellow, whose perfect utterance of the common thoughts and feelings of man makes him welcome everywhere; Bryant, with his heart open to Nature's still, small voice; Lowell, who

> "sees beneath the foulest faces lurking
> One God-built shrine of reverence and love;"

Holmes, who with all the art and none of the malice of Pope has for fifty years been saying the happiest things in the

[1] It may be well here to name others who have added in various ways to the literary life of America. Some of them may not be considered or may not consider themselves members of the Unitarian body, but all of them, I think, are in sympathy with its spirit. They are Jared Sparks, John Weiss, N. L. and O. B. Frothingham, Samuel Johnson, John S. Dwight, W. R. Alger, Bayard Taylor, T. W. Higginson, C. P. Cranch, Charles T. Brooks, Jones Very, Samuel Longfellow, Margaret Fuller.

happiest way, — all these are identified with Unitarian thought and life.

It is said of Dr. Holmes that he has always wished to be the author of a great hymn. It might be well to remind him that great poets have seldom written great hymns. Still, I cannot help thinking he has approached the desire of his heart in the hymn, —

"O Love divine, that stooped to share."

But whether Dr. Holmes has obtained his wish or not, Unitarianism has not been lacking in those who have won universal recognition for their hymns. The hymn of Sir John Bowring beginning —

"In the cross of Christ I glory,"

has struck the most vital chord of Christian feeling; Miss Sarah F. Adams in the hymn "Nearer, my God, to thee," has fitly voiced the universal aspiration of the heart of man after God; while the Christmas hymns of E. H. Sears go round the world on every Christmas day.

The first part of my task is finished. I have tried to recall the writers who have been more or less identified with Unitarianism; to show what a force those allied with it are in our literature. But now it may be asked by some one, What is the value of such an attempt? What use is there in recounting vanished glories or achievements, which after all have no vital relation to the actual mission of the church? I sympathize, although I cannot altogether agree, with such an inquiry. It is pernicious to recall memories of a glorious past if they are regarded merely as reasons for boasting, instead of incitements to doing something worth doing of our own in our own way. It is useless to remain satisfied with what has been done, while we fail to do the duty which lies at hand; and it will be idle for us to imagine that there is some necessary connection between Unitarianism and literary ability and achievement. Unitarianism in England has not been connected with the wonderful literary life that we have seen in New England. How did it happen to be an attractive influence here? By the fact that it was the only form of religious life in New England at the time which gave free scope to the awakening intellect. Other religious organizations were still fixed in the letter; still bound down to provincial interpretations of narrow systems. But men and women were beginning to see in a larger way than before; their conceptions of religious truth were in the process of transformation. The intellect revolted at the traditional theological thought, and at the forms of its manifestation. Unitarianism offered the only refuge to those who wanted a religious home, but were unwilling to purchase it by the denial of their sincere convictions. It was this that made it for years the church of those who have won a place in American literature.

That state of things has well-nigh vanished. The man of literature finds many religious homes, or is made at home in the church in which he was born and nurtured. Creeds can now be accepted " for substance of doctrine." Conditions of fellowship are large and elastic. The doctrines that once would have driven the literary man into the Unitarian fold are so kept in the background, are so little insisted upon and so broadly interpreted, that he does not care to make any protest. We may regret the present condition of things. It may seem at first sight as if this decline of relative literary predominance were a sign of failure in our denominational aim and purpose. In fact, however, it is nothing of the kind. It is the sign of a victory won. It indicates that a protest which was once needed is now needed less, because it was made so earnestly and so effectually. It means that the struggle of Unitarianism, begun so bravely against such overwhelming odds seventy years ago, has won larger religious freedom not only for its own followers but also for those who know nothing about it, who perhaps regard it with repugnance. It shows that then Unitarianism was in alliance with the powers that contend for the enlightenment of the mind and the freedom of the soul. We have a right to rejoice in the great literary names that cluster around our earlier history; not, however, because they belong to us, but rather because these found in us the first who were ready to welcome the larger thought and the clearer vision. That is our real ground for honest pride, and of that we should ever strive to make ourselves worthy.

In trying to present the second part of our subject, the expression of Unitarianism in literature, several difficulties at once appear. One difficulty lies in the fact that pure literature, as a rule, has little to say about strictly religious themes; and the little it does say is often hinted at obliquely, so that it is sometimes almost impossible to decide in any definite way just how much or how little may be inferred from any passage. Another difficulty rises out of the peculiar condition of the religious thought of the time, in which much that might be regarded as an utterance of Unitarian conviction will be claimed by members of other religious bodies as no less expressive of what they themselves believe. And still a third difficulty rises out of the nature of the Unitarian movement, which is not so much the means for diffusing certain well-defined opinions, as it is a tendency toward the creation of a free spirit, — a disposition to ask for reasons in religion as well as in politics or in science. It is not so much a definition as a point of view. It is less a tangible fact than an atmosphere which makes all things new. With the first of these difficulties we can do nothing except to make the most of the material we have, and to estimate what is less explicit by what we may find fully avowed. In regard to the second difficulty, namely, that many of the ideas which we associate with Unitarianism may be also found among bodies that stand in opposition to it, we have the right to urge that while in Unitarianism these ideas are a matter of course, in other religious bodies they are the rare exceptions; that while in it they are welcome, in them they are tolerated; in short, that while in Unitarianism they are the effect of a growth from within, in them they are the incident of a pressure from without. Because Prof. John Stuart Blackie is a member of the Church of Scotland, and writes, —

> "O sancte Socrates ora pro nobis,
> From silly flocks of petted lambs
> And from a faith that largely damns,
> Good saint, deliver us,"

it does not follow that that church adopts those words as the expression of its inmost conviction. Nor because the same writer declares, —

> "The errors of thy creatures praise thee, Lord,
> Not they who err are damned,"

are we compelled to believe that the church of which he is a member is prepared to preach the salvation of the heathen who never heard the Gospel. Nearly all such utterances are individual, and not, as in Unitarianism, representative. And as for the third difficulty, while it may be less easy to state particular propositions, in which all who call themselves Unitarians would be wholly agreed, there are lines of thought and points of view in which they are as much in harmony as any other religious body.

Unitarianism stands for the human element in religion. It believes that the highest revelation of the divine can be found only in the highest terms of the human. It sees in Jesus a revelation of God, because in him it finds a revelation of the religious nature of man. It does not manufacture any unscriptural and mechanical device for bringing together imagined opposites, like the divine and the human. It simply believes Jesus when he says, "He that hath seen me hath seen the Father." Unitarianism is also at one in its conviction that what is essential in religion does not depend upon the accidents of history. Instead of regarding the institutions and statements in which Christianity has manifested itself as necessary to it, it regards them as the transient forms for the embodiment of what the soul perceives as eternally true. It believes that revelation is not the exclusive gift of one race, or nation, or individual, however superior it may deem that nation or that individual to all others. It finds the revelation of God in the course of nature, and in the experiences of the soul of man. It regards the revelation of God as independent of accidents of time and place, and as present, inward, universal. And Unitarianism regards man not as a perverted, but an incomplete being; and instead of seeing in his stumblings, mistakes, and sins the result of a failure in the past, it sees only the incidents of a struggle from what man is towards the attainment of what he ought to become. It believes man is learning through experience, and that the experience he has is the experience through which he will learn wisdom and acquire strength. To it the thought of a God who punishes men for being imperfect, and with no view to deliverance from their imperfection, is simply blasphemous.

It believes that rewards and penalties are not attached to men, but grow out of what they are; in short, to use Dr. Hedge's profound aphorism, that "character is destiny." It sees the evil in man, it sees also the good; and it has an abiding faith that every soul will at last, through the loving though it may be hard discipline of God, be a redeemed soul. It makes no distinction between here and there, between the life that now is and the life to come. To it both are the same; and in both alike it sees the same law for man to learn, and the same love to trust.

These are some of the ideas which are implied in what is called Unitarianism. Do these ideas find expression in modern literature? It is somewhat singular that we find less of these ideas in many of those who are identified with the Unitarian organization than in those who have no connection with it. Bryant wrote little, and that little was written in relation to the aspects of Nature; and in his religious poems he has chosen to dwell upon the thoughts and feelings common to all forms of religious aspiration and trust. Longfellow never discusses religious problems. He deals with what is given in the spirit of the artist. In "Christus" he uses in this way the materials furnished him by the Gospel narrative. In reading it one would find it impossible to decide what the theological inclination of the writer really was. Lowell's poems, and, indeed, all his literary work for the most part, treat of subjects which afford little or no opportunity for the expression of theological ideas. Even in his Elegy on Dr. Channing there is nothing which reveals his religious thought, as indeed it was not necessary there should be. Perhaps the most distinctive expression of our thought is found in the "Cathedral" in its whole spirit, and especially in the passage where he declares his reverence for every shrine "which guards piety;" and in the lines, —

"Each age must worship its own thought of God,
More or less earthy, clarifying still
With subsidence continuous of the dregs;
Nor saint nor sage could fix immutably
The fluent image of the unstable Best,
Still changing in their very hands that wrought:
To-day's eternal truth To-morrow proved
Frail as frost-landscapes on a window-pane.
. . . .
Idle who hopes with prophets to be snatched
By virtue in their mantles left below;
Shall the soul live on other men's report,
Herself a pleasing fable of herself?"

In the poetry of Emerson there is nothing distinctive, but there is compensation for this in his prose, which, despite some criticism upon the "pale negation of Unitarianism," still preaches with "sweet reasonableness" the best of its affirmations. No one, however, can read the works of Dr. Holmes without being permeated with what is most characteristic in Unitarian thought. It is probable that he has done more to instil its views than any preacher ever had the power to do. After reading him one might be easily surprised that he had actually become a Unitarian without knowing it, as the men of whom Swedenborg tells in his "True Christian Religion" found to their surprise that without knowing it they had entered into the other world. As long as Dr. Holmes's works are read, — and read they will be so long as men and women can enjoy wit, — Unitarian ideas will not lack a preacher.

The poets whom we have been considering might be considered as either voicing the shibboleth of their own sect, or using the conventional terms of their own faith. It will therefore be well to inquire whether we find any expression of the ideas for which Unitarianism stands among those who without any such bias simply utter the thought that possesses them. As it would be impossible to bring before ourselves all that has been written, or to cite the expressions of faith to be found scattered through the voluminous literature of our time, I have thought it best to see what there is that voices our thought in a few of the leading contemporary poets.

It is only a few days since Whittier celebrated his eighty-first birthday. Dr. Holmes and he alone remain to remind the present generation of a period of poetic glory which in all likelihood New England will not soon see again. He stands apart from the fellow-poets of his own country in his preference for subjects which touch moral action and spiritual reflection. He has a deep interest in religious problems, and turns to them again and again. It is in this devout and free soul that we shall find in the clearest form some of the best utterances of what is most precious to the Unitarian spirit. That he is in close sympathy with the work, and a lover of the life, of Dr. Channing, his poem gives ample proof, —

> "In vain shall Rome her portals bar,
> And shut from him her saintly prize,
> Whom, in the world's great calendar,
> *All* men shall canonize."

Whittier knows nothing of the distinctions which are so often drawn by those who are wise above what is written, between here and there, now and then. To him every moment of existence is full of the Divine presence, and no place is without the revelation of the Divine goodness. He is sure

> "that life and death
> His mercy underlies."

He knows he

> "cannot drift
> Beyond His love and care."

He recognizes no moment when the mercy of God ceases and his love fails. This assurance is to be found in many of his poems, and it is clearly implied in the "Eternal Goodness." It is, however, in the poem "The Cry of a Lost Soul" that it finds distinctest utterance, A traveller on the Amazon hears the mournful cry of a bird; the guide crosses himself, whispers, "A lost soul!" and then says: —

> "'Saints strike him dumb! Our Holy Mother hath
> No prayer for him who, sinning unto death,
> Burns always in the furnace of God's wrath!'"

But the traveller, with a larger faith, declares: —

> " Thou lovest all: thy erring child may be
> Lost to himself, but never lost to thee.
>
> " All souls are thine, the wings of morning bear
> None from that Presence which is everywhere,
> Nor hell itself can hide, for thou art there.
> . . . .
> " Wilt thou not make, Eternal Source and Goal,
> In thy long years, life's broken circle whole,
> And change to praise the cry of a lost soul?"

Our poet is at one with the faith that includes all, and which sees in all men the same essential elements of faith and aspiration and trust. In one of his best poems, the hymn written for the dedication of Starr King's church at San Francisco, he gives in a single line his ideal of the church:

> "Thy church our broad humanity."

And in a poem read before the Quaker Alumni he thanks God

> "for the faith which embraces the whole,
> Of the creeds of the ages the life and the soul."

And again, —

> "For a sense of the Goodness revealed everywhere,
> As sunshine impartial, and free as the air;
> For a trust in humanity, Heathen or Jew,
> And a hope for all darkness The Light shineth through."

In his thought of the doctrines of Christianity he seeks the essential truth which they endeavor to reveal, or oftener still he concerns himself with their purely practical aspect. In "Trinitas" the great mystery is resolved in the experiences of the day, and he learns to see

> "The equal Father in rain and sun,
> His Christ in the good to evil done,
> His Voice in thy soul, — and the Three are One."

It is clear enough from this that the poet cares little or nothing for the doctrine of the Trinity beyond the suggestion it contains of the essential unity of the beneficence of Nature, the service of the loving heart, and the soul's perception of truth. Whittier finds the true thought of God neither in theological systems nor in great institutions alone, but in the unfoldings of the simple thought of tender and loving hearts. In one poem, "The Minister's Daughter," the minister in his morning sermon "had told of the primal fall, and how henceforth the wrath of God rested on each and all." But when in the afternoon he walks out with his daughter, the little girl whom he dearly loves, and tells her she ought to fear and love God, she says: —

> "Oh, I fear him,
> And I try to love him too;
> But I wish he was good and gentle,
> Kind and loving as you."

In these words, we are told, the minister discerned a revelation of God better than he had ever seen in system or creed. As Whittier finds the highest message of God in the experiences of the heart, so is he able to find the revelation of God

in Christ, because in him he finds revealed what is best in
man : —

> " So, to our mortal eyes subdued,
> Flesh-veiled, but not concealed,
> We know in thee the fatherhood
> And heart of God revealed."

The faith of Whittier in Christ and in the truths of Christianity does not rest for its support upon outward circumstances or written record. It is independent of all these. All the events of the history of Jesus are transformed by him into experiences of the inward life. No outward circumstance is needed to make him more real. He cries : —

> " Oh, the outward hath gone, but in glory and power
> The spirit surviveth the things of an hour ;
> Were my spirit but turned from the outward and dim,
> It could gaze even now on the presence of Him."

To Whittier, the judgment of Heaven is neither arbitrary nor incidental nor external; it is the result of what we have become. The inward conviction of the real inclination of our nature is the word of God within, accusing or excusing.

> " The stern behest of duty,
> The doom-book open thrown,
> The heaven ye seek, the hell ye fear,
> Are with yourselves alone."

If now we turn from the poets of our own land to those of England we shall find in them, as in our own simple Quaker poet, the same expression of much that is identical with the spirit of Unitarianism. In Tennyson, whose faultless verse has charmed the ears, and whose thoughts have brought comfort to the hearts of so many English-speaking people for half a century, we find that sympathy with freedom of thought in religion for which Unitarianism largely stands. He has no fear as he watches the transition through which religion is passing. He sees in it rather the sign of a providential order. To him there is more danger in having the life of the spirit entombed, although in splendor, in some letter of a creed or in some fossil of an institution : —

> "The old order changeth, yielding place to new,
> And God fulfils himself in many ways,
> Lest one good custom should corrupt the world."

He does not see in doubt an enemy to religion, but a tendency towards the discovery of a larger and deeper truth. Doubt of the form is the result of the conviction that there is something for whose manifestation the form is seen to be insufficient, —

> "There lives more faith in honest doubt,
> Believe me, than in half the creeds."

He has within the conviction of the Infinite Life, and that causes him to regard all systems that seek to explain it as partial and transient : —

> "Our little systems have their day;
> They have their day and cease to be;
> They are but broken lights of thee,
> And thou, O Lord, art more than they."

He finds a revelation of God in what may be learned of the smallest things. If he could know, all in all, the flower in the crannied wall, he would know what God and man is. He asks, —

> "The sun, the moon, the stars, the hills, and the plains,
> Are not these, O soul, the vision of him who reigns?"

And as he finds the revelation of God in and through the knowledge of Nature, so likewise does he find him revealed in and through human nature. In his thought humanity and deity are not seen sundered and opposed, but at one ; and in the human we learn to know the divine : —

> "Thou seemest human and divine,
> The highest, holiest manhood thou."

Man's thought of what is due him is taken as a token of what God will grant: —

> "Man thinks he was not made to die,
> And thou hast made him, thou art just."

In spite of all the contradictions of time and sense he proclaims, —

> "One God, one law, one element,
> And one far-off divine event,
> To which the whole creation moves."

With Whittier, Tennyson places punishment in no outward or arbitrary infliction, but in the formation of a character which finds the penalty of its sin in what it is. In the "Vision of Sin," the youth who has made himself the devotee of pleasure, and who yields himself to all its seductions, becomes as a natural consequence a miserable wreck of a man who has lost all sense of the dignity and worth of existence: —

> "The crime of sense became the crime of malice."

At the close of the same poem a voice is heard crying, "Is there any hope?"—

> "To which an answer pealed from that high land,
> But in a tongue no man could understand."

Here the final state of the sinful soul is left shrouded in mystery. Elsewhere, however, he trusts, though faintly, the larger hope, and cries, —

> "Oh yet we trust that somehow good
> Shall be the final goal of ill."

There is so much of the dramatic element in the poetry of Robert Browning that it is unwise to lay too much stress upon separate utterances, unless there is some good reason for believing that they are meant to express the personal conviction of the poet. But if we may not always know what Browning thinks by what appears in the utterances of his characters, we may learn much from the use he makes of them. We can see in the way in which God is revealed to different types of character how much he thinks man's knowledge of God depends upon what he is. Caliban, conscious only of brute impulses, knows God only as a greater brute. The philosophy of life is spoken by the Jewish sage, Rabbi Ben Ezra, while the deepest word of Christian faith comes through the lips of Saint John. In Browning, religion is independent of its historical incidents. The whole argument of the Apostle John, in "A Death in the Desert," is meant to establish as eternal convictions of the soul what had seemed to others to rest only upon the report of things seen and heard. And in "The Ring and the Book," the Pope, who here evidently reveals the mind of Browning, becomes aware of the danger of confounding religion with the report of its past manifestations, and asks: —

> " Whence need to bravely disbelieve report,
> Through increased faith in things reports belie?
> Correct the portrait by the living face,
> Man's God by God's God in the mind of man? "

It is true that he feels that this will produce evil results in some natures, who will only too readily take their lower inclinations for the law of their being; but when the historical witness to what is higher, and the visible institutions which embody it, avail so little, to fall back upon the inward and personal apprehension of religious truth may have a providential value for those

> "too obtuse
> Of ear thro' iteration of command
> For catching quick the sense of the real cry."

To Browning, all modes by which truth is communicated are useful, and all are temporal. In "A Death in the Desert" he unfolds his thought of the purely transient value of all usages and forms which seek to reveal the religious life.

> "Since all things suffer change, save God the truth,
> Man apprehends him newly at each stage;
> Whereat earth's ladder drops, its service done,
> And nothing shall prove twice what once was proved."

The faith which once rested upon the report of a miracle must now rest upon other supports. One who wrote a poem such as "The Ring and the Book" to teach

> "This lesson, that our human speech is naught,
> Our human testimony false,"

could never rest any vital conviction of religion even upon the best attested traditions. Again, in Browning the highest revelation of God rests upon a revelation of what is best in man. In "Saul," the boy David longs to comfort Saul, and believes that in his longing, which avails so little, there is implicitly contained the promise of the help of God, which is sufficient for everything: —

> "Would I fain in my impotent yearning do all for this man,
> And dare doubt he alone shall not help him, who yet alone can?"

In "Christmas Day," and again in "A Death in the Desert," the same thought recurs. Man has love; God cannot lack that, the lack of which would make him less than man.

> "For the loving worm within its clod
> Were diviner than a loveless God
> Amid his worlds, I will dare to say."

In "Easter Day" we have Browning's vision of the judgment of a soul that has preferred the things of this world to the life which knows and loves God. The choice is confirmed, and the punishment is but the necessary consequence of the choice. But the judgment is remedial. The loss of what seemed of no value compared with the glory of nature and art is seen to involve the loss of everything, and the soul cries out in its anguish, —

> "leave me not tied
> To this despair, this corpse-like bride,
> . . . .
> Only let me go on, go on,
> Still hoping ever and anon
> To reach one eve the 'Better Land.'"

That hope to reach "one eve the Better Land" is with Browning more than a hope. He feels sure of the final destiny of all. We are here indeed to make a choice, and that choice decides much, but it does not decide everything, nor does it decide forever. The Pope in "The Ring and the Book" says of Guido, "Not one permissible impulse moves the man;" but he also says: —

> "So may the truth be flashed out by one blow,
> And Guido see one instant and be saved,
> Else I avert my face, nor follow him
> Into that sad, obscure, sequestered state
> Where God unmakes but to remake the soul
> He else first made in vain."

And again in "Apparent Failure," as he looks upon "the three men who did most abhor their life in Paris yesterday," he says: —

> "My own hope is, a sun will pierce
> The thickest cloud earth ever stretched;
> That after Last returns the First,
> Tho' a wide compass round be fetched;
> That what began best can't end worst,
> And what God blessed once prove accursed."

Little known as Lewis Morris is in this country, he is well known in his own, where his longest poem, "Epic of Hades," published in 1877, has reached its twenty-second edition, and the approval of the best critics. His other poems are "The

Ode of Life," "Gwen," "Songs of Two Worlds," "Songs Unsung," "Gycia," and "Songs of Britain." More than any other poet he dwells upon the problems of religious experience, and there is no one in whom the Unitarian will find more reflection of his own thought. In one of his longer poems, called "The Wanderer," he portrays the experience of one who having tried all phases of life and forms of religious belief, and craving absolute knowledge, is at last convinced that he has not found what he sought because it is not best that man should find it; and that

> "Absolute truth revealed would serve to blind
> The soul's bright eye, and sear with tongues of flame
> The sinews of the mind."

In the same poem he speaks of the weakness of a faith that finds the revelation of God depending on the letter of a book: —

> "But if revealed he be, how to escape
> The critic who dissects the sacred page
> Till God's gift hangs on grammar, and the saint
> Is weaker than the sage."

In the poem, "The New Order," he views with somewhat of sadness many things that appear on the surface of our modern thought; nevertheless, all this only inspires him with the assurance that —

> "There shall rise from this confused sound of voices
> A firmer faith than that our fathers knew,
> A deep religion which alone rejoices
> In worship of the Infinitely True.
> Not built on rite or portent, but a finer
> And purer reverence for a Lord diviner."

Our poet does not regard any external attestation to a truth as conferring upon it any more value. To him religion is proved by its power here and now to convince the honest heart of its truth. In "Even-Song," speaking of Jesus, he says: —

"Nay! he is our Teacher indeed; little boots it to-day to seek
  To arraign with a labored learning the words that men heard him speak,
  Or to sneer at the wonders they saw him work, or believed they saw, —
  We who know that unbending sequence is only a phase of law.
  No wonder which God might do, if it rested on witness of men,
  Would turn to it our thoughts of to-day as it turned the multitudes' then;
  Nor proved would avail a whit, if the teaching itself was not pure,
  Nor if it were pure as his, would make it one whit more sure."

As religion does not with Lewis Morris rest on anything more or less secure than the perception of the soul of its goodness and truth, so also revelation is not confined to one person, nation, or race. While, as we have seen, confessing the pre-eminent worth of the revelation in Jesus, and while declaring in "Even-Song" that —

"'Twixt his rule of a Higher Mercy and that which the Rabbi taught
  Lies the gulf between glowing act and barren ashes of thought,"

and that "no teacher of old was full of mercy as ours, or pure," he at the same time maintains the universal revelation of God: —

"Yet God is not silent. Indeed, not seldom from every page,
  From the lisping story of eld to the seer with his noble rage,
  All are fired by the spirit of God.
  Each nation, each age has its laws whereto it shall stand or fall,
  But built on a wider law which is under and over them all.
  Nor doubt we that from Western wilds to the long-sealed isles of Japan
  There runs the unbroken realm of a law that is common to man."

As with Whittier, with Tennyson and Browning, punishment of sin or reward of good is seen by Lewis Morris to lie within, in what we are, and

> "We are ourselves our heaven and hell."

He is at one with them in his expression of the eternal hope. To him evil is that it may cease. In the "Epic of Hades" we have a vision of Tantalus in Tartarus, from whose lips the longed-for waters ever flee; who is receiving in this way the punishment of insatiable desire; and we hear him say,

"And yet there comes a healing purpose in my pain."

At the close of the terrible description of the sufferings of those whose guilt had incurred the heaviest doom, the poet hears a voice saying: —

"There is an end
Of all things that thou seest; there is an end
Of wrong, and death, and hell."

I think no one can read these poets without seeing how their spirit and tendency are in accord with the spirit and tendency of what is best in Unitarianism.

If we now turn to works of fiction, we shall find little expression of any distinctive religious thought among the great writers. They are artists, interested in the portrayal of what is, rather than in statements of what ought to be. Thackeray punctures the shams of our modern life in religion as in everything else, and George Eliot impresses upon her readers the unfailing consequence of the conditions in which we are placed, and of the principles upon which we act. The novels of George Macdonald have a more definite religious tendency, and deal more than almost any other with the religious life. These emphasize life rather than creed, and the spirit of some of them is found in that epitaph in "David Elginbrod," —

"Here lie I, Martin Elginbrod,
Ha' mercy on my soul, Lord God,
As I would do were I Lord God
And ye were Martin Elginbrod."

In so far as we have had religious novels they have tended towards the spirit which Unitarianism seeks to cherish. "Love and Theology," by Mrs. Celia Wooley, herself a Unitarian, is imbued with that spirit. In "John Ward, Preacher," the protest of the human heart against eternal punishment, and the conception of a God whose nature makes it possible, is uttered with unusual power. "Robert Elsmere," by Mrs. Humphrey Ward, brings before its readers in the most impressive way the relation of religion to history, and has wakened in thousands the inquiry whether a religion that has vital power must not depend upon the insight of the spirit rather than upon the uncertain results of historical criticism; upon present perception rather than upon the report of past happenings.[1] The fact is, that modern literature, even when it is not in general sympathy with Unitarianism, has much that helps it, and which makes its work easier to accomplish. Modern literature, like that of every age, has various tendencies, — positivist, agnostic, pessimistic. But there is no literature of great value which represents what is regarded as the orthodox and traditional systems of Christianity. This is a significant indication that the hearts of this century are not possessed by them. Literature is the best expression of the ideas and feelings which occupy the mind and heart of a generation. It was because the thought of Aquinas ruled all the life of his time that Dante wrote the "Divine Comedy," as it was because the ideas of Protestantism were so prevailing that Milton wrote his "Paradise Lost." Such works are impossible in our day, because

---

[1] We might include among those who in some way have uttered some portion of our Unitarian thought and feeling, although in many of their opinions they are far from being in accord with Unitarianism, men like Carlyle, Froude, Robert Buchanan, Dean Stanley, Jowett, Francis W. Newman.

the beliefs out of which they grew have lost their attraction and power. Since Pollok's "Course of Time," in which God is represented as one who

> "sees unmoved
> The endless tears of vain repentance fall,"

no poet has sung the thoughts of the old confessions. The creeds and systems remain, but the world's teachers have no faith in them; its noblest writers no longer care to give them utterance. A writer in a recent "Quarterly," who grows frantic over "Robert Elsmere," proposes that books like it should be banished from all Christian homes. That may be done; but to shut out the literature of an age, the subtle influences of poet and novelist and critic, is as impossible as to shut out sunlight and air. To succeed in such an attempt would mean intellectual death.

I rise from this review of Unitarianism and literature with the belief that Unitarianism has good reason to rejoice in the memories of its past history, in the consciousness of its harmony with the insight of gifted souls in the present, in its sense of its mission to make that insight the common possession of all, and in its assurance that the ideas and sentiments whose proclamation is its excuse for being, must inevitably be interwoven with the best life of the world for ages to come.

UNITARIANISM AND MODERN BIBLICAL CRITICISM.

BY JAMES DE NORMANDIE.

A FAMOUS critic, it is said, having gathered together all the faults of an eminent poet offered them a present to Apollo, who resolved to make him a suitable return for his trouble. He set before him a sack of wheat, as it had been thrashed out of the sheaf, and bid him pick out the chaff from among the corn and lay it aside by itself. The critic applied himself to the task with great industry and pleasure, and after having made the due separation was presented by Apollo with the chaff for his pains.

To many, criticism seems to be seeking only for the chaff, as if one were passing by the merits of a work to fasten upon its imperfections; and so it has to them an ungracious aspect. But ungracious or not, it is to this that we owe every improvement in manners, in morals, and in literature. Whether the critics come to find pleasure in their work of detecting errors or not, the profit is altogether ours. No error can be detected and confirmed unless it brings out a truth; the greater the magnitude of the error, the more helpful and permanent the revelation of the truth. In our school-boy compositions, how should we make any progress if it were not for the criticism which marks our faults, and thereby shows us the best way of expressing our thoughts. In manners, how grateful are we in after years to those who, even through our great mortification, cured us of awkwardness or of repulsive habits. In morals, how often the possession of many admirable qualities counts for nothing by reason of some one neglected and overwhelming passion. The law is universal, — we owe every advance to that criticism which, in seeking a higher truth, has to point out, even with some rudeness and an apparent pleasure, our faults.

The ungracious aspect of criticism is only deepened when it is applied to the Scriptures. In all other literature we confess its value, but here we have been afraid of its rude hand; and not a few have secretly longed, if not feared, that every Bible critic might share the fate of Uzzah, for touching this ark of God. So many cherished associations, so many lofty moments of devotion, so many of the deep experiences of life are bound up with the words of psalmist, prophet, or apostle, we have a strange misgiving that somehow or other criticism is to deprive us of their gracious message, or to bar us from sharing their spiritual experiences. Idle fears, and yet natural; and great pain have they brought even to many of the most reverent seekers after the truth of the Scriptures, who hesitated lest the destruction of some traditional opinion might carry with it the simple faith of some trusting heart. But we must learn — and we are learning it — that what is really valuable and divine in the past has "nothing to fear from the critic, whose labors can only put its worth in a clearer light, and establish its authority on a surer basis."

It is this principle which has been generally accepted by our body of the Christian Church, and which has made us hospitable to the results of modern Biblical criticism. Indeed, from the beginning, in this country, we have been committed unreservedly to the method of scientific criticism upon the Scriptures, even if we have not always followed it, or if sometimes we have shrunk a little from its results. And we must remember that here, as in every question which concerns morals, we are not to be much concerned about results; for if the principle is correct, the results may be left to themselves. Now, the principle is that "all knowledge must conform to scientific methods as a necessary condition of true knowledge. Every opinion is the product of reason; and even if swayed, biassed, or perverted by prejudice, reason is not discarded nor overthrown, but only misapplied, and made to sanction falsehood rather than truth. There is no difference in kind between opinions concerning God and opinions concerning the physical universe; they are both subject to the laws of thought, and must conform to the general principles which regulate the investigation of all truth." As all truth is one, so if we say that even in the most literal sense God gave us the Bible, — or if we call it in the most evangelical sense the Word of God, — from the same source surely came the faculty of reason with which to study the Bible; so that its true meaning is not to be measured by any traditional or preconceived theories, but determined by the method of scientific or reasonable research. Now this principle, I say, has been declared in every conceivable form, and with great emphasis, by our body from the beginning, and it really marks the widest line of division between us and all others.

"How," says Dr. Channing, "is the real meaning of Scripture to be understood? I answer, by reason. Of all books, perhaps the Scriptures need most the use of reason for their just interpretation."[1] "From a variety of possible interpretations we select that which accords with the nature of the subject and the state of the writer, with the connection of the passage, with the general strain of Scripture, with the known character and will of God, and with the obvious and acknowledged laws of nature.

[1] Channing's Works (Eng. ed.), p. 225.

We reason about the Bible precisely as civilians do about the Constitution under which we live; who, you know, are accustomed to limit one provision of that venerable instrument by others, and to fix the precise import of its parts by inquiring into its general spirit, into the intentions of the authors, and into the prevalent feelings, impressions, and circumstances of the time when it was framed."[1] And again: "Our leading principle in interpreting Scripture is this, — that the Bible is a book written for men, in the language of men, and that its meaning is to be sought in the same manner as that of other books."[2]

Even the most ardent follower of the Dutch school of Biblical criticism could ask no greater liberty for his investigations.

Now, although Dr. Channing was probably not in the least acquainted with the studies of the Scriptures then beginning to acquire some critical value in Germany, it is worthy of note that it was a few years before the last words I have quoted from him were written, that De Wette, the pioneer of historical Biblical criticism, had begun the publication of those remarkable works upon the Scriptures which have been followed to our day without one receding step. Dr. Channing adopted his conclusions out of the leadings of a liberal spirit; De Wette his, from following the strict laws of historical and scientific research.

The use of reason in the interpretation of the Bible, while it was itself the suggestion of, also made necessary an entire modification of, another doctrine before Biblical criticism could have any important results, — I mean the doctrine of inspiration. As long as theologians held that the Scriptures were the literal words of God, and that no human element was to be found in them, of course it was not only irreverent or impious, it was impotent and absurd to offer any

[1] Channing's Works (Eng. ed.), p. 279.   [2] Ibid., p. 278.

criticism of them; as much so as to criticise the laws of the physical universe, the flow of the tides, or the revolution of the seasons. In the Seventeenth Century, when the Protestant Church felt the necessity of some outward visible authority for the masses, with which to oppose the infallibility of Romanism, there grew up the doctrine of plenary inspiration, — that the writers of the Bible were not really human beings acting with any self-consciousness, but passive instruments of the Holy Spirit; so that even every word in the Bible was dictated by the unerring Spirit of God, and every idea and statement it in must be implicitly received as from the lips of the Almighty himself. Of course this view has to-day no acceptance among scholars, and yet its lingering influence is harmful to the last degree among multitudes. With us, however, there has been entire unanimity upon the principle of inspiration, if not always a clear vision, or a ready acceptance of its results.

Dr. Channing held that inspiration was a very secondary thing, a quality inferior to simple virtue.

"Suppose," he says, "the greatest truths in the universe to be revealed supernaturally to a being who should take no interest in them, who should not see and feel their greatness, but should repeat them mechanically, as they were put into his mouth by the Deity. Such a man would be inspired, and would teach the greatest verities, and yet he would be nothing, and would have no claim to reverence." [1]

And down to our day there seems to have been no deviation from the general principle that inspiration is to be regarded simply as a quickening of the mental faculties, a clearing of the soul-vision; and though we call it " in one case a process of nature, and in the other an operation of the Spirit, these

[1] Channing's Works (Eng. ed.), p. 249.

phrases do not alter the identity of the agent. Because the effects are different, is it not therefore the same God?"

With the acceptance of these two principles,— the use of reason, and the idea of inspiration as not different in kind but in degree in the writers of the Scriptures,— Biblical criticism began to play a most important part in the Unitarian movement in this country. It was first used with good effect in the Trinitarian controversy, and in combating the evangelical dogmas; and those who are familiar with the "Christian Examiner" thirty years ago, earlier and later, know how scholarly and well this work was done. The whole Orthodox system of faith was thoroughly and constantly enfiladed by a number of writers who were ever ready with the claims of reason, and the best results of criticism on the inspiration of the Scriptures; and although the criticism was generally a textual criticism, it is somewhat questionable if, according to the results of that time, there has been any work done quite so well since. The subjects of the articles and of the tracts of that day show what a spirited and controversial period it was. Whatever book or essay appeared in defence of the current dogmas of the church, met with an instant and able reply. So well was the textual bearing of the Bible against the popular form of expressing the Trinity employed, that many of its defenders were glad to confess that it belonged rather to the realm of metaphysics than of theology; and as a result of that controversy, no less an authority than W. Robertson Smith says in a recent work: —

"You will not find in the Bible any exposition of the doctrine of the Trinity, any definition of person and substance and essence, and all the other terms of which the chapter about the Trinity in every theological system is full." [1]

[1] Smith: The Old Testament in the Jewish Church, p. 11.

Still, beyond textual criticism there was a somewhat timid admission of any attempted criticism which went a little deeper. When Professor Norton published his "Translation of the Gospels," in which he says concerning Luke's narrative of the birth of Jesus, "It is in a style rather poetical than historical; with its real miracles the fictions of oral tradition had probably become blended, and the individual by whom it was committed to writing probably added what he regarded as poetical embellishments," one of our ministers, in a lengthy review of the work, remarked upon this passage: —

"We may grant that there is nothing more reasonable than such a supposition. But to define the limits of its application involves a serious embarrassment. Once admit that there is a legendary element mingled with the historical narratives of the Gospels, and an issue is opened in which men of equal wisdom, scholarship, and good judgment will array themselves as respectively the champions of the legend or the history; and the claims of the former will be pressed to the most serious consequences."[1]

The first results of German Biblical criticism were just being wafted to our shores, startling even those who dared to investigate them, while being held up by the evangelical church as the sure forerunner of atheism. Biblical criticism was just entering upon the scientific method. De Wette and Paulus, and Strauss and Schwegler were making their theories and studies known. Many generalizations were too hasty; many conjectures had to be modified or given up, many errors rectified, but results if not final, were of great value. They prepared the way for a rapidly increasing number of scholars, to study the Scriptures just as Dr. Channing had said they were to be studied. They brought to the work a strictly scientific method of inquiry, and that was the essential thing.

[1] Christian Examiner, July, 1855.

Results might be modified, but the principles knew no retrogression. Theological or traditional prepossessions were being thrown aside, to find out just what the Scriptures were,—their character and purpose, and age and authors. One cannot overlook those clergy who during these early years of our denominational life stood out boldly for the claims of reason, and met textual criticism with great skill against the popular dogmas of the church. Channing, Dewey, Gannett, the Wares, Ellis, Peabody, Walker, Noyes, are some of a list to be remembered with gratitude and even pride.

Thus far Biblical criticism was chiefly the keen scrutiny of the texts of Scripture, and their use in destroying the authority of some of the popular dogmas of the church; but it was about taking a more important step, and fraught with more momentous results. The study of the physical sciences was awakening serious doubts in many minds about the cosmogony of the Bible. I say physical science, because it is extremely unfortunate that we have not been able to preserve a more careful distinction in the use of terms; for science is simply what is known upon any subject, and the scientific method is simply the application of the reason to facts in any matter, to establish knowledge,—a method which we want to pursue in every department; but for the neglect of the distinction the studies into physical nature have appropriated the term "science," and bitter was the conflict a generation ago, and until very recent years, between science and theology, or science and religion. Every declaration of the naturalist, or every tentative hypothesis which he threw out as the result of his investigations, was regarded as a direct attack upon the supernatural revelation in the Bible. Those of us who recall the reception by the theological world of a book so reverent and according to the scientific triumphs and conclusions of our day so harmless as the "Essays and Reviews," and especially its essay upon the "Mosaic Cosmogony," are brought by memory into a warfare which seems to have belonged to centuries past. The researches and conclusions of the geologist, and the dawn of the Development theory, were big with peril to popular conceptions of the Bible. I remember that in the early years of my ministry I introduced into a sermon this sentence: "That whatever the conclusions of the naturalist might be in regard to the Development theory, certainly in morals and in spiritual things it offered us the great hope that if we had the endless past with its story of slow growth, we have the endless future to encourage our progress." It was a good while before I heard the last from that remark; but I have lived to hear one of our oldest ministers, who had been greatly troubled by my heresy, say that "he regarded the Development theory as the most helpful thing for the world that had ever been suggested either by science or by theology."

A dear good woman brought me some days after that sermon one of those cards quite common at the time, and issued to bring the theory into derision, on which by a series of almost imperceptible shadings of the lines the descent was traced from man to monkey, and wanted to know what I thought of that descent. I replied, I was not so much interested in the descent as in the ascent. I recalled it some years later when I read in "Nature" the story told about Huxley at one of the meetings of the British Association for the Advancement of Science. An English bishop closed a sarcastic speech against the Darwinians by turning to Professor Huxley, their leading representative, and saying, "Is the learned gentleman really willing to have it go forth to the world that he believes himself to be descended from a monkey?" Professor Huxley said in his quiet manner, "It seems to me that the learned bishop hardly appreciates our position and duty as men of science. We are not here to inquire what we would prefer, but what is true. The progress of science from the beginning has been a conflict with old prejudices. The origin of man is not a question of likes or dislikes, to be settled by consulting the feelings, but it is a question of evidence, to be settled by strict scientific investigation. But as the learned bishop is curious to know my state of feelings upon the subject, I have no hesitation in saying, that were it a matter of choice with me (which clearly it is not), whether I should be descended from a respectable monkey or from a bishop of the English Church who can put his brains to no better use than to ridicule science and misrepresent its cultivators, I should certainly choose the monkey."

Now, I am not here to accept in every detail the theory of Development, — there are some steps which Darwin himself says are still wanting for its establishment as a great law in the universe; but every addition to our knowledge in every realm brings some corroborative evidence. The great point is this, that the more it has influenced the criticism of the Bible, the less are we of to-day troubled by it. So in regard to geology. We have distanced that period of earnest and fierce discussion, only a generation past, so far as almost to have forgotten its issues, when we thought the foundations of religion were irretrievably shaken and overthrown if the cosmogony of the Bible were not literally accepted. Some began to say there could be no conflict between religion and science, or between theology and science. That was true, because creation must be the work of God quite as surely as the Bible; nevertheless, between current ideas of religion, or widely accepted dogmas of theology, there was a real and inevitable conflict of no doubtful result. Others began to say, when brought face to face with the accepted results of the naturalists, that the Bible was not intended to teach physical science, but only to give us a spiritual revelation, to teach us things man must ever be unable to learn for himself, — among which things physical truths could not be reckoned. This helped many over a shaky and crumbling bridge, — but they got safely over. It was a poor makeshift. If the general theory of inspiration were still accepted, it would be strange indeed if the Supreme Being, surely acquainted with all scientific as well as all spiritual truth, and seeing with omniscient vision all knowledge that man should finally attain, were to make statements conflicting with that future knowledge, and, accommodating himself to early ignorance, lend himself for ages to the perpetuation of error. What might not have been spared to the perplexing researches of naturalists, beset by the animosities and persecutions of theologians, from the Ptolemaic system down to the sad end of Hugh Miller, if only the Bible had taught the truths of physical science !

Still again, an attempt to harmonize the statements of the Bible and the results of geology was made by trying to revive something akin to that allegorical method which has been the bane of all scriptural interpretation. When it was found that geology carried the age of our world far back beyond anything the cosmogony of the Bible could be tortured to equal, it was said that the days of Genesis might be rendered as periods, or æons, or that the whole was a poetical description of creation. But Biblical criticism, under the guidance of the two principles we have steadily kept in view, made pretty quick work of all such attempts to create a harmony where there was only variance ; for if a day were to mean a period, or æon, in Genesis, it could as well mean an æon wherever it was found in the Bible. The fact was, and it had to be recognized, that there was no attempt at any mystical, or allegorical, or symbolical meaning. The description is simple, and maintained throughout with whatever scientific accuracy the age had, and modern scientific research was at liberty to modify it as was necessary in the advance of knowledge.

At the same time that physical science was influencing Biblical criticism there came another study of great importance, and with results of which Biblical criticism had to take serious account. I mean the study of comparative theology. As the Greek liked to designate everything outside of his borders "barbarian," and the Jew everything outside of his, "Gentile," so it has been customary for us to divide the world into Christian and Pagan. Christianity has generally been taught not as *a* religion, but as the *only* religion. God had made a revelation through Israel that was not only higher and more universal than any other, it was the only revelation he had made. He had not only inspired the prophets and teachers of the Bible with diviner truth than others, but they were the only ones he had inspired at all. Now, the study of comparative theology has done more to modify this view, during the past thirty years, than all the centuries before. The researches of Max Müller, of Renan, of Rhys Davids, of Kuenen, of Renouf, of Sayce, of Arnold, and others have swept away the assumption that ours was the only religion, while other peoples were only idolaters. It is not that they reveal to us that Judaism is necessarily borrowed or developed from Oriental religions; this idea of one nation borrowing its worship from another may have been carried altogether too far. Renouf says: "It may be confidently asserted that neither Hebrews nor Greeks borrowed any of their ideas from Egypt.

Purely external resemblances may no doubt be discovered in abundance, but evidence of the transmission of ideas will be sought in vain."[1]

But what we have learned is, that throughout all lands and peoples — outside of Judaism — we find worship, and worship which has in it the elements of true religion. There are prayers and hymns and sacrifices, and an acknowledgment of the Supreme Being, and a sense of sin, and an idea of providence, and a belief in a future existence. There are Scriptures held to be as venerable, and as reverenced, and as inspired among them, and as sacred as the most superstitious have ever regarded our own; and there are passages as full of true spirituality and piety, breathing the love of God and of man, — so that one cannot say we have all of what is Holy Scripture, or that theirs is not from the same source. No matter how superior we may confess our own to be, after the most impartial comparison (and I do believe it so to be), the difference is not so great as to be of kind and not of degree. The old Egyptian held his ritual for the dead to be quite as venerable and sacred as the Ten Commandments were to Israel, or the Beatitudes are to us. In that ritual we find this passage: —

"God is one in himself, sole, who produces all, the ancient of heaven, the oldest of the earth, the lord of time, the author of eternity. He is the causer of pleasure and light, maker of grass for the cattle and of fruitful trees for man, causing the fish to live in the river and the birds to fill the air, lying awake when all men sleep, to seek out the good of his creatures. He listens to the poor who is in distress, gentle of heart when one cries unto him, deliverer of the timid man from the violent, judging the poor, — the poor and the oppressed."[2]

[1] Egypt, pp. 254-256.
[2] English Positive Aspects of Unitarian Christianity, p. 156.

If the Romanist thinks his vast sacerdotal system is unique, he knows, if he is abreast of the studies of comparative theology, that Buddhism long before had its bells and rosaries and holy water, its shaven priests, its Virgin and Child, its fasts and purgatory, its shrines and pilgrimages, its monasteries and cathedrals, its Pope with a triple tiara on his head.

Now the results of these studies, accepted by all scholars, have been of profound significance when applied to our own Scriptures. Are we disappointed and envious to know that others as well have found the elements of the true religion, or have Scriptures they think come from the Eternal? Or, rather, have we gained a faith broader and grander as we think of them also as having found God, or rather being found of him? Are we the more earnestly stirred to find the superior merits of our own, out of that grand and universal law of development and of inspiration, and to have fresh springs of life unsealed within us as its greater spiritual purity lays heavier responsibilities upon us? All missionary efforts have thus far been carried on under the conviction that in other lands there was no true religion; and for this reason all missionary efforts have been comparatively fruitless; that is, upon the language or customs or morality or government or worship of the great world-religions they have left no perceptible traces, — nor will they until they are inspired by the truths which lie beneath the researches of comparative theology.

We are brought now to a question of Biblical criticism of no less importance than the others, which indeed inevitably follows them, of which we are just at the beginning, but to which the best scholarship looks for valuable results.

It has been the general consent of theologians, not only that the first books of the Bible *narrate* the earliest incidents of man and of creation, but also that they were the earliest written. " The laws of the Pentateuch, carefully written out by Moses himself, and preserved from his time, were held to have been the unvarying rule of faith and obedience before as after the Exile." We have all been taught that the Jews divided the Old Testament into the Law, or the Pentateuch, the Prophets, and the Hagiographa, and that this was the relative order of their age, — the Prophets coming before the Hagiographa, and the Law before the Prophets.

But the keen scrutiny of scholarship has for a long time found some difficulties here, natural as the order seems, and difficulties upon which for a long time no light seemed to dawn. I am not about to enter upon the interesting criticism of the different documents, especially the Jehovistic and the Elohistic, by which, through a line of eminent scholars like De Wette, and Vatke, and Reuss, and Graf, and Ewald, it has been sought to fix the composition and age of the earlier books, but merely to state even a later conclusion. If the Law was the oldest portion of the Bible to have been written and received into the canon, there were some difficulties, which grew only greater as the examination grew more accurate according to the best rules of historical criticism. Why, for example, if these books were universally received and known as authoritative at this early period, is it that none of the prophetical writers before the Exile ever appeal to the finished system of the Pentateuch? Or, there is the institution of the Sabbath; and if it was established at the end of the creative days, and for the reason that Jehovah rested from his creative work, and if this as a part of the Law was received as authoritative from the beginning, why do we not find any trace whatsoever of its observance? Not only do the Scriptures never speak of its being kept before the time of Moses, but they are silent about it from Moses to the end of David's reign, a period of four hundred and forty years. Is it strange that careful readers have been greatly perplexed at these omissions?

Difficulties which were utterly inexplicable under the old interpretations began to multiply as the historical criticism became more exact; and at last, for a working hypothesis, there came the explanation that perhaps the earliest in order of the canon might not have been the earliest arranged, and this seemed to throw a wonderful light upon many of the perplexities. Kuenen, whose investigations into the Pentateuch have been about the strongest thing in modern criticism, was one of the first to give this theory a full discussion, and it has had a hearty reception from many of the ablest scholars of our day. We may not accept all the conclusions of the Dutch school of theology, of which Kuenen is the acknowledged head; but of his own deeply religious spirit, and of his unquestioning, fervent acceptance of Christianity, there can be no doubt. In one of his lectures he writes so finely: —

"It is not for less but for more Christianity that our age cries out. The question only is, whether it will be able to take it to itself, and find in it a power for life, unbroken yet. For those who identify Christianity with the ecclesiastical form in which they themselves profess it, this question can hardly be said to exist. They expect the world to conform to them. They have no need to be reassured or encouraged. But those too — and they are many — who have no such confidence may be none the less at peace. The universalism of Christianity is the sheet-anchor of their hope. A history of eighteen centuries bears mighty witness to it; and the contents of its evidence, and the high significance they possess, are brought into the clearest light by the comparison with other religions." [1]

But while the great value of Dr. Kuenen's studies in Biblical criticism have been freely acknowledged by all scholars, it is

[1] Hibbert Lectures, 1882, p. 327.

to another careful student that this last theory of the date and composition of the Scriptures, to which we have referred, owes its exhaustive and apparently unanswerable defence.

In his " History of Israel," Wellhausen, who I suppose is acknowledged to be the chief of living biblical students, seems to me not only to maintain, but to demonstrate, that the first books of the Bible, known as the Pentateuch, or according to a better classing the Hexateuch, are not "remnants of the literature of ancient Israel," preserved in their present form from their departure from Egypt, or before they crossed the border, but that they grew up little by little, by this great law of development, from a Mosaic germ, and did not until the time of the Captivity assume their present order, completeness, and authority.

As Champollion found the key and opened the door of those strange writings of the Egyptians, so that we can enter into their mysterious knowledge, it looks as if Wellhausen had found the key to the chief perplexities which met the biblical student. At all events, the best scholarship is looking with great hospitality towards that theory. If it should not explain everything, it has already thrown a bright light upon many dark places. Robertson Smith — no mean authority, and himself fully accepting the hypothesis — says that "almost every younger scholar of mark is on that side."

It has been our privilege as a small body of the Christian Church — I might say our distinguishing privilege — to accept from our earliest association a few great principles in religion, which have made us hospitable towards, and fearless about, the results of Biblical criticism. It has often been charged that these were adopted from a spirit of pride, or intellectual sufficiency, or of scepticism and unbelief. But they come from the force of truth; and other bodies are finding by that same leading that they must rest upon the same principles.

Many think, and I fear even among us, that the need has passed for these questions; that it is a waste of time to be considering the authorship and canon of the Bible, while social life is full of pressing dangers, and of troubled and despairing hearts, and when the open talk is of multitudes drifting from every anchorage of faith in spiritual realities. But it is to assure us upon these very points that Biblical criticism has its own place and value; for if the principles upon which we have rested are safe, — the use of reason, the universality of inspiration, and the law of progress in God's universe, — then these questions do touch the everlasting problems of a living faith. They do touch the deepest problem of all, — of the ever-living, ever-present God. Errors, mistakes fall away; but every supreme truth abides.

UNITARIANISM AND MODERN SCIENTIFIC THOUGHT.

BY THOMAS R. SLICER.

Youth is ever taught by instances; manhood is taught by laws. — PROF. ASA GRAY.

THE subject assigned to me in this course of Lectures is the Relation of Unitarianism and Modern Scientific Thought. The statement of the theme very properly lays a restraint upon the lecturer; for I am required to furnish neither a theological argument nor a scientific demonstration.

Theology may be defined to be the statement, in terms of the intellect, of the report which the universe makes to the spiritual nature of man; it is the answer to the question, How does the universe interpret itself to the human soul? On the other hand, science may be defined as the statement, in terms of the intellect, of the report which the universe makes to the man concerning his place in the material world; it is the answer to the question, How does the universe interpret itself to the senses of man?

In comparing the theologic answer and the scientific answer three results are possible: (1) Both answers may be false, because men do not always understand what is said to them by the universe. The universe cannot be false, and the man may not be false; but there may be reasons why there is not a clear distinction of the sounds. The answer is not articulate and just. Results depend upon the material worked in. (2) One answer may be true and the other may be false, because the man may not be equally well developed in his soul and in his senses: he may "be alive unto God," or he may be "living after the flesh;" his senses may be keener than his spirit. (3) Both answers may be true. Even then the answer is not final. No soul is great enough, nor any sense keen enough, to do more than get an answer that will be provisionally or tentatively true ; the human mind is not yet perfectly developed, nor is the universe finished. Man is growing, and the universe is in process of creation. If we can get a good working-theory of the universe, we have done all that science requires and all that theology requires — when it is acquainted with the human soul.

These three conditions may be present, then, when the man is spoken to by the universe, and makes his theological and scientific interpretation : (1) Both answers may be false ; (2) One answer may be true and the other may be false ; (3) Both answers may be true. But in all cases the responsibility rests upon the interpreting man ; *the universe cannot be arrayed against itself !*

Unitarianism has an answer to the question, How is the soul of man related to the universe? Modern scientific thought has an answer to the question, What is man's place in the material world? The task assigned to me is to compare these two answers together, and to state whether they agree, or whether they contradict one the other; with this further thought implied, Has Unitarianism a good working-theory for the spiritual being who is thus face to face with the universe?

It is frequently said that all text-books of physical science must be rewritten every ten years ; the explorer must correct his maps, and the discoveries of scientific enterprise must be put on record. No man of science would be considered loyal to his task, who would refuse to accept any new scientific fact the moment its truth was established. What would be thought of the scientist who had made a discovery and refused to make it known to the world; or what disgrace would be equal to the treachery of the man of science who made a false report of what the universe had said to him? All the great and faithful labors of Charles Darwin would have been insufficient to atone for the infidelity which would have been justly charged upon him if he had hastened to print his hypothesis of the "origin of species," and had said nothing of the manuscript of Wallace, which that naturalist had sent to Darwin from the Southern Archipelago. Darwin was entitled to the discovery, which he had made prior to the reception of the communication of Wallace; he had also reached his conclusions by another path. But among scientific men, honor, honesty, fairness, every consideration demanded perfect openness to the light, and hospitality towards the truth from whatever direction it might come, and at whatever cost. It is not simply a code of honor, it is the very necessary temper of the truly scientific mind; and these are the only terms on which it can do its work, or be trusted with the secrets of the universe. Darwin's statement is very forcible on this point: "In the course of my life I have known but three cases of *intentionally* false statements in science."

The spirit in which Darwin devoted himself to his task is the essentially honest and sincere temper of one who feels sure that the universe may be trusted: "I cannot employ my life better than in adding a little to natural science. This I have done to the best of my abilities, and critics may say what they like, but they cannot destroy this conviction." Again he says: "I wish I could set less value on the bawble fame, either present or posthumous, than I do, but I think not to an extreme degree; yet, if I know myself, I would work just as hard, though with less gusto, if I knew that my books would be published forever anonymously."

I have quoted these few sentences from the vast literature of the devout confessions of scientists, in order to point out the spirit in which for the most part they approach their tasks. There is, I know, now and then an exception, — a narrow, self-seeking man, who like Lord Bacon regards the advance of scientific knowledge as a means to an end, that end being " the gathering of fruit," and "the good to men's estates." But how far this temper is from the scientific temper of to-day, may be gathered from the indignant protest of Professor Huxley against Bacon's undue elevation to be called "the originator of the inductive method in science." Of Bacon's attempt to sum up the past of science, and indicate the path which it must follow, Professor Huxley says: —

" The attempt was just such a magnificent failure as might have been expected from a man of great endowments, who was so singularly devoid of scientific insight that he could not understand the work already achieved by the true instaurators of physical science; yet the majestic eloquence and the fervid vaticinations of one who was conspicuous alike by the greatness of his rise and the greatness of his fall, drew the attention of all the world to 'the new birth of Time.'"

The application made is evident: —

" Nothing great in Science has ever been done by men who lack the divine afflatus of the truth-seeker. The great steps in its progress have been made, are made, and will be made, by men who seek knowledge simply because they crave it." [1]

[1] The Advance of Science in the Last Half Century. T. H. Huxley, F.R.S.

Dr. William B. Carpenter, a representative Unitarian and a distinguished scientific authority, was early impressed with the following statement of moral honesty and confidence respecting the order of the world : —

"Just as sedulously as the trader in knowledge severs his own peculiar science from all others, so does the lover of wisdom strive to extend its dominion and restore its connection with them. I say to restore, for the boundaries which divide the sciences are but the work of abstraction. What the empiric separates, the philosopher unites. He has early come into the conviction that in the dominion of intellect, as in the world of matter, everything is linked and commingled, and his eager longing for universal harmony and agreement cannot be satisfied with fragments. All his efforts are directed to the perfecting of his knowledge; his noble impatience cannot be restrained until all his conceptions have arranged themselves into one harmonious whole, till he stands at the central point of arts and sciences, and thence overlooks the whole extent of their dominion with a satisfied glance. New discoveries in the field of his activity, which depress the trader in science, enrapture the philosopher. Perhaps they fill a chasm which the growth of his ideas had rendered more wide and unseemly; or they place the last stone, the only one wanting to the structure of his ideas. But even should they shiver it into ruins, should a new series of ideas, a new aspect of Nature, a newly discovered law in the physical world, overthrow the whole fabric of his knowledge, he has always loved truth better than his system, and gladly will he exchange her old and defective form for a new and fairer one." [1]

Am I claiming too much for Unitarianism if I say, as I understand it, it is pledged to this course in all its search for truth? Unitarianism has no monopoly of truth, and does not make any such claim. But it is bound to accept all truth so soon as it is demonstrated to be truth; and it is bound to

[1] Schiller's Lecture on Universal History, quoted in "Nature and Man," Essays upon Natural Science, by the late William B. Carpenter: edited, with a Memoir, by J. Estlin Carpenter.

hold the judgment in suspense until the returns are all in, or manifestly on the way. For this reason Unitarianism refuses all formulated statements of belief, and is charged, in consequence, with being vague and inconsistent. But it does not care to refute the imputation. It is dealing with the very substance of life and experience, and cannot be of much service to those who know life only by its description, and have no experience of religion at first hand. This attitude of Unitarianism to truth is well expressed by Dr. Channing when asked why he did not defend from attack certain views which he had put forward confidently. He replied in substance that he feared too earnestly to defend his views, lest he should be too much taken up with their importance, and fail to go on in further pursuit of the truth.[1] This may be called a characteristic deliverance of Unitarianism, — as characteristic as the saying of Jesus, "While ye have the light believe in the light, that ye may be the children of light." The infidel, according to this view, is not the man who does not believe this or that proposition, but the man who is afraid to trust himself confidently to the spirit of light and truth. Unitarianism does not take much interest in the oft-repeated questions, "Will such a fact shake my faith?" "Can the old faith live with the new fact?" It stands with uncovered head at the door of truth, waiting with eager reverence to enter, sure that within those portals no harm can touch the child of God: for if "God is light and in him is no darkness at all," then all truth which lifts the reason to the control of life must be of God.

It is said that on one occasion the Count de Crillion remarked to M. d'Allenville, "If the universe and I professed one opinion and M. Necker expressed a contrary one, I

[1] See chapter on Channing, by Dr. Briggs, in this volume.

should be at once convinced that the universe and I were mistaken." M. Necker represents the infallible statute-book, the ancient creed, the church council, and all other consulting physicians, who must be taken into account before it can be determined whether it is safe for the light of truth to have free access to the human soul. Unitarianism keeps its system in repair by living under the open heaven. It is more important to keep the blood pure than to preserve the complexion. Unitarianism is not a formulated statement of opinions, but *a method of thought and a style of living.*

Having thus stated the claim of Unitarianism to open-minded devotion to the truth for its own sake, and having found in this candid temper the first point of contact between it and modern scientific thought, we will now turn to the consideration of the working-theory which each uses. Is this in each case the same?

I have said that Unitarianism refuses to stereotype its beliefs; it refuses "to put up the shutters in order to imprison the light already in." But does it believe nothing that it can state? As I conceive the matter, Unitarianism has no difficulty in affirming the principles on which it holds commerce with the universe.

It affirms one life, — One Life before all, above all, and through all. It repeats confidently the great announcement of Jesus, "God is a spirit." It discovers in man an appeal to consciousness as the final test of all experience; and since this consciousness has always been found looking beyond itself, sometimes with fear, sometimes with hope, in the most developed examples of humanity, with confidence which produces a literature forever after sacred to the religious sense of man, Unitarianism has learned to think that these two conscious beings — God and man — are conscious of each other;

that there is communion between them ; that the One Life
acts in both ; that man is the child of God. It goes even
further, this daring faith of ours, and thinks that if the same
life is in both, and each is conscious of the other, then if God
is a spirit, man is also a spirit : thus *it declares the essentially
spiritual nature of man.* This is fundamental to all the life
and thought of Unitarianism.

But Unitarianism goes even further in its declaration of the
terms on which it holds commerce with the universe, — *it takes
an oath of loyalty to the will of God.* It uses interchange-
ably the terms, Law, Will, Character, as applied to the Infinite
Spirit ; for we believe that there is perfect accord between the
being of God and the will of God ; in other words, the universe is administered in accord with the character of a perfect
Being. An evil universe cannot proceed from a Holy Source,
nor an imperfect world be formed by a Perfect Cause. We
find no difficulty in the adoption of the ancient words, "The
law of the Lord is perfect, the commandments of the Lord are
pure, the statutes of the Lord are right. the fear of the Lord is
clean, the judgments of the Lord are righteous altogether." So
the teachers of the religion we are considering are accustomed
to say that "*in all worlds moral character must be the same;*"
that sin is the violation of the law of the universe ; that retribution is the vindication of the law of the universe ; that to be
like God is the ideal of the children of God ; that he only is
being saved whose character is being transformed, developed,
according to the laws of the spiritual life in a spiritual being ;
that eternal life is not a remote condition, to be reached after
death, but *a present experience*, in which the man comes
into perfect accord with the conditions under which his being
reaches its best development.

What has been stated above has not in any instance taken

on the form of opinion or mere intellectual speculation; if I have at all succeeded in stating the matter, the impression is, that on these terms a spiritual being would adjust himself to the universe, — a universe of which an Infinite Spirit is the Final Cause, Life, and Revealer.

Now, having stated what the Unitarian believer thinks the universe says to the soul of man, it becomes next our duty to consider what modern scientific thought declares that the universe says to man concerning his place in it. It no longer says how the universe ought to have been formed; it has no scheme of creation to which it is pledged. Modern scientific thought has deliberately turned away from those who thought they could evolve the world out of their inner consciousness; and modern scientific thought has even threatened, if it were not left to work out its problem alone and undisturbed, to turn the tables on the priests and philosophers, and to show that so far from the world being evolved from our moral consciousness, our moral consciousness was evolved from — something else. This was such a terrible prospect, and threatened such destruction to all the stock in trade of the unscientific and dogmatic, that the inquiry has gone on unhindered, except by an occasional "resolution," passed in some convention that had charge of the universe on the old terms.[1]

I have referred to this matter because I desired to congratulate you that this state of things has, for the most part, gone by. It is an acute saying of Professor Huxley, "It is the fate of scientific discoveries to begin as heresies and end as superstitions!"

I think I may safely say that the devoted explorers of the scientific field have not been much interrupted by the fears

[1] At a meeting of a Synod at the South within the past year, it was resolved "that God originally made man out of *inorganic dust.*"

or anxieties of Unitarians. It was pointed out by another speaker in this course, Rev. James De Normandie, in "Unitarianism and Modern Biblical Criticism," that the modern scientific method had been applied to the study of the Scriptures with a result of the most important character, — a result no less than this, that the Bible has been restored to the thinking men of this generation. He reminded you that the same fears of the timid and obstinacy of the dogmatic accompanied the process that are now marking the application of the scientific method of the study of the material universe, and the consideration of the place of man in it. And, as was expected, this opposition led to misunderstanding and misrepresentation; the old defenders of the mechanical theory of creation, with its enthroned Deity and infallible statute-books, made haste to deny all the hypotheses of the scientists, — making the great mistake of not allowing the correcting agency of time, which is sure to drop the superlative in the interest of sober fact. On the other hand, the scientific inquirer, exasperated by the misconstruction of his motives, made his statements unnecessarily harsh; and he charged to the account of stupidity what was only want of knowledge. He denounced as fear what was for the most part reverence. But the man of science did one other thing which was most unfortunate, and went far to justify the fear of the man of theology; he cast his conclusions in the language of the baldest materialism; he became a grim prophet to whom no God had spoken, and the ruthless iconoclast, who could not tolerate the idol as a work of art which had ceased to mean anything as an idol, since there was now no God.

From this materialist position the man of science has had to recede, with what grace he has been able to assume; and he now admits, with rare exception, that the whole question of theism and atheism belongs to the metaphysician rather than to him. It really belongs to neither; it is the root-question in all departments of thought, and it belongs to no class of students, but to the human soul!

While it is undoubtedly true that we must not expect the scientist to speak dogmatically, or with authority, on the subjects which concern each religious man, yet if we can make use of the conclusions of modern scientific thought to confirm the position of the student of the soul's place in the sum of things, we have the right to do so, and to derive what courage we may from the comparison.

Unitarianism has for its fundamental hypothesis the statement that *all life is derived from one Life*. We apply to that one Life the highest name we know, and call it God. The fact is larger than the name, larger than all names, because it is the all-enclosing and ultimate fact in the universe. Now, what has modern scientific thought to say on this point?

In an earlier part of this lecture I have said that the time has gone by when a man need be ashamed to begin his thinking with God; he may still say in his heart "There is no God," if he desire to do so; or he may say anything which his reason will allow to his imagination, or his conscience will concede to his self-interest; but if he has been really troubled at the thought of expressing the conviction that the whole world of creation has a Cause sufficient for its origin, he may now take courage in the thought that though there are some who see no reason to believe it, there is no fact, as yet produced, that can be quoted by any competent man of science, to shame the devout believer in his reverent utterance of the name of God.

It is reported that the late Clerke Maxwell said, not long before his death, that he had "carefully examined all the agnostic theories of the universe known to him, and they all required a God to make them workable." This is given upon the testimony of Prof. Asa Gray. Professor Gray goes on to state the narrow limits to which the question is now reduced :

"It must be reasonable to all who have taken pains to understand the matter, that the true issue as regards Design is not between Darwinism and direct creationism, but between *any intention* or intellectual cause, and *no intention* nor predicable First Cause. It is really narrowed down to this; and on this line *all maintainers of the affirmative may present an unbroken front*. The holding of this line secures all; the weakening of it, in the attempted defence of unessential and now untenable outposts, endangers all. . . . Experience proves that the hypothesis 'no God' is possible, and some rest in it, *but few*, I think, *on scientific grounds*."

The argument is often used, which consists in the inference that as the human will certainly interferes with the action of the forces related to it, it is fair to suppose that there is a Will greater than ours which may also make its presence known. The argument has some of the weakness which all arguments from analogy must necessarily have; this, at least, may be maintained, — that the human will is conscious of making changes in its direction, and the easiest explanation of these changes is to refer them to a Force like its own, but greater than itself. This is a matter of consciousness. The ancient tradition places man in a scene of perfect peace and absolute mastery. His commission is, " Have thou dominion." Looking down, he finds an obedient host of forces ready to do his bidding; it seems the natural consequence that he should look up also, and say, "Thou hast beset me behind and before, and laid Thy hand upon me." Nature finds its limitation in man, and a part of its efficiency also in him as a cause; man finds his moral limitation in that nature higher than his own, and his efficiency is enhanced when he regards this as First Cause, and takes his moral direction from it.

To quote the words of Agassiz, justly called "one of the most eminent naturalists of this or any age": —

"Taking Nature as exhibiting [thought] for my guide, it appears to me that while human thought is consecutive, Divine thought is simultaneous, embracing at the same time and forever, in the past, the present, and the future, the most diversified relations among hundreds of thousands of organized beings, each of which may present complications again, which to study and understand even imperfectly, — as for instance man himself, — mankind has already spent thousands of years."

It may be objected that Professor Agassiz was not an Evolutionist, after the school of Darwin; this is true, but two facts must be borne in mind: (1) The quotation I have just offered is made by Professor Gray, a pronounced Evolutionist; (2) It was the Development Theory of Agassiz which made the Darwinian hypothesis easy of belief by the disciples of Agassiz.

In applying this quotation to the doctrine of the "Origin of Species," Professor Gray adds his testimony, as always, to creative design, thus: —

"In thus conceiving the Divine Power in act as coetaneous with the Divine Thought, and of both as far as may be apart from the human element of time, our author may regard the intervention of the Creator either as, humanly speaking, done from all time, or else as doing through all time. In the ultimate analysis we suppose that every philosophical theist must adopt one or the other conception."

Two great principles in modern science have fixed in the thought of this time this idea of the Life that includes all lives and is the spring of all being. These two principles are the Conservation of Energy and the Correlation of Forces. For the first of these, a good definition is given by Prof. Clerke Maxwell : —

" The total energy of any body or system of bodies is a quantity which can neither be increased nor diminished by any mutual action of these bodies, though it may be transformed into any one of the forms of which energy is susceptible."

The popular putting of this principle is : Any energy once present in the universe is always in the universe. In science, this principle holds the same grip on the thinking of the scientist that was once held upon the thought of a consistent Calvinistic theologian by the doctrine of the Final Perseverance of the Saints. The companion principle to the Conservation of Energy is the Correlation of Forces, and is thus described by Professor Le Conte :[1] —

" Until about forty years ago the different forces of Nature, such as gravity, electricity, magnetism, light, heat, chemical affinity, etc , were supposed to be entirely distinct. The realm of Nature was divided up into numbers of distinct and independent principalities, each subject to its own sovereign force, and each ruled by its own petty laws. About that time it began to be evident, and is now universally acknowledged, that all these forces are but different forms of one universal and *omnipresent energy*, and are transmutable into one another back and forth without loss. This is the doctrine of Correlation of Forces and Conservation of Energy, one of the greatest ideas of modern times. . . .

" But one force seemed to be an exception; life-force was still believed to be a peculiar, mysterious principle or entity, standing above other forces and subordinating them; not correlated with, nor transmutable into, nor derivable from, other and lower forces, and therefore in some sense supernatural. If this be true of living forces, it must follow that living forms are wholly different from other forms in their origin, — underived. . . .

[1] Evolution, and its Relation to Religious Thought.

"New forms of dead matter may be derived, but new living forms, underived. But it was soon discovered that vital forces were no exception. Vital forces were transmutable into and derivable from physical and chemical forces. Sun-force on the green leaves of plants is absorbed as light, to reappear as life."

It can be readily seen that the moment these twin principles took possession of the field of modern scientific thought the whole aspect of the universe was changed. The Energy which was always present refused to give standing-room for miracle in the sense of an intrusion of a foreign power, however benignant. Men trust the constant and distrust the inconstant. It was not long, therefore, before the reign of law took the place of the schemes of grace; and God, immanent, constant, and perfect, took the place of the arbitrary Oriental Sovereign who interfered for the benefit of those who were fortunate enough to get his ear or win his favor. The world expanded beyond the proportions of the patriarchal tent, and man was at home in the universe; for where the unfailing presence of the Eternal is, there the smallest atom and the most exalted organism must meet his eye. At last it was true,— true for the first time in the history of human thought, — "the heaven of heavens cannot contain God." The very dust became eloquent of his presence; nothing was any longer "common or unclean," for the divine Energy had made a temple of his creation, and the devout student of the mysterious universe put aside his selfish supplications that he might enter into the secret of the Eternal. The Divine Unity invited him to share in conscious communion the fellowship of God. The fine admission of John Stuart Mill is here in point: "It would be absurd to assume that the words we use exhaust the possibilities of being. There may be modes of it innumerable, which are inaccessible to our faculties, and which consequently we are unable to name."

The Unitarian takes the enlarged universe as the home of his soul, as well as the subject of his inquiry, and finds his trust and love and hope expand to meet the larger demand upon his experience of the religious nature of man. The thought of the Divine Unity has added dignity to life. It has put all Being within reach of each being. We read the old text with a new sense of its importance, — "Beloved, now are we the children of God, and it doth not yet appear what we shall be," but it must be something wonderful, to be worthy of such a start in life!

The watchword of this new security, which modern scientific thought has made familiar to all lips, is the word, Evolution. No word of our modern speech is more used, nor with greater inaccuracy of application. It has been elevated to the rank of an endowed Intelligence, and has shared with its prime minister, Natural Selection, the attributes of Being. But we must remember that even if evolution were a law, which it is not, it would not be entitled to this personality which is so constantly accorded to it. For law is not anything whatever. It is only the way in which natural phenomena report themselves; when these reports are found to be always the same under the same circumstances, the observer generalizes a law for the sake of convenience in describing these recurring phenomena. But evolution is not even a law; it is only a working hypothesis. For theology is not the only science which depends for a start in its processes upon a postulate or an hypothesis; so great an authority as Professor Huxley says that physical science rests on verifiable or uncontradicted hypotheses; and a great condition of its progress has been the invention of verifiable hypotheses.

"Any one who is practically acquainted with scientific work is aware that those who refuse to go beyond fact rarely ever get as far as fact; and any one who has studied the history of science knows that almost every step therein has been made by anticipating Nature; that is, by the invention of hypotheses which, though verifiable, often had very little foundation to start with, and, not infrequently, in spite of a long career of usefulness, turned out to be wholly erroneous in the long run."[1]

The very old theory of evolution is such a working hypothesis. It is as old as the time of Aristotle, and it might long ago have been where it stands to-day, but that for a thousand years the human mind was imprisoned by the fear that if it held too intimate an intercourse with matter, it would lose its communion with spirit, to which matter was the undoubted enemy. Since the age of the scholastic narrowness, evolution has been forging to the front through the crowd of contending theories of the constitution of the universe; and since Agassiz contributed his demonstration of the method of development, as Professor Le Conte has pointed out, "Scientific thought, like a rising tide which knows no ebb, through five hundred years has tended towards evolution with increasing pressure, but has been kept back by the one supposed fact of the supernatural origin of species. Darwin lifted the gate, and the in-rushing tide flooded the whole domain of thought." But it did not follow that because it flooded the whole domain of thought, all which floated in on that tide was true. What happened may be described in the words of Professor Gray: —

"In saying that the doctrine of 'evolution of species' has taken its place among scientific beliefs, I do not mean that it has been accepted by all living naturalists, for there are some who wholly reject it; nor that it is held with equal conviction and

[1] Advance of Science in the Last Half Century. T. H. Huxley, F.R.S.

in the same way by all who receive it, for some teach it dogmatically, along with assumptions both scientific and philosophical, which are to us both unwarranted and unwelcome ; more accept it with various confidence, and in a tentative way, for its purely scientific uses, and without any obvious reference to its ultimate outcome ; and some, looking to its probable prevalence, are adjusting their beliefs in it to cherished beliefs of another order. One thing is clear, — that the current is all running one way, and seems unlikely to run dry ; and that evolutionary doctrines are profoundly affecting all natural science."

The Unitarian position is not committed to any detail of this working-theory of evolution, but it finds itself helped along its own lines of a firm conviction of the progress of the race by the method of thought which evolution affords. Unitarianism is pledged to progress along all lines ; it looks for a Revelation which takes the whole race for its audience, all time for its duration, all themes for its subject, and all worlds for its field. Says Professor Gray : —

"When the naturalist is asked what and whence the origin of man, he can only answer in the words of Quatrefage and Virchow, 'We do not know at all.' We have traces of his existence up to and even anterior to the later climatic changes in our temperate zone ; but he was there perfected man, and no trace of an earlier form is known. The believer in a special creation is entitled to the benefit of the negative evidence. A totally unknown ancestry has the characteristics of nobility. The evolutionist can give one assurance, — as the wolf in the fable was captious in his complaint that the lamb below had muddied the brook he was drinking from, so those are mistaken who suppose that the Simian race can have defiled the stream along which evolution traces human descent. Sober evolutionists do not suppose that man has descended from the monkeys. The stream must have branched too early for that. The resemblances which are the same in fact under any theory are supposed to denote collateral relationship."

The sentimental objection to evolution is thus removed. But it must be admitted that the difficulty of accounting for man is not in the slightest degree reduced. The most that can be said for this admission is that it puts the deed of the property into the hands of an unquestioned family of brethren, without fear of the intrusion of the cousins-german to dispute the inheritance.

Unitarianism is pledged to the production of the highest style of life. This life it seeks to produce not by blind imitation, but by development from within; it is not startled by being told that the human family is derived from a family not human in its features at first, for if that hypothesis be proved, as it seems likely to be, then the fact that *we have become so nearly human as we now are* is a "sure word of prophecy" to which we do well to take heed. Our golden age is on ahead; we do not lament an Eden in which the tree of life is guarded so sternly; we have "the knowledge of good and evil," and we will yet find a way to eat of the "tree of life." We even dare hope that we shall live forever; and this, too, science has taught us to expect. I am little disposed to indulge in arguments from analogy, after the manner of that most overestimated book, "Natural Law in the Spiritual World;" yet analogy, which left to itself is like a railroad track, — two parallel lines which never meet, — may still be used, if they can be made to meet in that which travels on the track thus laid down. Well, modern scientific thought has pointed out to the hope of timid man that Nature is wholly ignorant of the most dreadful word in all our human speech: Nature does not know the word "death." Birth, Nature the fruitful mother knows well, and finds in it no fear. She fills the world with life. Her fecundity knows no limit; for when she bears more children than she can maintain, she but touches them with her magic wand and they are changed, but do not die. Nature knows two words well, — *change* and *continuance!* We think we shall not die!

There is a fine saying of Herbert Spencer: "Perfect correspondence would be perfect life. Were there no changes in the environment but such as the organism had adapted changes to meet, and were it never to fail in the efficiency with which it met them, there would be eternal existence and eternal knowledge."

A moral being seeking the good of all other beings is trying an experiment in perfect correspondence; such an one hails all the serious teachers of ethics, modern and ancient, to his aid in the endeavor to live upon a line of conduct which will fit the demand the universe makes upon its moral subjects.

A spiritual being seeking to know its spiritual environment is trying an experiment in perfect correspondence; such an one calls to his aid all those who know the human soul, not by description, but by a conscious experience, and he seeks with these to enter into the communion with the Highest so intimately that he shall not know where the will called human ends, and the will which is Divine begins; we call this *communion;* this is a synonym for eternal life.

But in all this we must not rest in second causes; that is fatal at once to scientific thought and to all discovery upon the part of the spiritual being who is seeking to find his relation to the universe. Most of the confusion which we have suffered has come from want of true spiritual enterprise, — a timid content with second causes.

The Unitarian, of all believers, is best equipped and least encumbered; he is committed to no past, except a past so remote that there are no records, — only here and there a bold handwriting made by the passing glacier on the imperishable rock; he is committed to no theory of ethics, save that which here and now will do honor to the perfect moral order of the world; he is pledged to no system of philosophy, save that which is indeed the love of wisdom. But one obligation is laid upon this man of whom we speak; each hour of his life, so little in its span, so tremendous in its vision, he shall renew his allegiance to the inviolable order of the universe, — a universe in which Cause and Effect are married together beyond the possibility of divorce. Let him make his life over to the keeping of this faith, that the universe cannot be arrayed against itself.

Perhaps no better illustration can be given of ideal Unitarianism in conscious harmony with the scientific temper and method than is to be seen in the life and work of the late William B. Carpenter; and as I began this paper with the quotation from Prof. Asa Gray, "Youth is ever taught by instances, manhood is taught by laws," so I will now close it with the words which Dr. Sadler uttered over the last resting-place of the mortal remains of the immortal seeker after truth: —

"At a time when religion and science have appeared too often unhappily divided, it is hardly possible to overestimate the significance of their union in him, of his steadfast avowal of his own faith, and his personal sympathy with and participation in Christian worship. It is hardly possible to overestimate the value of the contributions from his pen on religious subjects. To none of those who have given up all religious profession was a narrow and unspiritual theology more repellent than to him. But in the home of his childhood he breathed an atmosphere of religious freedom and of religious feeling, and was led by precept and example to think freely and earnestly on religious subjects; and the result was that his large intellectual culture did not repress in him a most devotional spirit, but gave it a wider range, and enabled it to soar up higher, foreshadowing, I trust, the way in which

> 'That in us which thinks and that which feels
> Shall everlastingly be reconciled,
> And that which questioneth with that which kneels.'" [1]

[1] Nature and Man.

THE LAW OF RIGHTEOUSNESS.

BY GEORGE BATCHELOR.

THERE are innumerable ways in which one might treat the subject assigned to me. Out of them all, I select that which seems to me most direct, practical, and easy of application. That which concerns us most to know is the motive *power* of the ethical life, and the way to get it under control.

Concerning this, the first thing which occurs to me to say is, that the sooner we drop the word "ethics" from common use, the sooner we shall be rid of one barrier between us and the popular heart. Ethics is a cold, scholastic, bloodless word, having little meaning except for scholars and for those who admire scholarship. No word that ends in "ic" or "ics" ever flashed into view on the crest of a wave of popular feeling.[1] Morals is a better word, because it is better understood. But it is not *much* better, because there is in it a suggestion of outwardness. Morality, to the popular imagination, suggests a polish of the surface without any deep stirring of the heart. Against this prejudice of the people it is useless to strive. In part it is right, and is to be taken as a traditional protest against an ordering of the life which is merely politic, conventional, and in motive selfish. There is many a man who answers to all the definitions of morality, who is hard, shallow, unloving, and unlovely; and the people are right when they repel and condemn what they mean when they speak of "mere morality."

[1] *Music* may be an exception.

But let it be remembered, always, that the morality for which Unitarians have stood has never been this bloodless ideal of correct behavior, but a more virile thing, which deserves a better name. What that thing is it will be my aim to set before you. The one word which has never been spoiled, because it is alive with the hot blood of heroic forms of human life, is "righteousness." A righteous man is wise as to what is right. Righteousness is right-wis-ness, — from the ancient verb, to wit, — right-wisdom, right-knowing, ending in right feeling and right acting. Ethics is the *science* of morality; but righteousness is the divine wisdom incarnate. Morals may be part of an external polish: righteousness can be nothing less than the outward expression of the deep-seated life. In our English language, this good word, from its earliest days, gathered about itself associations of the noblest kind. It easily connected itself with examples of wisdom, and traditions of heroism. Right-knowing-ness makes life massive, solid with virtues and motives which are of one kind within and without.

Now, to reach some definite conclusion as to the way in which this right-wisdom, or right-knowing-ness, is increased in the life of man, let us take first some of the more common and least regarded aids to the good life. Many of them have little regard to motive. They are often mere tricks of expediency, but they help to illustrate the principles which at last must have application as the tests of motives and the guides of life. You and I learn most quickly and practise with most willingness the virtues which aid us in getting a living and in the enjoyment of society. For this reason, business is a teacher of morality of the first order. Mr. Atkinson has recently stated a fact which illustrates. In business operations employing about eight hundred millions of dollars, he computes the losses from faithless creditors at about one fourth of one per cent. I once asked a seedsman, who scattered his little boxes of garden seeds all over the Northwest, leaving one at every little wayside grocery and provision store, whether he did not find great difficulty in making collections from such scattered and irresponsible agents. His reply, that he counted on losses of only one half of one per cent, greatly surprised me. Standing one day in the Hall of the Board of Trade in Chicago, an enthusiastic broker of great experience said to me, pointing at the howling mob who apparently were tearing each other in pieces in the wheat-ring, "There is more honor to the square foot on that floor than in any other spot in this world." In a certain way he proved his point. On that floor transactions, involving commonly thousands and often millions of dollars, have on record no evidence but the turn of a finger and a scratch in a note-book. Such transactions are often disastrous, and sometimes ruinous, to one or the other party; but, except in the rarest cases, the repudiation of a bargain is unknown. Honor, trust, fidelity, pluck, patience, fortitude, and uncommon honesty are the characteristic virtues of the Board of Trade.

What is true of the Board of Trade is true everywhere according to the measure of the necessity. Mutual service and mutual confidence are the solid foundations of the business of the world. Were these virtues not largely developed in human society, modern commerce and modern civilization would be impossible. Righteousness as right-knowing-ness has advanced so far. It is preparing soon to make another advance, and to say to the governments of the world, for instance, that slavery and war must stop, because business cannot afford the enormous waste of life and treasure which is now robbing industry of more than half the products of its toil. When business gives the command to call a halt, the kings of the world will take counsel together and will obey.

Business, I say, is a teacher of righteousness. But we must not forget to make the needed comment that business *may be* only a teacher of expediency. "Honesty is the best policy," is a business maxim which often reads the other way, "Policy is the best honesty." That is to say, a man may be commercially honest and morally a rogue. It does not always follow that he who has the virtues of his craft or trade has any other virtues, or that he practises *them* except when on duty as a business man. A man may be scrupulously exact in regard to a business transaction, and yet lie without a scruple concerning any fact which has no commercial value. I asked another broker concerning the social morals of these members of the Board of Trade. He had been a member of it twenty-three years. He said that they were subject to great vicissitudes of fortune, and therefore were often very irregular in their modes of life. A stroke of good luck was often followed by a champagne supper and excessive expenditure; and the temptation always is to resort to stimulants to keep their nerves up to concert pitch. Three or four years were about the limit of an average career. "Why," said he, "I have seen men enough go through this Board to make a city." So there I learned the good and the bad of it. The law was absolute trustiness as the condition of success. The exception, much too common, was a reckless disregard of that which alone makes success desirable. But, I reflected, the needed lesson will be taught. The law will endure; the exception will pass away. Business is competent to show the folly of such physical waste from a commercial point of view. The most efficient temperance work done to-day is done by business, which begins to discriminate between its agents who are sound in brain and nerve, and those who are excitable and unsteady. By this reference to business I wish to indicate one of the methods employed by Nature in the process of evolution to educate man to right-wisdom, or righteousness.

When business has finished its work in bringing out the trusty qualities in a man, society steps in and undertakes to complete the work by shaping the character of the gentleman. business teaches one what he must do to be trusted; then society teaches him certain decencies and graces which he must honestly and faithfully observe, at whatever cost to himself, in order to be accounted a gentleman. There is no virtue which at one time or another has not been so cultivated, in order to furnish the accomplishments of the gentle-*man* or the gentle-*woman*. The lady is simply "a perfect woman nobly planned."

Now right here Unitarianism has taken her stand, and has always affirmed that the right-wis-ness, or right-knowing-ness, of the business man is good, and that the gentle courtesy of the business man become a gentleman is better; that the great bulk of common honesty is real, and the most of the virtue of the world is not conventional, but genuine. She has seen the sham and detected the veneer. She has sometimes found beneath the methodical business life the greed of the ravenous beast not yet fully tamed, and under the polish of the conventional gentleman has sometimes detected the morals of the savage and the brute. How false a conventional ideal may become when used merely for the selfish purposes of society, is shown by an anecdote which, true or false in fact, is true to the life of a type of social development. In a foreign divorce case, an injured husband summoned as a witness a royal prince, whom he believed to have guilty knowledge of his wife's fatal defect. Now, the code of honor in such a case has always bound a gentleman to protect the reputation of a woman at any risk to himself. Of her character he might be careless, but not of her reputation or her good name. The royal prince took his oath, and, as his comrades said, "perjured himself like a gentleman."

Unitarianism has seen the evil thus masquerading under the similitude of goodness. But she has not, therefore, despaired of human nature. She has declared that the maxims, habits, customs, laws, of the well-ordered outer life are illustrations of laws eternal and divine. She has insisted that the law should be pondered and obeyed for its own glorious sake, and that deep within the heart must be hid the principles of integrity, out of which arise by native impulse all the strong and beautiful forms of life. Hence it has happened that she has furnished the world with incomparable examples of business integrity and refined culture. Her merchants have been filled with the spirit of right-knowing-ness. Her gentlemen have been without fear and without reproach. Her women have been angels of mercy and children of the light.

Nature has many such praiseworthy ways of educating her children. But it would take us too far from our main purpose to follow her into all the homes and haunts of men and women, and show how ceaselessly and how thoroughly she is educating the race through the common necessities of existence to the exhibition of virtues of every kind. There is no common task or most homely domestic necessity which has not its appropriate virtue. Patience, steadiness, steadfastness, courage, fidelity, order, decency, thrift, fortitude, public spirit, and the whole list of virtues manly and womanly, grow as naturally out of the soil of social and domestic necessity as "the earth bringeth forth her bud, and as the garden causeth the things that are sown in it to spring forth." Nature, — let me say Nature still, we shall reach a higher thought soon, — Nature puts before a human creature a possibility of a new relation or a higher relation or a nobler fulfilment of an old one; and she says: "There is your opportunity to get, to do, to be, the thing that for its goodness or its pleasantness invites you. You can have what you want, do what you like, and be what you please, If" — That "If" is the sign of a virtue. That "If" always stands for law, irreversible and enduring. It fixes conditions. If you would have, or do, or be, anything whatever, you must be, or you must do, that which matches your intent. The word "ought" is the sign of a relation of equality. The "If" means that you must even up on your side, over against what you wish or what you get. If you do not so even up by performance on your part, you are in debt. You owe. You ought. Now Nature is constantly giving us beyond our desert. She keeps us constantly in debt. Now and then, in some vision, or dream, or ideal or suggested opportunity, she shows us what kind of men and women we should be if we paid our debts; and then she leaves us to a noble chagrin, until we consent to pay in service and in being what we can never return in kind.

Among the noblest of these natural suggestions of which Unitarianism has always made much, is that related to the august words, "Our Country." Above the range of business, and with wider outlook than belongs to the simple gentleman, the Country reveals a whole constellation of possible duties, which have in them scarcely a suggestion of selfish advantage. The Country wants service which can be rendered only by loyal citizens, men and women of public spirit, — by lawgivers who are magnanimous, by judges who are incorruptible, by statesmen of great ideals, by heroes who have heart's blood to shed, and by women who will give their sons to die for the national honor. All these, and many other excellent forms of human character and service, the State demands, and must have or perish. Constantly the State confers benefit and increases our debt. Then she waits, offering meanwhile certain duties which must be done, suggesting certain forms of character which befit her servants, and holding up to the view of all the world the ideal service for which she invites competition. The Nation which needs and constantly wishes to have an ideal character of any kind seldom waits long with dream unfulfilled, whether she asks for hero or statesman, lawgiver or leader of men. In this way the virtues are produced even before men think of them and give them names. Nine tenths of what we call religion is, in form, Hebrew patriotism idealized and carried out into wider relations. The source of that which is noblest in American character is English love of home and country, transplanted and transfigured. The machinery for the production of virtue is always ready and always at work. That the products it turns out are not always good is due to the lack of an element which we are soon to consider, — the part that man consciously plays in the process of helping on the moral progress of the world. The machine must grind, and it grinds any grist. If it is not attended to, it turns out swindlers and rogues as well as incorruptible merchants and bankers. It turns out to-day the statesman and to-morrow the demagogue, and over against the Christian it exhibits the hypocrite. And this it does because the only motive thus far suggested is that of utility. That is useful which serves the purpose. Short cuts are often attempted. The seeming is often easier than the doing, and it may apparently serve the same purpose.

Right here Unitarianism takes her stand, and with much diversity of philosophic explanation has but one way of looking at human life and duty. Whatever may serve for transient expedients or may answer for a temporary purpose, nothing is worthy of a *man* which does not come from within, out of the human will and conscience. Outward necessities and superficial adjustment of conduct to occasion may, indeed, reveal the *forms* of duty, but can never supply the motive power of a man intent upon living his life in all its moods and tenses. Nature, through the utilities of life, does her work in fragments. She brings nothing to completeness. She seems to turn out enough for a sample, and then leaves it, as if to say, "There, that is what I mean: take it or leave it. But if you want any more of that kind, you will have to make it." She makes, for instance, one great statesman like Lincoln, or one military hero like Sheridan, to serve one immediate purpose. But she does not spend her time making more of them, unless man takes a hand consciously in the process. When we see that the virtues of the hero and statesman are lovely for their own sake, noble adornments of the perfect life, then a new order of things begins.

This new order begins by the association of another set of human experiences with these ideas of utility which have been developed in the frictions of social life. We cannot stop now to consider by what a devious road man came to his outlook on things eternal. But one thing is, to my mind, certain. When man first began to regard himself as part of a larger order of things, when he, for the first time, regarding himself as the offspring of Deity, began to hope for a continuance of being and an extension of opportunity, then morality "struck in," and virtue took on a finer quality. Rightness of thought, feeling, and conduct, was no longer limited to the exigency of the moment. It was no longer sufficient to ask, Does the deed fit the need? But the deeper question asked itself, Does the need itself fit the man? Is this an occasion worthy of one who has before him a great career?

We are brought now to the distinction between the two principal forms into which our thinking about right doing can be cast, — the only distinction of sufficient importance to press now upon your attention. Do you think first and most of the *ends* of moral action? Then you are a Utilitarian. Do you think first and most of the *quality* of the act and the life out of which it proceeds? Then you are a Transcendentalist. That is, if you do right because that is the best way to win money, or power, or friends, or happiness, or the favor of God, or a future life, or heaven itself, you are a Utilitarian. You may be a very good and lovely one, but you have not yet in you the root of the whole matter, and will not easily withstand temptation when on the right side there is no money nor any friends, nor prizes of power, popularity, and happiness. On the other side, you are a Transcendentalist if you do right things because they are true, honorable, just, pure, lovely, and gracious. You have the root of the matter within you. Your leaf shall not wither, and whatever you do shall prosper.

Now the great merit of Unitarianism has been that it has given due heed to both the quality of the *life* and to the consequences of *action;* and this it has done because it has, with even balance, held in equal honor both ethics and religion, blending them in that consummate compound, the wisdom of rightness, right-knowing-ness, about life and its objects.

There is a danger just here which the most practical person cannot afford to forget. All extremes are dangerous. Now the Utilitarian is the one who prefers the useful to the useless.

He who would make the most of his strength is especially liable to the temptation to neglect the quality of his own life, and to think of the useful ends to be attained. So long as they are good, why is not all well with him? We will not now speak of the low forms of moral conduct which may result from making the consequences of action the test of virtue; but we will strike right at the highest forms of pure Utilitarianism, and assert that, if the sole end of action be the attainment of something outside of yourself, then is your virtue in just so far superficial and shallow. Do you not see that it is all outside of yourself, both motive power and object? Even the power you exert is drawn out of you, not thrust out by abundance of inward strength. In this fact is to be found an explanation of that frequent spectacle, — a man or woman great, really great and good for some one noble exploit, and for all other things a disappointment both to others and to one's self. The greatness came out of an opportunity outside of the person, and was due to stirring motives which worked on the will through external prizes set in view; it was due to a drawing which, while it lasted, could take any common stuff of humanity, and show it in the colors of heroism and righteousness. This exhibition, with its after-story of failure, is often disappointing; but really it is an object-lesson of value. It shows what latent wealth is concealed in homely human lives. Now the one thing which can make that commonplace life, with its one streak of gold, to be golden throughout, is an inward law of conduct and an inward impulse to goodness, which shall be as strong to push as any external inducement can be to draw; and this is often shown in a case which might be set over against the last example as a companion picture. Some poor, unknown, wise man, with the right-wisdom in his heart, is forced into the bearing of burdens and the taking of responsibilities; and he goes on from the first with modest bearing and steady course, never failing, never shrinking, never disappointing the desire of his fellows, steadily growing in grace and power, and at last by common consent is called great, although in fact he is only one golden lump, well refined, extracted from the ore of our common nature by the heat and power of the self-fed and consuming fire of an inward purpose.

We see herein the reason why Unitarianism has been forced, in the interest of righteousness itself, to protest against all forms of moral teaching which set the motive for action outside of the individual reason and conscience. All virtue which takes its strength from the drawing power of the prize offered must be unsteady and superficial, even though the prize be the favor of God himself and the eternal enjoyment of his heaven. The Preacher said, " Better is it to have virtue and to have no children." Unitarianism goes further, and says, " Better is it to have virtue and to have no immortality than to be virtuous because the wages of virtue are great."

We come now to that which I shall make short for your patience' sake, but which I wish to leave in your mind as my final and inclusive statement. As I read history and human life, this interior, noble, self-compelling obedience to law, and this upspringing gladness and content to make right-wisdom the law of one's inner life and the shaper of one's outward conduct, never did, never will, and never can reach its highest form when entirely and wholly divorced from what we commonly mean by religious belief in its highest forms. I do not mean some general uplooking and uplifting of the will. I mean a definite and steady upreaching of the whole life towards moral being, not of this world, with some clearly defined and definite expectation of an opportunity to exercise the moral nature greater than this little life of ours ever has given or ever can give. Martineau would have been less great than he is, could he not have made his own the *naïve* confession which he puts into the mouth of the agnostic: "If once you allow yourself to think about the origin and the end of things, you will have to believe in a God and immortality."[1]

I stop but one moment to meet the objection that some of the noblest forms of ethical character are exhibited to-day by men and women who have none of this faith. Take, if you please, Matthew Arnold, with his famous formula, "A Power not ourselves which makes for righteousness," and George Eliot, with her still more famous and winning song, "The Choir Invisible;" and of both of them I say. The ideal they had they did not unfold. They took an ideal which had been wrought into their lives by others, and which they would have been powerless to create, and tried to adapt it to agnostic forms of thinking, and had little success in so doing. It is not always necessary that, in a given case, a noble religious belief shall accompany a high moral ideal; but before any man shall have attained to a high moral ideal, some man must have preceded him with that generous thought of human nature which always sees a chance for it better than earth and time can give. The winning ideal, once let loose in human thought, can live long outside its native air of heaven; but exiled too long, it must pine away and die.

Truth is the basis of duty. Right thinking is the guide of feeling, and furnishes the rule of conduct. Now it ought

[1] Study of Religion, Preface, p. vii.

not to be necessary to assert that duty is most nobly enthroned, and is most loyally obeyed, where God has been honored and man has been regarded as his offspring. But it does happen to be necessary to assert that just now, because our Christian civilization has produced a choice handful of noble-hearted men and women who, for the moment, do not connect in thought their enthusiasm for humanity with the great thought which gave it birth. Prove that through the ages no increasing purpose runs, and that man will never have any knowledge of this universe beyond what he can learn standing on the crust of this earth, or in flying perchance a league above it among the clouds, — prove that, and not instantly, but soon, the thought concerning the worth of human nature and its possibilities will begin to shrink. Some things that now seem worth doing for the poor, the sick, the wicked, will seem useless tasks and burdens, to be cleared away by harsh measures, if necessary.

I believe that men never began to work for Man until, latent or confessed, there began to stir within them the thought that Man was immortal, and that no pains taken in his behalf could be wholly fruitless. I do not believe that any man ever began to take interest in the refuse and dregs of human society, and to regard with compassion individuals who were horrible to contemplate, until into his thought, and from his thought into his imagination, and from his imagination into his sympathies, began to move the awakening suggestion that this brute, this beast, this demoniac outcast, was of kin to himself, and not only might have been a man, but might yet be one. At least, there must have been pity for one fallen from so high a place and so noble a fortune, and some desire to get the dreadful remains out of sight and decently cared for, — a suggestion which does not haunt us when we see a cur that has missed his destiny, "a dog that has had his day." As the imperious call of duty is not heard in the higher ranges of the soul until the soul-awakening truth is heard, so also the inspiring shout of freemen is never heard, and never has been heard anywhere around the girdle of the earth, until there has been proclaimed "the liberty of the sons of God." After that has been heard, liberty, fraternity, equality, may become the battle-cries of those who disbelieve in God and deny the immortality of man. But their inspiration is borrowed; or, rather it is the natural expression of a nature which by the truth has been set free.

It is for this reason that the benefactions and the training in righteousness of our church have been marked by such breadth of humanitarian zeal. Our church has taught us that we are not merely to do our duty to all men : it has also added the inspiring assurance that all men are worthy of our best. We have been taught that, even when a man discharges the most common obligations of the citizen, he is in a real sense doing that which may reach to the farthest bounds of the universe and the latest hour of time. Hence it follows that, so greatly out of proportion to the numbers of her children, our church has furnished the men and women who have done the public work of statesmanship, reform, and philanthropy.

When one is thinking of the external inducements to virtue, the prizes that religion offers may be somewhat lightly set aside on the ground that virtue that is paid for is not of the right tincture. But when one is thinking of the motives to the righteous life which spring up in profusion out of the great revelations and companionships which religion opens to man, he must be singularly blind to the causes and springs of action who can say that they can be left out of the account and man still retain all the motives of the righteous life. That capital " If," of which I spoke as the sign of virtue in the lower stages of the utilities, assumes majestic proportions when one thinks of himself as in debt for a universe, in debt to an Eternal Spirit for life, in debt for the gift of an immortal possibility. If you would be worthy of your kin, if you would have, or be, or do, what your kinship implies and requires of you, some very lofty virtues are in order. These virtues may or may not have commercial value. They may or may not assist us in the pursuit of what men call happiness. But they are imperative, nevertheless, on all who are moved by a sense of honor, and who have attained to the right-wisdom. The imperious sense of responsibility felt by all well-born creatures, the mysterious debt which oppresses the conscience of every man, and is confessed in that primitive word I *ought*, gets its final sanction only when one looks up with loving gratitude to the Giver of every good and perfect gift, and says, " I ought, because to Thee I owe life, love, liberty, and the delights of all my conscious being." In other ways we get our philosophy of ethics, in other ways we get our science of morals, in other ways we learn how to order the external affairs of life ; but for the supplying of motives no way has been invented so fruitful as the spirit of *sonship*, which is the essence of the noblest form of religion that has yet appeared upon the earth. Out of this flow reverence for that which is great and inimitable for the beauty of its goodness ; ambition to fill out somewhat the outlines of the noble career suggested to immortal creatures ; hope that the dream of goodness is not a delusion, but a reflection of the solid realities of the eternal life of which we are a part ; and, above all, love for human creatures, not merely because they are agreeable, but because they are our brothers by a tie which reaches above us all, and makes the distinctions of human society to be trivial. Benevolence flows from this in a stream which could never have been supplied by the (in comparison) petty sentiments of personal friendship, family affection, tribal partiality, the most magnanimous patriotism, or cosmopolitan sympathy. These grow thin as they widen. The Christlike spirit is intense in proportion to its breadth and the volume of its increasing stream. Every part and possibility of the universe which comes within our reach or our hope must be drawn upon, that the man of God may be thoroughly furnished for every good work; or, as Charles G. Ames puts it, "we need not only ethical culture, but total culture."

THE RELATION OF UNITARIANISM TO PHILOSOPHY.

BY CHARLES CARROLL EVERETT.

THE subject upon which I have been asked to speak to you is the Relation of Unitarianism to Philosophy. It is possible that to some this bringing together of Unitarianism and philosophy may seem artificial, if not meaningless. Unitarianism, it may be said, is not a philosophy. It is the simplest form of religious faith. It is a belief in God and in the soul's relation to him as Jesus taught them and manifested them in his life. It is thus something which is simple and clear, as free from the subtleties of metaphysics as from the complications of ritualism. Certainly, if we mean by philosophy a ponderous system of metaphysical speculation, Unitarianism is not, and does not represent, a philosophy. But philosophy, in itself considered, is something much simpler than this. It is not so much a system as it is the idea which takes form in a system. Every one of us is in a sense a philosopher. I do not mean that each one of us has a consciously held system of the universe, which he could state and defend; but each one of us holds, consciously or unconsciously, a certain view of the nature of the world and of the meaning of life, according to which his own life is in a great measure shaped. As I have intimated, we do not always know just what this theory or principle is. We might be surprised if we should suddenly discover according to what theory of life we are living. Many a man thinks that his faith is spiritual, while the real faith according to which he lives, and which by his life he proves to be what he really holds, is materialistic. Many a man who thinks he is a materialist may at heart be spiritual. The man who says, "Let us eat and drink, for to-morrow we die," has his philosophy of life; and when Paul cried, "For me to live is Christ, and to die is gain," he had his philosophy. In each case this philosophy might be expanded into a system. It has its assumptions that could be developed, illustrated, and defended; and the relation of all the facts of the universe, so far as they are known, to these assumptions could be set forth.

Unitarianism, in this sense at least, represents a philosophy. This philosophy could be, and indeed has been, developed with greater or less accuracy into various systems. The philosophy of Unitarianism would be the simplest form of the philosophy of religion. It would have to be differentiated on the one side from systems that are not religious, and on the other side from systems of religion which involve principles that Unitarianism disowns. You see how large is the task assigned to me, and will pardon me if I can hardly make a beginning in its accomplishment.

While Unitarianism stands, for the most part, in the simplicity of its faith, not troubling itself about the philosophical assumptions upon which it logically rests, any more than the tree cares for the roots which are hidden in the soil to which they bind it, it is confronted by systems that are antagonistic to its own, which are elaborated into organic completeness, and are defended by a subtle logic. The two forms of thought with which, as a philosophy of religion, it finds itself most directly confronted are agnosticism and materialism. As a form of faith it is obviously opposed to agnosticism; as a form of spiritual faith it is no less obviously opposed to materialism. There are also current, at the present day, forms of philosophy which are neither agnostic, materialistic, nor spiritualistic. The philosophy of Schopenhauer, for instance, and the Philosophy of the Unconscious, put forth by Von Hartmann, are of this sort. With such systems, however, I conceive that Unitarianism does not very often come into conflict. They are philosophies of the study, philosophies of philosophers, or of those who fancy that they are such. Agnosticism and materialism, on the other hand, in some shape or other are in the air. They are met in more or less complete form at every turn; and thus it is with them that Unitarianism stands in the most direct relation.

I have used the word "agnosticism" as if it had a single and definite meaning. In fact, the word varies in significance with the persons by whom it is used, or to whom it is applied. The word is simply a profession of ignorance, and ignorance may be of various sorts and degrees. In its popular use the word has its literal etymological sense. It means that the person who calls himself by this name, however wise he may be in regard to other matters, in regard to spiritual things knows nothing, and has no faith that soars where knowledge cannot climb. It is a striking fact that this age, which extends its investigations to the farthest star and to the most minute atom, should to so large an extent, by the use of the word "agnostic," proclaim its ignorance in regard to the highest themes that can occupy the human thought. The word may be, and sometimes is, used in humility. It expresses the awe of the spirit in the presence of the heights and depths of being. Sometimes it is used in a sense more definite than its etymology would imply, and expresses denial. Its modest meaning becomes transformed to pride, as it sweeps away with a breath, as childish and outgrown, the faiths which have been the solace and the inspiration of so many of the noblest lives. Sometimes it is used to express an utter bewilderment in regard to the whole region of religious thought. It is not strange that such bewilderment exists. The church itself is rent by opposing sects, and thus presents no solid front to the world. Outside the church, the air is full of criticism. Discussions that are aimed at the subversion of positive religious faith stand forth in stately volumes, and find a free field in our magazines. In the face of all this, we sometimes wonder that there are not even more to give up the thing in despair, and to say frankly, "I do not know." For the word, in this use of it, is the utterance of despair, or perhaps more often of an indolent indifference.

In the use of the word that we have been considering it has nothing to distinguish it from the word so freely used in the last generation, — the word "sceptic." Scepticism etymologically implies a little more activity of mind than the word agnosticism. It implies a certain looking about. It suggests a hope that at some time it may discover what is actually true. Agnosticism, on the other hand, expresses the blankness of a hopeless ignorance. Practically, however, the word "scepticism" meant for the most part a fixed attitude of mind. The sceptic too often forgot to look about; and thus the popular agnosticism is simply scepticism under another name. Like that, it is often, practically, a materialism that does not care to avow itself as such.

Why is it that there is this change of name when there is so little change of front? It is partly fashion. It is partly because the world having grown more tolerant of doubt and unbelief, it is convenient to drop a name that has been often used as a term of reproach, or which at least has had a bad odor. I think, however, the real reason that has given such currency to the word "agnostic" is, that it has been felt to have a certain philosophic dignity. Herbert Spencer has been by many regarded as the chief of agnostics, and the word "agnosticism" has been felt, therefore, to represent in some more or less definite, or more or less general way, his system. We have therefore to glance at the so-called agnosticism of Herbert Spencer.

I speak of Spencer's so-called agnosticism. I do not remember that he himself uses the term which Professor Huxley claims, I believe, to have been the first to use with the signification that we are considering. Herbert Spencer does, however, speak often of "The Unknowable." In his thought the Unknowable fills the place that God fills in the thought of theism. Since he speaks thus of the Absolute as the Unknowable, he might seem to be very properly classed among the agnostics, if not indeed to be their foremost representative.

The term "unknowable," however, has many different aspects and shades of meaning. A thing may be regarded as unknowable on account of its own nature, or, on the other hand, on account of the inadequacy of the human faculties, or on account of our own inadequate equipment or that of the age to which we belong. It may be well to make these distinctions clear by a few illustrations. Is the planet Mars inhabited? This we do not and at present cannot know. The thing is not unknowable in itself, any more than the fact of the peopling of some island in the South Sea. We, however, who are dwellers in this world, have no means of discovering whether Mars is inhabited or not. What is the precise diameter of Mars? Some of us, perhaps many of us, are agnostics on this point, not because the thing is unknowable or unknown, but simply because we do not happen to know, and have not at the moment at hand any authority that will determine the thing for us. Compare with such questions as these the questions, What is the extent of space? How many millions of miles would measure its diameter? That you cannot say. That no one can say. The difficulty is not, as before, with our mental powers or our means of information. We cannot tell because it is not to be told. Space cannot be measured, because it is immeasurable. In this sense we may say that the dimensions of space are unknowable. Let us take one or two examples of a different order. How long was the Chinese Wall in building? Here again we do not know. We are agnostics because we have no means of information. How long is eternity? This you cannot say, because eternity has no measurable length. It is immeasurable.

When you claim that the world will always be ignorant as to the habitability of Mars, you can defend your position by reasoning based upon the inherent limitation of telescopic power and of our own mental equipment. So far as this is concerned we are in hopeless ignorance. Our agnosticism in regard to the dimensions of space and the length of eternity, on the other hand, is based not upon the limitation of our powers, but upon the nature of space and of time. It is based, then, not upon our ignorance but upon our knowledge. Space being what it is and what we know that it is, and time being what it is and what we know that it is, we know that each is immeasurable; that if they were measurable they would cease to be what they are. When therefore we say that we cannot tell the dimensions of space or the length of eternity, it is our knowledge, not our ignorance, that speaks. What we called at first agnosticism, it appears, was gnosticism.

When Herbert Spencer speaks of the Unknowable, does he have reference to the imperfection of our faculties, or to the nature of that of which he speaks? Certainly it is the latter.

He shows, or he undertakes to show, that being what it is, the Absolute is and must be unknowable.

If he maintains that from its very nature the Absolute is unknowable, it must be because he assumes that he knows its nature. Indeed, he continually speaks of the Unknowable as manifesting itself. That must be a very helpless Absolute that should be continually manifesting itself and never make itself in the slightest degree manifested. This is not the place for an examination of the special position of Herbert Spencer. That is a matter for the schools. I wish merely to make clear that if he maintains that the Absolute from its nature is unknowable, it must be because he, so far, knows its nature. He speaks, not as an agnostic, but as a gnostic.

You will notice that the position is a paradoxical one. Spencer quotes Saint Augustine as occupying a position like his own. Saint Augustine, however, put the thing in the form of a paradox: *Cognoscendo ignorari, et ignorando cognosci,* — that is, our knowledge consists in the recognition of our ignorance. What Saint Augustine puts rhetorically as a paradox, Herbert Spencer puts dogmatically as a logical statement. If we say, however, that the Absolute, being what we know it to be, is not to be known, it is obvious that we confound knowledge and ignorance. Either we must do as the fiery Saint Augustine did, fuse knowledge and ignorance together into a paradox and hurl the burning phrase at the listener, or we must speak more calmly, and say that we know in part and only in part.

I have dwelt upon this to make it as clear as may be possible under the circumstances, that there is no agnosticism which has a philosophical foundation, in the proper sense of the words "agnosticism" and "philosophical." There is a popular agnosticism which is not to be distinguished from the old-fashioned scepticism, and there is the so-called philosophical agnosticism, which is simply a form of gnosticism which denies the name.

If there be no such thing as a philosophical agnosticism, the absolute, *a priori* barrier to thought does not exist, and the thinker has only to determine, by actual experiment in the use of his powers, what is the line that separates the known from the unknown, the knowable from the unknowable. This being so, we are not surprised that the foremost representative of Herbert Spencer's teaching in America, Mr. John Fiske, should take a step beyond his master, and in his admirable little book entitled " The Idea of God " should insist that we must assume the Absolute to be of the nature of spirit rather than of matter.

I have already intimated that what calls itself "agnosticism " is often a disguised materialism. Assuming that the spiritual realities which religion accepts cannot be known to exist, many put everything into materialistic formulæ, and the result is practically the same as if the material were everything. Materialism, indeed, or the tendency to this, is not infrequent in these days in which investigation has no limit, and thought no bound. This is not singular when we consider that the great discoveries of the age have been in regard to material things, that the lines of thought of the age run in the direction of material relations. Even the investigations and speculations in regard to human society and welfare concern for the most part the material well-being of men. I do not wish to do injustice to the other side of our modern life. We cannot deny, however, that the emphasis has been of late rather upon the material than the spiritual.

Materialism has much to commend it, at least to crude and superficial thought. It seems to make no demands upon faith. It does not stretch the thought beyond what is just at hand. It might perhaps be a little confused if it were asked what this matter is of which it talks so glibly. It might have no answer ready if it were asked to prove the existence even of this outer world. It might have to admit that here also faith and vision are inextricably intertwined. But these questions and difficulties do not trouble those who claim to take what they see and what they can handle, and to ask for nothing more.

On its side, materialism raises questions which the spiritualist finds it difficult to answer. So far even as our own spirits are concerned there are difficulties which might seem at the first glance not easy to be removed. The materialist points to what seems the absolute dependence of the body upon the mind. In childhood the mind is weak and cartilaginous like the body. In maturity it hardens into a firm tissue. It is strong and tenacious. In old age, when the body withers, the mind for the most part withers with it. If the brain becomes inflamed, the mind partakes of its fire, and raves and rages. A blow will take away consciousness; a removal of the pressure of the bone will bring back consciousness which takes up the story of life precisely where the blow interrupted it. From all these things, and many others of the same nature, it has seemed natural to many to assume that consciousness is simply a function of the brain; that, as one has said, the brain secretes thought as the liver secretes bile.

If these facts occasion difficulty to the spiritualistic view of life, there are difficulties also on the other side. Our consciousness is at every moment of our lives one; it is never divided. We hear sometimes, indeed, of a divided consciousness. There are freaks in the mental experiences. There are insanities in which the mind feels itself invaded by some foreign power, in which one seems to himself to be some one quite other than himself; in which he is, as we phrase it, "beside himself." But through all these changes the unity of consciousness at every moment is undisturbed. If the mind seems peopled by many personalities at once, the consciousness always identifies itself with one of these. The consciousness is at no moment dual or multiple. Look on the other hand at the brain. This is made up of innumerable atoms which, if the assumptions of science are correct, approach one another and recede from one another, but touch one another never. Though so near each other they are distinct, like the stars in heaven. These form themselves into molecules, and the molecules group themselves into cells, each of which has its special office. Where in all this multiplicity does the unity of consciousness reside? It cannot reside in one alone, for all are concerned in the work of thought. It cannot reside in all together, for it would be as multiple as they. Take a crowd, for example, that is animated by one thought and one purpose. Each member of it adds intensity to the fervor of the rest and catches intensity from their eagerness. We speak of a common thought and a common consciousness. There is no common consciousness. There is a multitude of consciousnesses. Each man in the crowd has a consciousness of his own, and this unity is never once disturbed. The brain is not one; it is manifold. It is made up, as we have seen, of a crowd, an innumerable crowd, of atoms and molecules and cells. What relation has the unity of consciousness to these? I cannot tell you. I know simply that it cannot be their product.

Materialism is thus unable to adapt itself to one of the most common facts of experience, to the most fundamental fact of human life,—the fact of the unity of consciousness. Here its formulæ fail. Just as its processes seem about to take possession of the whole, to swallow up thought and feeling as well as life, of a sudden its advance is checked. So the helpless Andromeda stood bound to the rock, watching the approach of the crawling monster that was to crush her beauty in its ravenous jaws; and so was its terrible approach suddenly checked. The awful form with which her defender confronted it had changed it to stone. The material universe, in the face of the fact to which I have referred, is seen to be simply the basis and the environment of that spiritual life of which it cannot be the source. I have just compared it to the terrible monster of the classic story. The comparison is in place only when the superficial theories of materialistic philosophers have distorted the material forces into something foreign to their real nature, have sought to make them invade the realm of spirit. In itself the material universe is sometimes terrible indeed, but for the most part helpful, and always beautiful. The sea is terrible when its encroaching waves threaten to sweep away the frail structures of man; but in its place it is man's helpful servant, bringing to his door the products of far-off lands, and yielding to him from its depths food that supports his life.

Unitarianism expresses a faith that shines out bright and clear over against the mists of agnosticism and the black clouds of materialism. It is a faith in spiritual realities by which the material universe is to it transfigured. It represents thus a spiritualistic philosophy. Before considering this, however, it may be well to place in contrast with Unitarianism certain forms of spiritualistic philosophy with which it stands in more or less sharp antagonism. I hardly know what to call such forms of religious belief. In these days, when creeds are so often taken "for substance of doctrine," and this substance is so often the merest shadow, it is difficult to know what men do, and what they do not, believe. My object, however, is not polemical, and it will serve my purpose to place Unitarianism in contrast with the unmistakable Orthodoxy of a former generation. What I shall call Unitarianism is unquestionably held to-day by many who call their own belief by another name.

Unitarianism maintains the substantial integrity and sanity of human nature. It recognizes imperfections and sins; but what it sees is to it the imperfection of incompleteness, not that of a ruin. This from a philosophical point of view is profoundly significant. To maintain, for instance, the substantial integrity and sanity of the human reason is to make philosophy possible. It alone can make even religion possible in any large and true meaning of the word. To deny the trustworthiness of the human reason is to make philosophy and religion, in any large sense of these words, impossible. To deny the trustworthiness of human reason, and to make this denial one of the fundamental principles in a philosophy or a theology, is to fall into the most absurd contradiction. A man who has what we call "a crooked sight," sees all things crooked. If you give him a mark to guide his sight, that will be seen by him as awry as all things else. He can correct this by thought. He can calculate his own personal equation. But if the mental sight be crooked, if reason itself be awry, what correction can be applied to that? How can even revelation help it? How can it distinguish between a true and a false revelation? And if it by chance accepts the true, how can it see this in its real significance? In this respect the philosophy accepted by Unitarianism stands in contrast alike with that of materialism and of a typical Orthodoxy. This philosophy alone recognizes the substantial sanity of man, the reliance that man may place upon his own instincts. He has, for instance, the passion to know. He instinctively trusts his thought. But if materialism be true, then his knowledge is a delusion. If the world has not an ideal content, if it be not the manifestation of spirit, then Herbert Spencer is right, and it is wholly unknowable. Then the only use for thought is to make ourselves as comfortable as we can; to seek to know, is like seeking to square the circle. If the typical Orthodoxy is right, human reason is a thing to be disowned and discredited. If, on the other hand, the philosophy which is assumed by Unitarianism and by kindred beliefs is true, if the world be the manifestation of spirit, and if man is in substantial harmony with his surroundings, then he may trust his reason. Then the world is rightly assumed by him to be transparent to his thought, and reason is rightly assumed by him to be his God-given instrument for learning the truth.

What is true of the intellect is also true of the heart. Materialism and the typical Orthodoxy unite in repressing the tenderest longings and aspirations of the soul. Materialism leaves no place for them; the typical Orthodoxy at once stimulates and crushes them.

I repeat, the philosophy represented by Unitarianism in contrast with that of materialism and of the typical Orthodoxy recognizes and guards the sanity of human nature. It leaves man free to develop what is most essential to his ideal nature. The intellect and the affections have open to them the freest and largest life.

What is true of human nature is also true of the world. This also is assumed, by the philosophy which Unitarianism represents, to possess a wholeness and a unity. Materialism, having no place for the highest spiritual development, indirectly represents the world as a beginning without completeness. The most marked developments of the world are without significance. To the typical Orthodoxy the world is a ruin. It is at best an imperfect machine that needs continual readjustment. The noblest and loftiest that appears upon it is something foreign. To the philosophy represented by Unitarianism and kindred beliefs the world is one. The divine power is in it, not as an occasional manifestation but as a persistent force. If what are called miracles be accepted, these are no interruptions of its course, but are the manifestations of some higher and persistent law. Jesus himself, the loftiest appearance among men, is in the true sense of the word the most typical of men. The light which was in him was the true light, because it was the light that according to his degree lighteth every man which cometh into the world.

Thus the philosophy of which we speak is that of a large optimism. Materialism on the one side and the typical Orthodoxy on the other see the world practically or avowedly as a failure. To the one it is a promise without fulfilment; to the other it is avowedly a wreck. To the spiritualistic philosophy which is represented by Unitarianism the world contains much that is obscure, much that makes terrible demands upon faith; yet it is one, it is sane, and through ways that are not clearly understood it is working out a noble end. Its promises are not in vain. Its beginnings are prophetic of a corresponding completeness.

Let us now look, so far as our circumstances permit, at the spiritualistic philosophy which is represented by Unitarianism and kindred beliefs.

This philosophy takes form in many different and often opposing systems. There are many ways by which the same results have been reached, and he who strikes out upon any one of these paths is very apt to maintain that it is the only one. Some of these attempts to find a basis for a spiritual philosophy have been mistakes; yet for the most part it is safe to say that each has called attention to some special form of the universal truth which all were defending. Each has erred for the most part in claiming for itself the sole right to be called the defender of the faith. All taken together may give results with a fulness that no one could reach alone. I shall not trouble you with the details of opposing systems of spiritualistic philosophy, but will simply call attention to certain fundamental principles or aspects of this philosophy.

This philosophy assumes that not matter but spirit is the basis and background of the universe; that spirit is not the product of matter, but that matter is the manifestation of spirit. If in matter there is, as has been said, "the promise and potency" of life and of spirit, it is because there is working in and through the material world a spiritual power, which is breathing into it and evolving out of it that which by itself it would be powerless to produce.

The first appearance of animal life upon the world may well excite our interest and wonder. In the earliest and lowest forms of animal structure there may seem at the first glance little to sharply discriminate them from the lifeless forms about them. Yet when we look at it there is a vast difference, one might almost say an infinite difference, between that which is moved and that which moves; and, above all, between that which is without feeling and that which feels. The lowest form of sensation, however vague, however imperfectly taken up into consciousness, marks a revolution the importance of which is hardly to be conceived. When I spoke of a difference that might almost be called infinite, I may have seemed to use the language of careless exaggeration; but with the introduction of feeling we have, however indistinct it may at first appear, a division of the world into subject and object. There is that which feels and that which is felt. Subject and object, although they may be never so inseparably joined together, yet stand in a relation of absolute antithesis to one another. They are so directly opposed, that between the senseless stone and the sentient creature that crawls upon it there is a difference that can hardly be over-estimated.

This lowest life, not only marvellous in itself, is marvellous in that to which it forms the introduction. It is, as we have seen, self-moved; it is self-centred. We are not surprised to see the self-centred forms of life gain in power and vastness. We watch with interest the development of the animal world into shapes of beauty or ugliness, of strength or cunning. We see each maintaining its own life and satisfying its own needs at the cost of whatever may oppose it. We see strife and carnage, and hear the cries of rage and suffering. But at once there is a revolution no less, perhaps even greater, than that in which conscious life was manifested upon the world. The principle of that was self-assertion; the new principle is that of self-sacrifice. There is the presence of a love that causes one living thing to forget itself, and to give itself for another. As in some musical composition, amid harsh, and it may be discordant tones, is heard a low, sweet movement that at first is overpowered and checked, which by degrees gains strength and fulness, until at last it dominates the whole, and the harsher strains sink away and are lost, — such is the presence of love in the world. It first manifests itself as almost alone in the midst of the rage and carnage of the lower life. We find it in the lion's den, where the mother lion watches over her young, which she would defend at the cost of her own life. We find it among creatures, no matter how fierce and untamable. Each new generation, as it enters upon the world in absolute helplessness, is watched over and guarded at the cost of privation or of life. In the lower forms of human life this presence of love may be hardly more marked than in that of the brute; but it has obtained a footing in the world of which it is one day, as we believe, to be the master. As history has advanced, we have seen its power expand. In the loftiest souls selfishness has seemed swallowed up in love. What was at first simply the devotion of the parent to the young, which was forgotten as soon as the young needed no further care, comes at last to know no difference of family or race. Wherever suffering is, wherever there is human need, it seeks to bring relief. We do not see as yet all things put under it, but we see the beginning and the spread of a kingdom, the slow yet sure advance of which is the prophecy, as we can but believe, of a yet wider supremacy. We see not as yet all things put under it, but we see Jesus, in whom is manifested the fulness of this power in its broadest sweep, in its complete mastery of the life, and in its claim to possess by right, and in the coming time in fact, the mastery of the world.

The spiritualistic philosophy insists that in this outcome of the world we have brought to light its deepest heart and mystery. It claims that the fountain cannot rise higher than its source; that the world that culminates in spirit must have spirit as its source; that self-forgetting and self-sacrificing love cannot be the offspring of mere material relations, and of the collision of the pitiless forces of Nature. It insists that spirit must have been born of spirit, and that love must have been born of love.

As man looks out upon the world he finds everywhere confirmation of this faith. The world about him, the ground beneath his feet, the heaven that soars above, seem all, as he looks closely at them, to be the manifestations of some vast, informing, and controlling mind. Not only are the movements of Nature in accordance with some principle of order, so that each thing knows its place and moves along its allotted path; all these elements co-operate. Each has its share in bringing about the magnificent results which we have just contemplated. From far back in the æons, when the solar system was but a measureless, nebulous cloud, through the ages in which this nebulous mass was whirled into solidity and form, through the ages of fire, through the ages of slime, through the ages of slowly organizing life, up to the highest thought and the tenderest love, the elements were working together to bring about this result. There seems to have been a steady path from chaos to spirit. Men used to try to prove the supremacy of man in the world by showing how all things are useful to him. Things were explained in their reference to him. The question what this or that was for, let us say mosquitoes, or the wild beasts of the desert, meant, What service do they perform for man? Now we see the supremacy of man in the fact that he is the organic head of the world. He is the capstone without which all is incomplete; or rather he is the type in which all lower forms and relations find themselves fulfilled. His appearance, and above all the appearance of the highest ideal in human life, brings a unity and a wholeness into Nature which it lacked before. It makes of the order of Nature an intelligent order.

Not only does man in the presence of the universe feel himself face to face with an intelligence kindred to his own, although so infinitely vaster, and so inconceivable by his best power of thought; he is conscious of even a closer bond which unites him to the earth, whose latest child he is. In the beauty of the world, in its sublimity, he feels himself in relation with something that is kindred to himself. He rejoices in the freedom of Nature as though it were his own freedom. The flowers smile at him. The forests seem to seek to open their heart to him. The glory of the heavens awes him; and yet there is a gladness in the awe as though the heaven itself were somehow akin to him. Even the laws of the material universe, so stern, so inexorable, fill him, as he contemplates them, with a solemn gladness.

In human life this inexorable law takes on a new aspect. Man feels its presence in its most awful form when it presents itself as duty. He who was so strong, so free, who felt himself the master of the world, finds himself in bondage. What sacrifice of the dearest and most precious does not the law of duty require? How does it break up what seemed the most solid, and bow down that which was the loftiest, and tear asunder those who seemed the most closely bound together! And yet when one has fairly yielded himself to it, how does duty seem as dear as before it seemed terrible. It is seen to be only the stern form which love assumes when its claims are trampled under foot; and when men have submitted their lives to it, they find that it is still love in its loftiest manifestation.

> "Stern lawgiver! yet thou dost wear
> The Godhead's most benignant grace;
> Nor know we anything so fair
> As is the smile upon thy face:
> Flowers laugh before thee on their beds,
> And fragrance in thy footing treads;
> Thou dost preserve the stars from wrong;
> And the most ancient heavens through thee are fresh
>   and strong."

The world in the manifestation of beauty becomes transparent to the spirit. The spiritual presence which is manifested in it seems almost to break through its concealing veil.

In the presence of that law of duty which controls his life, man feels himself in the very presence of that power which rules the worlds.

All these things, as I have said, make us feel that there must be a spiritual power which is manifested in and through the universe in which we dwell. But it may be asked, "Is not Spencer right? May there not be something which is neither spirit nor matter, but which, manifesting itself through both, is superior to both? May there not be something as high above spirit as spirit is exalted above matter?" Of course, we cannot exhaust in our thought the possibilities of being. Not only, however, can we conceive of nothing higher than spirit, we cannot conceive that there should be anything higher than it. We can find no place for it in our thought. Spirit is that which transcends itself. The stock or the stone, whatever is not spiritual, is shut up within itself. Its own self is closed to it. It does not even exist for itself. The stock or the stone is a stock or a stone *to us*. For itself it is nothing. Not only is it closed against itself, it is closed against all things else. It is affected by the things about it. The stone may be washed by the stream, or carried by the ice; it may be hurled through the air, or moss and lichen may cling to it; the sun may warm it, or the trees may bend over it. All these things, however, take place about it, but do not take place for it. It is as when we sleep and friends may come and go, the sun may shine or veil itself, the most stupendous transaction may occur, the fortunes of our life may be decided, as in Hawthorne's story of David Swan; but it is all nothing to us. Thus do the stock or the stone sleep only; they have no waking and no dream. This is not because they are material, but because they are not spiritual.

On the other hand, spirit transcends itself. Its own self is open to it. It stands as it were outside itself and contemplates itself. It exists not only for others, but for itself as well. It appropriates all its acts. While it transcends itself, its acts do not transcend it. It follows them with its sense of ownership. Yet further does it transcend itself. We, each standing in his own personality, have yet the freedom of the universe. My spirit presses back by its thought not merely to the time when I was not, but to the time when the world was not. For me that nebulous mass out of which the worlds were formed whirls into shape and order. For me the world rolled a mighty globe of flame. I, standing here, take into my thought the whole system of worlds of which ours is a part. All this is because I partake, however imperfectly, of a spiritual nature. We cannot conceive that anything not spirit should have this freedom of itself and of all things, should thus be open to itself, and should make all results of its power its own. We cannot conceive this, simply because all this constitutes the very essence of spirit. The tree manifests itself to us; we manifest ourselves to ourselves. We can define spirit in no other terms than that it is this completed circle; therefore it is that we cannot conceive that such largeness of being could be attained by any form of being that is not akin to spirit.

What is true of spirit in relation to this freedom and largeness is true of it also in its more inner and profound experience. We cannot conceive that there should be anything loftier than love. Just as the extremes of consciousness and unconsciousness exclude the possibility of conceiving of any third that is akin to neither, so there are two forms of life, one of which is the living for self, and the other is the living in and for others as well as one's self. The beauty of this latter is when the spirit, by its intelligence and its will, makes the self-surrender indeed its own. This is simply a roundabout way of speaking of love. We can conceive that there should be a love more exalted than anything that is known in our experience, so that love should be transformed and transfigured; but we cannot conceive that there should be anything so exalted above that which we know as love, as to be in its nature wholly foreign to this. We must then be forced to exclaim with Browning, that

> "the loving worm within its clod
> Were diviner than a loveless God."

Although, in the farthest reaches of our thought, we cannot conceive that there should be anything more exalted than spirit in its loftiest attributes, it may be urged that the facts of the world cannot be reconciled with the idea that it is the manifestation of such a spiritual life. There is in the world suffering; the possibility of suffering is coextensive with sentient life. There is probably no single sentient existence that wholly escapes suffering; while in the case of many this suffering is terribly intensified. There is not only suffering in the world, there is sin; there is not only love, there is hate. Hate is often triumphant over love, unrighteousness over righteousness. These are facts which no philosophy can either explain or explain away. We might be tempted to accept the ancient teaching of a dualism in Nature, and ascribe the good creation to a power of goodness, and that which appears evil to a power of evil. Further thought and a more profound knowledge show that this is impossible. Good and evil are so closely intertwined that it is impossible to extricate the one from the other. They both spring from the same root. The sweet and the bitter water flow often from the same fountain. Moreover, if science is sure of anything, it is of the unity of the universe. It confirms the one fundamental utterance of philosophy that all things are the manifestation of the one. Further, there is no caprice in Nature. This is another of the absolute propositions, we might say axioms, of science. We may say further that there is no indifference in Nature. In appearance, at least, she is either the one thing or the other. How carefully she provides for the gratification of the tastes, no less than the wants, of each one of her children. How remorselessly she provides for the destruction of each of them. We have then to face an apparent contradiction which it is impossible for us wholly to solve. We cannot, however, fail to recognize the fact that the great movement of Nature has been towards a fuller and a larger life, towards a tenderer and more widely embracing love. We cannot deny that there is a power in the world that makes for righteousness. Even the strife and suffering of the lower world, as our modern science proves, have been the instruments of working out this larger life. I cannot agree with Miss Cobbe, that the strife and suffering of the lower world press more heavily upon our thought when we find that, according to the theory of natural selection, they are bound up in the scheme of things. If they were merely accidents, there would seem no possibility of explanation. They are not accidents, they are instruments. The lower life is unconsciously, through necessity, doing what the highest life would do freely if the choice were given it.

It may be added also that it is the fashion at the present day to exaggerate the suffering of the lower life of the world, as it was in the former day to overlook it. The theory of natural selection has also its merciful and beneficent aspect. Its fundamental principle is the survival of the fittest. This shows that whatever survives does so through a certain fitness to its environment; that all existence, therefore, finds its environment to a certain extent favorable. In the spiritual world, we know how the highest moral attainments have been victories. Of such triumph the figure of Jesus stands as the central type. He was made perfect through suffering. In him the extremes of anguish and spiritual beauty meet. In him not only life, but the sorrowing life is glorified.

The extremes meet in every heart. You judge the world; you condemn it as imperfect; it is cruel, heartless, aimless. Who are you that judge? Are you a stranger from another universe? Do you stand over against the world? No; you are of the world. It is the power that made the world that in you condemns the world. The discord then must be in some sense apparent only. It is hard enough to reconcile the existence of evil with faith in a supreme goodness. Without such faith, however, it is impossible to understand the existence of love and of righteousness; and still more impossible to understand the stamp of divinity which love and righteousness wear. Even when they are, in outward seeming, crushed to earth, we reverence them still, while we scorn the triumphant wrong. Even he who dishonors the moral law in his life honors it in his thought. It shows itself thus the representative of that power which is the ruler of the earth.

Such, in imperfect presentation, is the relation of Unitarianism to philosophy. It assumes the unity of Nature; it assumes the sanity of the nature of the world and of the nature of man. It puts its faith in the prophecies of Nature, and in the most profound and tender instincts of the soul. It accepts the highest that it finds as the truest representative and manifestation of the power on which the worlds depend. It sees in Jesus the Son of God, because he is the truest Son of man. I confess that the philosophy which it and kindred beliefs represent seems to me to be the ideal philosophy; for as soon as we lose our faith in the integrity of the world without and the sanity of the world within, in the trustworthiness of human reason and of the fundamental instincts of the heart, what possibility is left for any philosophy that is worthy of the name?

ECCLESIASTICAL AND DENOMINATIONAL TENDENCIES.

BY GRINDALL REYNOLDS.

THE stint which has been appointed for our religious body is this: How to preserve unimpaired the liberty of the individual mind and conscience, and the absolute congregational freedom of the parish from outside dictation, and at the same time to make such liberty of the individual and such independence of the congregation consistent with a wide and ever-enlarging usefulness; to suffer no chains to rest upon our own souls; to seek to place none upon the souls of others; and yet to put into activity and to keep in activity methods full of highest and broadest spiritual influence.

This surely is a hard problem and a difficult work for any body of believers to undertake, — a problem which in all past religious history has not been satisfactorily solved. Who shall say that this work has as yet with any completeness been accomplished?

It may be asserted, I think, with truth that the first part of the desired result has to a reasonable degree been attained by us. That some contumely has been heaped upon opinions held to be not only new and strange but pernicious, that some brave explorers in the field of truth have found in the way some thorns, nobody would deny, — and few but would regret whatever in the clearer light of to-day we know to have been harsh and needless. But probably much of this was unavoidable. While human beings are limited, they are likely, on account of this very limitation, to ascribe to their own opinions, and even prejudices, an undue importance, if not sacredness. Still, as compared with any other period of Christian history, or with the experience of any other body of Christian believers, we may say that we have attained to liberty, — liberty for the individual, liberty for the religious society, and liberty for the whole body. Certainly, no courageous soul, no soul worthy to be the goodly vessel into which the new and higher spiritual truth shall be poured, has found any greater obstacles, any fiercer lions in the path, than such as are needful to keep heroism and faith in wholesome vigor. What we say then of sixty years of our church and denominational history is, that they have to a marvellous extent accomplished within our borders soul-liberty and congregational freedom. To have achieved this in the lifetime of two generations is not to have lived in vain.

But what of the second part of the desired result? Has our religious body made such freedom as consistent as it should be with an ever-enlarging and positive usefulness? No one would say that. By our mere existence we have accomplished a great deal. The first Unitarians — we may say it without egotism — were a remarkable body of men. In native capacity they were the equals of their opponents; in intellectual training they had in their day few peers, and no superiors. By the very fact that they were free, that they dared to look all moral and spiritual problems in the face, that at all risks they were ready, at the call of truth, to turn their backs upon the old and time-honored, and to espouse the new and despised, lifted them to the noblest moral and intellectual stature. What Priestley, Channing, Ware, Dewey, Parker, and the rest might have been, had they trodden in the ancient ways, no one can tell; but taking upon them the heroic attitude of dissent for conscience' sake, they became striking figures, rising above the monotonous level of ordinary humanity. Such persons could not live, think, speak, print, and act without leaving a deep impression. The life of New England, in every department, took some shape and hue from them. What has imparted so striking a quality to the life and activity, the organization and legislation of Massachusetts during the last half century as its philanthropic plans and enterprises? And from whom have those plans and enterprises received more glad sympathy and more constant support than from those who cherished most deeply the conception of human nature as innately noble? The creeds and especially the preaching in other folds have gradually assumed a milder type. What in doctrine is tenderest and most attractive has come more and more into the foreground; what is cruel and repulsive has not so much been cast out as permitted to fade out. For a long time there has been much truth in the sorrowful admission of the English preacher travelling in this country, that there was no sound Orthodox doctrine preached even in the so-called Orthodox churches of New England. It cannot be doubted that much of this change is due to the thought and speech of the fathers of American Unitarianism. In short, if useful work means exercising the necessary influence of cultivated and earnest souls, then in doctrine, in philanthropy, in literature, in the general life and opinion, our religious body has in the last sixty years achieved much.

But very little of what it might have done. Had Channing and his compeers believed in organization, had they felt the duty not only to do good, but to communicate, there is no measuring of the work which was within their power. Nothing is more striking than the way the Unitarian body came into existence in New England, a hundred and fifty churches strong. The old fable of Minerva springing forth from the head of Jupiter full armed was a real fact in our modern life. Methodism at its start was, in comparison, a feeble bantling. It looks as though the liberal faith might have swept over New England like a prairie fire. Instead of numbering four hundred churches, it might have counted thousands under its banner. But the early Unitarians feared organization. One almost questions whether they desired to increase their numbers. They broke the chains of dogma; they stood free souls, — and were satisfied.

The report of the past of our body may be stated thus: It has achieved individual and congregational freedom. It has exercised that incidental influence which large and free souls, living and acting their true selves, could not help exercising; but in the way of positive and organized work for the bettering of man's religious condition, it has until within a few years achieved but little, and has perhaps attempted to achieve less. It has grown rather because it could not help it than because it wished to grow.

Turn now to the present and the future. What at this time are our ecclesiastical and denominational tendencies? What are they likely to be in the time to come? Before we seek to answer these questions let us define what in this discussion we mean by ecclesiastical and denominational tendencies.

In churches like the Roman Catholic, Episcopalian, and Presbyterian, which have a more or less centralized form of government, when ecclesiastical tendencies are considered, at once questions like these arise: What methods of organization, what relations between minister and people, what ritual forms, are imperative, and therefore necessary conditions of lawful church existence? But when the drift of the Unitarian body is under consideration, no such questions are in order. There is no controlling authority to shape its growth. It is a collection of free churches, making their own organization, calling their own minister, settling him after their own fashion, determining what forms or lack of forms they will have, what charities they will support, what contributions they will make to the common weal. So when you look at the Unitarian body you cannot so much as think of a definite church polity, as you can when you regard more closely knit organizations. Our question is therefore an entirely different one. It is a problem of free church-life. It is an effort to ascertain into what ways of church government, into what forms of church worship, into what modes of Christian activity, our independent parishes, under the law of liberty, are insensibly growing. In short, what is the tendency and drift of the church life of congregations absolutely independent? For just as truly as in the outward universe there is a tendency towards certain ends, so is there in the spiritual universe.

The same general idea has to apply to our conception of denominational tendencies. We have no creed to determine what our churches shall believe. We have no central authority to say to what synod, conference, or association our churches shall belong. We have no statutes to appoint for our churches common work to do. As in our internal life, so in our external activity, we are free. All this is in the nature of the case. A Unitarian church may or may not have a creed. In any case, it is its own, and not another's. A Unitarian church may be rich in good works outside its borders, or it may keep in its own shell, and shut its gates and its heart against all appeals. Of course there is a certain unwritten agreement on the great spiritual themes, else we should fly apart like atoms having no bond of coherence. Of course there is a real unity of faith and of aims, or we should die. Still, as our ecclesiastical life is essentially free, so is our denominational activity. It is the natural trend of all, under the law of liberty, to definite purpose and action.

If now we consider a little what we are ecclesiastically tending from, perhaps we shall more clearly perceive what we are ecclesiastically tending toward. What we note first is this: The first Unitarian churches, while they stood for larger liberty of conscience, for a more rational interpretation of the Scriptures, for a more humane God and a diviner humanity, preserved in their church life, even to a greater degree than their theological opponents, Puritan simplicity. Their meeting-houses were commodious, rarely comfortable, still more rarely appealing to the sense of beauty or the sense of mystery. Often they were painfully cold, bald, and uninteresting. From the services was banished all richness of form. No special days were permitted to gather around them a wealth of sacred associations. Even the sermon, in its effort to be free from sensationalism, was apt to be more correct and thoughtful than stimulating. Any one whose memory of church-going runs back of 1830 will testify to the existence in Unitarian services of the quality, at any rate, of godly simplicity. This is easily explicable. The early Unitarian churches were largely the original local parishes. Witness the church of the Pilgrims at Plymouth, the church of Winthrop and John Wilson in Boston, the church of Higginson at Salem, the church of Hooker and Shepard at Cambridge, the church of Bulkeley at Concord, and a great number besides, scattered up and down the Commonwealth. The attendants upon the services were, to a great degree, the descendants of the men and women who founded those churches. It is easy to see why great ecclesiastical plainness went side by side with intellectual enfranchisement; for it is always less difficult to change our opinions than our habits.

Consider one other point, — what we may call shyness of dogmatic training. We had escaped the bondage of an iron system of theology; we did not wish to put on ourselves or our children any new chains. Not only did our churches banish creeds: I question whether, in our homes or in our Sunday-schools, we gave our children any fair knowledge of the religious opinions for which we stood. I was the son of a father who was a Unitarian twenty years before Channing spoke at Jared Sparks's ordination at Baltimore; yet I never had five minutes' or five seconds' explanation from his lips of our Unitarian position.

One thing, however, our fathers escaped; and that was the burning question of to-day, — how to bring church privileges to those in narrow circumstances. For many years, in Massachusetts, church rates took the form of taxation on property, and continued to do so till a late day in country towns. This of itself produced some parity between means and cost of worship. Plainly, then, what we are tending from in our church life is Puritan simplicity, and an almost morbid fear of imposing upon others dogmatic chains.

It is equally clear that in our church life to-day we are on the one hand tending toward greater richness, freedom, and variety in all that concerns worship and religious services; while on the other we are recognizing as never before our duty to give to our own children, at least, a firmer grasp upon the truth which is strength and joy to our souls. Our "trend" is, I say, in the first place toward greater richness, variety, and freedom in all that belongs to the public and social expression of religious life and needs. How evident this is! Begin at externals,—the church-building. A hundred years ago in New England the old meeting-houses had the venerableness which had gathered about them from their association with noble men and women, and from the heroic or pathetic town history with which they were indissolubly connected. But otherwise, what beauty had they to be desired; what majesty or tenderness to lift up any soul? Outwardly, they were for the most part rectangular structures, unbroken by any ornament, often unpainted,—not so shapely or elegant as a modern barn. Inside, you found a square box, glaring white, except where time and use had left their stains. By aisles and cross-aisles the floor was cut up into many little square boxes, miniatures of the building itself. No dim religious light shone through the dusty little panes. No fires made the building warm; no cushions made it comfortable. Even the relief of hymn-books and an organ was denied. All was bare and homely. This is no exaggeration. The picture of the Concord meeting-house of the time of the Revolution has been preserved. It was a barn-like building, square, apparently unpainted, absolutely unattractive, with no churchly appearance,—a good type, no doubt, of hundreds of the same plain but useful family.

Compare this with the modern ideal of a church, certainly in the Unitarian fold. The smallest hamlet that builds its little chapel demands, if it does not always get, beauty which shall at once tranquillize and stimulate. It would fain have the very wood and stone say to the passer-by, "A place of high thinking and lofty aspiring." Let me recall one fact which tells more than volumes would how much Unitarians have come to demand, even in the place of worship, something refining and uplifting. When the "Church Building Loan Fund" was created, the first requisite seemed to be plans. Our Methodist brethren, with a rare generosity, gave us permission to use their book of plans. But those plans had been dictated by a necessary economy rather than by any ideal conception of what a place of worship should be. As a result, no Unitarian society has ever used one. Whether this tendency to make church-buildings under all circumstances handsome and worshipful is always wise may admit of debate; that it often stands in the way of church extension is certain; but the existence of the tendency cannot be denied.

Pass to forms of worship and the keeping of times and seasons. The Puritan was called into being when times and seasons, forms and rituals, had come to exercise absolute tyranny over the free soul. They had replaced largely in church-life real soul experience, and were held to be sufficient of themselves, without inward faith and holiness. At any rate this was what the Puritan believed, and against this the Puritan rebelled. Days the most solemn, rites comely and grand, were to him mere formalism, standing between his unveiled soul and its God. Often he knew them to be used to crush out thoughts and aspirations that could not speak through the tongues of the past. I cannot doubt that his protest was a wholesome one, that a new influx of the spirit was what the time called for. Now, our Unitarian fathers inherited to the full the Puritan's dislike of the old church ways. It does not seem to me that I ever heard of Easter or Christmas till I reached manhood. Fast Day we had, and it was not a day of rioting. Thanksgiving was a great family and religious festival. New Year's brought the children the simple gifts which scanty means permitted. But Easter and Christmas, — where were they, what were they? Then the Sunday service, — mark its simplicity and uniformity! You might travel from Boston to New Orleans, the service was the same. Well we remember the order, — a hymn, " the long prayer," a reading from the Bible, a hymn, the sermon, a short prayer, a hymn, the benediction. The only innovation permitted was a transfer of the last prayer into an invocation ; and that probably dates from a later day, when defection from strict Puritan plainness had begun. Mark the change ! Easter and Christmas are observed among us almost as generally as with Catholics and Episcopalians. The improvements upon the order of service are absolutely bewildering. In each separate pulpit one has to give careful study, to know when the minister is to read alone, and when in response with the people ; where the anthems, the solos, and the organ are to come in. Nor is this all a matter of individual or parish caprice. Already the Association has prepared two forms of services, and these have been supplemented by a dozen more from private sources ; and now a commission of fifteen or twenty has been appointed to furnish a common form of worship, and so to evoke order out of chaos.

All this reaction was sure to come. Special circumstances and spiritual conditions made it necessary that our fathers should rebel against a whole system, which was then inextricably twined up with ecclesiastical formality and ecclesiastical tyranny. But days and forms have their place in human life : to that both secular and spiritual experience testify. The tendency, therefore, to find and keep what is good in religious forms and seasons has come to stay. We have not as yet discovered what best meets our wants ; we shall not probably find it easy to do so. There are many of us in whom the Puritan blood and the Puritan taste are too strong to feel anything to be so good as the old, plain simplicity. Still, we have to note as one of our marked ecclesiastical tendencies the disposition to give greater richness and variety to worship.

We mark again, as a distinct tendency in our church life, the disposition to give real instruction to our young people, especially in the Sunday-school. As we have already hinted, there was a time when our religious body was absolutely unsound in its views about the education of its young people. Its indisposition to proselyte reached monomania. Often in the home and in the Sunday-school almost unbroken silence was preserved on the great vital doctrines of religion and Christianity. The attention was altogether given to moral and spiritual instruction of a purely practical and personal character. Our youth grew up in entire uncertainty of belief about God, Jesus, man, or the future state. All the doubts and questionings about the Bible or miracles were kept from them. The result was, on the one hand, that many of our most earnest and devout young people had their minds (doctrinally speaking) empty, swept and garnished, ready for the first comer to enter in and convert them to a faith not that of their fathers; while, on the other hand, many, attacked by subtle and strange doubts, made shipwreck of faith. I was myself educated in a Trinitarian Sunday-school; and it was a thorough education, too. I was left in no doubt as to what was believed about the Trinity, total depravity, the atonement, election, or eternal damnation, or why these things were believed, or what texts were supposed to confirm them. In short, I received a very good theological education from fairly compètent hands, for which I have always been grateful, albeit I ever remained a heretic. Coming from such a training to be a teacher in a Unitarian Sunday-school, what surprised me was the absence of all education of this intellectual and theological sort. For lack of just such an intelligent training, whole families of children — I had almost said whole flocks of families — have been led back to the traditional faith out of which the fathers had emerged.

The tendency of our church life is now away from all this. It is something to be thankful for. We are coming to see that our children are rational beings; that it is safe to let them look at things as they are, and to know why they are so. If there are doubts about sacred things, which they are sure to meet, then in the proper season they should understand what these doubts are, upon what supposed foundations they rest, and how they may be honestly answered. On the other hand, we have convictions which are of inexpressible value to us. Should we not "pre-empt" these young souls? Should we leave error to take undisputed possession? The present ecclesiastical tendency to give a better religious education — yes, theological education — to the young is a sound and rational tendency. It ought to be cherished. What is it but fulfilling the simple duty of the parent to the child, the old to the young, — doing the best we can for them? The wonder is that we ever overlooked it.

We might add a word in respect to the plain tendency of our present church life toward larger church hospitality, — a most important tendency. For if anything should proffer to the world an all-inclusive invitation, it is religion, and especially that form which calls itself liberal. In a certain sense, church hospitality in Massachusetts is a need of late origin. While worship was wholly or mainly supported by taxation, the church was a home for all, not by charity, but by right, — a home, too, which they were compelled by law to frequent. How long this idea of the church as a home for all held sway in cities I know not, but in the country towns it lingered a great while. This, however, is certain: that in many churches the idea was effectually banished half a century ago. I recall perfectly, standing in the vestibule of a Boston church when I was a young man. The building would hold six hundred; the audience was less than sixty. Not only was no seat offered me, but the sexton absolutely refused to give me or several ladies near by a seat. This, no doubt, was an extreme case; but it shows at what an early date the question, "How to reach and feed all spiritually," came up, when a seat in the church had ceased to be a common right and depended upon the generosity or the selfishness of individual owners. And it shows, too, why in England some of the most radical of the dissenters object to the disestablishment of the Church.

In seeking to answer this question the Unitarians were perhaps first in the field. The Benevolent Fraternity of Churches in Boston came into being in the year 1834.[1] It was an honest effort to extend more widely moral and religious privileges. It has accomplished a great deal. The agitation of the free-pew system, dating back as far certainly as the gathering of the Church of the Disciples in 1841, was another effort to give a practical answer to the question, How shall religion reach all? I do not think it can be fairly said that we have made great progress in solving the problem of church hospitality. Nor is it an easy problem to solve: less easy perhaps in a country so free as ours, where class feelings, differences of culture and origin, assert themselves quite as frankly as anywhere. At any rate there is no patent remedy, applicable everywhere and to all cases. But the disposition among us to look the duty of church hospitality in the face is a wholesome tendency.

---

[1] The next year following the legal disestablishment of religious bodies in Massachusetts.

We see, then, that ecclesiastical life in our churches is directed, first, toward greater richness and variety in worship; second, toward greater fulness and precision in religious instruction; and finally, toward a more inclusive church hospitality.

We come now to our other question, What is our tendency as a denomination? Let us begin again by considering the conditions under which our religious body came into being. One sentence expresses the nature of those conditions and their actual influence. They were such as tended to foster the extremest independency of our churches. Our fathers did not intend to establish a separate religious body any more than the liberal Orthodox intend to establish one to-day. They resisted any disposition of that kind. What happened was this: In a large number of our societies, independently, by gradual and almost unperceived processes, Calvinism softened into Arminianism, and that into Unitarianism. When these societies were rejected by the Calvinistic wing, they had little organization. They were united by a common ostracism, more than by anything else. They cohered by sympathy of convictions. The tendency to independence growing out of this mode of origin was greatly increased by a morbid fear of ecclesiastical domination. Separation from old relations had had in it many elements of bitterness. The iron had entered the souls of our fathers, and there was a marked dread of any organization, however free. It is a well-known fact that at first Channing, Norton, and others looked with doubt, if not disfavor, upon the forming of the American Unitarian Association; and the first forty years of the history of that Association were years of penury, of feeble moral support by the body, and consequently of comparative inefficiency. When the creation of the National Conference was discussed, many of our older men seemed to fear that the road to ecclesiastical despotism might lead that way. We may say then, emphatically, that what our religious body is tending out of is an exaggerated and fruitless independency.

To what is our body tending? To external coherence. It has ceased to be like a handful of sand, which is free, certainly, but which cannot be united for any common and useful purpose but to fill a hole. Many things have been working to make such coherence possible. The existence of the Association, doing for forty years its modest work; the Sunday-School Society, for a period nearly as long, calling together a great body of earnest men and women; the various ministerial bodies, bringing our ministers into intimate acquaintance and friendship; our autumnal convention, precursor of the National Conference, — all these were developing our denominational consciousness. Still, I question whether, previous to 1865, threescore parishes ever in any one year contributed to our missionary fund, or whether their contributions in any one year ever reached the scanty sum of seven thousand dollars.

It was in that year, 1865, that our body, under the splendid leadership of Dr. Bellows, had its second birth. The National Conference, increasing steadily in interest and attendance, the local conferences, its true children, meeting frequently all over the country, have knit us together in a way unknown in the past. Sometimes these gatherings are stigmatized as picnics. We are asked, What good things have they done? All such talk is mere foolishness. They have done a great deal that is practical. But suppose they had not. They have changed us from a mass of brilliant, perhaps, but incoherent atoms into a living, throbbing, conscious, and growing organism; and they have done this with little if any loss of individual or congregational freedom. What more in reason can we ask?

To accomplish outward coherence, and that alone, might indeed be paltry work. But who thinks we are stopping there? Are we not advancing with steady step toward a more complete inward and spiritual union? Yea, under the guidance of perfect liberty, have we not already attained to a more real harmony than usually falls to the lot of religious bodies, — more real, because it is a harmony that wears no chains and is hemmed in by no walls? I am optimistic enough to believe so. When our little body had made its protest against harsh and unreasonable dogmas, when it stood a small group of dissenters in a large world, and when unmoved it had received the dread stamp "heretic," and had accepted a denominational name which it never desired, naturally enough there was a division as to future wishes and work. There were, and there must have been, a large portion who felt that we had achieved enough for one generation. Had we not won from the cruel grasp of Calvinism a humane God, a divine humanity, an honest salvation, and a hopeful eternity? Was it not well to stop and possess the country before we made farther advance, if indeed any farther advance was desirable? On the other hand, was it not equally sure that others would, forgetting the things behind, reach forward; that the error overcome would seem to them small compared with the error yet reigning; that the safety of possession would be as nothing compared with the fierce joy of overcoming? There is always a space between the advance and rear-guard; and they are both essential to the welfare of the army. So there were divisions in those days. Men doubted one another. On both sides were spoken words which both would regret to-day and gladly commit to oblivion. Still, to the impartial on-looker, the collision was inevitable.

What we have learned to-day is not that there are no differences; that would be like shutting our eyes and saying there are no clouds. What we have learned is that the differences are on the surface, the agreements at the heart of truth. Time will permit but one illustration, — the nature and office of Jesus. Upon what other subject can there be so much divergence as upon this? But have we not advanced so far that we are disposed to dogmatize with moderation concerning much lesser lights? Why does Shakspeare tower up among the poets like Mount Shasta among its foot-hills? Why is Michael Angelo a colossus, while just as earnest seekers after beauty and grandeur stand as pygmies under his shadow? Was the cause heredity; was it education; or were these men raised up by some deep law that we do not understand? Who shall say? Jesus, — was he the offspring of miracle, of wonder whose profound law (for law there must have been) we cannot fathom; was he the fruit of a long course of natural selection, running back through Joseph and Mary even to the sweet singer and greatest monarch of Israel; or was he, as Mr. Savage terms him, "the consummate flower of our common humanity"? On such questions men will differ; but have we not all reached the point where with united voice we can say "the great spiritual man of the ages, inspirer, teacher, example, and friend;" and is not this coming into genuine spiritual harmony, if not absolute intellectual agreement? What is true of the question in regard to Jesus is still more true of other vital religious questions. Under the guidance of the law of perfect liberty as a denomination, we are tending to a harmony at once rare and real, — rare because unforced, real because profound.

But to pass from individualism to outward coherence, and from outward coherence to spiritual union, however perfect, — does that justify the existence of a religious body, and fulfil all its duty? Certainly not. A denomination comes into being because it has a clear vision of some portion of the truth. It has not a monopoly of all the light that has broken forth, certainly not of all the light that shall break forth from God's word and God's world. I say that we have a clearer vision of some portion of the truth. I should be sorry were any bigoted enough to deny that other bodies had their vision of the truth; and very saddening it would be to believe that the truth is so bounded that our mortal eyes or minds could take it all in. But when one has something of real value, what duty does it bring with it? Suppose the discoverer of ether, which has assuaged so many pains and carried so many poor souls through fearful crises, had kept his discovery to himself, or had carefully confined its benefits within a narrow circle of favored ones; imagine an astronomer discovering some new law of the universe, or a navigator making some important geographical discovery, and remaining silent, and letting the knowledge die with him, — what should we say of these men? What should we say of any one who had found out in the world of body or mind what would help or comfort or enlighten his fellow-creatures, and should keep it as a private curiosity or a private luxury? We should hardly find language sharp enough for our condemnation. Nor can a denomination be excused for inaction, unless, indeed, you can prove that truth which concerns man's relations to God, to the universe, to his fellow-men, and to his permanent welfare, has less importance than a medical remedy or an astronomical or geographical fact; or unless you can show that truth is the one solitary gift of God, which can propagate and diffuse itself, and dissipate all darkness, and overcome all error without man's fidelity to help. But both these ideas are in fact untenable. Nothing makes so permanent an impression for good on mankind as higher moral and religious truth; and every advance in the knowledge and possession of such truth is largely dependent upon the faithfulness of some man or some body of men. Take out of modern history Christianity or the Reformation, and would not human life everywhere feel the loss? Where would Christianity have been if the apostles had gone to sleep? How long might the Reformation have been postponed if Martin Luther had contented himself with counting his beads and reading his missal? I hold, then, that the denominational tendency, which is so distinctly manifesting itself in these latter days, to accept truth as a trust held for the benefit of mankind, is eminently to be approved, and is one which is carrying us up to the climax of denominational duty. We may or may not have found out the best way to do good and communicate; but if we keep clearly before us that we have no moral option but to give to others what is a blessing to ourselves, we shall ultimately learn to walk in the ways of a wise fidelity.

The difference between our present ecclesiastical and denominational tendencies and those of the past may be thus defined: Whereas once we sought for truth and freedom, we are now desiring truth, freedom, *and usefulness*. Our first struggle was to enfranchise our own minds and souls; to put away from us what looked to be superstitious, irrational, or inhumane; to break every yoke of subjection to creeds however venerable, or to church authority however ancient, except as such yokes were the veritable truth of God. That was work which had to be done. We had to have our declaration of independence and our war of revolution, and in those days there were wise statesmen and good soldiers. But the chains are thrown off; the mental and spiritual independence is achieved. No doubt problems of truth remain and always will remain to be solved. But the chief problem of to-day is the problem of moral and spiritual usefulness, — how we shall make our own church life nourishing and instructive to young and old ; how we shall make our denominational life promote the sway in the world of a reasonable, humane, devout Christianity, fruitful in righteous character and noble works.

INDEX.

ABBOT, ABIEL, 173, 174.
Abelard: liberalism, 36; on original sin, 38; atonement, 40, 42; disciples, 41.
Absolute Religion, 228, 231–233, 237–242.
Absolute, the, unknowable, 333–336.
Achilles, comparison, 213.
Adam: sin, 38, 40; and Christ, 58; Geneva doctrine, 67; view of Socinus, 71. (See *Original Sin*.)
Adams Family, and Mayhew, 163.
Adams, John: on Gay, 158; leadership, 241.
Adams, John Quincy, 249.
Adams, Sarah Flower, hymn, 251.
Ætna, illustration, 203, 204.
Agassiz, Louis, character and opinions, 302, 306.
Agnosticism: requiring deity, 300, 301; confession, 324; defined and opposed, 331–337; mists, 339.
Agriculture, improved by convents, 31.
Alcott, A. Bronson, transcendentalism, 208, 212.
Alexandria: school, 20, 29; clergy, 21; fathers, 38.
Alger, William Rounseville, 250.
Allen, Joseph Henry: lectures, 1, 97; Christian History, 54; on transcendentalism, 219; Parker, 239.
Allenville, M. d', anecdote, 295.
Alton Riot, 192.
Ambrose, influence, 15.
America, discovered, 197.
American Literature: connection with liberal religion, 245–271; fiction, 246, 247; history, 247, 248; oratory, 248, 249; criticism, 249; essays, 249, 250; German study, 250; poetry, 250, 251, 256–261.
American Unitarian Association: publication of Parker's works, 109, 222; organized, 184, 367; liturgies, 363.
American Unitarianism: contact with German thought, 97–115; vast subject, 99; change, 112; great exponent, 173. (See *Channing, English, Unitarianism*.)
Ames, Charles Gordon, on culture, 328.
Ames, Fisher, 144.
Anabaptists, confounded with Unitarians, 79.
Andover Theological School: creed, 84; candidates, 144; doctrinal controversy, 183.
Andromeda, illustration, 339.
Anselm, on the atonement, 39, 40.
Antichrist, 44.
Antislavery Movement, 191–193.
Apollinaris Heresy, 22.
Apollo, fable, 272.
Apologists, early, 7.
Apostles' Creed, liberality, 156.
Apostolic Fathers: purpose, 7; doctrinal points, 10. (See *Church*.)
Apostolic Ministry, 125.
Appleton, Doctor, views, 158.
Apthorp, East, colonial mission, 164.
Aquinas, life and literature, 270.
Arianism: controversy, 6, 16, 34; laborious existence, 22; broken up, 69.
Arians: doctrines, 17; aristocratic favor, defeat, 21; semi, 35; ascendency, 40; new name in England, 80, 85; in Orthodox fellowship, 155; peculiar belief, 156; two dissenters, 168.

INDEX.

Aristides, heavenly hope, 59.
Aristotle, evolutionist, 306.
Arius, 21.
Arlington Street Church, pastors, 166, 182. (See *Federal*.)
Arminianism, a liberal movement, 48, 204, 367.
Arnold, Matthew: on miracles, 106; Philistines, 207; researches, 283; famous formula, 325.
Art Development, 197.
Asceticism: highly estimated, 28; once essential, 29, 30.
Asia Minor, spread of Christianity, 67, 68.
Astronomy, ignorance of, 333, 334.
Athanasian Creed: forcibly established, 28; antiquity, 34; revolt against, 35; devotees, 43; influence in England, 158: damnatory clauses, 216.
Athanasius, at Nicæa, 21.
Atheism: Parker accused of, 229; practical and theoretical, 236, 237.
Athenagoras, on the logos, 11, 12, 16, 17.
Atkinson, on business morals, 313, 316.
Audin, on Calvin, 65.
Augustine: unexpected issue of his teachings, 13, 15; sins, 27; City of God, 24; lauded, 36; predestination, 36, 37; theology restudied and rejected, 37; original sin, 38; atonement, 39; relation to Luther, 51, 60; standpoint, 62; agnostic saying, 335.
Austin, Attorney-General, 192.
Austria: liberal rule, 73, 76; four religions, 76.

BACON, FRANCIS: outgrowth of the Renaissance, 197; character, 293.
Bacon, Roger, 199.
Baltimore Sermon, 182, 184, 186, 360.
Bancroft, George: education and travel, 211; works, 248.
Baptism, heretical opinions about, 79.
Baptists: one of three sects, 83; creed-bound, 84; adoption of Unitarian theology, 86, 87.
Barker, Joseph, leadership, 93.

Bartholomew's Day, 83.
Bartol, Cyrus Augustus, 208.
Basil, falsehood, 31.
Batchelor, George, lecture, 312.
Baur, School of Criticism, 107, 111.
Beach, Seth Curtis, lecture, 48.
Beatitudes: a man of the, 174; imperative, 218; sacred, 284.
Beauty, its own reward, 200.
Beethoven, influence, 212.
Belknap, Jeremy: pastorate, 166; hymn-book, 167.
Bellows, Henry W.: on Channing, 181; leadership, 368.
Benevolent Fraternity of Churches, 366.
Bentley, William, pastorate, 168.
Bernard, Saint: opinions, 40; not interested in science, 198.
Berry Street Conference, established, 183.
Bible: indebtedness to convents, 32; French translation, 42; sufficiency, 43; pure system of faith, 44; Wiclif's translation, 46; studied, 79; taken from its sanctuary, 100; changed estimate, 107; relation to Protestantism, 122; Puritan use in worship, 131; Gay's arms, 158; Unitarian views, 182, 183; of different nations, 190; more light, 193; tribunal, 202; transcendentalism, 203; a large, 209; external authority, 218; idolatry, 229; Parker's view, 230, 232; transmission, 233; infallibility, 273; verbal inspiration, 276; restored to thinking men, 299; rational view, 359; doubts suppressed, 364.
Biblical Criticism: free, 64; in vogue, 222; relation to Unitarianism, 272–289; ungracious aspect, 273; scientific research, 274, 275; Dutch school, German investigations, 275; reason, 275, 277; inspiration questioned, 275–277; textual criticism, 277, 279; absence of metaphysical theology, 277; the fear of deeper criticism, startling tidings from abroad, 278; affected by physical science, 279–283; doctrine of evolution, 280–282; geol-

ogy and creation, 282, 283; Christianity compared with other religious systems, 283-285; God-given scriptures, 285; order of the historic books, 285-288; worth of the investigation, 289; scientific method, 299.
Biddle, John, career, 81, 82.
Blackie, John Stuart, satire, 254.
Blandrata, Giorgio: in Poland, 73; in Transylvania, 74; worshipping Christ, 76.
Board of Trade, honor in, 313-316.
Bogomite Sect, 41.
Bohemia, religious exiles, 103.
Bolsec, Jerome Hermes, theology and life, 63, 64.
Bonet, quoted, 65, 69.
Bossuet, on errors of Protestantism, 120.
Boston: early churches, 133, 143, 359; two Trinitarian pastors, 155; orators, 162; mission to, 164; Parker's influence, 227, 228, 230, 234; a small congregation, 366. (See separate names of churches, such as *King's Chapel*.)
Boston Association of Ministers, 162.
Boucher, Joan, burned, 79, 80.
Bowdoin, James, relation to Mayhew, 163.
Bowring, Sir John, hymns, 251.
Brain, relation to life, 338.
Brattle Square Church: pastorate, 153, 182; Webster, 248.
Briggs, George Ware: lecture, 178; allusion, 295.
Bristol, mission to, 164.
Broad Church: Quaker view, 82; opinion of miracles, 106.
Brooke, Stopford, on miracles, 106.
Brook Farm, 212.
Brooklyn, Connecticut, church, 174, 176.
Brooks, Charles T., literary work, 250.
Browning, Robert, liberalism, 270.
Brownson, Orestes A., change of opinions, 98.
Bruys, Peter de: sect, 41; death, 42.
Bryant, William Cullen, literary work, 250, 256.

Buchanan, Robert, liberalism, 270.
Buddhist Ritual, 285.
Bulkeley, Peter, pastorate, 359.
Burgundians, Arians, 40.
Burns, Robert, satire, 49, 61.
Business Morals, 313-316.
Byzantine Court, 31.

CALHOUN, JOHN C., theology, 249.
Calvinism: two hateful doctrines, 49, 50; view of human nature and sin, 58; Francis David's position, 74; broad stream, 82, 83; in different churches, melting away, 84; independence of English Presbyterian churches, 86; New England basis, 142; Boston changes, 143; obsolete type, 169; old school, 174; modern, 175; moral argument against, 184, 205; glory and dream, 204; sublime and awful, 204, 210; contrary teachings, 221; softened, 367; cruel grasp, 369. (See *Orthodoxy*.)
Calvinists: modern ministers, 158, 165; grip of one doctrine, 303.
Calvin, John: horrible decree, 49; on total depravity, 57; relation to Zwingli, 58, 61; predestination, 60; Life, 61, 64, 65; no help to Unitarianism, 62, 63; relation to three opponents, 64-70, 78; Willis's characterization, 65, 66; reign, 67; church liberalized, 77; partial reformation, 78; church property, 150.
Cambridge Platform, on ordination, 168.
Cambridge: church division, 144; Sanders Theatre, 162; mission to, 164; Divinity School, 213; churches, 359.
Caner's Answer, 164.
Carlyle, Thomas: wife, 69; volcanic, 210; literary work, 270.
Carmarthen Theological School, 95.
Carpaccio's Picture, 216, 217.
Carpenter, J. Estlin, 95, 294.
Carpenter's Ordination, text, 158.
Carpenter, William B., scientific temper, 294, 310.

Castellio, life and work, 63–65.
Cathari, sect, 41.
Cato, heavenly hope, 59.
Cause and Effect, 310.
Chalcedon Council, 16, 19, 22, 23.
Champollion's Discoveries, 288.
Change and Continuance, the great law, 309.
Channing Hall, 183, 184.
Channing Unitarianism, 184, 185, 190–193. (See *Unitarianism.*)
Channing, William Ellery: religious life, 112, 181; famous sermon, 157, 360; guest, 176; lecture, 178–195; man, theologian, and leader, 178; personal reminiscences of, 179, 180; preordination, 180; early days, 180, 181; religious experience and study, 181; settlement, 182; liberal sermons, 182, 183; fires of controversy, 183; exponent of the severed churches, 184; view of divine nature, 185; Jesus, 186; burning light and thought, 186, 187; estimate of human nature, 187; root idea, 188; regard for the soul, 189; religion natural to man, 189, 190; nourisher of noble minds, 190, 191; philanthropy, 191–193; steadfast faith, 193; patriotism, 194; native state, 194, 195; leadership, 205; prophetic sense, 206; hampered, 206, 207; close of period, relation to Parker, 221; moral questions, 222; literary rank, 246; poetic elegy, 256; loved by Holmes, 258; on the Scriptures, 274, 275, 278; inspiration below virtue, 276; textual criticism, 279; pursuit of truth, 295; heroism, 355; indifference to organization, 356, 367.
Chapels, era of, 83.
Character, superior worth, 54.
Charlemagne: schools, 36; era, 37.
Charles II., 134.
Charles V., 65.
Charlestown: first church, 133; pastorate, 139; division, 143, 144; bridge, 149.
Chateaubriand, 103.

Chauncy, Charles: early liberalism, 158–160; relation to Mayhew, 161; funeral prayer, 165.
Child, Lydia Maria, stories, 246.
Children, religiously taught, 364, 365. (See *Sunday-schools.*)
China: illustration, 3; wall, 334.
Christendom: war of words, 24; truth outside, 190.
Christian, a great name, 220.
Christian Church: injurious connection with state, 26; militant and triumphant, 30; redemptive power, 36; membership not insisted upon, 84; relation to parish in Massachusetts, 116-154; franchise restricted, 134; name and limits, 136; vital transmission, 124-128; Parker's views, 230, 232; wedded to Bible, 273; small Unitarian body, 288; political task, 15, 16; separation from the world essential to life, 128; privileged, 139.
Christian Conscience: type, 102; data, 104; creed, 105.
Christian Disciple, published, 183.
Christian Doctrine: first stage, 1, 10; early, 1–25; rapid development, 7; revolutionized, 8; second stage, 10; intellectual opinions, 13, 14; double current, 13, 15; old views continued, 34; Wiclif's enlightenment, 44; vital, 364.
Christian Examiner: contributions by Channing, 194; Parker, 227; anti-Trinitarian scholarship, 277; criticism, 278.
Christian History: first five centuries, 1–25; fifth to fifteenth century, 26–47; two seed-plots, 28; monasticism, 28–33; seeds scattered, 67; three great periods, 107.
Christianity: raw material, no geographical limitations, 5; nearly extinguished, state religion, 26; life in death, 28; procreant cradle, 32; contents neglected, 33; mustard-seed, 34; supernatural element, 98; special revelation, 106; transient and permanent elements, 109, 228, 229;

INDEX. 379

great purpose, 186; nothing left, 214; history and traditions, 222, 229; new notions, 226; universal religion, 228; substance, 229; tottering, 230; Parker's view, 230-232; relation to the absolute religion, 231, 232; institutions unjustly censured, 233; real gospel, 234; speculations, 236, 238; higher law, 240; modern conflicts, 242; supposed omission, 272; the only religion, 283; more needed, 287.
Christmas: not observed, 362; change, 363.
Christoffel's Biography of Zwingli, 58, 59.
Christology of Gospels, 170.
Chrysostom, 27.
Church and Parish: lecture, 116-154; irreconcilable differences, ordinances, 124; needful distinction, 124-126; Roman Catholic extreme, 126-128; legal subordination of the church, 126, 127; decision of Supreme Court, 129, 147, 148; choice of pastors, 137-141; *imperium in imperio*, 139; property questions, 141, 152, 153; parish regarded as a trespasser, 148, 150; church overshadowed, 151, 153; separation influenced by character of church-members, 153, 154; subsequent legislation, 154; means of support, 360; home, 365, 366. (See *Congregational Churches*.)
Church Building Loan Fund, 361, 362.
Church Fathers: overstudied, 2, 4; French translation, 42.
Church of the Disciples, 366.
Civilization, centred in monasteries, 31.
Clarke, James Freeman: scholarship, 100, 212; German leanings, 105; story, 108; relation to Parker, 109, 222, 241; popular type, 112; better way, 113; transcendentalism, 208; literary rank, 250.
Clarke, John, pastorate, 160.
Clarke, Samuel, liberal ideas, 156.
Clement of Alexandria, 20.
Clergy: vicious, 28; from convents, 33; maintenance, 131.

Cobbe, Frances Power, on suffering, 351.
Coherence, denominational, 368, 369.
Colenso, Bishop, on miracles, 106.
Coleridge, Samuel Taylor, 209.
Columbus: sailors, 198; allusion, 206; cry, 212.
Commenus, Alexis, 41.
Comparative Study of Religions, 241.
Concord: church, 359; picture, 361.
Conferences, 95. (See *National*.)
Confessors, class of Christians, 13.
Congregational Churches: in England, 83-86; American, 89; disturbed, 123, 124; subordinated by legal decisions, 126, 127; democratic position of the minister, 127; land grants, 130; property, 131; usage in worship, 131; defection, 142; ordination, 145; original basis, 148; gradual change, 182. (See *Church*.)
Congregationalism: name not doctrinal, 132, 133; blow at, 138; doctrinal causes of trouble, 142; two parties, 143; changes, 144.
Connecticut: Congregational churches, 169; little dissent, 169-177; Episcopal churches, 169; pastors, 173-176.
Conscience, identical with God, 236.
Consciousness, phenomena of, 338.
Conservation of Energy, 303, 304.
Consociations, 171-175.
Constantine: era, 7; religious edict, 21; baptism, 28.
Constantinople, 19, 21, 22.
Cooper, James Fenimore, novels, 246.
Cooper, Samuel, views, 165.
Copernicus, 69, 197.
Correlation of Forces, 303.
Correspondence, perfect, 309.
Cosmogony, 281-283.
Councils: œcumenical, 21; local, 34. (See *Nicæan, etc*.)
Cousin's Writings, 212.
Coventry, Connecticut, 173.
Cranch, Christopher P.: transcendentalism, 208; literary work, 250.
Cranmer, Archbishop, 80.
Creeds: of five centuries, 16; Luther's, 43; strengthened, 170; substance of

INDEX.

doctrine, 252; more tender, 356; Unitarian, 358. (See *Athanasian*.)
Crillion, Count de, 295, 296.
Criticism: scientific, 101; general, 272, 273. (See *Biblical*.)
Cromwell, Oliver, liberality, 82.
Crook, anecdote, 85.
Crusades, 23.
Culture, new, 328.
Curtis, George William, literary work, 249.
Cyprian, influence, 15.

DANTE, how influenced, 270.
Dark Ages: rightly named, 26; clergy, 33. (See *Middle*.)
Darwin, Charles: honesty of spirit, 292, 293; leadership, 306.
Darwinism: story, 280; steps wanting, 281; real antagonism, 301; Agassiz's position, 302.
D'Aubigné's History, 50, 53, 55.
Dauphigny Protestants, 43.
David, Francis: career, 72-77; church, 77.
Davids, Rhys, researches, 283.
Decalogue, 53, 284.
Dedham: early worship, 133; historic First Church difficulties, 116; legal victory, 122, 123; sympathy with defeated party, 129, 130; change of pastor, 144; separation, 145; litigation, 145-149; deacon, 146. (See *Church and Parish*.)
Deistic Writings, 103.
De Normandie, James: lecture, 272; allusion, 299.
Descartes, 197.
Development Theory, 280, 281. (See *Evolution*.)
Devil, personal, 71.
De Wette: scholarship, 108; on the Old Testament, 109; writings, 212; criticism, 275, 278, 286.
Dewey, Orville: usefulness, 179; leader, 205; textual criticism, 279; heroism, 355.
Dial, published, 227.
Dissenters, name first used, 83.

District Missionary Associations, 95.
Divinity School, Parker's residence, 223, 227. (See *Cambridge*.)
Doctrine, essential to salvation, 13. (See *Christian*.)
Doddridge, Philip, liberalism, 156.
Domestic Missions, 191, 192.
Donelly, Ignatius, on Shakespeare, 201.
Dover Church, 166.
Drummond, James, 95.
Dualism: ancient, 41; stage of religion, 231; in nature, 350.
Dublin Church, 174.
Dummer Academy, 173.
Duns Scotus, theories, 38.
Dutch School of Criticism, 275, 287.
Dwight, John S.: ordination, 193; transcendentalism, 208; German study, 211, 212; literary work, 250.
Dyer's Life of Calvin, 61, 64.

EASTER, 362, 363.
Eastern Church: speculations, 16; councils, 22, 34; division, 23; marriage rules, 33; peculiar theory, 36; heretics, 40. (See *Greek*.)
Eastern Empire: splendor, 31; Arians, 41.
Ecclesiastes, Book of, texts, 323, 330.
Ecclesiastical Laws in Massachusetts, 136. (See *Church*.)
Eckley, Doctor, 155.
Eck, the Papal champion, 51.
Edwards, Jonathan, transcendentalism, 203.
Edward VI., tolerant spirit, 80.
Egypt: lotus, 218; Greek and Hebrew ideas, 283, 284; key to records, 288.
Eliot, George: religious ideas, 269; song, 324.
Elizabeth, Queen, Protestant revival, 80.
Ellery Family, 180.
Ellis, George E.: lecture, 116; Half Century of Controversy, 148; textual criticism, 279.
Ellsler, Fanny, anecdote, 208, 209.
Elohistic Documents, 286.

INDEX. 381

Elsewhere, the, 214.
Emerson, Ralph Waldo: famous address, 98, 213-215; on Scriptures, 190; transcendentalism, 203, 208; anecdote, 209; mysticism, 212; saturnalia of faith, 213; compared to Achilles, 213; visionary, 214; beyond bounds, 221; magnetic voice, 226; influence over Parker, 242; depth, 242; literary rank, 246; religious poetry, 257.
England: Socinian refugees, 73, 79; fines for non-attendance at church, 135; Society for Propagating the Gospel in Foreign Parts, 163, 164; Renaissance, 197; transcendentalism, 210, 211; patriotism, 319.
English Baptists, 83-87.
English Church: political relations, 26, 27; Wiclif and Wesley, 46; a powerful antagonist, 83; liberal movement, 86, 87; amendments needed, 87; prestige, 91; denial of miracles, 106; liberal tendencies, 156, 157.
English Common Law, rights of women, 33.
English Independents, freedom, 83.
English Literature: expressing liberal religion, 261-271; poetry, 261-269; fiction, 269-271. (See *American* and *Literature*.)
English Methodists, becoming Unitarians, 93.
English Presbyterians: one of three great sects, 83; becoming Unitarians, 84-86, 89; old families, 92.
English Unitarianism: lecture, 78-96; date and name, earliest facts obscure, 78; undercurrent of thought, 81; organic movement, 83; creedless soil, 84; evolution of other sects, 84, 85; first church, 88, 89; relation to America, 89, 90, 156, 168; two influences, 91; Methodist societies, 92, 93; steady growth, 96; aspects, 284.
English Unitarians: confounded with other heretics, 79; woman martyr, 79, 80; persecuted by other Protestants, 80; last burnings for heresy, refugees, 81; distinguished adherents, 82; a great leader, 85-87; cramped by controversy, 91; home missions, 91, 92; famous discussion in lectures, 93, 94; ecclesiastical taxes, 94; educational movements, lay preaching, 95; not influential in America, 156; sympathy of Bentley and Freeman, 168; recent views, 169; writers, 170.
Environment, 309.
Ephesian Council, 22.
Episcopacy: not Congregationalism, 132; efforts in New England, 163-165; organization, 357; festivals, 363.
Epistles, single texts overstudied, 2. (See *Paul*.)
Erasmus: on predestination, 51; Renaissance, 197.
Erigena, 37.
Eternal Life, present, 297. (See *Immortality*.)
Ethics: bloodless word, 312; culture, 328.
Eutychian Heresy, 23.
Everett, Charles Carroll: book, 106, 111; lecture, 329.
Everett, Edward, oratory, 248, 249.
Evolution: relation to religious thought, 303; scientific place, antiquity, 306; working theory, 307; prophecy, sentimental objection, 308; moral methods, 316. (See *Development*.)
Evolutionists: Gray, 302; assurance, 307; monkeys, 307.
Ewald's Researches, 286.

FABRICIUS, 53.
Faith: necessary to salvation, 38; relation to experience, 53.
Farley, Frederick Augustus, ordination, 187.
Farrar, Archdeacon, on Gregory, 27.
Fast Day, 362.
Feathers' Tavern Petition, 88.
Federal Street Church, 166, 182. (See *Arlington*.)
Fénelon, life, 194.

Fetichism, 231.
Fichte: leadership, 210; influence, 212.
Final Perseverance of the Saints, 303.
First Church in Boston: formed, 133; change, 143; pastorate, 159.
Fiske, John, works, 336.
Foxcroft, Thomas, pastorate, 160.
France: heresy, 41; Latin not understood, 42; Renaissance, 197; transcendentalism, 211.
Franklin, Benjamin, 241.
Freedom, of church and individual, 354, 355.
Freeman, James: liturgy, 89, 90; career, 167-169.
Free Religion, 242.
Free Will: essential to sin, 38; element in salvation, 39; not well named, 50; Roman Catholic view, 50, 51.
French Revolution: illustration, 14; anti-religious fury, 102, 103.
Frothingham, Nathaniel L., literary activity, 250.
Frothingham, Octavius Brooks: scholarship, 111; History of Transcendentalism, 204; literary rank, 250.
Froude, James Anthony, 270.
Fuller, Margaret: transcendentalism, 208; anecdote, 209; German study, 212; literary service, 250.
Fuller, on Wyclif, 45, 46.
Funeral, first prayer, 165.
Furness, William Henry: writings and opinions, 109; better way, 113; transcendentalism, 208; literary service, 249, 250.

GALILEO, 197.
Gannett, Ezra Stiles, textual criticism, 279.
Garrison, William Lloyd, fame, 192.
Gay, Ebenezer: career, 157. 158; allusion, 160; relation to Mayhew, 161.
General Court, rebuked, 159, 160. (See *Massachusetts.*)
Genesis, Book of, days, 282, 283.
Geneva: liberalized, 67, 77; made safer, 67; Italian Protestants, 68; property transferred, 150. (See *Calvin.*)
Gentiles, 283.
Gentilis, Valentine, 78.
Gentleman and Gentlewoman, 316.
Geography, ignorance of, 333, 334.
Geology and Scripture, 281, 282.
German Language, indispensable, 108.
German Theology, contact with American thought, 97-115. (See *Philosophy.*)
Germany: Socinian refugees, 73; Renaissance, 197; new thought, 210; American scholars, 211; philosophy, 222; Bible criticism, 275, 278.
Giles, Henry: pastorate, 93; literary service, 249.
Gnosticism and Gnostics, 12, 41.
God: personified attributes, 17-20; begetting another deity, 18; with man, 26; suffering, 35; Schleiermacher's opinions, 104; excluded from certain metaphysical systems, 112; Channing's views, 185, 186; his own witness, 203; creative mind, 210; naturally known, 218; love, 225; Parker's idea, personality, and nature, 231; indwelling spirit, 235, 304; ever-living, 236, 289, 304; perfect cause, 237; motherhood, 240; independence of revelation, 255; knowledge of science, 282; great problem, 289; light, 295; spirit, 296; inspiring loyalty, 297; statute-books, 299; life, 300; not an Oriental sovereign, 304; unity, 305; will, 309; effect on philanthropy, 324-326; unknowable, 333-335; Idea, 336; seen in nature, 346, 347; loveliness, 350; humanity, 359, 369; ignorance about, 364. (See *Holy Spirit, Jesus Christ, Life, Trinity.*)
Goethe: relation to Carlyle, 210; influence, 212.
Golden Age, 308.
Good Hope, Cape of, 197.
Goodness, no delusion, 327.
Gospels: facts explained, 109-111; for disciples, 125; legends, 278.

Gothic Arians, 40.
Gottschalk's Heresy, 37, 38.
Graf's Researches, 286.
Gray, Asa: motto, 290, 310; on agnosticism, 301; evolutionist, 302, 306, 307.
Greece: mighty spirits, 197; Egyptian ideas, 283, 284; barbarians, 283.
Greek Church: phrase in creed, 35; view of original sin, 38. (See *Eastern*.)
Greek Language: genders, 12; studied, 174.
Green, Joseph, ordination, 158.
Greenwood, Francis W. P., leadership, 205.
Gregory of Nyssa: theory, 20; lies, 27.
Guide-books, illustration, 215.
Gunpowder, invented, 197.

HALE, EDWARD EVERETT, stories, 247.
Hallam's History, 67.
Hall's Orthodoxy and Heresy, 62.
Hamont the Martyr, 81.
Harvard College: benefits, 166; Parker, 223, 224. (See *Cambridge* and *Divinity School*.)
Hawthorne, Nathaniel: stories, 247; David Swan, 348.
Haynes's Reply, 85.
Hebrews: spiritual prophets, 163; heroes, 191; hymns, 251, 257, 258; in Egypt, 283, 284; not the only recipients of revelation, 283. (See *Jews*.)
Hector, 213.
Hedge, Frederic Henry: scholarship, 100, 212; German study, 105, 106, 211; leadership, 106; work, 111; better way, 113; transcendentalism, 208; literary service, 250; aphorism, 256.
Hegel School, 99, 106, 111.
Henricians and their Founder, 42.
Henry VIII. and the Reformation, 119.
Heresies, forty, 12.

Herford, Brooke, lecture, 78.
Hexateuch, 288.
Hibbert's Lectures, 287.
Higginson, Francis, pastorate, 359.
Higginson, Thomas Wentworth, 250.
Hincmar, 37.
Hindus: mysticism, 212; flower of the spirit, 218.
Hingham Church, 157. (See *Gay*.)
Holland Land Company, 171, 172.
Holland: Socinians, 73; refugees, 79; American sermon, 157; Renaissance, 197.
Hollis, Thomas, generosity, 166.
Holmes, Oliver Wendell: stories, 247; wit, 249; literary ability, 250; poetry, 257.
Holy Spirit: logos, 9; Pauline doctrine, 10; unity with the Son, 11; personality, 22, 57; procession, 35; Melancthon's view, 56. (See *God, Jesus*.)
Homo-ousian Controversy, 21, 35.
Honesty and Policy, 315.
Honor, false ideas of, 316, 317.
Hooker, Thomas, pastorate, 359.
Hopkins, Samuel: views, 169; disinterestedness, 187.
Hornbrooke, Francis Bickford, lecture, 245.
Howard, Doctor: ordination, 158; relation to Boston Association, 162.
Huidekoper, H. J., strong Unitarian, 172.
Human Nature: belief in, 50, 188; Zwingli's view, 57, 58; exaltation, 189; fourfold analysis, 225; integrity, 340; sense of duty, 347; reliability, 352, 353.
Hungary: Unitarian root, 74-76; nobility, 76; congregations, 77.
Huns, 24.
Hussite Wars, 104.
Huxley, Thomas Henry: anecdote, 280, 281; on Bacon, 293; acute saying, 298; Advance of Science, 306.
Hypostasis, 20, 56, 57.
Hypotheses: necessary for investigation, 306, 307; in agnosticism, 333.

IF, force of the word, 318.
Immortality: Schleiermacher's view, 104; its own witness, 233; sure, 239; relation to philanthropy, 234–237; Parker's belief, 238–240; ignorance about, 364.
Independents, creed-bound, 83, 84.
Indian Evangelization, 161, 164, 165.
Infidelity, the real, 295.
Inquisition, persecutions, 41, 66.
Insanity and Sanity, 337–341.
Inspiration: Parker's view, 223, 230; universal, 233; inferior to virtue, 276; outside of the Hebrews, 284.
Italy: precursors of Protestantism, 43; free-thinkers, 70; Renaissance, 196.

JEFFERSON, THOMAS, 241.
Jehovistic Documents, 286.
Jerome, bad character, 27.
Jerusalem, overthrown, 8.
Jesus Christ: nature and office, 6; deified, 6, 11; logos, 9; simply a saviour from sin, 10; Son and Spirit, 11; double nature, 16; pre-existence, 17; an inferior divinity, 21, 22; without human personality, 22; absorbent of divine nature, 23; divinity with man, 25; supreme deity denied, 35, 36; adoption into godhead, 36; relation to faith and salvation, 38; ransom, coequal divinity, 39; relation to justification, 40; only intercessor, 44; prayer to, 56; extent of salvation, 58, 59; greatest martyr, 67; Socinian theory, 71; true rank, 78, 80; foundation of the Mass, real benefit, 79; Schleiermacher's theory, 104; miracles as natural acts, 109; special facts, 109, 111, 114; true nature, 155–157; full indwelling of God, 170; Unitarian doctrine, 182, 183; Channing's view, cruel death and its relation to sin, 186, 187; real authority, 214, 228; conflicting reports, 232; Parker's view, 233, 238; rescued from mystery, 240; beloved, 255; in poetry, 261; revelation, 268; characteristic saying, 295; intensity, 328; loftiest appearance, 342; fulness of power, 345; central type, 352; truest son of man, 353; manhood, 364; flower, 370. (See *Logos, Messiah, Miracles, Trinity*.)
Jesuits, attacking Socinianism, 72.
Jews: messianic hope, 7, 8; catastrophe, 9; hot-bed of tradition, 67, 111; expelled from Spain, 73; confounded with Unitarians, 78, 79; synagogues, 150. (See *Hebrews*.)
John of Gaunt, 45.
John's Epistles, text, 305.
John's Gospel: logos, 9; proem, 10.
John the Evangelist: nature, 20; fearlessness, 192.
Johnson, Samuel: Oriental Religions, 241; literary service, 250.
Johnson's Answer, 164.
Jonah, story of, 202.
Jouffroy's Ethics, 212.
Jowett's Works, 270.
Judaism: distinguished from Christianity, 7; worship, 284.
Judd, Sylvester, great story, 247.
Justification by Faith, experimental, 53.
Justin Martyr: doctrinal works, 8–10; apologist, 9; logos, 16; unexpected results, 23.
Justinian Code, 32.

KANT: leadership, 210; influence. 212.
King's Chapel: liturgy, 89, 168; rector, 164; freedom, 167.
King, Thomas Starr, church, 259.
Kuenen's Researches, 283, 287.

LANCASHIRE LIBERALISM, 92, 93.
Latin Church, view of original sin, 38. (See *Roman, Western*.)
Latin Language: not understood in worship, 42; Unitarian treatise in, 81.
Latitudinarians, 87.
Laymen: preaching, 95; right to ordain, 138.
Lecky's History of Rationalism, 61.
Le Conte, on development, 303–306.

INDEX. 385

Leggatt, Bartholomew, Unitarian martyr, 81.
Lenox Meeting, 192.
Leonard's Pastorate, 174.
Leo the Great: power, 1, 15; boundary line, 5; formula of faith, 23; first among the popes, 24.
Leper Church, 72.
Lessing: impulse to theology, 100; life, 102.
Lewis, John, Unitarian martyr, 81.
Lexington, Parker family, 222, 224.
Liberal Christianity, permeating literature, 227. (See *Unitarianism.*)
Liberalism: vague form, 142; in Boston, 143.
Life: one pervading, 296-300, 308, 309; debt to Eternal Spirit, 327; first appearance, 343; lowest forms, 344.
Lincoln, Abraham, a model, 320.
Lindsey, Theophilus: church, 78, 89; career, 87-89; liturgy, 89.
Literature: Unitarian authors, 245-253; writers on religion, 253-271.
Liverpool Controversy, 93, 94.
Locke, John: theology, 82; philosophy, 204, 214.
Logos: early doctrine, 9-20; soul of Christ, 22; Luther's view, 56. (See *Word.*)
Lombard, Peter, doctrines, 40.
Lombardy Arians, 40.
London: Unitarian church, 78, 88, 89; synods, 81; Dr. Priestley, 90; domestic missions, 91.
Longfellow, Henry Wadsworth, religion, 256.
Longfellow, Samuel, literary service, 250.
Long Parliament, 82.
Lord's Supper, controversy, 74.
Love: among animals, 344, 345; solution, 345, 346; roundabout definitions, 350. (See *God.*)
Lovejoy Riot, 192.
Lowell, James Russell: criticism, 247, 249, 250; religion, 256.
Luke's Gospel, poetic element, 278.
Lutheranism: Socinus, 70; F. David, 74; traditions, 97.

Luther: inferior to Wiclif, 43; view of transubstantiation, 44; predestination, 50, 51, 60; depravity, 50, 51; reticence about the Trinity, 52, 56; ceremonies and commands, salvation by faith, 53; not a believer in the doctrine of character, 54; rejecting reason, 54, 55; yet aiding it, 55, 63; disciples, 56, 57; relation to Zwingli, 58; Melancthon, 62; era, 69; Francis David, 74; partial reform, 78; Renaissance, 197; heroism, 372.

MACDONALD, GEORGE, 269.
Macedonia, spread of Christianity, 67, 68.
Macedonius' heresy, 22.
Mahometan Lands: captives, 34; rejection of the Trinity, 35, 36.
Manchester New College, 95.
Mansfield Church, 169-172.
Man: spiritual nature, 297; made of dust, 298; offspring of deity, 320; inspired work for, 325; relation to the universe, 346, 347. (See *Human Nature.*)
Mappa, Colonel, 171, 172.
Maronites: heresy, 23; type, 41.
Marriage: protected by the Justinian Code, 32, 33; of clergy, 119.
Martha's Vineyard, 161.
Martineau, Harriet, theology, 69.
Martineau, James: preaching, 69; defence, 94; Oxford, 95; Study of Religion, 104; leadership, 106; literary service, 250; greatness, 324.
Martyrs: class of believers, 13; Servetus and Jesus, 67; English Unitarians, 79-81.
Mary, Queen, reign, 80.
Massachusetts: ecclesiastical laws, 123, 129, 136; Supreme Court, 129; General Court, 130; privileged heritage, clergy, 131; townships, 132; theory and practice, 132, 133; four orders passed, 134, 135; choice of pastors, 137-141; legalized trespassers, 149, 150; fraudulent devices, 159; legis-

lation, 356; oldest meeting-houses, 359; church-rates, 360; hospitality, 365; church disestablished, 366. (See *New England*.)

Mass, significance of the name, 125, 126. (See *Roman Catholic*.)

Materialism: disguised, 336–339; illustration, 337; repressive, 341; failure, 342.

Matter, product of spirit, 343.

Maury, 65.

Maxwell, Clerke, 300, 301, 303.

Mayflower, era, 81.

Mayhew, Jonathan, career, 160–166.

May, Samuel J.: pastorate, 176; anti-slavery sentiments, 191, 192.

Meadville Theological School, 95, 172.

Meeting-houses, description of earliest, 359, 361.

Melancthon: liberality, 56, 57, 62; relation to Servetus, 70; Socinus, 70; F. David, 74.

Messiah: office, 1; Jewish, 7; Son of Star of Jacob, 8; hope extinguished, 10; perishing, 16; in prophecy, 108. (See *Jesus*.)

Methodists: becoming Unitarians, 93; personal experience, 203; earliest, 357; building-plans, 362. (See *English*.)

Michael Angelo, 370.

Michelet, on two worlds, 196, 197.

Middle Ages: ignorance, 196; change, 201; heart, 210. (See *Dark*.)

Migne's Patrologia, 4.

Mill, John Stuart, admissions, 304, 305.

Miller, Hugh, death, 282.

Milton, John: theology, 82, 270; essay on, 194.

Mind, as the logos, 11–13, 16–20.

Minerva, fable, 357.

Ministerial Conference, 183.

Ministers: election, 137–141; compulsory support, 140; a new one settled, 141; life-tenure, 143; quarrel over, 144, 145; Unitarian models, 177. (See *Clergy*.)

Ministry at Large, 91.

Miracles: believed by early radicals, 98, 99, 106, 107; definition, 106; in New Testament, 114; authority, 214, 215; no test, 218; doubt suppressed, 364.

Missionaries, mistaken methods, 285.

Monasticism: genial soil, 28–33; refuge for useful arts, 31; scholarship, 31, 32; Bible, 32.

Monotheism, 231. (See *God, Unitarianism*.)

Montaigne, 65.

Moore the Innkeeper, 172.

Morals, the word, 312.

Moravians, 103.

Morris, Lewis, poetry, 266–269.

Morse, Jedediah, pastorate, 168.

Moses, books of, 285–287.

Motley, John Lothrop, histories, 248.

Motte, Mellish I., ordination, 187.

Müller, Max, researches, 283.

Music: growth, 211; word, 312; illustration, 344.

NAPOLEON BONAPARTE, essay on, 194.

National Conference, 367, 368.

Natural Law, in spiritual world, 308.

Natural Selection, 305.

Nature: love for, 236, 237; no death in, 308, 309; education of her children, 317, 318; few models, 320; expression of mind, 345, 346; duality, 350, 351; indifferentism, 351; unity and prophecy, 352.

Neander: on Luther, 51, 56; Zwingli, 58, 60; fame, 101.

Necker, anecdote, 295, 296.

Nestorian Heresy, 22.

Newbury: church tax, 134, 135; mission to, 164.

New England: Unitarianism, 105; scholarship, 111; one preacher of Universalism, 160; Hopkinsians, 169; earliest defence of Unitarianism, 172; creeds, 179, 180; transcendentalism, 196–219, 222; colonists, 200, 201; hardy soil, 201; many-sided minds, theocracy, 202; witnesses to religious life, 203; dead Calvinism, 204; sober habits, less provincial, 209; ferment, influential scholars, 211 : isolation, 224 ; new notions in religion, 226 ; phantom ship, 227 ; material for years of thought, 233 ; sermons, 246 ; history, 248 ; oratory, 248, 249 ; literary life, 252 ; poetry, 258 ; influence of Unitarian heroes, 356 ; birth of Unitarianism, as a prairie fire, 357 ; church-buildings, 361. (See *Church and Parish, Massachusetts*.)

New Hampshire: History, 166 ; liberal influences, 174.

New Haven, influential resident, 169.

New London, missionary to, 164.

Newman, Francis W., writings, 270.

Newman, John Henry, narrow faith, 2.

New Orthodoxy anticipated, 79.

Newport: Hopkins, 169 ; Channing, 179, 180, 194 ; sermon, 189.

New Testament: leading idea, 7 ; plainly read, 78 ; Tyndale's, 79 ; smuggled, 80 ; Unitarianism, 85 ; miracles, 113 ; church pattern, 132 ; Abbot's study, 174 ; ethical principles, 247. (See *Bible, Miracles*.)

Newton, Sir Isaac, theology, 82.

New Year's Gifts, 362.

New York State, first liberal society, 171.

Nicæan Council: decision, 21, 22 ; barren conflict in the dark, 25 ; era, 35.

Nicene Creed: adopted, 21 ; expanded, 22 ; on nature of Christ, 35 ; adherents persecuted, 40 ; anti-Trinitarian, 156, 157. (See *Athanasian, Creeds*.)

Northampton, ordination, 179, 193.

Norton, Andrews: address, 98 ; letters to, 99 ; representative of an older school, 100 ; insistence, 102 ; dislike of certain phrases, 103 ; on Schleiermacher, 104 ; controversy, 106 ; on Old Testament, 108 ; relations to Furness, 109 ; on infidelity, 112 ; tendency, 113 ; leadership, 205 ; compared to Hector, 213 ; conservatism, 214 ; on myths, 278 ; doubtful about organization, 367.

Novatian: character and works, 6 ; blunt opinion, 18.

Noyes, George R.: scholarship, 100 ; on Hebrew prophecy, 108 ; leadership, 205 ; textual criticism, 279.

Numa, heavenly hope, 59.

ŒCOLAMPADIUS, letter, 65.

Old Dissent, 91.

Old South Church: Trinitarian, 155 ; during the Revolution, 168.

Old Testament: Jesus revealed in, 38 ; inspiration, 41 ; lectures by three scholars, 108 ; De Wette, 109 ; great sermon, 109 ; divisions, 286.

Olshausen, 110.

Opinions, organic growth, 1.

Ordinations, 27, 28.

Organization, neglected, 356, 357.

Oriental Religions, 241.

Origen, era, 20.

Original Sin: doctrine advocated and opposed, 38, 39, 58 ; horror of abated, 60.

Orthodoxy: liberal leaven, 206 : contrary teachings, 221 ; fear of infidelity, 229 ; disarmed, 232 ; Wendell Phillips, 248 ; literature, 270 ; former generation, 340 ; types, 340-342 ; unsoundness, 356 ; Sunday-schools, 364 ; liberal wing, 367. (See *Calvinism, Trinitarianism*.)

Osgood, of Medford, 173.

Otis, James, correspondence, 163.

Ought, the word, 327.

Owen, on Unitarian poison, 82.

PALESTINE: not the limit of Christianity, 5 ; sect, 8.

Palfrey, John Gorham: lectures, 108 ; estimate of Mayhew, 162 ; literary service, 248.

Pantheism: ancient form, 37 ; approaches to, 61 ; allies, 112 ; stage of religion, 231.

Parish and Church, 116-154. (See *Church*.)

Parker, Theodore: on miracles, 99, 106 ; scholarship, 100, 109 ; study of

Strauss, 110; tendency, 113; transcendentalism, 212; career, 220-244; unsectarianism, 221; popular representative of new ideas, 221; an oak, indebtedness to Channing, a disturbing preacher, 222; birthplace, 222, 223; ancestry, man of inspirations, 223; passion for work, 223, 224; college and parish, 224; armed host of thoughts, fourfold analysis of human spirit, prayers, 225; friendships, 225, 226; courage, knowledge, method, tact, sentiment, logic, satire, language, oratory, 226; not an originator, 226, 227; removal to Boston, theology magazine articles, 227; new questions, 228; the Absolute Religion, 228; famous sermon, 228-230; style, 229; chief book, 230-235, 238; signal for revolution, 232; diverse effects, 233; qualities for leadership, 233, 234; country parish, 234; energizing outlook, 235; nature and deity, 236; on atheism and theism, 236, 237; mission of Jesus, 238; personal conviction of future life, 238-240; inward revelation, 239; love of truth, 240; anti-slavery, 240, 241; study of historic religions, 241; free religion, 242; pulpit tonic, 242; stimulating influence, 242, 243; persecuted followers, solid labor, 243; premature end, 243, 244; relation to Phillips, 248; heroism, 355.
Parkman, Francis, histories, 248.
Parsee Religion, 218.
Patriotism: of Mayhew, 163; Channing, 178; a nursery, 223; wide outbreak, 318-320; Jewish, 319.
Paulician Heresy, 40, 41.
Pauline Epistles, dividing line, 7.
Paul the Apostle: on messianic office, 1; boundary line, 5; era, 7; doctrine of spirit, 10: nature, 20; precept, 44; predestination text, 54; reason, 55; heavenly hope, 59; charitable spirit, 193; "to live is Christ," 330.
Paulus: representative name, 107; commentary, 110; criticism, 278.

Peabody, Andrew Preston: lectures, 26, 155; literary service, 250; textual criticism, 279.
Peabody, Elizabeth, transcendentalism, 208.
Peabody, Ephraim, leadership, 205.
Penn, William, theology, 82.
Pentateuch, date, 285-288. (See *Moses*.)
Persia: dualism, 41; mysticism, 212; rose, 218.
Personal Equation, 340.
Personality of God, 231.
Peterborough Church, 174.
Petersham Church, 176.
Peter the Apostle: theology, 3; heavenly hope, 59; symbol, 200.
Petrobrussian Sect, 41, 42.
Pew-rents, 95.
Philanthropy, dependent on religion, 324-326.
Philistine Gospel, 207.
Phillips, Wendell: speech, 192, 193; literary work, Orthodoxy, 248.
Philo, doctrine of, 9.
Philosophy: relation to Unitarianism, 329-353; a universal possession, 329, 330; various systems, 330; special German systems, 331; agnosticism not included, 335, 336; materialism defective, 338, 339; spiritualistic philosophy, 339-353; large optimism, 342; spirit the basis of the universe, 343, 344.
Philpot, Jhon, 80.
Photographs, composite, 4.
Pictures: labelled, 200; illustration, 215-218.
Piedmont Protestants, 42.
Pindar, and Zwingli, 59.
Pisano, Niccolà, sculptor, 212.
Plato: tribute to, 59; transcendentalism, 212.
Plotinus, 212.
Plymouth Pilgrims and Church, 359.
Poe, Edgar Allan, writings, 250.
Poland: liberal religion, 68-77 *passim*; influence in England, 81.
Pollok's Course of Time, 271.
Polytheism, 231.

INDEX. 389

Pond, Enoch, on the Dedham case, 148.
Portsmouth: missionary, 164; hymn-book, 168.
Positivism, ancient form, 37.
Prayers, by Parker, 225. (See *Public Worship*.)
Predestination: doctrine virtually set aside, 36; logical result, 37, 38; conditional, 39; horrible, 49; revolt against, 50; Luther's belief, 50, 60; Catholic view, 51; protest against Paul, 54; views of Swiss reformers, 60; liberal form, 61; Genevan belief, 67.
Presbyterianism: English, 83; different from Congregationalism, 132; in Boston, 166; organization, 357.
Prescott, William Hickling, histories, 248.
Price, Richard, theology and politics, 156.
Priesthood, 189, 190.
Priestley, Joseph: clear sight, 85; leadership, 87, 88; in America, 90; heroism, 355.
Primitive Christianity: five centuries, 1; wrongly identified, 2; point of view, 3.
Printing, 197.
Protestantism: principles, 43; no finality, 122; result, 123; shocked at its own teachings, 150; speculative errors, 232; needing authority, 276.
Protestant Reformation: precursors, 43; head, 66.
Protestants, diversity, 120.
Providence, ordination sermon, 187.
Psalms of David: clean heart, 53; besetting God, 301.
Ptolemaic System, 282.
Public Worship: Puritan usage, 131; fines for non-attendance, 135. (See *Prayers, Ritual*.)
Puritanism: national influence, 81; narrow, 84; old ways changed, 148; a nourisher, 223.
Puritans: faithful stewards, 53; clergy ejected, 83; heritage, 127-129, 132;

joyless, 201; simplicity, 359, 360; rites and holidays, 362; conservative blood, 363.
Purvey's Translation, 46.

QUAKERS, inner light, 203, 208.
Quatrefage, quoted, 307.
Quincy, Josiah, 241.

RACOW SOCINIANS, 71, 72.
Rationalism, 61, 63. (See *Philosophy, Reason*.)
Realism: philosophy, 17; theology, 19.
Reason: personified, 9-20 *passim*; rejected by Luther, 54, 55; supreme tribunal, 202; reasonable limits, 204-206; trustworthiness denied, 340.
Reformation: relation to Unitarianism, 48-77; not a Unitarian movement, 48; harsh side, 50, 51; advance and retrogression, 51, 52; rational theologians, 61; new chapter with Calvin, 62; doctrinal system running to seed, 101, 102; era, 116; success, 118; earlier reformers, 118, 119; wrong causes assigned, 119, 120; leaders blind to the outcome, 121, 122; transfer of church property, 150; great souls, 244; possible postponement, 372.
Regulus, illustration, 53.
Religion: to be dealt with religiously, 3; not limited, 58, 59; mother's lesson, 102; Parker's Discourse, 230-238; made possible, 340.
Religious Life: swift current, 4; and thought, 112, 113.
Renaissance: in New England, 196-219; re-birth, 196; double discovery, 196-198; in music, 211; living faith, 213; right term, 219.
Renan's Works, 283.
Renouf's Researches, 283.
Retribution, personal, 44.
Reuss's Researches, 285.
Revelation: not limited to one nation, 283; universal, 307. (See *Bible*.)
Revolutionary War: era, 149; anecdote of Gay, 158; Chauncy's ser-

vice, 159; Channing's birth, 180. (See *Mayhew, Patriotism.*)
Reynolds, Grindall: lecture, 354; early training, 360, 364.
Rhode Island: "a gentleman from," 164; slave-trade, 167; Channing's early home, 95, 179, 180. (See *Newport.*)
Righteousness: law of, 312–328; best word, defined, 313; taught by business, 313–316; added grace, mostly real, 316; false code of honor, 316, 317; mercantile integrity, 317; the power of *if*, 318; wider reach, 318, 319; a few great models, 320; end or quality of moral action, 321–323, 326, 327; temptations, 322; connection with religion, 323–328.
Ripley, George, and Wife, 99, 106, 208, 212.
Ritual: substitute for duty, 30; splendid, 33. (See *Public Worship.*)
Robert Elsmere, the novel, 108, 270, 271.
Robinson, John, earnestness, 193.
Roman Catholic Church: devotion to creed, 43; pecuniary exactions, 45; Luther's challenge, 50, 51; not spiritually purified, 116–120; no reform from within, 116; claims, 116, 117; breath, systematization, 117; errors, 118, 119; unity, 120; rites, 125; separation of church and people, 126, 127; clerical rule, 127, 128; monuments of piety, 150; priestly comfort, 198; opposed to progress, 198, 199; symbol of Peter, 200; speculative errors, 232; infallibility, 276; likeness to Buddhism, 285; organization, 357; feast-days, 363.
Roman Empire: Gothic invasion, 24; civilization, 26; subversion, 30; laws, 32, 33; fraudulent devices, 159; mighty spirits, 197.
Rome, City of: courts, 15; pantheon, 22; potent voice, 24; ambiguous silence, 35; Christianity in, 67, 68; basilicas, 150.
Ruskin, John, on a great picture, 216, 217.

SAADI, transcendentalism, 212.
Sabbath, 286.
Sabellian Controversy, 6, 16.
Sabellius: work, 6; mysticism, 20; opponent, 21.
Sacraments: value, 129; neglected, 151.
Sadler's Sermon, 310, 311.
Salem: turnpike, 149, 150; mission to, 164; pastor, 168.
Salvation: doctrine essential to, 13, 14; and faith, 38; for non-Christians, 38; relation to character, 53, 54; joint result, 56.
Samosatians, condemned, 57.
Sanity, of the world within, 353. (See *Insanity.*)
Savage, Minot Judson, on Jesus, 370.
Sayce's Researches, 283.
Scepticism, like agnosticism, 332.
Schaff, Philip, 101.
Schelling: leadership, 210; transcendentalism, 212.
Schiller's Lecture on History, 294.
Schleiermacher: era, 97, 115; influence, 99; career, 101, 102; first strong impressions, 102; views, 103, 104; veil, 104; miracles, 106; compromises, 108; pivot of appeal, 113; transcendentalism, 212.
Scholarship, in convents, 31, 32.
Scholasticism, 32, 36.
Schopenhauer's Philosophy, 331.
Schwegler, on Biblical criticism, 278.
Science: in theology, 3; teaching unity, 188; relation to Scripture, 279, 282; progress, 281; text-books, 290, 291; continually rewritten, 292, 293; two great principles, 302–305; harmony with religion, 310, 311.
Scientific Method, in Biblical study, 274, 279.
Scientific Thought: relation to Unitarianism, 290–311; definition, 290; answer, 290, 291; man's place in the material world, 291; evolution of moral consciousness, 298; sometimes harsh, 299; material position assumed and forsaken, 299, 300; conclusions, 300; new dignity in life,

the watchword of new security, 305; verifiable hypotheses, 305, 306; origin of man, 307, 308; touching immortality, 308; organism and environment, 309. (See *Philosophy*.)
Scientists: strict honor, 292; sincerity, 292, 293; devout confessions, 293, 294; devoted explorers, 298, 299.
Scipios, the two, 59.
Scotch Presbyterians, separated from English, 84.
Scotus, Duns, 38.
Scotus, John: doctrine, 37; heresy, 38. (See *Erigena*.)
Sculpture, revolutionized, 212.
Sears, Edmund Hamilton: works and views, 109; Heart of Christ, 110; hymns, 251.
Secker, Archbishop, 164.
Sects, result of Protestantism, 120, 121.
Seneca, tribute to, 59.
Sensationalism, in pulpit, 259.
Servetus: burned, 48, 57, 70, 78; career, 65-69; high rank as a martyr, 67; worshipping Christ, 76.
Shakespeare: relation to Renaissance, 197; transcendental sentence, 198; Puritan estimate, 201; lectures, 249; Mount Shasta, 370.
Shepard, Thomas, pastorate, 359.
Sheridan, General, heroism, 320.
Sherman, John: liberal views, 169-173; allusion, 175.
Sherman, Roger, correspondence, 169.
Sibylline Oracles, 38.
Sight, crooked, 340.
Sigismund, John, 73-75.
Sin: salvation from, 186; Channing's view, 187. (See *Original*.)
Slicer, Thomas Roberts, lecture, 290.
Smithfield Martyrs, 80.
Smith, Samuel Abbot, pastorate, 174.
Smith, W. Robertson, on the Trinity, 277, 288.
Socinianism: movement begun, 48; term of contempt, 69, 85; expelled from Poland, 73; Latin treatises, 81.
Socinus, Lælius and Faustus, 61-65, 69-71, 76.

Socrates, heavenly hope, 59.
Son of God: among men, 14; theory of Servetus, 65. (See *Jesus*.)
Sonship, implying subordination, 19.
Soul: respect for, 189; relation to universe, 291, 292.
Spain: theological revolt, 35, 36; Jews, 73. (See *Servetus*.)
Sparks, Jared: ordination, 182, 184; literary service, 250; ordination, 360.
Spencer, Herbert: on correspondence, 309; agnosticism, 333-336; something higher, 348.
Spinoza, 197.
Spirit: and matter, 343, 347-349; transcends itself, 349; freedom, 349, 350. (See *Holy*.)
Sprague's Annals, 174.
Spurgeon, Charles H., leadership, 86.
Stanley, Dean: use of liturgy, 87; literary work, 270.
Stetson, Caleb, transcendentalism, 208.
Stewart, Samuel Barrett, lecture, 220.
Stowe, Harriet Beecher, novels, 246.
Stowe, the historian, 79, 80.
Strangeways Church, free, 94.
Strauss: representative of thought, 107; theory, 110, 111; criticism, 278.
Stuart Dynasty, overthrown, 83.
Subject and Object, 344.
Suffering: universal, 350, 351; exaggerated, 351, 352.
Sufi Garden, 218.
Sumner, Charles, oratory, 248, 249.
Sunday-schools: without a pastor, 92; lacking in knowledge, 360, 365, 366; doctrines, 364, 365.
Sun, illustration, 20.
Swedenborg, quoted, 57.
Symbol, Unitarianism a, 220.
Symbolism of Language, 103, 104.
Symonds, on the Renaissance, 196.

TAYLOR, BAYARD, literary work, 250.
Temperance, encouraged by business laws, 315, 316.
Tennyson, Alfred, religion in poetry, 208, 261, 263, 268.

Thacher, Peter, pastorate, 101.
Thackeray, William Makepeace, on shams, 269.
Thanksgiving Day, 362.
Theism, 233, 236, 237.
Theology: conflicts, 242; defined, 290; questions, 290, 291; not the only science dependent on hypotheses, 305, 306.
Theophilus of Alexandria, character, 27, 28.
Tholuck, influence, 101.
Thom, John Hamilton, pastorate, 95.
Ticknor, George, literary work, 248.
Tiffany, Francis, lecture, 196.
Time Spirit, 221.
Titans, 203, 210.
Tories, in Revolution, 158.
Total Depravity: revolting doctrine, 49; Luther's view, 50; Zwingli's, 57; ameliorated, 60. (See *Human Nature, Sin.*)
Town Meetings, 201.
Transcendentalism: called Infidelity, 100; in New England, 196–219; illustration from mountain-climbing, 199; sublime sentences, 200; History, 204; genuine notes, 208; travesty, 208, 209; characteristic feature, 209; imported influences, 209, 210; foreign travel and study, 210, 211; a native growth, 211, 212; bearing on Unitarianism, 212, 213; connection with miracles, 215; root idea illustrated, 217, 218; effect, 219; leaven, 222; freight, 227; Parker's view, 230; unselfish, 321.
Transcendentalists: the pioneer, 203; early leaders, 207, 208; relation to ancient and modern thinkers, 212; effect of Emerson's address, 213, 215; crowning glory, 218.
Transubstantiation. 44.
Transylvania: Unitarianism, 68, 73–77; sympathy with England, 96.
Trenton Church, 171, 172.
Trinity: not taught in early church, 2, 3, 11; first formal treatise, 6; germ of the doctrine, 17; of attributes, 20; formally stated, 22; coequal personalities, 35; three aspects of deity, 36; later opposition, 50; Reformation leaves the doctrine unchanged, 52; Luther, 52, 56, 57; Melancthon, 56, 57; Augsburg Confession, acceptance and denial, 57; Dialogues, 65; Errors, 65, 66; challenged, 68; Genevan views, 69; Italian rejection, 70; Socinianism, 71; opposition suggesting Judaism, 79; Sandy Foundation Shaken, 82; increasing silence about, 84; Lindsey's rejection, 88; Schleiermacher's opinions, 104; change in eighteenth century, 155; name retained, 156; omitted from a hymn-book, 167, unscriptural, 168; doubted by Sherman, 170; voted essential, 175; absurdities, 205; anti-Trinitarian colony, 220; Whittier's poetry, 260; not Biblical, 277. (See *God, Jesus, Unitarianism.*)
Tritheism, 36.
Truth, its own reward, 200.
Tübingen School, 111.
Tuckerman, Joseph: in England, 91, 92; religious life, 112; correspondence, 176.
Tyndale's Translation, 79.

UNCONSCIOUS, PHILOSOPHY OF THE, 331.
Unitarian Churches: thoughts gladly welcomed, 245; denominational tendencies, 354–373; individual and congregational liberty, 334, 335; no definite polity, 358; creedless, 358; early organizations, 359; buildings, 359, 361, 362; teaching of children, 360, 364, 365, 367; taxation, 360; ritual, 362–364; hospitality, 365, 366; field of benevolence, 366. (See *Church, Congregationalism.*)
Unitarian Home Missionary Board, 95.
Unitarianism: not found in early Christendom, 2, 3; relation to Reformation, 48–77; restricted sense, 48, 65; larger meaning, name, 48;

INDEX.

confession, 50, 59; free-will, 50, 51; Actual Condition, 52, 77; indebtedness to Luther, 52, 53; in character, 53; reasonable, 54; relation to Luther, 54-57; Zwingli, 59; theologically considered, 65; Early Sources, 65, 69; era in America, 67; Poland and Transylvania, 68-77; aristocratic, 75; in England, 78-96; way open in the United States, 90; relation to German thought, 97-115; hard to trace in early New England, 155; old creeds, 156, 157; earliest printed defence, 172; objections answered, 183; carnival of reason, 205; decline of Channing's interest, 206; serious limitation, 206, 207; relation of transcendentalism, 212, 213, 219; Parker's influence, 220-244; broadened, 220, 242; name not restricted, influx of new thought, end of first period, 221; polemical and philanthropic, 222; dust of speculative workshop, 238; relation to modern literature, 245-271; coeval, 246; writers identified with, 251; connection with English movement, fold of refuge, 252; age of struggle, 253; expression in literature, 253, 256, 257; nature of the movement, 253; ideas found in other sects, 254; what it stands for, 255, 256; pale negations, 257; spirit, 258; poetic harmony, 269; in modern novels, 270, 271; harmony with great writers, 270, 271; happifying memories, 271; relation to modern Biblical criticism, 272-289; relation to modern scientific thought, 290-311; answers to questions, 291; working theory, 291; pledged to search for truth, 294-296; beliefs not stereotyped, 296; loyalty to God's will, 297; word of the universe to the human soul, 298; all life from one Life, 300; finding an enlarged universe, 305; not committed to the philosophy of evolution, 307; pledged to highest style of life, 308; best equipped and least encumbered, 309, 310; clear-sighted, 317; suggestions, 318-320; great merit, 321; recognizing the supreme value of righteousness, 323; relation to philosophy, 329-353; representing a philosophy, standing for simple faith, 330; antagonism to certain forms of philosophy, 331; bright contrast to agnosticism, 339, 340; integrity of human nature, 340; wholeness and unity thereof, 341; relation to the world, 341, 342; spiritualistic philosophy, 342. (See *American, Calvinism, God, Orthodoxy, Parker, Trinity.*)

Unitarians: anciently not so called, 36; martyrs, 78-81; generosity to other sects, 91; causing trouble in Massachusetts, 142; early in New England, 155-177; influenced by England, 156; first public avowal, 168; recent views, 169; model Christians, 177; controversy over Parker, 228, 229; his exhortation, 232; noted in literature, 245-270; novelists, 247; historians, 248; orators, 248; essayists, 249, 250; scholarship, 250; poets, 250, 251, 256-270; an honored list, 279; standing for good behavior, 313; remarkable body of men, 355; affecting Orthodoxy, 356; dislike of forms, 362; no separation intended, 367; reaction, 363; united by common ostracism, 367; independency lessened, 367, 368; external coherence, 368, 369; spiritual advance, 369; differences in unity, 370; duty of imparting truth, 371, 372; future work, 373. (See *Socinians.*)

United States: fraudulent devices, 159; patriotism, 319, 320.

Universalism: part of Unitarianism, 48; Zwingli's view, 58-60; not formerly believed in New England, Chauncy's position, 160; Channing's words, 186.

Universe: wise source of, 297; filled with infinite spirit, 298.

Unknowable, the, 333-335.

Usefulness, the present need, 372, 373.

Utilitarianism, 321–323.
Uzzah, fate of, 273.

VANDALS, Arians, 40.
Van der Kemp, Adrian, refugee, 171, 172.
Vasari's Story, 212.
Vatke's Researches, 285.
Venice, Accademia, 216.
Very, Jones, literary work, 250.
Vesuvius, in New England, 204.
Vicarious Atonement: doctrine late established, 39; theories, 40.
Vincent of Lerins, test of Orthodoxy, 36.
Virchow's Writings, 307.
Virginia, Channing's residence, 181.
Virgin Mary: mother of God, 23; allusion, 71; worshipped, 76.
Virtue: its own reward, 200; superior to inspiration, 276; inducements to, 326, 327. (See *Utilitarianism.*)
Von Hartmann's Philosophy, 331.
Voysey, Charles, denial of miracles, 106.
Vulgate, English translation, 46.

WALDENSES, founder of the, 42.
Wales, Prince of, anecdote, 316, 317.
Walker, James, textual criticism, 279.
Wallace's Discovery, 292.
Ward, Mrs. Humphrey, story, 270.
Ware, Henry: religious life, 112; controversy, 183; textual criticism, 279; heroism, 355.
Ware, Henry, Junior: household, 98; textual criticism, 279.
Ware, William, stories, 246, 247.
Washington, George, sermon on, 241.
Watts, Isaac, sermon, 170.
Webster, Daniel: bust, 162; Parker's sermon, 241; oratory, 248.
Weiss, John, literary work, 250.
Wellhausen's History of Israel, 288.
Wesleyans, 46.
Wesley, John, 103.
West Church, Boston: pastors, 158, 160–166.

Western Church: practical side, 15; councils, 22, 34, 35; marriage protected, 33; peculiar adoptive theory, 36. (See *Latin, Roman.*)
West Roxbury Church, 224, 228, 234.
Whipple, Edwin P., literary work, 249.
Whitefield, George, fiery apostle, 203.
White Mountains, 199, 200.
Whitney, Josiah, colleague, 175.
Whittier, John Greenleaf, religion in poetry, 250, 258–261, 263, 268.
Wiclif, John, life-work, 43–47.
Wigglesworth, Edward, gift, 166.
Wightman, Edward, burned, 81.
Will, one great, 301.
William III., charter, 163.
Williams, Roger: illustration, 6; spirit, 180, 181; colony, 195.
Willis, on Servetus and Calvin, 165, 166.
Willson, Luther, career, 174–176.
Wilson, John, pastorate, 359.
Wilton Church, 173.
Winthrop, John, church, 133, 359.
Winthrop, Robert C., literary work, 248.
Wisdom, personified, 9–13.
Wooley, Celia, literary work, 270.
Worcester, Noah, leadership, 205.
Word of God: logos-doctrine, 9–13; made flesh, 14; importance of doctrine, 16–20; indwelling, 22; relation to Holy Spirit, 57; Bible, 274, 275; more light, 371.
World: shape indifferent, 198; transparent to spirit, 347, 348.
Worlds, two discovered, in the Renaissance, 197, 198.
Worship: Puritan usage, 131; barren, 362; changes, 363. (See *Public, Ritual.*)
Wright, Richard, missionary spirit, 92.

YANKEE QUESTIONS, 202. (See *New England.*)

ZWINGLI: views, 57–63; church, 77.

www.ingramcontent.com/pod-product-compliance
Lightning Source LLC
Chambersburg PA
CBHW062040080426
42734CB00012B/2513